AF897735

Personal Data Architectures in the BRICS Countries

Personal Data Architectures in the BRICS Countries

Edited by

LUCA BELLI

Professor of Digital Governance and Regulation, Getulio Vargas Foundation Law School, Brazil

WALTER BRITTO GASPAR

Researcher and Project Lead, Center for Technology and Society, Getulio Vargas Foundation, Brazil

OXFORD
UNIVERSITY PRESS

OXFORD
UNIVERSITY PRESS

Great Clarendon Street, Oxford, OX2 6DP,
United Kingdom

Oxford University Press is a department of the University of Oxford.
It furthers the University's objective of excellence in research, scholarship,
and education by publishing worldwide. Oxford is a registered trade mark of
Oxford University Press in the UK and in certain other countries.

© Luca Belli and Walter B. Gaspar 2025

The moral rights of the authors have been asserted.

All rights reserved. No part of this publication may be reproduced, stored in a retrieval system, transmitted, used for text and data mining, or used for training artificial intelligence, in any form or by any means, without the prior permission in writing of Oxford University Press, or as expressly permitted by law, by licence or under terms agreed with the appropriate reprographics rights organization. Enquiries concerning reproduction outside the scope of the above should be sent to the Rights Department, Oxford University Press, at the address above.

You must not circulate this work in any other form
and you must impose this same condition on any acquirer.

Public sector information reproduced under Open Government Licence v3.0
(https://www.nationalarchives.gov.uk/doc/open-government-licence/)

Published in the United States of America by Oxford University Press
198 Madison Avenue, New York, NY 10016, United States of America.

British Library Cataloguing in Publication Data
Data available

Library of Congress Control Number: 2025943834

ISBN 9780198974482

DOI: 10.1093/9780198974468.001.0001

Printed and bound by
CPI Group (UK) Ltd., Croydon, CR0 4YY

MIX
Paper | Supporting
responsible forestry
FSC® C013604

The manufacturer's authorised representative in the EU for product safety is
Oxford University Press España S.A. of Parque Empresarial San Fernando de Henares,
Avenida de Castilla, 2 – 28830 Madrid (www.oup.es/en or product.safety@oup.com).
OUP España S.A. also acts as importer into Spain of products made by the manufacturer.

Dedication

This volume is dedicated to the memory of Danilo Doneda (1970–2022), a friend, a mentor, and an incredible professional and human being. The idea to develop this study was first discussed with Danilo in the context of the CyberBRICS project, run by the Center for Technology and Society at Fundação Getulio Vargas Law School Rio de Janeiro, and resulted in the seminal paper by Luca Belli and Danilo Doneda, 'Data Protection in the BRICS Countries: Legal Interoperability through Innovative Practices and Convergence' (2023) 13(1) International Data Privacy Law 1–24 that inspired development of this volume.

Contents

Contributors

Luca Belli is Professor at FGV Law School, Rio de Janeiro, Fundação Getulio Vargas (FGV), Brazil. https://orcid.org/0000-0002-9997-2998

Sofia Chang Nogueira, LLM is Research Fellow, Center for Technology and Society, Fundação Getúlio Vargas Law School, Rio de Janeiro, Brazil. https://orcid.org/0009-0009-2559-9113

Larissa Chen Yi Qian, is PhD Candidate at Tsinghua University, Beijing, China.

Anna Churshina, LLM is a legal professional specializing in privacy and data protection law across multiple jurisdictions. https://orcid.org/0009-0006-3077-1289

Walter Britto Gaspar, MPH is Researcher and Project Lead, Center for Technology and Society, Getulio Vargas Foundation, Brazil. https://orcid.org/0000-0002-5585-7963

Anna Kruglikova is Senior Legal Counsel, ERA Capital, London School of Economics, London, United Kingdom

Melody Musoni, PhD, LLM, LLB, and PG Dip is Digital Policy Analyst, ECDPM, Maastricht, Netherlands

Pablo Andres Palazzi, LLM is Director Center of Technology and Society, University of San Andres, Buenos Aires, Argentina

Smriti Parsheera, PhD candidate, School of Public Policy, Indian Institute of Technology Delhi, India. https://orcid.org/0000-0001-8985-0594

Sizwe Snail ka Mtuze, LLB (UP) LLM (SA) is Adjunct Professor, Mercantile Department and Attorney at Snail Attorneys @ Law, Nelson Mandela University, Ghebhera, South Africa, FGV - CTS, Rio de Janeiro, Brazil

Wayne Wei Wang is PhD Candidate in Law and Technology, Faculty of Law, University of Hong Kong, Hong Kong, and Non-Resident Fellow, FGV Rio Law School, Rio de Janeiro, Brazil. https://orcid.org/0000-0002-2278-9933

About the Authors

Luca Belli, PhD, is Professor of Digital Governance and Regulation at Fundação Getulio Vargas (FGV) Law School, Rio de Janeiro, where he directs the Center for Technology and Society (CTS-FGV) and the CyberBRICS project. Luca is also editor of the *International Data Privacy Law* (IDPL) journal, published by Oxford University Press, and Director of the Computers Privacy and Data Protection Conference Latin-America (CPDP LatAm). He is currently a member of the Brazilian Presidency's National Cybersecurity Committee, board member of the Global Digital Inclusion Partnership, and member of the Steering Committee of the Forum for Information & Democracy. He is author of more than fifty publications on law and technology, exploring Internet access, data governance, cybersecurity, AI regulation, and digital transformation. He has been consulted by several intergovernmental organizations and national regulators, including the Council of Europe, the International Telecommunications Union, and the French Telecoms Regulator, and his works have been quoted by numerous media outlets, including *The Economist*, *Financial Times*, *Forbes*, *Le Monde*, BBC, China Today, *The Beijing Review*, *The Hill*, *O Globo*, *Folha de São Paulo*, *El Pais*, and *La Stampa*. Luca holds a PhD in Public Law from Université Paris Panthéon-Assas and can be found on LinkedIn and on Twitter as @1lucabelli.

Walter Britto Gaspar is a lawyer with a master's in Public Health from UFRJ (2017), studying the interface between innovation, intellectual property, and access to medicines policies in Brazil. Walter was a grantee of the Fundación Botín Programme for the Public Interest in Latin America (2013), a researcher in the Fiocruz and Shuttleworth Foundation project on intellectual property and access to medicines (2017), a National Coordinator of the NGO Universities Allied for Essential Medicines (2013–16), and a Certified Graphic Designer by the Istituto Europeo di Design (2018). Currently, he is a researcher in the CyberBRICS project at FGV's Center for Technology and Society and a PhD candidate at the Public Policies, Strategies and Development Programme at the Economics Institute of the Federal University of Rio de Janeiro (UFRJ). Walter is a Substitute Advisor to the Municipal Council for the Protection of Personal Data and Privacy of the city of Rio de Janeiro.

Sofia Chang is a research fellow at the Fundação Getulio Vargas Law School in Rio de Janeiro, contributing to the CyberBRICS project, delving into the regulatory landscape of digital technologies and cyberspace in China and Brazil. Sofia holds an LLM from Peking University, an LLB from Universidade Federal de Minas Gerais, and has gained diverse academic experiences through exchange programmes at The Hague University of Applied Sciences and National Taiwan Normal University. She currently works with the implementation of privacy, data protection, and AI governance in one of the world's biggest digital banks.

Larissa Chen Yi Qian is a lawyer and part-time researcher at the Center for Technology and Society at FGV and participates in the CyberBRICS Project. She holds an LLM in Chinese law from Tsinghua University, China, where she is currently pursuing a PhD in law. She has a postgraduate degree in Digital Law from the Institute of Technology and Society in partnership with the State University of Rio de Janeiro, and a degree from the Brazilian Institute of Capital Markets. She translated the Chinese Civil Code into Brazilian Portuguese and is a lawyer registered at the Brazilian Bar Association.

Anna Churshina is a privacy and data protection lawyer with extensive expertise in managing legal and compliance activities for privacy and data protection. With a diverse background spanning in-house, consulting, and law firm roles, she brings a wealth of experience in navigating international privacy frameworks. Anna holds an LLM from the Queen Mary University of London, and an LLM from the Higher School of Economics, Moscow.

Anna Kruglikova is a corporate lawyer focusing on private equity and venture capital transactions, mergers and acquisitions, and general corporate matters. She currently serves as a Senior Legal Counsel at a private investment fund. Anna received a Bachelor of Laws from the Russian State University for the Humanities and is currently pursuing an LLM at the London School of Economics and Political Science (LSE).

Melody Musoni is Policy Officer at the European Centre for Development Policy Management, The Netherlands. Before joining ECDPM, Melody worked as a data protection senior expert and advisor at the Southern African Development Community (SADC) Secretariat. Melody has a decade-long experience in both legal practice and academia where she specialized in privacy law, cybersecurity, and information technology law. Melody recently finished her PhD degree in cybercrime law and cloud computing law. She holds a Master of Laws degree and a Bachelor of Laws degree from the University of Witwatersrand.

Pablo Palazzi is the Director of CETYS, the Center for Technology and Society of Universidad de San Andres, Buenos Aires. He has been a Professor at UCA, UDESA, and Visiting Professor at Fordham Law School and FGV Law School, Rio de Janeiro. He has written extensively on data privacy and was advisor to the Council of Europe and to the Ibero American Networks on Data Protection for the drafting of their respective Standard Contractual Clauses for personal data transfers. He has been a partner of Allende & Brea since January 2012. He obtained his degree at the School of Law of Universidad Católica Argentina. In May 2000, he obtained an LLM from Fordham Law School in New York with a focus on IP & IT matters. Mr Palazzi is admitted to practise law in Argentina and in New York. He also worked as an associate at Morrison & Foerster LLP in New York where he was admitted to the NY Bar, and was also a law clerk in the Supreme Court of Argentina and a legal counsel in the Ministry of Economy. Before becoming a lawyer Mr Palazzi was a computer programmer.

Smriti Parsheera is a PhD candidate at the Indian Institute of Technology Delhi. Her research interests include privacy, data governance, and digital rights. Until recently she was the India Fellow at the CyberBRICS Project. Before that she led the technology policy vertical at New Delhi's National Institute of Public Finance and Policy. She has also worked for the Competition Commission of India and UNDP India. Smriti studied law at the National Law School of India University, Bangalore, and obtained her LLM from the University of Pennsylvania with a Certificate in Law and Business from the Wharton School. She recently edited the book *Private and Controversial: When Privacy and Public Health Meet in India* (HarperCollins 2023).

Sizwe Snail ka Mtuze is an Admitted Attorney of the South African High Court. He holds an LLB from the University of Pretoria and an LLM from the University of South Africa and is a practising attorney with the law firm Snail Attorneys at Law. Sizwe is registered with the University of Fort Hare for an LLD. Sizwe is an Adjunct Professor at the Nelson Mandela University, Mercantile Law Department (2020 to date) and has been a Research Fellow since 2014 as well as Lecturer in the field of cyberlaw at the University of Fort Hare since 2018. Sizwe is also a Visiting Professor at CTS-FGV University, Rio de Janeiro since 2022. Sizwe was a member of the South African Information

Regulator (IR) from 2016 to 2021 and served on the National Cyber Security Advisory Council of the DTPS from 2014 to 2016. He was deputy chair and chair for the Law Society of South Africa (LSSA) E-Law Committee (2013 to 2021). He has been an Advisory Member of the Cyber BRICS, FGV Rio de Janeiro, Brazil from 2019 to date. Sizwe was the co-editor and author of *CyberlawSA III: The Law of the Internet in South Africa* (2012) and also *CyberlawSA IV: The Law of the Internet in South Africa* (2022).

Wayne Wei Wang is a PhD candidate in Law and Technology at the University of Hong Kong (HKU), and a Fellow-in-Rio at FGV Rio Law School (FGV Direito Rio) in Brazil. Trained in Engineering and Law, Wayne focuses his research interests on Intellectual Property, Data Protection, Algorithmic Governance, and S&T Studies, with a special focus on Law, Innovation, Technology, and Entrepreneurship in the Automating Global South. He has also held academic affiliations with universities and institutions in the USA, the UK, Germany, Poland, and Singapore. Prior to his PhD studies, Wayne completed his LLM in Intellectual Property with Dean's Scholarship jointly conferred by the World Intellectual Property Organization (WIPO) and Queensland University of Technology (QUT) in Australia. He also worked as a data analyst at a legal technology start-up in Shenzhen. Wayne graduated with his double bachelors in Engineering and Law as well as MPhil from Huazhong University of Science and Technology (China), with China National Scholarship from the Ministry of Education of PR China and University Outstanding Graduate Award.

1
UNDERSTANDING THE BRICS COUNTRIES, THEIR DIGITAL COOPERATION, AND THEIR EMERGING DATA PROTECTION ARCHITECTURES

Luca Belli

1.1. Introduction

The BRICS countries—Brazil, Russia, India, China, and South Africa, and their expanding group of partners—are an unusual grouping;[1] even more unusual is the thought that such countries may be trailblazers regarding personal data protection. Indeed, while their economic and geopolitical relevance can hardly be denied and, on the contrary, is attracting the interest of an increasing number of countries[2] notably from the so-called 'Global South', 'Majority

[1] In 2001, the Goldman Sachs economist Jim O'Neill, also known as Lord O'Neill of Gatley, coined the expression BRICs, without the capital 'S', to refer to Brazil, Russia, India, and China. South Africa joined the grouping later, at the third BRICS Summit, in 2011, when the group adopted an uppercase 'S' in the acronym, officially including the African country. The countries were originally grouped as, according to O'Neil's projections, they would experience a similar and particularly relevant phase of new and advanced economic development. See Jim O'Neill, 'Building Better Global Economic BRICs' (2001) 66 Goldman Sachs Global Economic Papers <https://www.goldmansachs.com/insights/archive/archive-pdfs/build-better-brics.pdf> accessed 7 October 2021.

The long-term projections of the BRICs' growth were further described by O'Neill's colleagues, Dominic Wilson and Roopa Purushothama, in 2003. See Dominic Wilson and Roopa Purushothaman, 'Dreaming With BRICs: The Path to 2050' (2003) 99 Goldman Sachs Global Economic Papers <https://www.goldmansachs.com/insights/archive/archive-pdfs/brics-dream.pdf> accessed 8 October 2021.

[2] At the fifteenth BRICS Summit, the group heads of state 'decided to invite the Argentine Republic, the Arab Republic of Egypt, the Federal Democratic Republic of Ethiopia, the Islamic Republic of Iran, the Kingdom of Saudi Arabia and the United Arab Emirates to become full members of BRICS from 1 January 2024'. BRICS, XV BRICS Summit, Johannesburg II Declaration (Sandton, Gauteng, South Africa, 23 August 2023), para 91 <https://web.archive.org/web/20250207002847/https://brics2023.gov.za/wp-content/uploads/2023/08/Jhb-II-Declaration-24-August-2023-1.pdf>; Carien du Plessis,

Luca Belli, *Understanding the BRICS Countries, their Digital Cooperation, and their Emerging Data Protection Architectures* In: *Personal Data Architectures in the BRICS Countries*. Edited by: Luca Belli and Walter Britto Gaspar, Oxford University Press. © Luca Belli and Walter B. Gaspar 2025.
DOI: 10.1093/9780198974468.003.0001

World', or 'Global Majority',[3] the human rights records of some of the group members is far from stellar, and some BRICS members have been routinely accused of gross violations of fundamental rights. From the perspective of Western[4] scholars, notably European ones, whose approach to data protection

Anait Miridzhanian, and Bhargav Acharya, 'BRICS Welcomes New Members in Push to Reshuffle World Order' (*Reuters*, 24 August 2023) <https://www.reuters.com/world/brics-poised-invite-new-members-join-bloc-sources-2023-08-24/>; 'What is BRICS, Which Countries Want to Join and Why?' (*Reuters*, 21 August 2023) <https://www.reuters.com/world/what-is-brics-who-are-its-members-2023-08-21/>; Julian Borger, 'BRICs to More than Double with Admission of Six New Countries' *The Guardian* (24 August 2023) <https://www.theguardian.com/business/2023/aug/24/five-brics-nations-announce-admission-of-six-new-countries-to-bloc>.

[3] Over the past two decades, the 'Global South' term has enjoyed an increasingly relevant use by academics, policymakers, and other stakeholders alike in discussions related to an ample spectrum of world politics issues. As stressed by Haug, Braveboy-Wagner, and Maihold, this prominent concept is used 'as a general rubric for the decolonised nations located roughly, but not exclusively, south of the old colonial centres of power' and encompasses multiple understandings, including 'socio-economic marginality, multilateral alliance-building and resistance against global hegemonic power'. Sebastian Haug, Jacqueline Braveboy-Wagner, and Günther Maihold, 'The "Global South" in the Study of World Politics: Examining a Meta Category' (2021) 42(9) Third World Quarterly 1923–44. Although it represents a powerful concept, the 'Global South' label may be less useful as regards digital governance and data governance, as the digital and data power dynamics do not necessarily reflect old colonial relationships, ie domination by former colonizers of former colonies. In this perspective the use of the terms 'Majority World' or 'Global Majority' may be more interesting. The latter terms refer to all countries formally designated as 'Developing Countries', 'Least Developed Countries', or even 'Third World Countries'. While 'Majority World', 'Global Majority', and 'Global South' can interchange, the former may be preferable as it defines the community based on the demographic and social majority it represents. Thus, it brings a less geographical and more demographic conception, while still identifying the territories and nations that have been invaded, looted, and violently subjugated by colonizers over the past centuries—in some cases until the late 1970s—and which often continue to be subject to new globalized forms of control. Anibal Quijano, 'Coloniality of Power, Eurocentrism, and Latin America' (2000) 1(3) Nepantla: Views from South 533–80; Everisto Benyera, *The Fourth Industrial Revolution and the Recolonisation of Africa: The Coloniality of Data* (Routledge 2021). Similarly, the 'Global Majority' term is also used, although less frequently, to describe people of African, Asian, Latin American, and Arab descent, who constitute approximately 85 per cent of the global population. See Rosemary M Campbell-Stephens, *Educational Leadership and the Global Majority. Decolonising Narratives* (Palgrave Macmillan 2021).

[4] Stuart Hall's work provides a fascinating analysis of the conception of 'the West', highlighting that this term has been constructed to describe a type of social, political, and economic system, supposedly indicating development, compared with 'the rest'. The idea of the West can be traced back to the Enlightenment as an indicator of modernity, tending to impose European categories and norms to assess global phenomena. The concept is not connected to a fixed geographical location, although typically includes Europe and the US. Stuart Hall, 'The West and the Rest: Discourse and Power' in Stuart Hall and others (eds), *Modernity: An Introduction to Modern Societies* (Blackwell Publishers 1996) 184–227. This book refers to Western legal systems when considering the systems whose core elements were initially defined by Roman law and subsequently by French, German and US legal thinking, based on Legal Formalism, which dominated legal doctrine in the late nineteenth century, until the rise of Legal Realism at the turn of the twentieth century. These evolutions have been accompanied by consecration of three key feature of contemporary Western political culture: the limitation of government, through the rule of law; some degree of institutional separation of the economy and of science from government and religion; and the organization of popular participation into governance through elections. The formalization of these features has become an essential element of so-called 'liberal democracies', forming the conceptual basis from which Western observers inevitably assess other systems. Karlson Preuß, 'Legal Formalism and Western Legal Thought' (2023) 14(1) Jurisprudence 22–54; Erich Weede, 'Ideas, Institutions and Political Culture in Western Development' (1990) 2(4) Journal of Theoretical Politics 368–89. This book starts from the assumption that all the above elements

is solidly grounded on fundamental rights, a certain scepticism about the BRICS grouping in general and their personal data frameworks may be understandable. Indeed, several rankings categorize some of the BRICS as 'partly free', 'not free' or even 'authoritarian regimes'.[5] Russia notably left the Council of Europe, ceasing to be a party to the European Convention on Human Rights, in September 2022, after the members of the human rights body voted to suspend the Russian Federation's rights of representation, due to its invasion of Ukraine.

The authors of this volume are well-aware of the abundant critiques[6] regarding the human rights records of some BRICS countries and of the importance of carefully considering this issue when assessing the extent to which a given system effectively protects personal data. In this respect, each of the following chapters dedicated to a BRICS member includes an introductory section providing further human rights-related context, so that the data architectures described in this volume can be understood in their complexity. Indeed, the reason why the term 'architecture' has been chosen is precisely to stress how the combinations of regulatory, institutional and technological choices of the BRICS countries give rise to specific structures shaping their approaches to data governance.

are neither universally defined nor uniformly applicable, and entail significant costs related to enforcement, legal infrastructure, and managing legal and bureaucratic complexities. S Haggard, A Macintyre, and L Tiede, The Rule of Law and Economic Development (2008) 11 Annual Review of Political Science 205–234. Hence, they cannot be seen as a monolithic and homogeneous, but need to be considered in light of the cultural and economic idiosyncrasies of specific nations. Hence, while Western legal and political thinking has proven to be a valuable combination of rule of law, democracy, and human rights, it would be incorrect to assume that the same combinations produced by Western systems are necessarily the best possible options, or should be considered the only basis on which other systems can or must be assessed, or can be easily replicable without relevant resources that western democracies have often extracted from former colonies. Indeed, it is crucial to recognize that the vast majority of current liberal democracies are former colonizers whose ability to build robust institutions has been substantially—if not predominantly—facilitated by the immense wealth extracted through violent colonial exploitation over several centuries. This dynamic of subjugation and extractive colonialism provides an essential, yet largely ignored, explanation for both the advanced institutional development observed in former colonizing nations and the persistent poverty and institutional weakness experienced by former colonies. This relationship is systematically demonstrated in the meticulous reconstruction of global trade flows and balance of payments between colonies and European powers from 1800 to 2025, as highlighted in the work of Thomas Piketty and Gastón Nievas. G Nievas and T Piketty, *Unequal Exchange and North-South Relations: Evidence from Global Trade Flows and the World Balance of Payments 1800-2025*, World Inequality Lab Working Paper 2025/11.

[5] See for instance the Global Freedom Scores, the Internet Freedom Scores, and the Democracy Scores elaborated bi-annually by Freedom House and available at <https://freedomhouse.org/countries/freedom-world/scores>.

[6] See for instance, Jan Czarnocki and others, 'Government Access to Data in Third Countries' (Study prepared by Milieu under Contract No EDPS/2019/02-13 for the benefit of the European Data Protection Board (EDPB) 2019).

While all BRICS countries have adopted data protection legislation, the unrestricted access that some of the BRICS members' governments enjoy to their citizens' personal data may undermine the very essence of data protection principles, especially in terms of the full enjoyment of informational self-determination. As stressed in the introductory sections of each chapter, unchecked governmental capacity to access personal data poses a significant threat to the rule of law, due process, and individual rights. This book, however, strives to adopt a balanced stance, acknowledging that government's capacity to steer research and development regarding the processing of (personal) data is also an essential yet underappreciated factor in terms of collective enjoyment of informational self-determination, that can have significant socio-economic benefits, thus playing a fundamental role in building what can be defined as 'data sovereignty'.[7]

These considerations are particularly relevant for Global South countries, where the capacity to utilize data in the national interest can prove essential to enable policymakers to design and implement more effective, targeted, and evidence-based policies and projects. Yet it should be emphasized that the promotion of data usage, even if in the national interest, cannot be seen as a justification for the lack of proper safeguards regulating government's ability to access and process vast amounts of citizens' data, which inevitably raises concerns about mass surveillance, censorship, and the suppression of dissenting voices. Indeed, while it is acknowledged that the development of data protection is a process and may take years or even decades to achieve effectiveness, and that each country has its own cultural and institutional specificities, it must be stressed that unchecked government access is likely to erode trust in data protection regimes.

[7] Data sovereignty should be seen as the capacity to promote the full enjoyment of informational self-determination, from both an individual and collective perspective. It can be defined as 'the capacity to understand how and why (personal) data are processed and by whom, develop data processing capabilities, and effectively regulate data processing, thus retaining self-determination and control'. See L Belli, WB Gaspar, and S Singh, 'Data Sovereignty and Data Transfers as Fundamental Elements of Digital Transformation: Lessons From the BRICS Countries' (2024) 54 Computer Law & Security Review 1–15. This conceptualization is constructed upon the complementary definitions of digital sovereignty and artificial intelligence (AI) sovereignty proposed in previous works, defining digital sovereignty as the capacity to 'exercise agency, power and control in shaping digital infrastructure, data, services, and protocols' and AI sovereignty as the 'capacity of a given country to understand, develop, and regulate AI systems'. These definitions are provided by Min Jiang and Luca Belli, (eds), *Digital Sovereignty from the BRICS Countries: How the Global South and Emerging Power Alliances Are Reshaping Digital Governance* (CUP 2024); L Belli, 'To Get Its AI Foothold, Brazil Needs to Apply the Key AI Sovereignty Enablers (KASE)' in Steven Feldstein (ed), *New Digital Dilemmas: Resisting Autocrats, Navigating Geopolitics, Confronting Platforms* (Carnegie Endowment for International Peace 2023); L Belli and WB Gaspar, *The Quest for AI Sovereignty, Transparency and Accountability* (Springer 2025).

However, it should be also emphasized that it is not the goal of this initial chapter, nor of this volume, to analyse how personal data are or may be misused by BRICS governments, but rather to introduce the BRICS systems, so that the reader can understand their complexity. This effort is aimed at exploring the characteristics of the normative and institutional frameworks that are emerging in these increasingly influential countries, and determining to what extent they can allow 'legal interoperability'[8] as regards data governance.

Studying and striving to understand these leading emerging economies is therefore essential to comprehend why other Majority World countries are increasingly attracted by their models and leadership, despite the shortcomings of some group members in terms of the rule of law, democracy, and human rights. In this perspective, the recent BRICS expansion and its increasing willingness to enhance cooperation on digital matters deserves particular attention.[9] Since the publication of the seminal paper on 'Data Protection in the BRICS Countries: Legal Interoperability through Innovative Practices and Convergence', which openly called for legal interoperability amongst BRICS

[8] The CyberBRICS research has illustrated the interest of legal interoperability in the field of data governance for BRICS countries since 2020, being positively received by most interlocutors in the grouping. L Belli, *Data Protection in the BRICS Countries: Enhanced Cooperation and Convergence towards Legal Interoperability* (Chinese Academy of Cyberspace Studies 2020).

The term 'legal interoperability' is the property fostering compatibility of rules concerning the same topic within different jurisdictions or different administrative levels within a state. Like technical interoperability, legal interoperability stimulates the exchange of information within different systems. Technical interoperability is usually described as 'the ability to transfer and render useful data and other information across systems, applications, or components'. See International Telecommunication Union, 'Interoperability in the Digital Ecosystem' (GSR discussion paper, ITU 2015). Interoperability is therefore the property enabling the exchange and use of information across heterogeneous technologies and systems. This concept is increasingly important as interconnected technologies, continuously receiving and transmitting data, are becoming the norm. From a technical perspective, interoperability is fostered by adopting shared technical standards and protocols that allow all Internet users to exchange information and to utilize services in a cross-border fashion. The concept of interoperability has been associated with different benefits, fostering openness and positively affecting competition and innovation, while also increasing efficiency in the provision of a greater diversity of content and services. Interoperability is also associated with reductions in the cost of technologies, as it promotes scalability. Similar benefits may be achieved through the promotion of interoperability from a regulatory perspective—ie through legal interoperability—rather than from an exclusively technical one. As such, interoperability of both technical and legal systems allows individuals—particularly Internet users—to access and provide services in a cross-border fashion and to enjoy equal rights protection within different systems thanks to compatible (or common) rules, principles, and procedures. Shared rules and principles amongst various juridical systems have the potential to reduce transaction costs, deflating barriers to cross-border trade, and foster non-measurable benefits such as the protection of fundamental rights. See R Weber, 'Legal Interoperability as a Tool for Combatting Fragmentation' (2014) 4 Global Commission on Internet Governance Paper Series; L Belli and N Zingales, 'Interoperability to Foster Open Digital Ecosystems in the BRICS Countries' in Chinese Academy of Cyberspace Studies, Xinhua Institute, China Institute of International Studies (eds), *Shared Vision for the Digital World: Insights from Global Think Tanks on Jointly Building a Community with a Shared Future in Cyberspace* (The Commercial Press 2023).

[9] This point will be explored in the upcoming sections.

data governance frameworks,[10] the grouping has not only enlarged, including new members and partners, but has also started to explicitly advocate

> the design of a fair and equitable *global framework for data governance*, including cross-border data flows, to address the principles of collection, storage, use and transfer of data; ensure the *interoperability of data policy frameworks* at all levels; and distribute the monetary and non-monetary benefits of data with developing countries.[11]

It is therefore essential to analyse what types of data governance conceptions and contexts the BRICS are departing from, to understand what their vision of a 'global framework for data governance' could be. One must not forget that BRICS are emerging economies with very different levels of maturity from typically 'Western' countries, as well as very strong cultural and legal specificities, which need to be considered, especially when trying to promote shared approaches to specific norms. These considerations are even more relevant when applied to the new BRICS members, ie Egypt, Ethiopia, Indonesia, Iran, Saudi Arabia, and the United Arab Emirates, which bring additional layers of complexity to the group. While all except Iran have very recently approved general data protection laws,[12] the human rights records of the new BRICS countries, repeatedly criticized by numerous observers, can hardly be said to improve the average of the grouping.[13]

Rule of law, democracy, and human rights are considered key pillars of effective data protection, and in many countries, they represent essential criteria for the evaluation of adequacy decisions authorizing international data transfers. The adoption of data protection frameworks by the BRICS countries is

[10] L Belli and D Doneda, 'Data Protection in the BRICS Countries: Legal Interoperability through Innovative Practices and Convergence' (2023) 13(1) International Data Privacy Law 1–24 <https://doi.org/10.1093/idpl/ipac019>.

[11] BRICS, 'Strengthening Multilateralism for Just Global Development and Security' (XVI BRICS Summit, Kazan Declaration (Kazan, Russia, 23 October 2024), para 71 <https://dirco.gov.za/xvi-brics-summit-kazan-declaration-strengthening-multilateralism-for-just-global-development-and-security-kazan-russian-federation-23-october-2024/>)(emphasis added).

[12] On 13 July 2020 Egypt adopted its Law on the Protection of Personal Data, under Resolution No 151 of 2020; Ethiopia enacted its Personal Data Protection Proclamation, Proclamation No 1321/2024, on 24 July 2024; in the United Arab Emirates, the Federal Decree-Law No 45 of 2021 regarding the Protection of Personal Data became effective on 2 January 2022; Indonesia's Personal Data Protection Law (PDP Law) No 27 was adopted in 2022; in Iran, the Ministry of Communications and Information Technology announced the Draft Protection of Personal Data Law in 2018, but the text is still awaiting review by the Islamic Parliament of Iran; the Kingdom of Saudi Arabia's Personal Data Protection Law (PDPL) was issued on 16 September 2021 and then amended on 27 March 2023. The frameworks of the 'new' BRICS will be briefly explored in the concluding chapter of this volume.

[13] See for instance Economist Intelligence Unit, 'Democracy Index 2023. Age of Conflict' (The Economist 2023) <https://www.eiu.com/n/campaigns/democracy-index-2023/>.

particularly interesting as it allows us to consider the impact of such regulatory innovations on democracy, human rights, and rule of law, and vice versa, the extent to which these core elements can be seen as an essential precondition for the effectiveness of personal data regulations. Table 1.1 provides a brief overview of the BRICS countries' governance structures, and of the level of independence of each country's data protection authority. Furthermore, each country-specific chapter of this volume is opened by a section exploring the constitutional and human rights framework in each of the five original BRICS countries, to provide additional context to the reader.

While not exempt from criticism, established democracies such as Brazil, India, and South Africa demonstrate robust constitutional governance, characterized by judicial independence and adherence to separation of powers. However, only South Africa amongst the BRICS members can be said to have a completely independent data protection authority. In contrast, the introduction of data protection law in regimes commonly criticized for their rule of law and human rights records, such as China, Russia, Egypt, and Ethiopia, alongside absolute monarchies such as Saudi Arabia and the UAE, and theocracies such as Iran, raises important questions in terms of implementation, particularly as regards capacity to exercise oversight independently from governmental interference. These considerations are particularly relevant as strong enforcement disparities persist, especially as regards implementation of the law on governmental entities, across BRICS members. These patterns underscore the tension between formal legal and institutional frameworks and political realities, particularly in contexts where personal data governance remains nascent or politically constrained.

However, when approaching this book, the reader is invited to try to understand—and respect—that the aim of this volume is not to assess how each BRICS country is faring in terms of rule of law, democracy, and human rights, but to provide the first concrete account of the existing BRICS data architectures, from BRICS perspectives and comparing BRICS perspectives without using Western referentials, stressing how BRICS architectures are shaping our conceptions of data governance. This account is particularly important to assess if and how the emergence and increasing rapprochement of BRICS digital policies can lead to a 'post-western model of data governance'[14] able to shape the regulatory, institutional, and technological frameworks governing international flows.

[14] L Belli, 'New Data Architectures in Brazil, China, and India: From Copycats to Innovators, towards a Post-Western Model of Data Governance' (2022) 18(2) Indian Journal of Law and Technology 1–58.

Table 1.1 Characteristics of Personal Data Protection Architectures in BRICS Countries

Country	Political System	Data Protection Authority
Brazil	Federal Presidential Republic	**Formally independent.** The National Data Protection Authority (ANPD) is formally independent, but its budget is controlled by the Ministry of Justice.
Russia	Federal Semi-Presidential Republic	**Not independent.** Roskomnadzor depends from the Ministry of Communications and Mass Media of the Russian Federation.
India	Federal Parliamentary Democracy	**Formally independent.** The Data Protection Board of India has not yet been established. Interim oversight is provided by the Ministry of Electronics and Information Technology (MEITy).
China	Unitary Marxist-Leninist One-Party State	**Not independent.** The Cyberspace Administration of China (CAC) enforces data law, amongst other digital regulations, and is not an independent body.
South Africa	Constitutional Parliamentary Republic	**Fully independent.** The Information Regulator was established as an independent body.
Egypt	Semi-Presidential Republic	**Not independent.** The Data Protection Authority depends from the Ministry of Communications.
Ethiopia	Federal Parliamentary Republic	**Not independent.** The Data Protection Authority depends from the Ministry of Innovation and Technology.
Iran	Theocratic Presidential Republic	**Not independent.** The Supreme Council of Cyberspace oversees all data-related laws, aligning with state interests.
UAE	Federal Absolute Monarchy	**Not independent.** The Data Protection Office depends from the Dubai International Financial Centre; a UAE-wide authority is still lacking.
Indonesia	Unitary Presidential Republic	**Not independent.** The Personal Data Protection Authority has not been established yet. Interim oversight is provided by the Ministry of Communication and Information Technology.
Saudi Arabia	Absolute Monarchy	**Not independent.** The Saudi Data and Artificial Intelligence Authority (SDAIA) oversees AI/data, but is not an independent body.

Source: The authors.

Such an effort seems necessary to explain why BRICS systems are exercising mounting appeal[15] amongst Majority World countries, as it seems particularly evident in the recent BRICS + expansion.[16] BRICS systems continue to have international impact, despite Western efforts to contain, 'de-risk'[17] from, and ostracize some BRICS members through heavy, yet arguably ineffective, sanctions. This impact is manifest not only in the growing mutual influence amongst BRICS countries, but also in their capacity to shape how third countries—which are either traditionally influenced by BRICS or have entered more recently the BRICS countries' sphere of influence—are adapting to normative and institutional innovations they have introduced. Being large and complex developing countries with very recent data privacy cultures, the BRICS offer very relevant teachings for other low- and middle-income countries as they face challenges shared by the Global South.[18]

Conspicuously, one of the most widespread challenges is a very limited or simply non-existent 'data protection culture',[19] which makes it extremely difficult to comply with newly 'transplanted'[20] data protection frameworks. Indeed, in the Global Majority, data subjects are frequently unaware of their data rights, public and private entities typically do not know how to correctly comply with data protection obligations, and regulators themselves may face enormous shortfalls of the intellectual and financial resources necessary to implement the law and build a data protection culture through education and effective enforcement. While taking inspiration from consolidated European models is completely understandable, developing countries face many challenges that Western countries are

[15] See Council of Councils, 'The BRICS Summit 2023: Seeking an Alternate World Order?' (Global Memo by ORF, SWP, SAIIA, SVOP, SIIS, RSIS, FGV, and CFR, 31 August 2023) <https://www.cfr.org/councilofcouncils/global-memos/brics-summit-2023-seeking-alternate-world-order>.

[16] See above (n 2).

[17] M Schaus and K Lannoo, 'The EU's aim to de-risk itself from China is risky . . . yet necessary' (CEPS, 7 September 2023) <https://www.ceps.eu/the-eus-aim-to-de-risk-itself-from-china-is-risky-yet-necessary/>; P Blenkinsop, 'EU agrees to de-risk from China and debates what this means' (*Reuters*, 30 June 2023) <https://www.reuters.com/world/eu-leaders-pledge-de-risk-china-debate-what-this-means-2023-06-30/>.

[18] See L Belli, 'New Data Architectures in Brazil, China, and India: From Copycats to Innovators, towards a post-Western Model of Data Governance' (2022) 18(2) Indian Journal of Law and Technology <https://www.ijlt.in/journal/new-data-architectures-in-brazil%2C-china%2C-and-india%3A-from-copycats-to-innovators%2C-towards-a-post-western-model-of-data-governance>.

[19] Professor Stefano Rodotà, one of the most influential scholars and intellectuals in the data protection field, used to consider the 'data protection culture' as the assimilation by society of the crucial importance of data protection. This process consists in the gradual understanding of the instrumental value that data protection plays for the realization of citizenship and the sustainable development of society, economy, and democracy. See L Belli and D Doneda, 'O que falta ao Brasil e à América Latina para uma proteção de dados efetiva?' *Jota* (2 September 2021).

[20] The import, or even copying, of influential foreign frameworks into another country's legislation is a phenomenon typically defined 'legal transplant'. Alan Watson, *Legal Transplants: An Approach to Comparative Law* (University of Georgia Press 1974). Data protection offers a telling example of this practice.

not used to dealing with. In this sense, the analysis of leading emerging economies' experiences offers much more realistic illustrations of how data protection plays out in the Global South, both in terms of the problems that need to be faced and the innovations that could help solve such problems.[21]

Hence, this volume endeavours to analyse and compare some extremely relevant yet enormously understudied frameworks, acknowledging that BRICS countries are very influential leaders both in their own regional environments and, to a lesser but increasingly relevant extent, globally, as tellingly illustrated by the recent expansion of the BRICS grouping.[22] Such evolutions only emphasize the need for carefully studying their policy choices, including understanding why their data—and constitutional—architectures are different from Western ones. In this perspective, it is also acknowledged that researchers and policymakers should analyse the BRICS systems from a critical standpoint. Indeed, the BRICS frameworks are not exempt from criticism, especially as regards the very light safeguards they might offer against abusive data processing practices perpetrated by public organs.

To start exploring this unusual coalition of emerging powers, the next section will briefly analyse how and why these very heterogeneous countries decided to establish their own process of club governance.

1.1.1. The BRICS: From Acronym to Alliance

Originally, the BRICS acronym was coined to describe some of the largest and fastest-growing economies, to identify leading emerging powers with some shared economic characteristics, with no intention to suggest any possibility of political or normative cooperation.[23] However, some years after the creation of the acronym by Goldman Sachs economist Jim O'Neill,[24] the BRICS countries started to sense the enormous potential of the acronym, which represents

[21] See above (n 14).

[22] At the time of this writing, the BRICS grouping is 'composed of eleven countries: its five original members—Brasil, China, India, Russia, and South Africa—and six new members admitted in 2024–25—Egypt, Ethiopia, Indonesia, Iran, Saudi Arabia, and the United Arab Emirates. The group was originally composed of Brasil, Russia, India, and China in 2006; South Africa adhered in 2011; the new expansion, effective as of 2024, derived from the Johannesburg Declaration, from August 2023. Partner Countries According to the mandate agreed upon through the Johannesburg Declaration, the leaders approved the creation of the BRICS partner country category during the Kazan Summit in 2024. The BRICS partner countries are: Belarus, Bolivia, Cuba, Kazakhstan, Malaysia, Nigeria, Thailand, Uganda, and Uzbekistan'. BRICS, 'BRICS Brasil: About the BRICS' (20 January 2025) <https://brics.br/en/about-the-brics>.

[23] See n 2.

[24] ibid.

an alternative 'post-Western'[25] system of global governance, led by emerging economies. In this sense, the BRICS club has been created to foster a multi-polar order where Global Majority leaders could play a relevant role in global governance and development, considering the increasing relevance of developing countries.

Initially, the BRICS countries started to increase their synergies on the margins of the G7/8 summits. In fact, the members of the G7/8 understood the mounting global relevance and influence of large emerging economies and began engaging with them through their so-called 'outreach process'.[26] Besides facilitating interactions among the BRICS countries, their inclusion in the G7/8 outreach process proved to be a useful learning experience, letting these emerging powers understand the functioning of global club governance and the benefits brought by high-level summit processes.

In this spirit, the BRICs countries—with a small 's', as South Africa would join later—organized their first *ad hoc* informal meeting, in 2006, on the margins of that year's UN General Assembly. Two years later, the global financial crisis and the euro crisis considerably weakened the traditional Western powers, creating a vacuum of global leadership and stressing the need for better coordination of Global Majority leaders. Indeed, as leading emerging economies, the BRICs had largely escaped the crises, and jointly agreed to establish their own stand-alone summitry process, driven by a newly found sense of self-confidence.

Russia organized the first BRICs heads of state meeting, in 2009, as an informal club-like summit with a notable international profile. Since then, no head of state has ever missed any of the summits,[27] which have been held with

[25] In this sense, see O Stuenkel, *Post-Western World: How Emerging Powers Are Remaking Global Order* (Polity Press, 2016).

[26] The most relevant such process was the 'G8 Outreach Five', which included Brazil, China, India, Mexico, and South Africa at the 2005 G8 summit (Russia was still part of the G8 then, before being expelled for annexing Crimea). However, while the outreach model recognized the relevance of emerging economies—notably the future BRICS members—it also perpetrated a shared sense of exclusion, as the countries kept on being merely invited as external guests with a marginal role, compared to the G8 members.

[27] The only exceptions have been Vladimir Putin's online participation at the XV BRICS Summit, due to the pending International Criminal Court (ICC) arrest warrant issued in connection with the Ukrainian war, and Luiz Inacio Lula da Silva's absence to the Kazan meeting due to medical treatment. See Nomsa Maseko and Kathryn Armstrong, 'Putin Will Not Attend BRICS Summit—South African Presidency' *BBC News* (19 July 2023) <https://www.bbc.com/news/world-africa-66247067>; International Criminal Court, 'Situation in Ukraine: ICC Judges Issue Arrest Warrants Against Vladimir Vladimirovich Putin and Maria Alekseyevna Lvova-Belova' (17 March 2023) <https://www.icc-cpi.int/news/situation-ukraine-icc-judges-issue-arrest-warrants-against-vladimir-vladimirovich-putin-and>; Marcela Ayres. 'Brazil's Lula cancels BRICS trip to Russia after minor brain hemorrhage'. (*Reuters*, 21 October 2024) <https://www.reuters.com/world/americas/brazils-lula-cancels-trip-brics-summit-kazan-medical-advice-2024-10-20/>.

a rotating presidency among the members, adopting a similar format to other informal high-level processes, such as the G7/8 and G20. In 2011, the original BRICs club became a larger BRICS, with the full integration of South Africa, and, in 2014, the bloc established the BRICS-led New Development Bank (NBD)[28] and Contingent Reserve Arrangement, which can be seen as its most prominent institutional achievements.

Importantly the BRICS grouping has been discussing expansion for almost a decade and, since 2021, the New Development Bank has admitted Bangladesh, Egypt, the United Arab Emirates, and Uruguay as new members.[29] Furthermore, at the 2023 BRICS Summit, the grouping leaders jointly agreed to enact the largest expansion of the alliance, inviting six new members—Argentina, Egypt, Ethiopia, Iran, Saudi Arabia, and the United Arab Emirates[30]—that were chosen amongst the twenty-three countries that have formally applied and the more than forty that expressed interest in joining the BRICS grouping.[31]

Since the club's inception, the number of governmental and multistakeholder gatherings, partnerships, and initiatives has been growing steadily, reaching more than 100 official initiatives per year.[32] However, it is important to emphasize that BRICS is neither an intergovernmental organization with a constitution and a headquarter, nor a decision-making body with binding regulations, but rather a club governance[33] mechanism aimed at coordinating shared positions. The NBD is the only existing BRICS-led institution. In June 2022, under the Chinese rotating presidency the grouping decided to strengthen its own outreach process, the BRICS+ ('BRICS plus') initiative, and as a consequence numerous emerging economies, especially large producers of commodities, requested formally to join the grouping, being attracted by the BRICS potential for Majority World coordination. This evolution opened a new chapter for the club, while also strengthening its participatory legitimacy.

[28] See <https://www.ndb.int>.

[29] New Development Bank (NDB), NDB member countries <https://www.ndb.int/about-us/organisation/members/>.

[30] See above (n 6). Importantly, Indonesia was invited at later stage, but its adhesion to the grouping was already confirmed in January 2025, at the beginning of the Brazilian rotating presidency of the grouping. See above (n 21). <https://web.archive.org/web/20250207002847/https://brics2023.gov.za/wp-content/uploads/2023/08/Jhb-II-Declaration-24-August-2023-1.pdf>.

[31] Tim Cocks, 'More than 40 Nations Interested in Joining BRICS, South Africa Says' (*Reuters*, 20 July 2023) <https://www.reuters.com/world/more-than-40-nations-interested-joining-brics-south-africa-2023-07-20/>.

[32] For detailed overviews of the evolution of BRICS, see O Stuenkel, *The BRICS and the Future of Global Order* (Lexington Books 2016); and the same author, quoted above at n 25.

[33] See ibid (Stuenkel 2016); C Brandi, 'Club Governance and Legitimacy: The Perspective of Old and Rising Powers on the G7 and the G20' (2019) 26(4) South African Journal of International Affairs 685–702 <https://doi.org/10.1080/10220461.2019.1697354>.

Crucially, despite their remarkable differences, the BRICS countries find commonalities, not only in some of their economic characteristics, but also in their shared grievances regarding imperialist attitudes and the very recent colonialist past of Western countries, as well as the perceived unfairness of Western-led global governance and institutions, such as the World Bank and the International Monetary Fund. Hence, to understand the BRICS, it is important to remember that while the existing global governance system is accepted by Global South countries, it was established at a time when most of the Global South countries were still colonies, a position of dominance that some European countries tried to retain with extremely violent repression and gross human rights violations well into the 1960s and 1970s.[34] Ignoring these essential aspects means having a very selective conception of history. In this context, most Global Majority countries have been complaining about the injustice of the existing global institutional system for decades, and have long criticized the arguably hypocritical stance of former colonial powers in evaluating the adherence of former colonies to human rights, democracy, and the rule of law, given that these very principles were systematically breached by the colonizers for centuries.[35] Although such complaints have had very meagre success, they have supported a shared endeavour to counterbalance existing institutions and acquire further prominence via what came to be known as 'South–South cooperation'.[36]

This is the background where the Non-Aligned Movement and its Group of 15, the Group of 77, the IBSA Trilateral,[37] and, finally, the BRICS and BRICS +,

[34] I Surun, M Pešta, and G Metzler, 'Empire and Colonialism in Contemporary History (ca. 1900–2000)' in J Hansn and others (eds) *The European Experience. A Multi-Perspective History of Modern Europe, 1500–2000* (OpenBook Publishers 2023) <https://doi.org/10.11647/OBP.0323>. For a visual representation, see: The Map as History, 'Decolonization after 1945' <https://www.the-map-as-history.com/Decolonization-after-1945>.

[35] Nearly all developing countries were colonized by European nations—now characterized as liberal democracies—during the eighteenth, nineteenth, or early twentieth centuries, during which local populations experienced violent subjugation, exploitation, exclusion from public affairs, and systematic dehumanization. See e.g. H. *Arendt Imperialism. Part Two of The Origins of Totalitarianism,* Harper Collins Publishers, 1968; A. Quijano, 'Coloniality of Power, Eurocentrism, and Latin America', *Nepantla: Views from South,* (2000) 1(3), 533–580; C. Elkins. *Imperial Reckoning: The Untold Story of Britain's Gulag in Kenya.* St. Martins Press-3PL, 2005.

[36] In 1990, the Report of the South Commission, chaired by former Indian prime minister Manmohan Singh, who was a key figure in the establishment of the BRICS, called for the establishment of a South–South cooperation, stressing that 'the emerging development patterns of the North clearly suggest that the Northern locomotive economies will not pull the train of Southern economies at a pace that will satisfy its passengers—the people of the South. The locomotive power has to be generated to the maximum extent possible within the economies of the South themselves'. See The South Commission, *The Challenge to the South: The Report of the South Commission* (OUP 1990) 286 <https://www.southcentre.int/wp-content/uploads/2013/02/The-Challenge-to-the-South_HRes_EN.pdf>.

[37] IBSA is a trilateral forum which brings together India, Brazil, and South Africa to foster consultation and coordination on global and regional political issues; collaboration on concrete projects; and to assist other developing countries through the IBSA Fund. See <http://www.ibsa-trilateral.org/>. This organization became well-known to Internet Governance scholars in 2011, when it put forward a

can be seen as subsequent attempts of the Global South, driven by the 'locomotives of the South'[38] to reclaim relevance.[39] This striving for relevance aims at establishing an alternative to what has been perceived as an arbitrary and frequently discriminatory system, led by former colonizers and frequently biased in favour of these latter countries.[40]

Recent BRICS developments provide substantial evidence both of the importance that digital technologies have acquired for the grouping and of the relevance these countries have gained regarding global digital policies.[41] In this perspective, the purpose of this introductory chapter is to note that, after having looked at European and Western models for reference over several years, the BRICS are starting to become real innovators in terms of data policy, governance, and regulation[42] and are establishing a Global Majority-driven approach to global data governance.[43] Furthermore, while keeping a low profile, and raising frequent yet not always justified criticism from observers, the BRICS are continuously coordinating and expanding their agenda, sharing information and best practices, mutually influencing each other, and explicitly

proposal for a UN Committee for Internet-Related Policies, which was strongly contested at that year's UN Internet Governance Forum and, despite the contestations, endorsed by the Indian government at the 66th Session of the UN General Assembly in October 2011. See L Belli, 'Internet governance v. Internet government' *MediaLAWS* (7 November 2011) <https://www.medialaws.eu/internet-governance-v-internet-government/>.

[38] The report of the South Commission vocally stressed that Global South countries could not expect former colonizers and imperialist forces to be the drivers of their development. Such locomotive force had to be found within the South itself. See above (n 35). See also L Belli, ' BRICS: The New Digital Locomotives' *Beijing Review* (11 July 2022) <https://www.bjreview.com/Opinion/Voice/202207/t20220711_800300500.html>.

[39] Interestingly, the website of the South African chairmanship of the BRICS 2023 Summit provides an eloquent infographic that explicitly situates the grouping as the latest evolutionary step of a struggle for Global South relevance which started with the First Asian–African Conference held in Bandung in 1955 and the subsequent creation of the Non-Aligned Movement in 1956 and the Group of 77 in 1964. See BRICS, 'Evolution of BRICS' (2023) <https://web.archive.org/web/20231228223804/https://brics2023.gov.za/evolution-of-brics/>.

[40] The Group of 15, which emerged within the Non-Aligned Movement in 1989, the IBSA Trilateral created in 2003, and eventually the BRICS since 2009, have all been driven by this yearning for a multipolar word and less Western-centric global governance. A compelling review of how such events unfolded and why a South–South cooperation was born and evolved is provided by V Prashad, *Poorer Nations: A Possible History of the Global South* (Verso 2012).

[41] See section 2.2. For an analysis of BRICS digital policies and most recent developments, particularly in the field of cybersecurity, see L Belli (ed), *CyberBRICS: Cybersecurity Regulations in the BRICS Countries* (Springer 2021); L Belli, 'Cybersecurity Policymaking in the BRICS Countries: From Addressing National Priorities to Seeking International Cooperation' (2021) 28 The African Journal of Information and Communication 1–14.

[42] On this point, see, notably L Belli, 'New Data Architectures in Brazil, China, and India: From Copycats to Innovators, towards a post-Western Model of Data Governance' (2022) 18(2) Indian Journal of Law and Technology 1–58<https://www.ijlt.in/journal/new-data-architectures-in-brazil%2C-china%2C-and-india%3A-from-copycats-to-innovators%2C-towards-a-post-western-model-of-data-governance>.

[43] This point will be discussed in the following sections and in the concluding chapter of this volume.

committing to enhance their cooperation on digital matters. Data governance, cybersecurity, and cybercrime are critical domains in which this enhanced cooperation is especially apparent, as clearly evidenced by the adoption of the recent United Nations Convention against Cybercrime—a process propelled and made possible primarily through the active engagement of the BRICS nations.[44]

As will be discussed in this volume, all the BRICS have adopted, renewed, or tabled data protection frameworks and consider data governance as one of their key priorities. This trend is to be welcomed, especially in countries frequently accused of democratic deficit, as some BRICS members frequently are, as even relatively partial advancements can have a considerable impact for the countries' enormous populations. However, such a trend should also be considered with a degree of caution. It would be naïve to argue that the BRICS' interest in data protection is exclusively motivated by a sudden intention to champion human rights. Indeed, economic, developmental, strategic, or even protectionist considerations play a key role in these countries' approach to data governance.

This latter point is key to understanding why and how BRICS countries' data-related policies innovate, as their rationales and motivations may differ from those of Western, and especially European, countries—and be harder to grasp for Western observers. However, being able to leverage data for development arguably represents the main rationale and motivation leading most Global South countries to regulate personal data. In this context, their adoption of data protection frameworks and the establishment of new institutional and normative arrangements offer a very interesting perspective on how and why emerging economies regulate data, and why BRICS are becoming innovators and even world leaders in data-related policymaking.

It is important to understand that the blend of developmental and normative strategies produces incredible evolutions for large emerging economies. As an instance, in less than a decade, BRICS countries have become not only some of the most connected countries in the world[45] but also global leaders

[44] Deliberately vague, the text of the Convention is not without criticism, particularly regarding its potential for abusive implementation. Nevertheless, it is important to emphasize that the adoption of a BRICS-led treaty on such a critical issue clearly marks a significant shift in the global influence of these countries. For further information about the Convention, see United Nations General Assembly, Draft United Nations Convention Against Cybercrime (7 August 2024; A/AC.291/L.15.

[45] See the country reports on 'Connectivity across BRICS Countries' developed by the CyberBRICS Project and included in L Belli and L Magalhães (eds), 'SmartBRICS: How Brazil, Russia, India, China, and South Africa Are Shaping Their Digital Transformation into Smart Countries' (2024) <https://cyberbrics.info/connectivity-across-brics-countries/>.

in data-intensive sectors such as instant online payments.[46] This latter example is particularly telling as, in the past five or six years, India and China have climbed the world ranking, becoming the first and second country with the highest number of real-time online payments in the world and, even more staggeringly, Brazil has reached the top ten, starting from the bottom, in only four years since the introduction of Pix, the Brazilian national digital payment system.[47] These trends should be considered in parallel with the evolving discussions on data and digital sovereignty, which find in the BRICS grouping some of the most fascinating examples of heterogeneous initiatives and expressions of the concept.[48]

It is also important to emphasize that, as demonstrated by the latest Russian developments, normative and institutional frameworks regarding data protection—as virtually any other type of framework—may be repurposed to fit the national security needs of countries at war. In this respect, the Russian experience is useful not only to study the country's data protection system, but also to predict which kind of developments one might expect from countries with poor human rights records entering a war.

Considering the complex scenario depicted above, this chapter aims at offering to the reader the elements necessary to grasp the evolutions of the BRICS, two decades since the first mention of this acronym.[49] This introductory chapter must be seen as instrumental to understanding the increasingly relevant role played by the grouping members in the data governance field and the intensification of digital governance alignments between BRICS members.

[46] Particularly interesting and up-to-date data are available in the ACI Worldwide global data reports on 'Prime-Time for Real Time', which track and analyse real-time payments volumes, growth, and dynamics in forty-eight global markets. See ACI Worldwide, 'Global Data. Prime Time for Real-Time' (April 2022) <https://www.aciworldwide.com/real-time-payments-report>.

[47] In 2024, the Pix systems processed more than 5.6 billion transactions per month. All Pix statistics are updated on a monthly basis on the website of the Brazilian Central Bank <https://web.archive.org/web/20250131212351/https://www.bcb.gov.br/en/financialstability/pixstatistics>. According to the ACI Worldwide global data report mentioned at n 44, already in 2022, 'Brazil's PIX system has gotten off to a flying start, passing a billion transactions within months of launching and continuing to go from strength to strength. There are now more than 100 million PIX users'. See ibid p 8.

[48] Digital sovereignty is an increasingly debated issue, which does not yet have a universal definition. For an analysis of the concept and how its various dimensions can be understood in the BRICS context, see above n 7. For a digression on why emerging economies might be keen on building digital sovereignty narratives, see L Belli, 'BRICS Countries to Build Digital Sovereignty' in L Belli (ed), *CyberBRICS: Cybersecurity Regulations in the BRICS Countries* (Springer 2021); L Belli, 'Building Good Digital Sovereignty through Digital Public Infrastructures and Digital Commons in India and Brazil. G20's Think20 (T20)' (June 2023) <https://t20ind.org/research/building-good-digital-sovereignty-through-digital-public-infrastructures/>.

[49] See the 2001 paper by Jim O'Neil quoted above (n 1).

1.1.2. Methodology and Research Structure

This book stems from research performed during the CyberBRICS project,[50] which is the first—and to date only—initiative aimed at producing a comparative analysis of digital policies of the BRICS countries. This chapter focuses on the ongoing development and increasing rapprochement of BRICS data protection frameworks, stressing the existence of a tendency towards convergence,[51] highlighting that the grouping can be considered as an example of 'enhanced cooperation'[52] for Internet governance, and stressing the innovative character of some of the policy and governance elements that BRICS are introducing in their frameworks.

This chapter, first, provides context to understand the BRICS and their efforts to cooperate on digital affairs, analysing official documents issued by the grouping, reviewing existing literature and presenting relevant data on the countries' interactions. While setting the scene, it explores how an enhanced cooperation on the governance of information and communication technologies (ICTs) has been unfolding in the BRICS agenda. Subsequently, the chapter briefly presents some key elements of the BRICS countries' data protection frameworks. Based on the empirical research developed by the CyberBRICS team,[53] the existence of a tendency towards convergence of several aspects of the BRICS national data protection framework is investigated. In this perspective, the chapter argues that the existence of a shared data protection skeleton and increased interest in cooperating on digital matters fosters legal interoperability. Building upon these introductory considerations, the subsequent country-specific chapters and the concluding chapter of this volume will explore some concrete examples of how BRICS countries are innovating data protection, developing new institutions and strategies, as well as new generation of data protection tools that can inspire other countries.

[50] See <www.cyberbrics.info>.

[51] For an introduction to the policy convergence phenomenon, see Colin J Bennett, 'What Is Policy Convergence and What Causes It?' (1991) 21(2) British Journal of Political Science 215.

[52] In Internet governance parlance, this term finds its origin in the UN-sponsored World Summit on Information Society—commonly referred to as WSIS—and was consecrated in the outcome of the second phase of the Summit, held in Tunis in 2005. While this concept has never been detailed, after having been consecrated by the Tunis Agenda for the Information Society, world leaders have agreed on 'the need for enhanced cooperation in the future, to enable governments, on an equal footing, to carry out their roles and responsibilities, in international public policy issues pertaining to the Internet'. See Tunis Agenda for the Information Society (adopted 18 November 2005; WSIS-05/TUNIS/DOC/6(Rev. 1)-E (Tunis Agenda)) para 69 <https://www.itu.int/net/wsis/docs2/tunis/off/6rev1.html> accessed 8 October 2021.

[53] For a detailed comparison of the normative elements in the BRICS data protection frameworks, see 'BRICS Data Protection Map' (CyberBRICS Project 2021) <https://cyberbrics.info/data-protection-across-brics-countries/> accessed 8 October 2021.

Hence this introductory chapter can be considered as a teaser of the country-specific chapters of this volume, which will analyse in detail the data architectures of each BRICS member. Although each chapter is structured in a slightly different fashion, reflecting the specificities of each country's system, a 'core structure' has been followed by all authors to facilitate comparison. Each chapter: i) introduces the legal system of each country with a particular focus on their human rights and rule of law track record, so that the reader can understand how the normative frameworks analysed are *de facto* applied; ii) describes the normative networks in the context of which each country's data protection law must be considered; iii) analyses the national data protection framework; and iv) scrutinizes the institutional mechanism dealing with the oversight and implementation of the normative framework. Furthermore, each country-specific chapter includes the English translation of the national data protection law as an annex.

Lastly, the concluding chapter of the book adopts a prospective stance, focusing on the possibilities of BRICS countries' cooperation regarding personal data flows, trying to understand which types of mechanisms would be more suitable to foster sustainable transborder data exchanges, to foster digital trade and cooperation while guaranteeing that data subjects' rights are respected and data security is fully enforced.

1.2. Background: Contextualizing the Increasing Interest of the BRICS in Digital Cooperation

Some figures are key to understanding the relevance of the BRICS in general and, particularly, the impact of their digital policies and data protection regulations on a global scale. These countries together represent over 40 per cent of the world population, being home to 3.2 billion individuals (ie 3.2 billion data subjects or data producers, depending on the perspective), and account for 26 per cent of the world's gross domestic product and a share of over 16 per cent of world trade.[54] Hence, the digitalization of the BRICS economies and societies represents a major opportunity for individuals and businesses in these countries, while also creating considerable challenges.

[54] These figures increase further when taking into account not only the core BRICS countries but also the recently admitted members. See the official website of the Brazilian 2025 Presidency of BRICS <https://brics.br/en/about-the-brics/brics-data>.

The members of the BRICS grouping have realized that digital transformation is an essential element for the future of their economies and societies,[55] and that data protection is a key priority to fostering thriving digital environments, where data subjects' rights are protected, businesses benefit from legal certainty, and 'data colonialism'[56] from foreign tech giants can be avoided or at least mitigated. At the same time, BRICS are well-aware of the risks that massive adoption of and dependency on foreign ICTs may generate, and that sound policies are vital not only to regulate how individuals and businesses interact but, chiefly, to protect the vital interests of the state.

In this sense, it is possible to argue that the disclosures by former US National Security Agency (NSA) contractor Edward Snowden played a major role as a triggering event for the intensification of digital policymaking in the BRICS countries. Indeed, since 2013, the BRICS have elaborated and implemented an extensive range of data-related strategies, laws, and regulations. Besides increasing personal data protection, these regulations have been aimed at strengthening cybersecurity[57] and constructing—and experimenting with their own conceptions of—what is currently characterized as 'digital sovereignty'.[58]

It is worth remembering that the Snowden disclosures were a particularly severe and acute wake-up call for the BRICS countries, with the revelation that the Brazilian president's personal phone had been wiretapped,[59] together with the communications of a wide number of members of the Brazilian government.[60] It is also useful to emphasize that, since the revelations, Mr Snowden has been exiled in Russia. It is therefore not a coincidence that, since 2013, the protection of personal data and cybersecurity measures have emerged as increasingly essential issues for BRICS countries to assert their (digital) sovereignty.

[55] L Belli and L Magalhães Special issue on Digital Transformation in the BRICS Countries. *Computer Law & Security Review*, 2024 <https://www.sciencedirect.com/special-issue/10VRL9GGMQG>.

[56] The concept of 'data colonialism' is eloquently discussed in N Couldry and UA Mejias, *The Costs of Connection: How Data is Colonizing Human Life and Appropriating it for Capitalism* (Stanford University Press 2019).

[57] See Belli (2021) (n 41).

[58] See above (n 7, 48).

[59] -See Sonia Bridi and Glenn Greenwald, 'Documentos revelam esquema de agência dos EUA para espionar Dilma' (*Fantástico*, 1 September 2013) <http://g1.globo.com/fantastico/noticia/2013/09/documentos-revelam-esquema-de-agencia-dos-eua-para-espionar-dilma-rousseff.html> accessed 14 October 2021.

[60] See 'EUA grampearam Dilma, ex-ministros e avião presidencial, revela WikiLeak' (*O Globo*, 4 July 2015) <http://g1.globo.com/politica/noticia/2015/07/lista-revela-29-integrantes-do-governo-dilma-espionados-pelos-eua.html> accessed 14 October 2021.

When the BRICs leaders met for the first time in 2009, before becoming BRICS with a capital S, the terms 'digital' or 'cyber' were not mentioned even once in their first Joint Statement. These terms are featured twenty-seven times in the XVI BRICS Summit Kazan Declaration, adopted on 23 October 2024. In the aftermath of the Snowden revelations, BRICS leaders included for the first time an explicit reference to the 'paramount importance' of the adoption of 'universally accepted norms, standards and practices [on] the security in the use of Information and Communication Technologies'[61] in their annual BRICS Summit declaration. Since the 2013 Summit, the BRICS ministers for science, technology, and innovation have established continuous cooperation, meeting for the first time in 2014, intensifying their relations and defining partnerships.

Through an increasing number of shared documents on ICT cooperation,[62] starting from the Memorandum of Understanding on Cooperation in Science, Technology, and Innovation,[63] the grouping has structured the design of the legal frameworks within which intra-BRICS coordination, partnerships, and synergies could be developed. As will be stressed in the next section, this evolution culminated with the recent call for the establishment of 'legal frameworks of cooperation among BRICS States [and] a BRICS intergovernmental agreement on cooperation'[64] on cybersecurity and the recent adoption of the United Nations Convention against Cybercrime, whose proposal was intensely lobbied for by Russia, China, and India and brokered thanks to the essential role of Brazil and, to a lesser extent, South Africa.

The process aimed at creating partnerships, promoting joint research projects, and fostering policy synergies may be considered an example of what in Internet governance vernacular is commonly referred to as 'enhanced cooperation'.[65] This context has spurred renewed efforts to build and modernize

[61] See BRICS, V BRICS Summit, eThekwini Declaration (Durban 2013), para 34.

[62] For an analysis of such documents and their impact see Vladimir Kiselev and Elena Nechaeva, 'Priorities and Possible Risks of the BRICS Countries' Cooperation in Science, Technology and Innovation' (2018) 5(4) BRICS Law Journal <https://web.archive.org/web/20221114213642/https://www.bricslawjournal.com/jour/article/view/193> accessed 8 October 2021.

[63] See BRICS, Second BRICS Science, Technology and Innovation Ministerial Meeting, BRICS Memorandum of Understanding on Cooperation in Science, Technology and Innovation (Brasília, 18 March 2015) <https://www.gov.br/mre/pt-br/canais_atendimento/imprensa/notas-a-imprensa/ii-reuniao-de-ministros-de-ciencia-tecnologia-e-inovacao-do-brics-documentos-aprovados-brasilia-18-de-marco-de-2015> accessed 8 October 2021.

[64] BRICS, XIII BRICS Summit, New Delhi Declaration (9 September 2021) <https://web.archive.org/web/20231015202017/https://brics2021.gov.in/brics/public/uploads/docpdf/getdocu-51.pdf> accessed 8 October 2021.

[65] The concept of 'enhanced cooperation' is introduced by paras 69 and 71 of the Tunis Agenda for the Information Society. See n 50. Importantly, the United Nations Economic and Social Council has acknowledged that 'the Tunis Agenda underlines the need for enhanced cooperation to enable Governments to carry out their roles and responsibilities in international public policy issues

digital policies in general and data governance frameworks in particular. Conspicuously, while elaborating their frameworks, the BRICS have enjoyed the advantage of having the most modern data protection standards—chiefly, the European General Data Protection Regulation (GDPR) and the updated OECD Guidelines on the Protection of Privacy and Transborder Flows of Personal Data—as a source of inspiration, while adapting the norms to their domestic legal traditions and political systems.

Importantly, the enhancement of BRICS digital policy cooperation and the movement towards personal data protection are producing particularly interesting outcomes. Being 'late-movers', BRICS countries have learned from first movers' successes and failures, thus not only 'transplanting'[66] foreign best practices into their domestic frameworks, but also innovating data protection practices.[67] Furthermore, by taking inspiration from the same sources, BRICS frameworks are triggering policy convergence and enabling 'legal interoperability', due to the increasing compatibility of the BRICS normative frameworks regulating the protection of personal data. As will be pointed out in the next section as well as in the conclusion of this volume, this latter point has now officially entered the BRICS agenda, having been explicitly included as part of the BRICS commitments since the 2024 Summit.

1.2.1. Enhanced Cooperation on ICT Governance

As an outcome of the fifth BRICS Summit, held in the South African city of Durban in 2013, the BRICS leaders for the first time agreed on enhancing 'cooperation on combating cybercrimes and we also recommit to the negotiation of a universal legally binding instrument in that field [considering] that the UN has a central role in this matter'.[68] This commitment was reiterated at the subsequent fifth Summit, in Fortaleza, and expanded at the seventh BRICS Summit,

pertaining to the Internet [but does] not specify how the process of enhanced cooperation should be designed, the means by which enhanced cooperation could be achieved or how the desired results should manifest themselves in practice'. See United Nations (General Assembly, Economic and Social Council), 'Enhanced cooperation on public policy issues pertaining to the Internet, Report of the Secretary-General' (4 May 2011, A/66/77–E/2011/103).

[66] The concept of 'legal transplantation' is well-known in comparative law studies and refers to 'the moving of a rule or system of law from one country to another'. See A Watson, *Legal Transplants: An Approach to Comparative Law* (University of Georgia Press 1974) 21.
[67] See L Belli above (n 17).
[68] BRICS, V BRICS Summit, eThekwini Declaration (27 March 2013), para 34 <https://brics-ysf.org/sites/default/files/5th_Summit.pdf>.

held in the Russian city of Ufa in 2015, when the BRICS Declaration asserted the 'inadmissibility of using ICTs and the Internet to violate human rights and fundamental freedoms, including the right to privacy, and reaffirm[ed] that the same rights that people have offline must also be protected online'.[69] At the same time the Ufa Declaration stressed that 'a system ensuring confidentiality and protection of users' personal data should be considered' and BRICS leaders reiterated their 'condemnation of mass electronic surveillance and data collection of individuals all over the world, as well as violation of the sovereignty of States and of human rights, in particular, the right to privacy'.

While the reader might be forgiven for thinking that such a commitment might sound peculiar, coming from some countries that have less than stellar records in terms of privacy protection, the consideration of the abovementioned elements is key to understanding the rationale behind the successive policy developments at both international and domestic BRICS level in the subsequent years. To operationalize their stated intentions and enhance their cooperation and coordination, BRICS leaders established a BRICS Working Group on ICT Cooperation so that 'members could actively lead and cooperate to strategize synergies, . . . sharing of information and case studies on ICT policies and programs in creating an enabling environment'.[70]

It is important to realize that the goal of the working group is to foster exchange of policy strategies adopted at domestic level and facilitate the development of shared positions at the international level, primarily at the UN level, which is considered by all BRICS as the only legitimate forum having a central role to play as regards the establishment of global regulatory frameworks, notably with regard to ICT and data regulation. The subsequent Goa Declaration, resulting from the eighth Summit, adopted a more assertive posture regarding BRICS-led policymaking efforts, stressing the potential for cooperation amongst the BRICS countries that could 'work together for the adoption of the rules, norms and principles of responsible behaviour of States including through the process of the United Nations Group of Governmental Experts (UNGGE)'.[71]

By explicitly mentioning the joint elaboration of rules, norms, and principles, BRICS leaders crossed the Rubicon, willingly showing a clear intention to enhance cooperation in international digital policymaking. Subsequent

[69] See BRICS, VII BRICS Summit, Ufa Declaration (9 July 2015) <https://web.archive.org/web/20231015210449/https://brics2021.gov.in/BRICSDocuments/2015/Ufa-Declaration-2015.pdf> accessed 8 October 2021.

[70] ibid.

[71] ibid.

years witnessed the establishment of several initiatives aimed at making co-operation on technological and digital matters more tangible, such as the BRICS Digital Partnership,[72] the BRICS Science & Technology Enterprise Partnership (BRICS-STEP, subsequently renamed STIEP), the BRICS Partnership on New Industrial Revolution (PartNIR), the Innovation BRICS Network (iBRICS Network), and the BRICS Institute of Future Networks.[73]

1.2.2. A New Phase for BRICS Digital Cooperation

The abovementioned policy and operational initiatives emphasize 'the importance of continuing BRICS scientific, technical, innovation and entrepreneurship cooperation',[74] as well as that of understanding that the development of technology and innovation is a key vector to convey the values that are traditionally part of policies and regulations. This posture culminated in the elaboration of an Enabling Framework for the Innovation BRICS Network (iBRICS Network), 'a mechanism for direct dialogue among actors of innovation of the BRICS countries, which will promote mutual support, joint projects and the exchange of best practices with a view to advancing BRICS systems of innovation'.[75]

Besides the Enabling Framework, the 2019 BRICS Summit, organized under the Brazilian Presidency, led to the adoption of two relevant innovations, corroborating the thesis of an ongoing enhanced cooperation: the new BRICS Science, Technology, and Innovation Work Plan 2019–2022[76] and the establishment of a new BRICS Science, Technology, and Innovation (STI) Architecture.[77] Notably, the BRICS STI Architecture aims at defining an 'agile cooperation governance structure' to improve and prioritize the coordination

72 See BRICS Working Group on ICT Cooperation, 'ICT Development Agenda and Action Plan' (Bengaluru, 11 November 2016).

73 ibid.

74 See Ministério das Relações Exteriores, 'BRICS Informal Leaders' Meeting on the Margins of the G20 Summit—Joint Media Statement—Osaka, 28 June 2019' <https://www.gov.br/mre/en/contact-us/press-area/press-releases/brics-informal-leaders-meeting-on-the-margins-of-the-g20-summit-joint-media-statement-osaka-28-june-2019> accessed 8 October 2021.

75 See BRICS, 'Enabling Framework for the Innovation BRICS Network "iBRICS Network"' (2019) <https://web.archive.org/web/20220120134725/http://brics2019.itamaraty.gov.br/images/documentos/Enabling_Framework_iBRICS_Network__Final.pdf> accessed 8 October 2021.

76 See BRICS, 'BRICS Science, Technology and Innovation Work Plan 2019–2022' (October 2019) <https://web.archive.org/web/20210919232524/http://brics2019.itamaraty.gov.br/images/documentos/BRICS_STI_Work_Plan_2019-2022__Final.pdf> accessed 8 October 2021.

77 See BRICS, 'A New BRICS STI Architecture' (September 2019) <https://web.archive.org/web/20210919230350/http://brics2019.itamaraty.gov.br/images/documentos/The_New_BRICS_STI_Architecture__Steering_Committee__Final_19_9_19.pdf> accessed 8 October 2021.

and management of BRICS STI activities, at measuring and evaluating STI initiatives, to minimize their development risks and optimize their impact, and at ensuring dissemination of BRICS STI activities amongst different stakeholders.[78]

The BRICS-led initiatives and particularly the BRICS STI Architecture highlight the potential but also the remaining challenges to be faced to achieve concrete results through cooperation. This is clearly not an easy task, due to the very elastic configuration of BRICS, the mounting number of members, and the lack of a coordinating body: there is no stable 'BRICS Secretariat': the Presidency is rotating, thus increasing the difficulty of monitoring the effective execution of all existing initiatives. However, history demonstrates that, despite their different perspectives, their diversity of approaches has always been acknowledged as a point of richness rather than a weakness, and considerable results, such as the establishment of the NDB, have been achieved.

In this spirit, the twelfth BRICS Summit culminated with the adoption of a new Strategy for BRICS Economic Partnership 2025, featuring Digital Economy as one of the three key pillars of the strategy around which to 'define a development path of BRICS and set the framework for cooperation of its members'.[79] Indeed, as stressed by the Strategy, the 'development and adoption of digital technologies becomes a determinant of sustainable economic growth of the grouping'[80] and, for this reason, BRICS countries 'acknowledge the importance of digital governance in the era of global digitalization and cooperate with each other in the area of digital governance' and have committed to take steps to 'exchange experiences and explore approaches to regulatory issues of digital transformation of economy'.[81] These latter document is particularly relevant as it clearly states the importance of jointly considering developmental, governance and regulatory issues, highlighting that this is a key BRICS feature of the grouping approach to digital matters.

The BRICS Leaders 2021 Declaration represented a further milestone, as the countries have started recognizing explicitly the value of enhanced cooperation in these issues. Indeed, the 2021 Declaration contains an explicit commitment of BRICS heads of state to the 'respect of the right to privacy of individuals' and the promotion of cybersecurity,

[78] ibid.

[79] See BRICS, 'Strategy for BRICS Economic Partnership 2025' (November 2020) <https://web.archive.org/web/20210919232524/http://brics2019.itamaraty.gov.br/images/documentos/BRICS_STI_Work_Plan_2019-2022__Final.pdf> accessed 8 October 2021.

[80] ibid 8.

[81] ibid 8–9.

> *advance[ing] practical intra-BRICS cooperation in this domain*, including through the implementation of the BRICS Roadmap of Practical Cooperation on ensuring Security in the Use of ICTs and the activities of the BRICS Working Group on Security in the use of ICTs, and underscore[ing] also the importance of *establishing legal frameworks of cooperation among BRICS States on this matter* and acknowledge[ing] the work towards consideration and elaboration of proposals, including on *a BRICS intergovernmental agreement on cooperation* on ensuring security in the use of ICTs and on *bilateral agreements among BRICS countries.*[82]

Hence BRICS' enhanced cooperation has been developing on three different fronts: i) through the research and scientific initiatives highlighted above; ii) through the establishment of a joint institution, the NDB, aimed at providing funding for development projects; and iii) through the policy coordination that, as anticipated above, may find its most structured example in the process that led to the adoption of the new UN Convention against Cybercrime. Indeed, for almost a decade, BRICS members have coordinated their digital-policy approaches, identifying as the common denominator the need to craft a universal regulatory framework on cybercrime under the aegis of the United Nations.

It is important to note that in August 2024 this vision came to fruition with the adoption of the new UN Convention against Cybercrime, an effort that RIC countries, chiefly Russia, had been trying to promote at least since the early 2010s.[83] Until recently, the mere idea that the proposal of a global cybercrime treaty led by Russia and China and backed by BRICS countries and their Global South partners could be adopted by the UN was considered less than seriously by most observers. Recent developments compellingly demonstrate how everything is relative and things can significantly change. Crucially, despite the criticisms that can legitimately be raised about the Convention[84]—whose scope is so broad that it could facilitate surveillance and repression—its adoption represents a concrete instance of the impact that BRICS coordination and joint action may have regarding international digital policymaking.

[82] BRICS, XIII BRICS Summit, New Delhi Declaration (9 September 2021) <https://web.archive.org/web/20231015202017/https://brics2021.gov.in/brics/public/uploads/docpdf/getdocu-51.pdf> accessed 8 October 2021 (emphasis added).

[83] M Ballard, 'UN Rejects International Cybercrime Treaty' *Computer Weekly* (20 April 2010) <https://www.computerweekly.com/news/1280092617/UN-rejects-international-cybercrime-treaty>.

[84] T Hassan, 'Upcoming Cybercrime Treaty Will Be Nothing But Trouble' *Human Rights Watch* (7 August 2024) <https://www.hrw.org/news/2024/08/07/upcoming-cybercrime-treaty-will-be-nothing-trouble>.

In this respect, the BRICS should be seen as a laboratory for policy coordination of Global South leaders. The push towards cooperation and convergence is increasingly involving governance, policymaking, and regulatory areas, besides research, development, and trade partnerships. The following section posits that the recent BRICS data protection developments provide useful material to observe how the elaboration of domestic frameworks, together with their shared international aspirations, are offering an opportunity to align BRICS data policies. This objective has been clearly emphasized by the most recent Kazan Declaration, where BRICS + heads of state openly advocate for a 'global framework for data governance, including cross-border data flows, to address the principles of collection, storage, use and transfer of data [to] ensure the interoperability of data policy frameworks'.[85]

This objective builds upon an already established willingness to strengthen cooperation on e-commerce issues, as clearly expressed by the India-chaired 2021 Summit that adopted the BRICS Framework for Ensuring Consumer Protection in e-Commerce. This document recognized that '[a]dequate safeguards and measures are needed to ensure privacy and security of the consumers [and resolved] to enhance cooperation through the BRICS E-commerce Working Group', while also emphasizing 'the role of the digital economy as an important tool for modernization and transformation of the industry, promotion of inclusive economic growth, support of seamless global trade and business conduct, thus helping BRICS economies meet their Sustainable Development Goals'.[86]

As this volume will illustrate, many data protection policy elements are already remarkably similar in the BRICS countries and, given this already existing compatibility, the enhancement of their legal interoperability, perhaps through the adoption of a 'BRICS Data Protection Framework' or a 'BRICS Data Security Framework', may respond to the call for 'a legal framework of cooperation' highlighted above, and should be considered as a strategic priority for the BRICS. Moreover, as will be suggested in the following sections, in their effort to regulate data protection, BRICS are putting forward some innovative elements that should be utilized as 'experiences' to be exchanged, as suggested by the Strategy for BRICS Economic Partnership 2025. Non-BRICS countries would also benefit from studying such alternative 'experiences', which

[85] See above (n 11).
[86] BRICS, 'Framework for Ensuring Consumer Protection in e-Commerce' (2021) <https://web.archive.org/web/20240616213528/https://brics2021.gov.in/brics/public/uploads/docpdf/getdocu-44.pdf>.

provide useful approaches to tackling challenges that are faced by virtually all countries.

1.3. Data Protection in the BRICS

To understand why BRICS digital policies and, particularly, their data protection frameworks are especially relevant, it is necessary to consider not only that these countries encompass roughly 40 per cent of the world population, but that more than 40 per cent of global Internet users are also from the BRICS.[87] Personal data refer to and are generated by individuals. Hence, a population of 3.2 billion individuals, of whom more than half are connected to digital technologies, makes the BRICS grouping the largest producer of what is currently deemed the world's most valuable resource and a 'new asset class'.[88] Data governance is therefore essential, not only for the functioning of economy and society but also for the assertion of (digital) sovereignty.[89]

Importantly, the large number of connected individuals contributes not only to the creation of enormous consumer bases and consequent data pools. It also expands remarkably the number of potential developers that can shape the evolution of technology well beyond the BRICS countries.

The abovementioned considerations and the mounting economic and geopolitical relevance of personal data have triggered intense data-related policymaking efforts in all BRICS countries. The Snowden revelations elevated 'security in the use of Information and Communication Technologies (ICTs)' to the level of 'paramount importance',[90] while the ninth BRICS Summit Xiamen Declaration enshrined the countries' commitment to jointly 'advocate the establishment of internationally applicable rules for security of ICT infrastructure, data protection and the Internet'.[91] In this context, alignment in data-related policies has been growing.

This section explores some of the results of the comparative research developed by the CyberBRICS project, regarding data protection. While the BRICS frameworks deserve in-depth analysis, this section highlights some of the most striking commonalities, highlighting the existence of a certain degree of

[87] 'Internet Users by Country' (Internet Live Stats, 2016) <https://www.internetlivestats.com/internet-users-by-country/> accessed 8 October 2021.
[88] World Economic Forum, *Personal Data: The Emergence of a New Asset Class* (WEF 2011).
[89] See above (n 7, 48).
[90] See BRICS (n 18) para 34.
[91] See BRICS, IX BRICS Summit, Xiamen Declaration (4 September 2017) <http://www.mea.gov.in/uploads/publicationdocs/28912_xiamendeclaratoin.pdf> accessed 8 October 2021.

compatibility.[92] All BRICS countries have undertaken major regulatory developments regarding data protection in recent years, elaborating new legislation, updating existing laws, or establishing new regulatory agencies.

The most recent developments include:

- In Brazil, the adoption in August 2018 of a new General Data Protection Law (Law 13.709/2018)[93] that entered in force in September 2020, the establishment of a new National Data Protection Authority (ANPD)[94] in late 2020, and a new National Council on Privacy and Data Protection. In February 2022, the new fundamental right to data protection was enacted in the Brazilian Constitution,[95] and the transformation of the ANPD into a formally independent agency between 2022 and 2023.[96]
- Russia, in late 2020, amended its general data protection law (Federal Law No 152-FZ on Personal Data), having reinforced its data localization obligations in 2019, with the adoption of the so-called 'Sovereign Internet Law'. The localization of major Internet companies in Russian territory was introduced in July 2021; in September 2022 new data security requirements entered into force, together with the state system for the detection, prevention, and elimination of consequences of computer attacks (GosSOPKA).
- In India in August 2017 the Supreme Court recognized privacy as a new fundamental right, thus opening the path to the elaboration of a new Data Protection Bill, which was introduced in Parliament in December 2019 and considerably reshaped by subsequent Parliamentary Committees and consultation processes. The final version of the Bill was adopted in August 2023 as the Digital Personal Data Protection Act 2023. India is also experimenting with electronic consent frameworks within its Data Empowerment and Protection Architecture (DEPA), in the context of the so-called 'India Stack' aimed at propelling a new vision of Digital India, leveraging Digital Public Infrastructures (DPIs).

[92] See above (n 10).

[93] See CyberBRICS Project, 'Brazilian General Data Protection Law—Unofficial English version' (2020) <https://cyberbrics.info/brazilian-general-data-protection-law-lgpd-unofficial-english-version/> accessed 8 October 2021.

[94] The official website of the new Brazilian Data Protection Agency is available at <https://www.gov.br/anpd/pt-br>.

[95] In May 2020, Brazil's Supreme Court recognized a fundamental right to data protection in the 1988 Brazilian Constitution, derived but not coincident with the right to privacy and the 'habeas data' writ.

[96] See CyberBRICS Project, 'Non-official Translation of Executive Order n. 1124/2022, Which Transforms the Brazilian Data Protection Authority into an Independent Administrative Agency' (2022) <https://cyberbrics.info/non-official-translation-of-executive-order-n-1124-2022/>.

- China formally considers data as a factor of production since 2019. In August 2021 it adopted its new Personal Information Protection Law (PIPL), having in January 2021 adopted a new Data Security Law in June 2021 and having also introduced new rights to privacy and the protection of personal information in its new Civil Code. China also adopted stringent measures on security assessment of outbound data transfers in September 2022, later announcing in September 2023 that this would be made more flexible.
- South Africa in 2017 established its new data protection authority, the Information Regulator, to oversee implementation of the 2013 Protection of Personal Information Act (POPIA), which entered fully into force in July 2021. In 2022, the Information Regulator established its Enforcement Committee, an essential organ to fully implementing and being able to enforce POPIA.

In a very condensed timeframe, BRICS countries have revolutionized their domestic data protection frameworks, introducing major developments in their legal systems. Interestingly, despite the absence of any formal agreement mandating the harmonization of their national frameworks, several regulatory elements are emerging in an extraordinarily similar fashion. The main reason for such convergence is likely the common inspiration from existing frameworks, particularly the European General Data Protection Regulation (GDPR), the Council of Europe Convention 108, and the OECD Guidelines on the Protection of Privacy and Transborder Flows of Personal Data.

While the BRICS domestic frameworks on data protection present a shared skeleton highlighting several similarities, it is important to stress that there are also considerable differences. Some of the similarities include: (i) the definition of personal data in itself, which all BRICS countries consider as the information related to an identified or identifiable natural person; (ii) the core principles and individual rights upon which the data protection architecture is erected; (iii) the set of obligations for data controllers and processors; (iv) recognition of the essential role of international data transfers for the (digital) economy;[97] (v) the extraterritorial reach of data protection laws; (vi) the application of these norms to government activities, although with multiple exceptions and varying levels of intensity; and (vii) the creation of data regulatory authorities to support the application of these laws.

[97] See Belli, Gaspar, and Singh (n 7).

Conversely, some divergences include (i) the different stances toward data localization; (ii) the suite of available legal tools for international data transfers; and (iii) particularities of some BRICS data protection laws, such as the possibility to use DPIs as consent managers in India, the Chinese requirement for major online platforms to establish independent oversight committees for personal information protection, or South Africa's 'personal data' rights extending beyond natural persons to include legal persons as well. These, in sum, are indicators of the convergence and divergence of BRICS states around a shared 'data protection skeleton', which showcase points of potential tension and legal interoperability. These points will be analysed in more detail in the following chapters and the conclusion of this volume.

1.4. Towards Legal Interoperability on Data Protection in the BRICS?

As the following chapters will illustrate, a shared data protection skeleton is emerging in the BRICS, but the national frameworks also include remarkably different and unique elements that should be studied carefully. It would be naïve to argue that the rising relevance of data protection in the BRICS is merely due to global policy trends, such as the so-called 'Brussels effect' triggered by the adoption of GDPR, or the numerous data-related scandals. As argued previously, a key element is the increasing awareness of the economic and strategic value of data, in this context, the understanding that personal data laws are essential—although clearly not sufficient—to foster well-functioning and cybersecure digital economies, while strengthening digital sovereignty.[98]

In this context, the BRICS' willingness to protect personal data and enhance their cooperation regarding digital policy stems from the consideration that compatible regulations may be enormously beneficial to foster digital trade and online businesses, while achieving their shared cybersecurity goals. Hence, the establishment of compatible BRICS solutions for data governance may be seen as an experiment aimed at scaling up such solutions 'for the design of a fair and equitable **global framework for data governance**, including cross-border data flows', as proclaimed by the 2024 BRICS Declaration.

[98] ibid. See also, above 7 and 48, and L Belli, 'From BRICS to CyberBRICS: New Cybersecurity Cooperation' *China Today* (13 November 2021) <http://www.chinatoday.com.cn/ctenglish/2018/tpxw/201911/t20191113_800184922.html> accessed 14 October 2024.

The governments of the BRICS nations clearly understand that each of their citizens is a producer of personal data that, combined, have not only immense economic relevance, but also unmatchable strategic value.[99] Moreover, the demand for data protection is growing amongst the billions of people in the BRICS, as many individuals are beginning to understand the potential value of their data, the risks that personal data processing may entail, and the subjective dimensions of data sovereignty.[100]

In this context, modern and compatible frameworks are instrumental to protecting individual rights and providing legal certainty for businesses, while also being a key pillar of international digital trade. As this introductory chapter has argued, BRICS countries have already developed a remarkably homogeneous normative basis. This aspect of BRICS data protection regulations will be expanded upon in the following chapters, dedicating particular attention to potential vectors of legal interoperability in the concluding chapter of this volume. However, the following chapters of this volume will also illustrate the many differences that exist, and that it is indeed in the interest of the grouping to work toward the enhancement of digital cooperation in general and legal interoperability in data-related policy in particular. Lastly, it is also important to keep in mind that the drive towards legal interoperability can be influenced by several factors, including global geopolitical and regulatory trends, the concrete economic incentives and strategic interests that can foster—or hinder—cooperation and harmonization efforts, and the public support for or aversion to such efforts. Legal interoperability in data protection brings multiple benefits, spanning from the reduction of barriers to cross-border data flows, thus increasing economic growth and partnership opportunities in research, development, and innovation, while also strengthening cybersecurity through the adoption of shared information security standards.

From this perspective, as argued in the concluding chapter of this volume, the promotion of legal interoperability in data governance is likely to strengthen data sovereignty through a collaborative effort. Indeed, the definition of shared regulatory arrangements for data governance and data transfers can enhance transparency, accountability, security, and control over personal data, thus extending the reach of data subjects' rights while increasing legal certainty for data controllers as well as for regulators.

[99] See above (n 87).

[100] See above 48 and Anja Kovacs and Nayantara Ranganathan, 'Data Sovereignty, of Whom? Limits and Suitability of Sovereignty Frameworks for Data in India' (2019) Data Governance Network Working Paper 03 <https://cyberbrics.info/data-sovereignty-of-whom-limits-and-suitability-of-sovereignty-frameworks-for-data-in-india/> accessed 14 October 2021.

As stressed in the earlier sections of this chapter, over the past decade the BRICS countries have been constructing the basis of their legal interoperability through multiple BRICS declarations and high-level documents, but also an increasing number of concrete partnerships. The latest evolutions expressed in the BRICS 2024 Declaration suggest that the path towards legal interoperability in data governance is a firm choice, driven by global trends, economic incentives, and shared strategic interests. While their unique national idiosyncrasies present challenges, the benefits of promoting shared solution to data governance are clear. Importantly, it should be understood that by working together to enhance digital cooperation and achieve legal interoperability in data-related policy, the BRICS can act as a policy laboratory for Global South-driven solutions, defining the basis of a more inclusive digital economy.

2
THE PERSONAL DATA ARCHITECTURE OF BRAZIL

Walter Britto Gaspar

2.1. Introduction: Legal Architecture of Data Flows in Brazil

This chapter is concerned with the legal architecture of personal data flows in Brazil. In particular, it will deal with the legal instruments involved in the collection and processing of personal data in the country, as well as the institutions involved in that processing. This entails looking at the laws that may influence personal data processing operations, as well as other types of norms and guidance documents. Each of these will be presented and their main points highlighted to explain how they fit in the personal data protection architecture.

Reference should also be made to legal instruments that deal with information security in its various instances, be it when data is stored or in transit, by public or private actors. This is an aspect of data architectures that runs in parallel to personal data protection, but in many ways overlaps with it—since information security deals with aspects of data processing that are instrumental to the realization of the right to data protection.

Brazil currently has no overarching data security law such as China's or South Africa's, although there have been many normative policy and planning documents on the subject so far and the country has signed and internalized the Budapest Convention on cybercrime.[1] The most recent effort in this direction was the enactment of a new National Cybersecurity Policy, rooted in concepts of national sovereignty and protection of fundamental rights; and

[1] Ministério da Justiça e Segurança Pública, Convenção de Budapeste é promulgada no Brasil, 17 April 2023 <https://www.gov.br/mj/pt-br/assuntos/noticias/convencao-de-budapeste-e-promulgada-no-brasil>; Luca Belli and others, *Cibersegurança: Uma Visão Sistêmica Rumo A Uma Proposta De Marco Regulatório Para Um Brasil Digitalmente Soberano* (FGV Direito Rio 2023) <https://cyberbrics.info/ciberseguranca-uma-visao-sistemica-rumo-a-uma-proposta-de-marco-regulatorio-para-um-brasil-digitalmente-soberano/>.

Walter Britto Gaspar, *The Personal Data Architecture of Brazil* In: *Personal Data Architectures in the BRICS Countries*. Edited by: Luca Belli and Walter Britto Gaspar, Oxford University Press.
© Luca Belli and Walter B. Gaspar 2025. DOI: 10.1093/9780198974468.003.0002

the resulting discussions around the creation of a National Cybersecurity Authority to unify regulation, inter-agency coordination and oversight of the subject nationally.[2] This cybersecurity blueprint makes up a backdrop for the personal data architectures described and discussed herein.

Brazil has had a long but sparse trajectory on these subjects up until recently. Unification of personal data protection rights under one overarching law is a recent development in the Brazilian legal landscape. This means new legislation enters a field populated not only by other specific laws, but also by other institutions in general, including bureaucratic bodies and processes, specialized judicial actors, and law enforcement practices. All this unfurls in the face of ongoing public discourse that in many ways reflects global dichotomies between protection of rights and structures of vigilance.[3]

Beyond all that, new norms are being discussed or implemented on topics that intertwine with data architectures. One relevant recent example is the draft Artificial Intelligence Bill,[4] currently awaiting discussion in the country's Chamber of Deputies after approval in the Federal Senate. Although focused on AI applications, due to the very nature of these technologies, it will also touch upon matters of personal data collection and flows.

It should also be noted that Brazil is a presidential democracy with regular elections and a normative framework under the Federal Constitution of 1988, with a comprehensive approach to fundamental rights rooted in human dignity. The Constitution upholds human rights among its principles in international relations and ensures internal validity of international human rights treaties approved under special proceedings at the same level as constitutional amendments. Brazil has been classified as 'Free' under Freedom House's Freedom in the World report[5] for the last five years, a highlight being the

[2] Gabinete de Segurança Institucional, CNCiber (Comitê Nacional de Cibersegurança) <https://web.archive.org/web/20250417144230/https://www.gov.br/gsi/pt-br/colegiados-do-gsi/comite-nacional-de-ciberseguranca-cnciber/CNCiber> accessed 27 March 2025; Rafael Bucco, 'Governo Publica Nova Política Nacional de Cibersegurança' *TeleSíntese* (27 December 2023) <https://telesintese.com.br/governo-publica-nova-politica-nacional-de-ciberseguranca-com-anatel-no-comite/>; Redação, 'Criado o Comitê de Cibersegurança' *TeleSíntese* (14 February 2024) <https://telesintese.com.br/criado-o-comite-de-ciberseguranca-cnciber/>; Secretaria de Comunicação Social, 'O que é a Política Nacional de Cibersegurança, marco no combate aos crimes virtuais', (29 December 2023) <https://www.gov.br/secom/pt-br/fatos/brasil-contra-fake/noticias/2023/12/o-que-e-a-politica-nacional-de-ciberseguranca-marco-no-combate-aos-crimes-virtuais>.

[3] Shoshana Zuboff, *The Age of Surveillance Capitalism: The Fight for a Human Future at the New Frontier of Power* (Profile Books 2019).

[4] Walter Britto Gaspar, Eduardo Mattos, and Luca Belli, 'Non-Official Translation of the Brazilian Artificial Intelligence Bill, n. 21/2020' (*CyberBRICS*, 25 October 2021) <https://cyberbrics.info/non-official-translation-of-the-brazilian-artificial-intelligence-bill-n-21-2020/>.

[5] Freedom House, *Brazil: Freedom in the World 2023 Country Report* (Freedom House 2023) <https://freedomhouse.org/country/brazil/freedom-world/2023>.

polarized electoral process and political scenario of the most recent presidential elections, in 2022. It has been classified as 'Partly free' in the Freedom on the Net report[6] by the same entity in the last five years, noting provisions contained in the country's 'fake news' bill, actions taken against disinformation during elections, and issues related to the economic exclusion of minorities, among others. All in all, Brazilian institutions, including regular elections, have been through tempestuous times lately, but the country has managed to maintain its constitutional democratic system.

In terms of the protection given to personal data under this framework, there have been significant developments in recent years. Even before the General Data Protection Law fully entered into force, in 2020, in a case discussing the legality of sharing telecommunication services' customer data with the National Statics Institute (IBGE), an important judicial interpretation was set. The case evidenced the existence of an autonomous fundamental right to personal data protection under the Brazilian Constitution—echoing, in BRICS, the significance of the *Puttaswamy v Union of India* case in India, which recognized the existence of an autonomous fundamental right to privacy in the country's Constitution as a consequence of the protection of human dignity (art 1, III; art 5, X), the right to habeas data (art 5, LXIX), the protection of due process (art 5, LIV) and the protection of private life (art 5, X).[7] This was later reinforced by the inclusion of section LXXIX to article 5 of the Constitution via amendment no 115 of 2022, adding the protection of personal data as a fundamental right.

All these factors shall be dealt with in the following discussion, focused on the legal architecture of personal data protection in Brazil—its accomplishments so far and challenges to come.

2.2. The Pre-LGPD Normative Framework

The Brazilian normative landscape regarding data protection has seen significant advances lately with the enactment of the country's General Data

[6] Freedom House, *Brazil: Freedom on the Net 2023 Country Report* (Freedom House 2023) <https://freedomhouse.org/country/brazil/freedom-net/2023>.

[7] Bruno Ricardo Bioni and Renato Leite Monteiro, 'A Landmark Ruling in Brazil: Paving the Way for Considering Data Protection as an Autonomous Fundamental Right' (Future of Privacy Forum, 9 June 2020) <https://fpf.org/blog/a-landmark-ruling-in-brazil-paving-the-way-for-considering-data-protection-as-an-autonomous-fundamental-right/>.

Protection Law (LGPD, in the Portuguese abbreviation)[8] and creation of its National Data Protection Authority (ANPD). However, there existed a previous legal structure regarding privacy rights and information rights, which paved the way to the current architecture.

2.2.1. The Federal Constitution and the Civil Code

Firstly, it is relevant to stress that the civil and constitutional legal orders in Brazil give space and importance to personality rights, among which is the right to privacy. In fact, the Brazilian Civil Code (law no 10.406/02) has a chapter (c II, arts 11–21) dedicated to 'personality rights', and within it one finds, alongside image rights, bodily autonomy, and other personality rights, specific protection to private life in article 21[9]:

> Art. 21. Private life of the natural person is inviolable, and the judge, upon request by the interested party, shall adopt the necessary procedures to avoid or stop any act contrary to this norm.

In the 1988 Federal Constitution[10] this is reflected in a series of fundamental rights: inviolability of intimacy, private life, honour, and image (art 5, X); inviolability of the homestead (art 5, XI); and secrecy of communications, correspondence, data communication, and telephone communications (art 5, XII). The latter gave rise to debate within the Brazilian legal scholarship on the extent of the right to privacy of data: whether it was to be restricted to data in transit or should also apply to stored data. In other words, if protection was given to communications or to data itself.[11]

This controversy hints at the limited reach of dealing with issues of data protection solely on privacy grounds: the challenges of the information age, summarized by Zuboff[12] as surveillance capitalism, require an approach that

[8] Luca Belli and others, 'The Brazilian General Data Protection Law (LGPD). Unofficial English Version' (*CyberBRICS*, January 2020) <https://cyberbrics.info/brazilian-general-data-protection-law-lgpd-unofficial-english-version/>.

[9] Brazil, Código Civil (l. n. 10.406/02) (10 January 2002) <http://www.planalto.gov.br/ccivil_03/leis/2002/l10406compilada.htm>.

[10] Brazil, Constituição Federal (1988) <http://www.planalto.gov.br/ccivil_03/constituicao/constituicao.htm>.

[11] Danilo Doneda, *Da Privacidade à Proteção de Dados Pessoais: Fundamentos Da Lei Geral de Proteção de Dados*, 2ª (Thomson Reuters Brasil 2019) 262; Danilo Doneda, 'Panorama Histórico Da Proteção de Dados Pessoais' in Danilo Doneda and others (eds) *Tratado de Proteção de Dados Pessoais* (Forense 2021) 11–12.

[12] Zuboff, *The Age of Surveillance Capitalism* (n 3).

tackles data processing in a more adequate manner. This would become increasingly clear in Brazilian legal practice and public discourse, with issues involving not only secrecy of intimate data, but of control over personal data flows arising.

One more instance where the subject of personal information is detailed in the Constitution is the fundamental right to habeas data, that is, the right to access information concerning oneself and to correct erroneous information (art 5, LXXII). Habeas data is further regulated in a specific law (no 9.507/97)[13]. Habeas data reflected a mounting demand for control of the use of personal data, especially in accordance with the country's redemocratization process. It was also influenced by earlier foreign specific data protection concerns—especially, in the United States, the National Data Center debate in the 1960s and 70s.[14] The constitutional remedy has a very limited scope, though, directed at knowledge and correction of personal data held in public or public interest databases, and thus was equally unsuited to responding to the full scheme of data protection issues presented by a connected society.

2.2.2. A New Fundamental Right to Data Protection

These would have been the sole mentions of privacy or, by interpretative extension, data protection in the Brazilian Constitution up until recently. However, in October 2021 the Brazilian Senate unanimously approved a constitutional amendment project,[15] promulgated as Constitutional Amendment no 115 on February 2022,[16] that added an autonomous right to data protection into the roster of fundamental rights in article 5 of the Constitution:

> Art. 5º All are equal before the law, without distinction of any nature, being assured to Brazilians and foreigners residing in the Country inviolability

[13] Brazil, L. n. 9507/97 (1997) <http://www.planalto.gov.br/ccivil_03/leis/l9507.htm>.

[14] Doneda, 'Panorama Histórico Da Proteção de Dados Pessoais' (n 11).

[15] Agência Senado, 'Senado Federal Aprova Proposta de Emenda à Constituição 17 (PEC 17/2019) Que Inclui a Proteção de Dados Pessoais No Rol de Direitos e Garantias Fundamentais' *Gov.br* (26 October 2021) <https://www.gov.br/anpd/pt-br/assuntos/noticias/senado-federal-aprova-proposta-de-emenda-a-constituicao-17-pec-17-2019-que-inclui-a-protecao-de-dados-pessoais-no-rol-de-direitos-e-garantias-fundamentais>.

[16] José Carlos Oliveira, 'Promulgada PEC Que Inclui a Proteção de Dados Pessoais Entre Direitos Fundamentais Do Cidadão' *Portal da Câmara dos Deputados* (10 February 2022) <https://www.camara.leg.br/noticias/850028-promulgada-pec-que-inclui-a-protecao-de-dados-pessoais-entre-direitos-fundamentais-do-cidadao/>.

of their right to life, liberty, equality, security and property, in the following terms:

...

LXXIX—it is assured, as dictated by law, the right to personal data protection, including in digital media.

This makes Brazil the BRICS country with the best-defined independent constitutional right to data protection, whereas others, such as India and South Africa, derive this right from the right to privacy. The amendment also determines that the Federal government is responsible for organizing and enforcing personal data processing and protection, as well its sole competence for proposing legislation on the matter.

This development came shortly after the enactment of an overarching data protection law in the country and the creation of its National Data Protection Authority, as will be discussed below, and indicates the growing awareness of the need for specific personal data protection regulation. There are, however, yet other laws that pre-date the General Data Protection Law which merit mention beforehand.

2.2.3. The Brazilian Consumer Code

One noteworthy legal reference is the Brazilian Consumer Code.[17] Article 43 of the Code establishes the rights of the consumer regarding databases containing their information. Similar to the habeas data legal remedy, access and rectification rights are granted to the data subject. However, the Consumer Code also establishes duties for controllers of such data (the providers of goods and/or services):

1. A duty to inform that the data is being registered.
2. A duty to inform the origin of the data, ie, when, how and why it was collected.
3. A duty to provide access in a manner that is 'objective, clear, truthful' and using 'easily understandable language'.
4. A limit of five years to store negative records concerning consumers.

[17] Brazil, L. n. 8078/90 (11 September 1990) <http://www.planalto.gov.br/ccivil_03/leis/l8078compilado.htm>.

All these foreshadow rights, duties, and principles that later were important in the rise of the LGPD and currently make up the personal data protection framework of Brazil and other countries. This sort of consumer data protection is another unique characteristic of Brazil in comparison to other BRICS countries.

2.2.4. The Access to Information Law

Another important reference is the Access to Information Law.[18] Although it is focused on access to information regarding the public administration, this law contains norms on access to personal information contained within these public records. As such, it contains the first legal definition of 'personal data' (named, in this case, 'personal information') in the Brazilian legal order: personal information is 'that [information] related to an identified or identifiable natural person' (art 4, IV). This definition is in line with that which would later be given in the LGPD[19] and is similar to those in other BRICS countries, including China and India.[20]

Besides that, the law also builds a personal information micro-system based on the secrecy by default of such data, which can only be exempted by the subject's explicit consent or in a few hypothetical situations:

1. When there is a specific law which would allow access to such information.
2. For medical treatment of the subject, given that they are incapable of giving consent.
3. For statistical and scientific research of 'evident general or public interest', with a legal basis, and barred the identification of the subject.
4. When it is necessary to comply with judicial orders.
5. When necessary to defend human rights.
6. To protect an overwhelming general and public interest.

[18] Brazil, L. n. 12527/11 (18 November 2011) <http://www.planalto.gov.br/ccivil_03/_ato2011-2014/2011/lei/l12527.htm>.

[19] Gabriel da Silva Barros, Lorena dos Santos Silva, and Clarissa Schmidt, 'Public Records and Personal Data: The Access from the Perspective of the Brazilian General Personal Data Protection Law and the Brazilian Access to Information Law' (2019) 9 *Revista Do Arquivo* 22–39.

[20] Art 4 of China's PIPL defines personal data as 'various kinds of information related to identified or identifiable natural persons recorded by electronic or other means, excluding the information processed anonymously'; section 2(t), of India's Digital Personal Data Protection Act defines it as 'any data about an individual who is identifiable by or in relation to such data'.

Of interest, still, is the determination that those who access such information shall be responsible for its misuse; and that this access restriction shall not be used to defend against scrutiny related to irregularities or to bar historical research of greater relevance.

It is interesting to note how the system put forth in the Access to Information Law brings to the fore some matters that would later be tension points in the application of the LGPD. The question of how liability should be applied to the various actors in the chain of data processing is still open.[21] This is especially true regarding artificial intelligence applications which use personal data, where there have been attempts to establish a subjective liability scheme, and strong opinions to the contrary due to the technical and political disparity between data subjects and controllers.[22]

The credit scoring law[23] regulates the creation of credit score databases. This law shows a greater proximity to modern-day concepts of data protection,[24] with mention of sensitive information[25] and adequacy, necessity, and purpose limitation (although not under these denominations, the concepts are implicit in linking processing activities to the intended purpose and prohibiting excessive collecting of information) included among its articles.

Additionally, the law establishes information duties (art 3) comparable to those enacted by the consumer code, the right to access and rectification, to solicit cancelling of the record, to be informed of credit analysis criteria, and to request revision of solely automated decisions (art 5). Finally, it establishes strict liability for material and moral harms caused by database administrators, data sources, and consultants of the database (art. 16).

[21] Maria Celina Bodin De Moraes, 'LGPD: Um Novo Regime de Responsabilização Civil Dito "Proativo"' (2019) 8(3) *Civilistica.Com* 1–6; Bruno Bioni and Daniel Dias, 'Responsabilidade Civil Na Proteção de Dados Pessoais: Construindo Pontes Entre a Lei Geral de Proteção de Dados Pessoais e o Código de Defesa Do Consumidor' (2020) 9(3) *Civilistica.Com* 1–23.

[22] André Lucas Fernandes, 'Os Erros Do PL 21/2020, Que Regula a Inteligência Artificial' *JOTA* (1 November 2021) <https://web.archive.org/web/20250812175205/https://www.jota.info/opiniao-e-analise/artigos/pl-21-2020-inteligencia-artificial>; Consultor Jurídico, 'Especialistas Questionam Artigo Do PL Do Marco Legal Da IA' *ConJur* (27 October 2021) <https://www.conjur.com.br/2021-out-27/especialistas-questionam-artigo-pl-marco-legal-ia>.

[23] Brazil, L. n. 12414/11 (9 June 2011) <http://www.planalto.gov.br/ccivil_03/_ato2011-2014/2011/lei/l12414.htm>.

[24] Doneda, 'Panorama Histórico Da Proteção de Dados Pessoais' (n 11).

[25] Defined as those relating to 'social or ethnic origins, health, genetic information, sexual orientation and political, religious and philosophical convictions', art 3, §3.II.

2.2.5. The *Marco Civil da Internet*

Finally, the *Marco Civil da Internet* (MCI), or Internet Civil Framework,[26] a law created to regulate various aspects of Internet use—from net neutrality to liability of content intermediaries—was built on the basis of data protection, containing specific provisions on the matter. It establishes privacy and data protection as separate principles of Internet use in Brazil (art 3) and establishes the inviolability of intimacy and private life and of the confidentiality of communications (in flow and stored) as rights of the internet user, summarizing in one article (art 7) many aspects of the discipline of privacy described so far in other laws.

Article 7 also determines that processing and sharing of personal data by controllers is dependent on the subject's 'free, explicit and informed' consent. It further mentions purpose limitation and a duty of exclusion of data when the purpose of its collection (the contract between the internet application provider and the internet user) ends. Finally, it sets record-keeping periods of connection records and records of access to internet applications to one year and six months, respectively.

The MCI marks a crucial step in internet regulation in Brazil, prioritizing fundamental rights at a time when the foundations of the current data-based platforms and markets were being set. Its role as a 'constitution' of the internet is reflected in this substantive aspect as well as in its process of discussion, based on rounds of online participatory consultations at a time when this had seldom been attempted. It is a unique feature of the Brazilian personal data architecture among BRICS countries, indicating the country's early involvement with digital rights discussions.

A significant step toward modern-day data protection schemes, the Framework's focus on consent as the legal basis for data processing would prove a limited approach, due to the complexity of implementing meaningful consent in fast-paced internet relations.[27] This point would later be addressed by the LGPD through an expansion of legal bases and of information, transparency, and accountability duties, among others.

[26] Brazil, L. n. 12965/14 (23 April 2014) <http://www.planalto.gov.br/ccivil_03/_ato2011-2014/2014/lei/l12965.htm>.

[27] Luíza Couto Chaves Brandão, 'O Marco Civil Da Internet e a Proteção de Dados: Diálogos Com a LGPD' (2019) XX(3) *Cadernos Adenauer* 35–48.

2.2.6. A Multifaceted Data Protection Framework

The access to information law, the consumer code, and the credit scoring law, alongside the habeas data constitutional remedy and law and the Internet Civil Framework, are commonly referenced as a basis for the Brazilian data protection framework prior to the LGPD. However, there are many normative instances where personal information is involved. One impactful example is given by Louzada,[28] discussing genetic profile databases in Brazil.

These profiles are used in law enforcement and investigations; thus, the General Data Protection Law—which excludes such activities from its ambit—does not regulate them. However, due to the LGPD's extension of part of its data protection framework even to those areas excluded from its scope (art 4, §1), the genetic profile databases niche must abide by the LGPD's overarching principles and ensure some of the rights contained therein.

This is likely to involve changes to the current normative landscape (composed of a specific law, no 12.564/2012, and a decree published by a Steering Committee). There are currently considerable gaps in regulation which need to be addressed. First, there is no provision as to the immediate discarding of the biological sample after the profile is registered. There is also a lack of purpose limitation rules and procedures and a need for better communication of the purposes and procedures involved in the collection of these materials. There is a need for better documentation of the whole production chain of these genetic profiles and for more specified and secure procedures regarding the security and quality of samples extracted; among other needs.[29] This case is but one example of potential harmonization efforts needed in the future because of the new regime implemented by the LGPD.

One other area where personal data are regulated and heavily transacted is banking. Besides the 2001 Banking Information Secrecy Law (no 105/01), Brazil recently began implementing an open banking scheme aimed at operationalizing interoperability and portability between financial institutions. This was put in motion via a joint regulation by the National Monetary Council and the Brazilian Central Bank[30] and is implemented via APIs that allow sharing data such as identification and account information between

[28] Luiza Louzada, 'Princípios Da LGPD e Os Bancos de Perfis Genéticos: Instrumentalizando a Garantia de Direitos No Processo Penal' (2019) 144 *Revista Do Advogado* 90–98.

[29] ibid.

[30] BCB and CMN, Res. Conj. n. 01/20 (1 May 2020) <https://web.archive.org/web/20200506105501/https://www.bcb.gov.br/pre/normativos/busca/downloadNormativo.asp?arquivo=/Lists/Normativos/Attachments/51028/Res_Conj_0001_v1_O.pdf>.

registered institutions. The system is based on the user's 'free, informed, previous and unambiguous' consent (art 2, VIII) and excludes sensitive data from the data-sharing scheme.

Other notable instances are:

- The Digital Medical Charts Regulation, through which patients' medical records are allowed to be digitized, provided appropriate security measures are in place. The regulation is promulgated by the National Medicine Council (CFM)[31] and the information security and secrecy standards are set by CFM in partnership with the Brazilian Society of Health Informatics.[32] These standards include digital identity certification under the National Digital Identity Certification Structure; audits, security certifications, and seals; and a series of security requirements according to the type of system being implemented.
- Notary offices and public registry laws and regulations. These entities operate under oversight and are regulated by the judicial branch, via the National Justice Council (CNJ). Laws and regulations in the area cover the digitization of documents and registries, data security standards, and liability schemes, among others.[33]
- Electoral processes. These are regulated by the Superior Electoral Tribunal (TSE), which even before enactment of the LGPD had already made certain provisions on the processing of personal data. Specifically, donation or purchase of databases containing contact information of potential voters was restricted together with the means of massive electoral propaganda, such as references to consent to inclusion in mailing lists and opt-out options.[34]

In conclusion, the many normative developments in recent decades[35] point to a progressive path from a framework focused on intimacy and private life

[31] CFM, Res CFM n 1821 (23 November 2007) <https://www.normasbrasil.com.br/norma/resolucao-1821-2007_105431.html>.

[32] CFM and SBIS, 'Cartilha Sobre Prontuário Eletrônico' (2012).

[33] Rodrigo Ichikawa Claro Silva and Ana Cláudia Corrêa Zuin Mattos do Amaral, 'Ônus e Bônus Da Evolução Tecnológica No Tratamento de Dados Por Serventias Notariais e Registrais' in Tarcisio Teixeira and Américo Ribeiro Magro (eds), *Proteção de Dados: Fundamentos Jurídicos* (JusPodivm 2020) 139–65.

[34] Walter Britto Gaspar, Eduardo Magrani, and Samara Castro, 'Vácuos Eleitorais, Desinformação e a Desgovernança de Dados', *Estadão* (15 June 2020).

[35] One potential regulatory subject that merits mention is the recent move toward legislating neurorights, that is, those rights related to the use of data derived from brain functions, for example via brain–machine interfaces. Chile is a frontrunner in this regulatory area, having approved legislation inscribing neurorights into its Constitution: María Izabel Cornejo Plaza, 'Neuroderechos en Chile: Consagración Constitucional y regulación de las neurotecnologías', *Somos Iberoamérica* (blog,

to one focused specifically on data protection aspects adapted to information society challenges. Detailed information duties, purpose limitation, adequacy and necessity rules, and the establishment of qualified consent as the basis for personal data-intensive relations gradually joined access and rectification rights. As stated by Gomes,[36] the 'traditional' data protection rights already present in sectoral regulations were joined by 'new' rights brought about by the LGPD (and corresponding duties), such as data portability, revocation of consent, and anonymization, among others. The LGPD would come into play to unify all these aspects and add further norms to cater to the needs of a society of ubiquitous connection, considering both demands for the protection of fundamental rights and for innovation and flexibility in data flow schemes.

2.3. The General Data Protection Law

In 2018 Brazil enacted an overarching data protection law which covers all personal data processing activities by natural or legal purposes.[37] In 2019 the country's National Data Protection Authority was created. This constitutes a new, unified data protection framework in the country, in the sense that all previous and subsequent regulation must adapt to the architecture put forth by the LGPD.

This means there are bound to be areas where balancing efforts will be necessary. The LGPD recognizes this by stating that its sanctions do not substitute those laid down in other laws, whether civil, administrative, or penal in nature (art 52, §2). It does, however, represent a true architecture of data protection in Brazil, since it lays out the foundations, principles, duties, and rights to be observed whenever personal data are processed.

A few preliminary aspects of the law should be highlighted. First, the definition of 'personal data' is similar to that mentioned earlier, referring to 'identified and identifiable' natural persons—a feature of all BRICS countries' personal data architectures, except for that of South Africa, which extends this

1 February 2023) <https://www.somosiberoamerica.org/tribunas/neuroderechos-en-chile-consagracion-constitucional-y-regulacion-de-las-neurotecnologias/>. In Brazil, proposed bill no 522/2022 would alter the LGPD to include neural information as sensitive personal data: Brazil and Câmara dos Deputados, PL 522/2022 (9 March 2022) <https://www.camara.leg.br/proposicoesWeb/fichadetramitacao?idProposicao = 2317524>.

[36] Maria Cecília Oliveira Gomes, 'Novos Direitos' (2019) 18(4) GV Executivo 35–37.

[37] An unofficial translation of the LGPD is available at <https://web.archive.org/web/20250917173907/https://cyberbrics.info/brics-data-protection-laws/>.

protection to juristic persons. Personal data processing is allowed under ten legal bases (art 7), including consent, legitimate interests of the controller or third parties, for the protection of health (public health and the subject's life and wellbeing), and for the execution of contracts, among others. There is a specific legal basis for processing done for the execution of public policies and another for research purposes.

Sensitive personal data have a more restricted list of legal bases, excluding legitimate interests and the execution of contracts (art 11). It is important to note that sensitive personal data are defined in a closed list, being those related to 'racial or ethnic origin, religious conviction, political opinion, enlistment in labour union or religious, philosophical or political organisation, data referring to health or sexual life, genetic data or biometric data' (art 5). Creating a separate category of personal data that is afforded special protection is a characteristic shared by almost all BRICS' personal data architectures, except for the Indian law. The approach varies among BRICS countries. China's PIPL presents an illustrative list of sensitive personal data—defined as data 'that can easily lead to the infringement of the personal dignity of natural persons or the harm of personal or property safety once leaked or illegally used' (art 28, PIPL). Russia and South Africa, similarly to Brazil, refer to closed lists of types of data, but with varying scopes—Russia's FZ-152 law contains a shorter list, whereas South Africa's POPIA goes beyond that of Brazil in some aspects. These discrepancies may present challenges when structuring legal interoperability schemes between BRICS countries' personal data architectures.

Another point of note is the treatment given to personal data of minors, which is subject to the same legal bases, but, as per article 14 of the law, needs to be processed exclusively in the minor's best interest. This wording is aligned with how Brazilian law approaches rights of minors, an aspect that was recently reiterated by the ANPD in an official announcement.[38]

As mentioned earlier, the LGPD does not apply to criminal enforcement and investigation activities, nor to public security, national defence, or state security, referencing the enactment of specific legislation on these subjects. A Commission of Jurists brought together by the Brazilian Chamber of Deputies in 2019 is developing this proposed legislation, commonly called the 'Penal' or 'Criminal' LGPD. A first draft was released, but there is as yet no clear timeline of its parliamentary debate and possible enactment.[39]

[38] ANPD, Enunciado no 1 de 2023 (2023) <https://www.gov.br/anpd/pt-br/assuntos/noticias/anpd-divulga-enunciado-sobre-o-tratamento-de-dados-pessoais-de-criancas-e-adolescentes/Enunciado1ANPD.pdf>.

[39] STJ, 'Comissão Entrega à Câmara Anteprojeto Sobre Tratamento de Dados Pessoais Na Área Criminal' *Portal do STJ* (5 November 2020) <https://www.stj.jus.br/sites/portalp/Paginas/Comunica

The LGPD also excludes other hypotheses, such as data processing for strictly personal purposes; for journalistic, artistic, and academic purposes; and of data that is stored in Brazil from countries with an equal level of protection and which are not transferred to other controllers in Brazil. On this point, comparison among BRICS countries reveals significant variety, with India, Russia, and China having the broadest exemptions (with general exemptions relating to national sovereignty, security, and public interest, and a few oversight mechanisms).

Finally, an important preliminary note is that the law has extraterritorial application. This means it will apply even to those controllers or operators not located in Brazil. Extraterritorial application is triggered when the processing operation aims at providing goods or services in Brazil; when the data processed are relative to people located in Brazil; or when the data processed have been collected in Brazil.

2.3.1. Structure and Content of the LGPD

The LGPD is framed by ten data protection principles—eleven, if counting amongst them good faith (*boa-fé*), mentioned in the *caput* of article 6. These are similar to those of the European General Data Protection Regulation (GDPR), which inspired the Brazilian law, and also echo those of other BRICS countries' personal data protection laws. This explicitly principles-based approach is not found in the Indian Digital Personal Data Protection Act of 2023, which contains no section dedicated to principles of data protection, although elements of the following principles (purpose limitation, data minimization and accuracy, security, etc.) are reflected in data principals' rights and data fiduciaries' obligations throughout the Act. The LGPD's personal data protection principles are:

(i) Purpose (legitimate, specified, and explicitly informed to the data subject, barred further processing for incompatible purposes).
(ii) Adequacy (the data processed must be related to the stated purpose).
(iii) Necessity (data minimization, barring the collection and processing of excessive data).

cao/Noticias/05112020-Comissao-entrega-a-Camara-anteprojeto-sobre-tratamento-de-dados-pessoais-na-area-criminal.aspx>.

(iv) Free access (a data subject must be allowed to access their own data in an easy and inexpensive manner).
(v) Quality (data must be up to date, correct, and clear).
(vi) Transparency (the data subject must be clearly informed of the processing and the processing agents involved).
(vii) Security (adequate technical and administrative measures must be taken to establish a secure data environment).
(viii) Prevention (necessary measures to prevent incidents involving the data must be taken).
(ix) Non-discrimination (data processing must not be done in a discriminatory manner or for discriminatory purposes).
(x) Accountability and responsibility (the data controller must be able to demonstrate compliance with the law).

The mention of 'good faith' is important since it references a long-standing interpretative tradition of contracts in Brazilian civil law whereby juridical dealings are to be interpreted according to a series of contextual elements, such as the behaviour of the contracting parties, the habits and current market practices and the context of the negotiation of the contract. It is interesting to note that 'good faith' is also mentioned in article 5 of China's Personal Information Protection Law (PIPL)[40] in a list of principles for the processing or personal information.

This matters in analysing how data protection principles are observed in practice, since the law seeks to adopt a regulatory approach that allows personal data flows and does not impose disproportionate barriers to them. From a perspective of contextual privacy,[41] it makes sense to consider the legitimate expectations of the parties involved, their relative positions towards each other in terms of information and power, and the reasonable intent of each party when entering into a personal data-intensive relation to measure the degree of compliance with data protection law. As summarized by Bioni:

> Contextual privacy resides exactly in the trust deposited by the issuer of information to their recipients, in the legitimate expectation that their personal data will be used and shared according to the context of a pre-established relationship or the original purpose that originated the publicization of the

[40] People's Republic of China, Personal Information Protection Law (2021) <https://personalinformationprotectionlaw.com/PIPL/article-5/>.

[41] Bruno Ricardo Bioni, *Proteção de Dados Pessoais: A Função e Os Limites Do Consentimento* (2nd edn, Forense 2020).

> data; particularly, in the hope that the flow of their personal information will not hamper and betray their capacity to fully and freely develop their personality and social participation.[42]

In other words, besides precise obedience to all duties and rights granted by the law, and besides observance of the ten principles set out in article 6, context matters in interpreting the relations regulated by the LGPD. This is further reinforced by the law's risk-based approach to data protection regulation, embracing a paradigm of prevention and mitigation as well as considering such measures when determining sanctions.

Heavily inspired by the GDPR,[43] many aspects of the LGPD are akin to the European regulation. There are, however, unique aspects to the Brazilian legal context, as well as possible connections to personal data architectures of other BRICS countries.

The law creates specific data subject rights, including access, rectification, deletion and opposition (traditionally named 'ARCO rights' in Latin American data protection schemes). These are similar in content to those found in the GPDR (chapter 3) and PIPL (chapter IV), with the rights to access, correct or complete, delete, and copy data present in all three.

Portability is another right granted to the data subject by the LGPD. Related to this, there are provisions that data processed by public authorities should follow interoperability standards (art 25) and that the Data Protection Authority may provide interoperability standards to enable portability (art 40). In spite of this, interoperability standards do not feature in the Authority's 2021–23 Strategic Plan,[44] leaving portability rights under a degree of uncertainty for the time being. On this point, the Authority might find inspiration in China's legal framework, where portability is also present in PIPL art 45 and was recently specified in the Network Data Security Management Regulation.

[42] ibid 229.

[43] The GDPR's influence over the LGPD and other national data protection laws is well documented. Besides the aforementioned similarity in data protection principles, the LGPD draws on the GDPR in terms of user rights (including, eg, data portability), definitions (eg, of personal data and of sensitive, or special category, data), data retention and deletion requirements, record-keeping, its extraterritorial scope, and others. The LGPD is, however, broader and less proscriptive in its text than the GDPR, leaving much to the interpretation of the Brazilian National Data Protection Authority. See Raymond H Geistel, 'GDPR, PIPL & LGPD: Privacy Regulations & Policies Across the Globe' *Cybersecurity Undergraduate Research*, ODU Digital Commons 11 (22 November 2021); Laila Neves Lorenzon, 'Análise Comparada Entre Regulamentações De Dados Pessoais no Brasil e na União Europeia (LGPD e GDPR) e Seus Respectivos Instrumentos De Enforcement' *Revista do Programa de Direito da União Europeia* 1 (15 March 2021) 39–52; Abigayle Erickson, 'Comparative Analysis of the EU's GDPR and Brazil's LGPD: Enforcement Challenges with the LGPD' (2019) 44(2) *Brooklyn Journal of International Law* 859.

[44] ANPD, 'Planejamento Estratégico 2021–2023' (Brasília, 2021).

According to the latter, portability is available under the following conditions: '(i) verifying the true identity of the data subject; (ii) the legal basis for processing the concerned personal information must either be consent or contract necessity; (iii) the transfer is technically feasible; and (iv) the transfer will not harm the legitimate rights and interests of others'.[45]

Finally, a few other highlights of the Brazilian Data Protection Law are as follows. The law dedicates a full chapter to data processing by public authorities. In summary, this kind of processing must be attached to a public interest purpose, a specific public agency's mandate, and under strict transparency rules. Public–private partnerships are regulated by the same chapter, enacting a general rule that forbids data transfers from public entities to private entities, as well as shared used of data between them, except in a closed, albeit extensive, list of hypotheses (arts 26 and 27). As stated before, some obligations are made immediate in the case of public authorities, such as the interoperability of databases, communication of the agreements involved in public–private partnerships to the Data Protection Authority, and the nomination of a data protection officer.[46] Others, however, lack sufficient specificity or result in counter-intuitive interpretations—eg, the aforementioned extensive exemptions to public–private sharing of personal data in articles 26 and 27 and their use of undefined concepts.

International transfers of personal data under the LGPD are allowed in a few instances which play a comparable role to the legal bases mentioned earlier. The law mentions adequacy decisions by the Authority regarding foreign countries' protection level as well as safeguards offered by the controller, such as specific or standard contractual clauses, global corporate norms, and seals and certificates. Other hypotheses are given, related to the execution of public policies, international agreements, and protection of life and wellbeing.

[45] Carolyn Bigg and others, 'CHINA: Enhanced and Clarified Data Compliance Obligations on Handlers of "Network Data", Covering Personal Information and Important Data, and Operators of Online Platforms from 1 January 2025' (*Privacy Matters*, 16 October 2024) <https://web.archive.org/web/20241019153622/https://privacymatters.dlapiper.com/2024/10/china-enhanced-and-clarified-data-compliance-obligations-on-handlers-of-network-data-covering-personal-information-and-important-data-and-operators-of-online-platforms-from-1-january-2025/>.

[46] In general, the law demands a DPO for any processing operation; however, a recent regulation by the Data Protection Authority (Eduardo Mattos and others, 'Application of LGPD to Small-Sized Processing Agents: Non-Official Translation of the ANPD Regulation' (*CyberBRICS*, 31 March 2022) <https://cyberbrics.info/application-of-lgpd-to-small-sized-processing-agents-non-official-translation-of-the-anpd-regulation/>) has excepted this rule for small and medium businesses and start-ups—see Curzi and others, 'LGPD Regulation for Small Agents: Highlights, Advances and Future Paths' (*CyberBRICS*, 30 March 2022) <https://cyberbrics.info/lgpd-regulation-for-small-agents-highlights-advances-and-future-paths/>.

One note on this aspect of the law is that its text, as is, does not fully clarify these hypotheses. For adequacy decisions, global corporate rules, and contractual safeguards, the Authority has enacted further regulation specifying their requirements and giving detailed contours of these cases. ANPD Resolution no 19, of August 2024, sets out a more detailed set of international transfer rules as well as model contractual clauses to be used.[47]

In other instances, the wording of the law is unclear, and the Authority will need to exercise its interpretative capacity to make the rules enforceable. For example, when the law authorizes foreign transfers that 'result in a commitment undertaken in an international cooperation agreement' (art 33, VI), the strict wording creates a state of uncertain legality between the time of the transfer of data and the signature of said agreement—it will only have been legal if the commitment is undertaken under the agreement. This seems excessively complex and prone to confusion or misuse, and a better wording would potentially have focused on the instrumentality of said data to the negotiation process, and left out considerations of whether it results in a commitment. A second controversy comes when data transfers are authorized if 'necessary for international judicial cooperation between public intelligence, investigation and enforcement agencies' (art 33, III). Further specification of what kinds of activities fall under this hypothesis is necessary, since the law excludes from its application criminal investigation and enforcement activities, public security, and national and state defence, as pointed out earlier.

One last, but no less important, point relates to collective litigation in data protection rights under the LGPD. Zanatta[48] recounts how Brazil has a 'very strong tradition of diffuse and collective rights, which left a mark in the institutional and judicial development of the last 30 years in the country'.[49] This collectivization, as the author calls it, takes the form of Civil Public Actions (*Ações Civis Públicas*, or ACP; Zanatta also refers to the denomination 'Privacy Class Actions'[50]). In the LGPD, they are legitimized by articles 22 and 42, §3, which recognize the possibility of collective action against violations of data protection rights. This is a unique feature of the Brazilian data protection architecture, in comparison with other BRICS countries.

[47] Brazil (ANPD), 'Resolução CD/ANPD n. 19/2024', *Diário Oficial da União* (23 August 2024) <https://www.in.gov.br/web/dou>.

[48] Rafael Zanatta, 'A Tutela Coletiva Na Proteção de Dados Pessoais' (2019) 144 Revista Do Advogado 201–8.

[49] ibid 204.

[50] ibid 203.

The next section will highlight some of the notable cases involving this class of action in the realm of data protection, before and after the LGPD went into force. However, it is important to note that this process of collectivization is a reflection of the nature of the rights under protection, which, although referring to individuals, have profound collective roots and consequences due to the very risks involved in the operationalization of digital markets.[51]

These are the general aspects of the Brazilian LGPD. One can see a linear progression, from strict privacy conceptualizations under intimacy and private life doctrines, rooted in the intimate sphere and the right to be let alone, and a broadening of this approach in successive laws in response to technological advancements, to a point where a specific personal data protection framework becomes necessary. This is all rooted in the idea of allowing the full realization of personality, largely translated into digital identities in the form of personal data and thus requiring special protection. The following section will discuss some recent developments in the institutional framework of data protection in Brazil and how they relate to the rights of the data subject.

2.4. Regulatory Developments

There are many moving parts in Brazil's data protection framework. Existing public agencies need to coordinate their activities under the new law and with a new National Data Protection Authority given ample control capacities. The Authority has entered a field rich with other institutional actors—courts, prosecutors, consumer protection agencies, and other regulatory agencies—and will need to coordinate with them, as well as provide guidance as to how the law should be interpreted, and concrete instruments for private actors to comply with to mitigate risks.

2.4.1. The Initial Application of the LGPD

From a judicial perspective, the State Prosecution of the Federal District (MPDFT) had a proactive role in data protection beginning in 2018, when it created a Specialized Unit on Data Protection and Artificial Intelligence.[52]

[51] ibid 202.

[52] MPDFT, P. N. PGJ n. 539/18 (12 April 2018) <https://web.archive.org/web/20211207214852/https://www.mpdft.mp.br/portal/pdf/comissao_protecao_dados_pessoais/Portaria_PGJ_n2018_0539.pdf>.

With the LGPD not yet in force, the State Prosecution conducted some high-profile investigations into cybersecurity incidents involving personal data of Brazilian citizens—one involving Netshoes,[53] an e-commerce service, one against Uber,[54] and one against Banco Inter;[55] all regarding undue access to personal data of users of these services. Since the LGPD entered into force, the agency has prosecuted two notable cases of commercialization of personal information databases: against Infortexto Ltda, a company which offered structured databases of personal data of Brazilian citizens, and against Serasa Experian, a Brazilian credit protection agency that owns one of the biggest consumer databases in the world.[56]

The Federal Prosecution (MPF) has also had an important role in asserting data protection rights since the enactment of the LGPD. In 2021, it published a joint recommendation alongside the ANPD, the National Consumer Protection Office (SENACON), and the Brazilian Competition Bureau (CADE) regarding the change in WhatsApp's privacy rules.[57] This prompted the messaging service to delay the mandatory rollout of the new rules and, in the end, to decide not to cut access to the app to any users who did not accept the new terms.[58] The MPF also demanded information from the Health Minister regarding a personal data breach under investigation involving the

[53] MPDFT, Rec. n. 01/18 (Netshoes) (25 January 2018) <https://web.archive.org/web/20221020184831/https://www.mpdft.mp.br/portal/pdf/comissao_protecao_dados_pessoais/Recomendacao_Comissao_Protecao_Dados_2018_01.pdf>.

[54] MPDFT, Port. n. 01/18 (Uber) (6 February 2018) <https://web.archive.org/web/20230614163110/https://www.mpdft.mp.br/portal/pdf/comissao_protecao_dados_pessoais/Instauracao_de_PP_Uber.pdf>.

[55] Alberto Alerigi Jr, 'Banco Inter Faz Acordo de R$1,5 Mi Com Ministério Público Em Caso de Vazamento de Dados' (*uol.com.br*, 19 December 2018) <https://www.uol.com.br/tilt/noticias/reuters/2018/12/19/banco-inter-faz-acordo-de-r15-mi-com-ministerio-publico-em-caso-de-vazamento-de-dados.htm>.

[56] MPDFT, 'MPDFT Ajuíza 1ª Ação Civil Pública Com Base Na LGPD' (22 September 2020) <https://web.archive.org/web/20250720040546/https://www.mpdft.mp.br/portal/index.php/comunicacao-menu/sala-de-imprensa/noticias/noticias-2020/12384-mpdft-ajuiza-1-acao-civil-publica-com-base-na-lgpd>; MPDFT, 'MPDFT Obtém Decisão Que Suspende a Venda de Dados Pessoais Pela Serasa Experian' (23 November 2020) <https://web.archive.org/web/20240513200024/https://www.mpdft.mp.br/portal/index.php/comunicacao-menu/sala-de-imprensa/noticias/noticias-2020/12586-mpdft-obtem-decisao-que-suspende-a-venda-de-dados-pessoais-pela-serasa-experian>; Matheus Garzon, 'Após Ação Do MPDFT, Justiça Manda Tirar Do Ar Site Que Vende Dados Pessoais' (*Metrópoles*, 22 October 2020) <https://web.archive.org/web/20230109004938/https://www.metropoles.com/distrito-federal/justica-distrito-federal/apos-acao-do-mpdft-justica-manda-tirar-do-ar-site-que-vende-dados-pessoais>.

[57] Convergência Digital, 'Cade, ANPD e MPF Alertam WhatsApp Que Compartilhamento Compulsório Viola a LGPD' (*Convergência Digital*, 7 May 2021) <https://web.archive.org/web/20250120183343/https://www.febrac.org.br/clipping/clipping-diario-no-3904-10-de-maio-de-2021/#cade>.

[58] ANPD, 'Após Esforço Interinstitucional, WhatsApp Se Compromete a Atender Às Recomendações Sobre Sua Política de Privacidade' (*Gov.br*, 23 August 2021) <https://www.gov.br/anpd/pt-br/assuntos/noticias/apos-esforco-interinstitucional-whatsapp-se-compromete-a-atender-as-recomendacoes-sobre-sua-politica-de-privacidade>.

'ConecteSUS' system, used to register vaccination and other health data connected to the use of the Brazilian Unified Health System (SUS).[59]

Finally, the MPF has published technical studies and opinions on matters related to data protection in Brazil, such as the announced plans to privatize SERPRO, the Federal Data Processing Service—which, among other things, holds in its databases the tax information of all Brazilian citizens, including government authorities;[60] and the proposed 'Criminal LGPD' draft.[61] Recently, the MPF has been called upon by a coalition of civil society organizations to investigate and prosecute 'Córtex',[62] a system spearheaded by a branch of the Justice and Public Security Ministry with the potential to unify 160 databases and provide persistent electronic monitoring of 360,000 people.[63]

2.4.2. Continuing Fragmentation, Despite the ANPD

On the other side of the bench, the National Data Protection Authority will also need to coordinate efforts with the various judicial decision-making bodies and instances. A joint research project conducted by the Brazilian Institute of Teaching, Research, and Development (IDP) and JusBrasil looked at 274 decisions of lower courts in all Brazilian states between September 2020 and August 2021. Their analysis concludes, among other aspects, that many of these courts have applied the LGPD as a complement to other legislation and has not engaged deeply with data protection doctrine or theory. Most discussions revolved around the first two chapters of the law, containing introductory aspects, definitions, principles, foundations and legal bases for personal

[59] André Rigue and Julyanne Juca, 'MPF Pede à PGR Que Solicite Esclarecimento a Queiroga Sobre Ataque Ao ConecteSUS' (*CNN Brasil*, 18 December 2021) <https://www.cnnbrasil.com.br/nacional/mpf-pede-a-pgr-que-solicite-esclarecimento-a-queiroga-sobre-ataque-ao-conectesus/>.

[60] The MPF's position was that it would not only violate the LGPD, but also pose considerable national security risks: PGR, 'Privatização Do Serpro Contraria Legislação e Ameaça Segurança Nacional, Afirma MPF Em Nota Técnica' (*MPF.mp.br*, 25 February 2021) <https://web.archive.org/web/20210303032552/http://www.mpf.mp.br/pgr/noticias-pgr/mpf-alerta-para-restricoes-previstas-no-anteprojeto-de-lei-de-protecao-de-dados-para-a-persecucao-penal/>.

[61] The MPF's position was that it would impose disproportionately restrictive obligations on data transfers between authorities, among other issues: PGR, 'MPF Alerta Para Restrições Previstas No Anteprojeto de Lei de Proteção de Dados Para a Persecução Penal' (*MPF.mp.br*, 1 March 2021) <https://web.archive.org/web/20210303032552/http://www.mpf.mp.br/pgr/noticias-pgr/mpf-alerta-para-restricoes-previstas-no-anteprojeto-de-lei-de-protecao-de-dados-para-a-persecucao-penal/>.

[62] Gabriela do Vale, 'Sociedade Civil Pede Ao MPF Investigação Do Sistema Córtex' (*TeleSíntese*, 10 February 2022) <https://www.telesintese.com.br/sociedade-civil-pede-ao-mpf-investigacao-do-sistema-cortex/>.

[63] Conectas Direitos Humanos and others, 'Rep. Sistema Córtex' (February 2022) <https://www.telesintese.com.br/wp-content/uploads/2022/02/representacao-controle-externo-da-atividade-policial.pdf>.

data processing, followed by data subjects' rights in third place, and legal bases for sensitive data processing in fourth.[64]

Additionally, the São Paulo State Court (TJSP) presented a substantially larger number of decisions compared to other state courts and other instances.[65] Although this is not discussed in the findings, this may be related to the fact that São Paulo is a state whose consumer protection unit (Procon-SP), as well as the Brazilian Consumer Defence Institute (IDEC), have been very active in matters of data protection. IDEC proposed a Civil Public Action against the operator of one of the state's subway lines (ViaQuatro) for its plan to implement facial recognition at its stations. A final decision fined ViaQuatro in 100,000 reais and forbade the company from reactivating its facial recognition initiative.[66] In 2022, IDEC and others moved a new against the state's general subway operator, 'Metrô de SP, to bar the use of facial recognition, requesting the immediate suspension of the system and an indemnification of at least 42 million reais.[67]

Another study, conducted by the Opice Blum law firm, which specializes in digital rights, focused on 2021 and revealed more data on the first steps of the LGPD in courts. The study analysed 465 decisions in courts in seven states and three federal and regional courts. A few interesting findings were:

(i) The greater concentration of decisions at the São Paulo State Court, observed in the previous study by IDP and JusBrasil, was also observed in this study.
(ii) Seventy-seven per cent of all decisions did not result in sanctions.
(iii) Almost 40 per cent of the cases analysed involved security incidents.
(iv) Around 90 per cent of decisions considered that moral damages reparation required proof of damage, ie, damages were not considered *in re ipsa*.
(v) When sanctions are applied, they go from 600 reais to 100,000 reais, with most (88 per cent) between 2,000 and 11,000 reais.[68]

[64] Laura Schertel and others, 'LGPD Nos Tribunais' (*JusBrasil*, October 2021) <https://www.jusbrasil.com.br/static/pages/lgpd-nos-tribunais.html>.
[65] ibid.
[66] IDEC, 'Idec Obtém Vitória Contra Reconhecimento de Emoções No Metrô de SP' (*idec.org.br*, 10 May 2021) <https://idec.org.br/noticia/idec-obtem-vitoria-contra-reconhecimento-de-emocoes-no-metro-de-sp>.
[67] Idec, 'Ação Quer Vedar o Uso de Tecnologias de Reconhecimento Facial Pelo Metrô de São Paulo' (*idec.org.br*, 3 March 2022) <https://idec.org.br/release/acao-quer-vedar-o-uso-de-tecnologias-de-reconhecimento-facial-pelo-metro-de-sao-paulo>.
[68] Opice Blum, 'Relatório Anual de Jurimetria 2021' (27 January 2022) <https://images.jota.info/wp-content/uploads/2022/01/relatacc83c2b3rio-anual-jurimetria-24-01-versacc83o-final.pdf>; Letícia Paiva, 'LGPD: 77% Das Decisões Não Resultaram Em Condenação Em 2021' (*Jota*, 27 January

FGV's E-commerce studies centre (NEEC) also conducted research that supplements these findings, confirming a significant concentration of cases regarding consumer relations and the LGPD at the São Paulo State Court and reiterating the issue of *in re ipsa* moral damages derived from personal data incidents as a pivotal legal debate.[69]

The issue of the application of the law in courts will be informed by the institutional arrangements that come up while the Authority attempts to exercise its legal capacities. This is due to the determination that the Authority give the final interpretation of the LGPD (art 55-J, XX; art 55-K, sole paragraph), as well as its executive capacities as overseer of the law's application, such as requesting information, publishing regulation and technical opinions, analysing data subject requests, and applying sanctions, even regarding public bodies' processing activities (art 55-J). This is seemingly in conflict, firstly, with judicial instances' independent analysis and interpretation of facts and law; and, secondly, with the independence of the judicial branch ensured by the separation of powers. The latter is especially evident when considering that the Authority is not structured as an independent entity, but as a branch of the Federal administration.

The LGPD does not resolve this conflict, as it only mentions the need to coordinate actions with other authorities, and will need to be dealt with in the future. One institution that the ANPD will need to coordinate with on this is the National Justice Council, a judicial organ that is constitutionally (Federal Constitution, art 103-B, §4) and legally (Civil Procedure Code, art 196) competent for administrative proceedings of the judicial branch in Brazil.[70]

2.4.3. The Role of the Supreme Court

Even before the Authority was in place and the LGPD was in effect, the country's Supreme Court had made an important and consequential judgment on the matter of the constitutional standing of data protection in Brazil.

2022) <https://web.archive.org/web/20230331211329/https://www.jota.info/justica/lgpd-condenacao-77-das-decisoes-nao-27012022>.

[69] Erica Bakonyi, 'LGPD em números. Resultados e tendências no contexto "E-commerce"' (2ª reunião do NEEC, Rio de Janeiro, January 2023) <https://direitorio.fgv.br/sites/default/files/arquivos/apresentacao-lgpd-em-numeros-neec.pdf>; NEEC, '2ª Reunião do Núcleo de Estudos em E-Commerce' (Reuniões do NEEC, Rio de Janeiro: FGV Direito Rio, January 2023) <https://direitorio.fgv.br/sites/default/files/2023-01/direito_rio_livro_neec_ap3_v3.pdf>.

[70] CDTV, *9º E-Fórum TIC Na Justiça* (CDTV Youtube, 2021).

IBGE, the Brazilian Institute of Geography and Statistics, was authorized, via presidential order no 954/2020 (MP 954/20), to obtain from telecommunications companies the contact information of 200 million individuals. The justification was that the institute would need to conduct the national census via telephone due to the Covid-19 pandemic. This was seen by many as a highly disproportionate measure, since in-person interviews for the census are usually conducted with a statistically representative sample of households, besides the evident deviation of the telecoms companies' original purpose for collecting and processing those data.

A complete narration of the case would require at least a chapter of its own, but Bioni and Monteiro[71] portray the impact of the judgment. In addition to establishing data protection as an autonomous fundamental right rooted in informational self-determination under the Brazilian Constitution and highlighting the importance of procedural guarantees to its realization,[72] the case also marked a decisive change in the position of the Court:

> In previous case-law, the Court struggled to recognize stored data, such as subscribers data, as data protected by Art. 5, XII. Long standing precedents only granted such type of protection to data in motion, like ongoing telephone calls or data being transmitted. Acknowledging the need to update this understanding in light of new technologies and the impact that the misuse of data can have upon individuals and the society, another argument was presented: the need to recognize the right to protect personal data as an autonomous fundamental right.[73]

One more data protection case currently in the Supreme Court's docket is Direct Unconstitutionality Action no 6649, which refers to Presidential Decree no 10.046. This Decree creates a general shared data regime between government agencies, including biometric data, family life, and labour information, among other aspects of individual identity. The constitutionality of the Decree is in question for violation of the constitutional provisions regarding privacy and by referring to the same Court's decision on the *IBGE* case, described

[71] Bruno Ricardo Bioni and others, 'A Landmark Ruling from the Brazilian Supreme Court: Data Protection as an Autonomous Fundamental Right and Informational Due Process' (2020) 6 European Data Protection Law Review 615.

[72] Gaspar Pisanu, Rafael AF Zanatta, and Mariana Marques Rielli, '"Please Do Not Share": Brazilian Supreme Federal Court Rules in Favor of Privacy' (*Access Now*, 14 May 2020) <https://www.accessnow.org/brazilian-supreme-federal-court-rules-in-favor-of-privacy/>.

[73] Bioni and others (n 71).

above.[74] The case is ongoing, and its results might inform how personal data processing and sharing by governmental entities is interpreted—including by the ANPD.

2.4.4. A Complex Relation with the Judiciary

Still in the area of the ANPD's relations with the judicial branch, one particularly sensitive subject might be the publicity of judicial proceedings and decisions. There is notice of efforts to institute secrecy of such proceedings based on the LGPD,[75] and the country's Supreme Court has recently accepted a case where the matter is at hand. The latter is particularly interesting because it discusses the subject of publicity of judicial proceedings applied not to courts, but to private judicial aggregators, ie, sites specialized in indexing judicial decisions[76] ('Escavador' and 'JusBrasil' being two prominent examples in Brazil).

The issue of access to information in opposition to data protection rights has also been emerging in other areas. The Superior Electoral Court (TSE) has recently been called upon to decide whether campaign donation data, among other information involving personal data of people participating in electoral campaigns, should be made secret due to data protection concerns. The President of the Court, however, recently declared that, although the issue is complex and merits a long and wide discussion, and that case-by-case analysis should reveal instances where the balance favours privacy, the rule, for the time being, is for transparency in favour of the public interest.[77]

There have also been cases where the executive branch refuses to provide public interest information based on the LGPD. Machado[78] describes how fear

[74] Gilmar Mendes, ADI 6649 (23 December 2020); OAB, 'Petição Inicial, ADI 6649' (*STF*, 18 December 2020) <https://redir.stf.jus.br/paginadorpub/paginador.jsp?docTP = TP&docID = 754736097&prcID = 6079238#>; Ferreira, Lucia Maria Teixeira and Comissão de Proteção de Dados e Privacidade da OAB-RJ. 'Parecer sobre a legalidade dos Decretos no 10.046/2019 e 10.047/2019 em face das normas que disciplinam os direitos fundamentais à proteção de dados e à privacidade no ordenamento jurídico brasileiro'. Parecer técnico (Rio de Janeiro: OAB-RJ, January 2020) <https://www.oabrj.org.br/sites/default/files/parecer_final_rev._30_jan_2020_lucia_dec._10.046-_comissao_prot_de_dados.docx.pdf>.

[75] Dânton Zanetti, 'Proteção de Dados Pessoais e Publicidade Processual: Um Contrassenso?' (*Migalhas*, 15 April 2021) <https://www.migalhas.com.br/depeso/343796/protecao-de-dados-pessoais-e-publicidade-processual-um-contrassenso>.

[76] Severino Goes, 'Decisão Abre Debate Sobre Direito à Informação e Uso Da LGPD' (*ConJur*, 18 May 2021) <https://www.conjur.com.br/2021-mai-18/decisao-abre-debate-direito-informacao-uso-lgpd>.

[77] José Marques, 'Fachin Descarta TSE Impor Sigilo Sobre Dados de Doações Eleitorais' (*Folha de S. Paulo*, 23 February 2022) <https://www1.folha.uol.com.br/poder/2022/02/fachin-descarta-tse-impor-sigilo-sobre-dados-de-doacoes-eleitorais.shtml?origin = folha>.

[78] Cecília Machado, 'Há Retrocessos Na Lei Geral de Proteção de Dados' (*Folha*, 28 February 2022) <https://www1.folha.uol.com.br/colunas/cecilia-machado/2022/02/ha-retrocessos-na-lgpd.shtml?origin = folha>.

of the LGPD's sanctions has been moving public servants toward caution and secrecy in sharing public interest data, such as the educational microdata yearly published by INEP, a research institute linked to the Education Ministry, since the 1990s.[79] These are invaluable data to allow oversight regarding the quality of education in the country.

Other similar situations abound, some of which were recounted during a Chamber of Deputies' public hearing on balancing the Access to Information law and the LGPD, held in 2021. The examples brought to the fore on the occasion included refusals to provide information to the MPF in the course of investigations; the establishment of a 100-year secrecy rule for various public interest information; and refusals to provide data to journalists conducting investigations and to other interested parties under personal data protection justifications.[80] Resolving the necessary balancing of the application of the Access to Information Law ("LAI" in the Portuguese acronym) and the LGPD will require coordination with various organs and entities and a careful look at regulatory and technical solutions to providing access to information while preserving privacy.

2.4.5. Blending the LGPD with Consumer Law and Competition Law

Another field where the National Data Protection Authority will need to seek coordination and cooperation proactively is consumer protection. SENACON, a specialized office subject to the Justice and Public Security Ministry, oversees the National Consumer Protection System. This system is composed of a variety of units of 'Procons', state or municipal offices of consumer protection responsible for processing consumer requests, amounting to 981 units in Brazilian territory.[81]

Some of these units have been particularly active in personal data protection, such as São Paulo state's Procon (Procon-SP). Besides publishing a basic

[79] Maria Angélica Minhoto, Pedro Arantes, and Soraya Smaili, 'A Quem Interessa Impedir o Acesso Aos Microdados Do Inep?' (*Folha*, 24 February 2022) <https://www1.folha.uol.com.br/blogs/sou-ciencia/2022/02/a-quem-interessa-impedir-o-acesso-aos-microdados-do-inep.shtml>.

[80] Câmara dos Deputados, 'Fiscalização Financeira e Controle – Execução Da LGPD/LAI' (Câmara dos Deputados (YouTube), 16 November 2021) <https://www.youtube.com/watch?v=jA5yIsFkSZM>; Lara Haje, 'Acesso à Informação Não Pode Ser Prejudicado Por Conta de Lei de Proteção de Dados, Dizem Especialistas' (*Portal da Câmara dos Deputados*, 18 November 2021) <https://www.camara.leg.br/noticias/828370-acesso-a-informacao-nao-pode-ser-prejudicado-por-conta-de-lei-de-protecao-de-dados-dizem-especialistas/>.

[81] SENACON, 'Sindec Boletim – 2019' (Brasília, 2019).

data protection guide to inform the general public,[82] the unit has under its belt cases and notifications against Serasa,[83] some of the major telephone companies in the country,[84] and TikTok.[85] Coordinating understandings with these entities will prove invaluable to executing the ANPD's vision for the application of the LGPD.

The ANPD has made cooperation agreements with SENACON, CADE,[86] and NIC.br. The latter is the operational branch of the Internet Steering Committee in Brazil (CGI.br), and the partnership is aimed at building know-how and sharing information.[87] It also has a technical cooperation agreement with the Superior Electoral Court[88] and the two have published a guide to data protection during election times.[89] The Authority has also recently published guidance to small and micro enterprises regarding cybersecurity,[90] guidelines on the definition of processing agents,[91] and guidelines for data processing by the public administration.[92]

In terms of regulation, as well as norms creating governance bodies and bylaws and setting regulatory agendas, it has published six norms. One deals with its regulatory process, establishing guidelines such as social participation

[82] PROCON-SP, EPDC, and Gov. do Estado de SP, 'Lei Geral de Proteção de Dados: O Que Você Precisa Saber' (December 2020) <https://www.procon.sp.gov.br/wp-content/uploads/2021/02/Cartilha-LGPD-2021.pdf>.

[83] For a data breach involving the personal data of 220 million Brazilian citizens, PROCON-SP, 'Procon-SP Notifica Serasa' (*Procon.sp.gov.br*, 28 January 2021) <https://www.procon.sp.gov.br/procon-sp-notifica-serasa/>.

[84] Also for a data breach, this time involving data of 100 million mobile phones, PROCON-SP, 'Procon-SP Notifica Claro, Oi, Tim, Vivo e Psafe' (*Procon.sp.gov.br*, 17 February 2021) <https://www.procon.sp.gov.br/procon-sp-notifica-claro-oi-tim-vivo-e-psafe/>.

[85] Requesting information on the company's safeguards regarding children's data on the platform, PROCON-SP, 'Notificação TikTok' (*Procon.sp.gov.br*, 14 May 2020) <https://www.procon.sp.gov.br/notificacao-tik-tok/>.

[86] João Paulo Vieira Tinoco and Mauricio Koki Matsutani, 'CADE Firma Parceria Com ANPD – Congresso Em Foco' (*Congresso em Foco*, 10 October 2021) <https://web.archive.org/web/20240625225131/https://congressoemfoco.uol.com.br/tipo/patrocinado/salve-seus-dados/cade-firma-parceria-com-anpd/>.

[87] ANPD, 'Convênios e Transferências' (*ANPD.gov.br*, 17 January 2021) <https://www.gov.br/anpd/pt-br/acesso-a-informacao/repasses-e-transferencias-de-recursos-financeiros>.

[88] ANPD, 'ANPD e TSE Assinam Acordo de Cooperação Técnica' (*ANPD.gov.br*, 24 November 2021) <https://www.gov.br/anpd/pt-br/assuntos/noticias/anpd-e-tse-assinam-acordo-de-cooperacao-tecnica>.

[89] ANPD, 'Em Ano Eleitoral ANPD e TSE Publicam Guia de Eleições' (*ANPD.gov.br*, 3 January 2022) <https://www.gov.br/anpd/pt-br/assuntos/noticias/em-ano-eleitoral-anpd-e-tse-publicam-guia-de-eleicoes>.

[90] ANPD, 'Guia Orientativo de Segurança Da Informação Para Agentes de Tratamento de Pequeno Porte' (ANPD, 2021).

[91] ANPD, 'Guia Orientativo Para Definições Dos Agentes de Tratamento de Dados Pessoais (Operadores e Controladores) e Do Encarregado' (ANPD, May 2021).

[92] ANPD, 'Tratamento de Dados Pessoais Pelo Poder Público (Guia Orientativo)' (ANPD, January 2022) <https://www.gov.br/anpd/pt-br/documentos-e-publicacoes/guia-poder-publico-anpd-versao-final.pdf>.

and simplification of processes;[93] one on its inspection, control, and sanctioning activities;[94] one establishing a special data protection regime for small and micro enterprises and start-ups;[95] one on communication of security incidents;[96] one on the role of data protection officer;[97] and one on international data transfers.[98] These norms were created following public hearing processes held via digital participation platforms as well as live online sessions.

The first two determine organizational and procedural aspects of the Authority's functions, highlighting the significant space given to preventive and pedagogic action relating to data protection risks and controllers' activities. The third regulation implements a series of adaptations of the law to the context of smaller companies and start-ups: an exemption to the indication of a DPO, longer procedural deadlines in administrative processes, and simplified recording and security policy requirements, among others.[99] The definition of the scope of the regulation was careful to exclude from this simplified regime entities whose data processing might 'significantly affect fundamental rights and interests of data subjects' (art 4.I.b), among other criteria aimed at ensuring a balance between protection and flexibility.

The ANPD's activities have been conducted in parallel to ongoing discussions on its independence and institutional format. In 2022, a Presidential Decree, later confirmed into law by the National Congress, transformed the Authority from an organ of the Federal Government into an independent authority—called a 'special autarchy' in Brazilian public law. This ensures the Authority's technical, administrative and financial autonomy, stability of its directors' mandates, and legitimizes it as a party in moving collective rights

[93] ANPD, 'Portaria Nº 16, de 8 de Julho de 2021' (*DOU*, 8 July 2021) <https://www.in.gov.br/en/web/dou/-/portaria-n-16-de-8-de-julho-de-2021-330970241>.

[94] ANPD, 'Resolução CD/ANPD Nº 1, de 28 de Outubro de 2021' (*DOU*, 28 November 2021) <https://www.in.gov.br/en/web/dou/-/resolucao-cd/anpd-n-1-de-28-de-outubro-de-2021-355817513>.

[95] ANPD, 'Resolução CD/ANPD Nº 2, de 27 de Janeiro de 2022' (*DOU*, 27 January 2022) <https://www.in.gov.br/en/web/dou/-/resolucao-cd/anpd-n-2-de-27-de-janeiro-de-2022-376562019#wrapper>; unofficial translation by Mattos, Eduardo, Walter Britto Gaspar, Yasmin Curzi, and Luca Belli, 'Application of LGPD to Small-Sized Processing Agents' (*CyberBRICS*, March 2022) <https://cyberbrics.info/application-of-lgpd-to-small-sized-processing-agents-non-official-translation-of-the-anpd-regulation/>.

[96] Imprensa Nacional, 'Resolução CD/ANPD Nº 15' (*DOU*, 24 April 2024) <https://www.in.gov.br/web/dou>.

[97] Imprensa Nacional, 'Resolução CD/ANPD Nº 18' (*DOU*, 16 July 2024) <https://www.in.gov.br/web/dou>.

[98] Imprensa Nacional, 'Resolução CD/ANPD Nº 19' (*DOU*, 23 August 2024) <https://www.in.gov.br/web/dou>.

[99] Luca Belli, Nicolo Zingales, Yasmin Curzi, Walter Britto Gaspar, and Erica Bakonyi, 'LGPD Regulation for Small Agents: Highlights, Advances and Future Paths' (*CyberBRICS* (blog), March 2022) <https://cyberbrics.info/lgpd-regulation-for-small-agents-highlights-advances-and-future-paths/>.

actions involving data protection issues in the Brazilian judiciary.[100] Despite this new form, the ANPD still struggles with budgetary limitations, as do other independent autarchies, since their budgetary plan is subjected to the regular annual national budget plan, leaving them vulnerable to budget cuts and retention of funds by the Executive.[101]

2.4.6. Automated Personal Data Processing

Regulation of Artificial Intelligence (AI) has been an ongoing and controversial discussion in Brazil for some time. Initial efforts to enact a dedicated Artificial Intelligence Act were met with initial opposition to the contents of the proposed text and to the hastened legislative discussion process. In response, a commission of jurists was created to discuss and propose a new version of the proposed act. Its results have been exhaustively discussed and recently approved in the Brazilian Senate, awaiting further appreciation by the Chamber of Deputies. In the absence of specific regulation, and considering the superposition of AI use cases and the need to process personal data, data protection regulation in Brazil is a relevant legal source for AI, be it in general personal data protection rules and principles as explained so far, or in its specific terms regarding automated processing of personal data.

Article 20 of the LGPD creates a right to revision of solely automated decisions which 'affect [the data subject's] interests, including decisions aimed at determining their personal, professional, consumer and credit profiles and aspects of their personality' (art 20). This right was originally meant to provide human revision of such decisions, but a presidential veto removed it, and the final wording did not mention revision by natural persons.

Importantly, the right also includes (at paragraph 1) a duty to inform the data subject on the criteria and procedures adopted to take an automated decision that can impact any interest of the data subject (paragraph 2), the possibility of an audit by the ANPD, conditional to the failure to provide said information and focused on investigating discriminatory decision-making. The detailed

[100] Fabricio da Mota Alves, 'ANPD como autarquia federal: o que muda para a proteção de dados?' (*JOTA Jornalismo*, 14 June 2022) <https://web.archive.org/web/20250114072810/https://www.jota.info/artigos/anpd-como-autarquia-federal-o-que-muda-para-a-protecao-de-dados-no-brasil>.

[101] Plenário, Acórdão 240/2015 (Tribunal de Contas da União, 11 February 2015); Paulo Sampaio, 'A Independência Real Das Agencias Reguladoras No Brasil' (2013) 5(1) Revista de Direito, Estado e Telecomunicações 135–74 <https://www.academia.edu/4220021/A_Independencia_Real_das_Agencias_Reguladoras_no_Brasil>.

contours of this right, including technical matters related to explainability of AI systems, are still to be determined by the Authority.

Besides these normative aspects, Brazil has had a period of dispersed AI public investments and programmes followed by the implementation of a Brazilian AI Strategy, which was heavily criticized for lacking strategic and planning elements. This was followed by a revision effort to produce a new AI Strategy, which was announced recently but has not yet resulted in a new document; and the publication of a Brazilian AI Plan, which amounts to a public investment plan divided between immediate actions and structural actions. This plan is heavily focused on developing capacity in algorithms and computational capacity. It is, however, merely a guiding document, with no binding power.[102]

In summary, Artificial Intelligence regulation in Brazil is less of an architecture and more of a blueprint. Even where it sits on the more solid foundations of an actual law—the automated processing part of the LGPD—it lacks precise technical definition.

2.5. Conclusion

A unified Brazilian data protection system is a recent development. Before the LGPD, many sectoral regulations were the basis not only for privacy and data protection rights in particular instances, but also for institutional structures built around these rights. On top of that, the path from strict privacy interpretations to data protection rights has followed hand in hand with this normative progression. This amounts to a scenario with many moving parts, rooted interests and established bureaucracies revolving around the subject.

This chapter aimed to present a general image of the complexity of this scenario, from rules to institutional actors and their interests. Attention was paid to raising issues and cases related to personal data protection in an attempt to highlight tension points that will need to be addressed by the Authority in its administrative and regulatory capacities.

The new data protection system and its main guardian and operator, the National Data Protection Authority, need to build the avenues for cooperation with these pre-existing institutional arrangements. Some issues might prove

[102] Germano P Johansson Neto, Viviane C Farias da Costa, and Walter Britto Gaspar, 'Brazil's Artificial Intelligence Plan (PBIA) of 2024: Enabler of AI Sovereignty?' (2024) 34 The African Journal of Information and Communication (AJIC) 1–15 <https://doi.org/10.23962/ajic.i34.20424>.

controversial and harder to resolve, such as competence disputes. However, the Authority has demonstrated a proactive stance in seeking out relevant institutional actors to coordinate visions and build understanding.

The administrative capabilities of the Authority are extensive, and on top of its regular attributions it must provide clarity to the many unanswered questions left open in the LGPD. If it takes too long to answer, uncertainty and recourse to other decision-making bodies might ensue, which could fragment the personal data protection system in the long run. Time will tell how these relations will unfurl.

Looking at the broader context of BRICS personal data architectures may provide insights into these challenges. The administrative and enforcement structures built in other BRICS countries vary significantly—from an authority structured as an organ of government, in Russia, to an independent authority without normative powers, such as the Data Protection Board of India.

Brazil's ANPD is independent; however, its capacity is constrained by budgetary limitations. Since its creation, it has demonstrated an increasingly active stance, having enacted nine sanctions via administrative sanctioning processes, one against a private company;[103] acted on matters of relevant national impact, such as cases involving the sharing of data between WhatsApp and its parent company, Meta[104] and usage of personal data drawn from Meta's user base for AI training; established a pay-for-biometric data scheme by Tools for Humanity;[105] and enacted regulations on international data transfers, the role of the *Encarregado*, communication of security breaches, and the sanctioning process. Overall, its more prolific work outside of actual sanctions applied might reflect a more preventative and educational focus, as well as its budgetary. However, some areas and cases still require more careful attention and further regulation and control.

One such issue is automated decision-making, which has rapidly become more relevant since the enactment of the LGPD due to the widespread use of popular generative AI tools. Their indiscriminate use of personal data,

[103] Fabrício Guimarães Madruga Lopes, Coordenação-Geral de Fiscalização, Relatório de instrução nº 1/2023/CGF/ANPD (ANPD 2023).

[104] ANPD, 'ANPD Conclui A Análise De Adequação Da Nova Política de Privacidade do WhatsApp à LGPD' (*Autoridade Nacional de Proteção de Dados*, 11 May 2022) <https://www.gov.br/anpd/pt-br/assuntos/noticias/anpd-conclui-a-analise-de-adequacao-da-nova-politica-de-privacidade-do-aplicativo-a-lgpd>; ANPD, 'Após Esforço Interinstitucional, Whatsapp se Compromete a Atender às Recomendações Sobre Sua Política De Privacidade', (*Autoridade Nacional de Proteção de Dados*, 20 August 2021) <https://www.gov.br/anpd/pt-br/assuntos/noticias/apos-esforco-interinstitucional-whatsapp-se-compromete-a-atender-as-recomendacoes-sobre-sua-politica-de-privacidade>.

[105] Miriam Wimmer, Conselho Diretor, Votos no recurso em processo administrativo de fiscalização nº 00261.006742/2024-53 (ANPD 2025).

including sensitive data, scraped from the internet, without notice, record or any further necessary caution, is an issue that has been faced by authorities in many countries,[106] but has fallen on deaf ears in Brazil.[107] On this point, a look to the Chinese efforts to rein in AI and algorithmic recommendation might provide an interesting reference: companies are required to provide transparency and explainability to the state controller, including code and plain-language explanations, of how algorithmic recommendation tools work; and to label generative AI content and ensure legitimate sources are used in training of such models.[108]

Another crucial matter is the specification of technical elements that are mentioned, but not exhaustively defined, in the LGPD. This includes interoperability as well as anonymization standards. These gaps are present in other BRICS countries' data architectures, with the exception of China, that has published specifications on the matter of data portability and interoperability. These gaps could be paths for future collaboration, with specification of BRICS technical standards.

Brazil's personal data architecture, while inspired by the GDPR, is rooted in a long tradition of personality rights and digital rights, with the notable case of the MCI as a landmark in terms of legislative process and innovative contents at its time. Its adoption of a GDPR-style data protection law did not create a clean slate, but rather a fruitful and complex frame in which the fundamental right to data protection has since been given form and structure. This is an ongoing process and among its many moving parts special note is given to the country's Data Protection Authority, which has had to deal with significant challenges and changes since its inception and still struggles to find the right balance between orienting and sanctioning.

[106] Stephanie Borg Psaila, 'Governments vs ChatGPT: Investigations around the World – Diplo' (*DiPLO*, 20 April 2023) <https://www.diplomacy.edu/blog/governments-chatgpt-investigations/>.

[107] Luca Belli, Walter Britto Gaspar, and Natalia Couto, 'Por que o ChatGPT descumpre a LGPD' (*Jota*, 25 August 2023) <https://web.archive.org/web/20250917211743/https://www.jota.info/opiniao-e-analise/artigos/por-que-o-chatgpt-descumpre-a-lgpd-parte-2>; Luca Belli, 'Por que o ChatGPT descumpre a LGPD e por que peticionei à ANPD' (*JOTA Jornalismo*, 23 May 2023) <https://web.archive.org/web/20250917211409/https://www.jota.info/opiniao-e-analise/artigos/por-que-o-chatgpt-descumpre-a-lgpd-e-por-que-peticionei-a-anpd>.

[108] Ashyana-Jasmine Kachra, 'Making Sense of China's AI Regulations' (*Holistic AI*, 12 February 2024) https://www.holisticai.com/blog/china-ai-regulation; AI Watch, 'Global Regulatory Tracker – China' (White & Case LLP, 13 May 2024) <https://www.whitecase.com/insight-our-thinking/ai-watch-global-regulatory-tracker-china>; Rogier Creemers, Graham Webster, and Helen Toner, 'Translation: Internet Information Service Algorithmic Recommendation Management Provisions—Effective March 1, 2022' (*DigiChina*, 10 January 2022) <https://digichina.stanford.edu/work/translation-internet-information-service-algorithmic-recommendation-management-provisions-effective-march-1-2022/>.

In conclusion, this chapter aimed to present and discuss a double coordination challenge for the Brazilian personal data architecture as it stands today. Internally, the main actor in interpreting and implementing the vision of data protection rights of the LGPD, the National Data Protection Authority, needs to simultaneously resolve issues of regulatory coordination with other authorities, fill in the legal gaps left by the law, give clarity to data controllers, and establish its supervisory role in face of data protection violations. Some of these goals have been pursued more actively than others, as has been shown. Externally, the country needs to find tools to coordinate its own personal data architecture with other relevant commercial and diplomatic partners, such as the BRICS countries. Many convergences and divergences were highlighted in this chapter, that give hints as to what opportunities and challenges for legal interoperability of BRICS personal data architectures exist.

3
THE PERSONAL DATA ARCHITECTURE OF RUSSIA

Anna Churshina and Anna Kruglikova

3.1. A Brief Overview of the Russian Legal System

3.1.1. General Background

Russia's legal structure developed at a fast pace during the 1990s. During this time, significant reforms were made to support the country's transition toward a market economy, including liberalization of markets and trade, privatization, and fiscal stabilization.

The Russian legal system is generally classified as a civil law system. It is based on the Constitution, federal and regional laws, and municipal acts. Primary legislation is supported by decisions of ministers, Russian government decrees, and Presidential executive orders.

The Constitution, which was adopted in the national referendum of 12 December 1993, states that both universally recognized principles of international law and international treaties to which Russia is a party are components of the Russian legal system. Consequently, when an international treaty provides for provisions contrary to those envisaged in domestic law, the international treaty provisions shall prevail. At the same time, the Constitution takes precedence over any controverting statements of an international treaty.

The Russian Civil Code (the 'Civil Code') sets out the main provisions of civil law, applicable to private individuals and businesses. A number of significant amendments to the Civil Code with regard to corporate law and contract law were introduced in September 2014 and June 2015. The key changes included the introduction of certain concepts into Russian law which had for a long time been common in international practice but had been previously absent from the Russian regulatory framework, such as the concept of warranties (as used in contracts under English law), the concept of reimbursement of

Anna Churshina and Anna Kruglikova, *The Personal Data Architecture of Russia* In: *Personal Data Architectures in the BRICS Countries*. Edited by: Luca Belli and Walter Britto Gaspar, Oxford University Press.
© Luca Belli and Walter B. Gaspar 2025. DOI: 10.1093/9780198974468.003.0003

losses arising from the occurrence of certain circumstances or conditions specified in a contract (an equivalent of indemnity in English law), new types of civil law contracts, such as options and framework agreements, new mechanisms to ensure the performance of contractual obligations by the parties, and a few others. While the Civil Code does not explicitly address personal data, it contains provisions relevant to personal data processing, such as article 152, which protects an individual's honour, dignity, and reputation. Inappropriate use of personal data can infringe upon these rights, potentially leading to claims for compensation.

Similarly, the Brazilian Civil Code includes specific provisions protecting privacy, such as article 21, which declares the inviolability of private life and empowers judges to take necessary actions to prevent or halt violations of this right. The General Principles of Civil Law of the People's Republic of China also stipulate that 'the personal information of a natural person shall be protected by law', reinforcing the legal protection of personal data and establishing safeguards against unauthorized disclosure or use. In summary, while Russia, Brazil, and China each have distinct legal frameworks, they all emphasize the protection of personal data and privacy through various provisions in their civil codes and specific laws, highlighting the importance of safeguarding individuals' personal information.

Russian legislation has evolved rapidly over the past decade, and Russia's data security laws are no exception. As the data economy has grown, lawmakers have increasingly sought to regulate transparency over how personal data is used and to clearly define the rights of businesses and individuals to personal data, with steps being taken to implement the core international principles of privacy and security laws.

3.2. Russian Data Protection Laws: Historical Overview and Current Trends

Fundamental provisions of personal data protection are laid down in the Constitution of the Russian Federation,[1] international treaties, and Russian specific laws. The Russian Constitution (enacted in 1993) guarantees privacy and data protection rights. Article 23 of the Constitution establishes the right

[1] The Constitution of the Russian Federation, 25 December 1993.

to privacy as one of the principal rights of citizens of Russia (this right may be challenged only by a court decision),[2] and article 24 creates the basis for the right to data protection, confirming 'consent' as one of the main legal bases for data processing. It requires that 'the collection, keeping, use and dissemination of information about the private life of a person shall not be allowed without his or her consent'. Enactment of specific laws and regulations is required to support these rights' execution. It is important to note that the Brazilian Constitution also guarantees the right to both privacy and data protection.

As a logical step in the further development of personal data protection, in 2005, Russia ratified the Council of Europe Convention for the Protection of Individuals with regard to the Automatic Processing of Personal Data 1981. Several countries have built their data protection regime based on the Council of Europe Convention.

In order to ensure the effective implementation of the Convention and the adoption of country-specific technical requirements for the processing of personal data, in 2006 Russia's State Duma adopted two primary laws governing personal data protection: Federal Law No 149-FZ 'On information, information technologies and data protection' (the 'Data Protection Act') and Federal Law No 152-FZ 'On Personal Data' (the 'Personal Data Law').[3] The Personal Data Law is mainly based on Directive 95/46/EC on the protection of individuals with regard to the processing of personal data and on the free movement of such. The experience of its application and interpretation in Europe allows us to resolve issues related to personal data in the Russian Federation.

The Data Protection Act serves to protect information in general and partially covers personal data. Article 2(7) of the Data Protection Act is an important pillar for the right to confidentiality. It guarantees confidentiality of information and requires a person who has access to information to seek the consent of the owner of such information, prior to transferring it to third parties (clause 7, art 2).

The Personal Data Law regulates many aspects of data protection, including but not limited to the definition of personal data, data types, and technical and

[2] Art 23: '1. Everyone is entitled to privacy of personal life, personal, and family secrets, protection of one's honour and good name. 2. Limitations of this right shall be allowed only by court decision'. Translation of the Constitution provided by Garant Service (Garant.ru).

[3] An English version of the law can be found at the website of the CyberBRICS project <https://cyberbrics.info/>.

organizational measures that must be applied by those who process personal data. Unlike European law, the Personal Data Law does not distinguish between data controllers and data processors. Therefore, any individual or entity working with personal data is considered a personal data operator governed by the Personal Data Law.

Thus, both acts play a significant role in guaranteeing privacy and confidentially of information.

Personal Data Law is the main legislative act that regulates relations concerning the processing of personal data, and defines the principles, conditions, and rules for the processing of personal data. According to article 3 of the Constitution, the regulation of relations concerning the processing of personal data is carried out exclusively at the federal level. Federal subjects of the Russian Federation cannot adopt legal acts in this area.

Additionally, the leading regulator of data protection—the Federal Service for Communications, Information Technology and Mass Communications Supervision (Roskomnadzor)—was established in 2008. It is controlled by and reports to the Ministry of Digital Development, Communications, and Mass Media of the Russian Federation (*MinTsifry Rossii*). This government ministry is responsible for telecommunications, media, and the post. Thus, Roskomnadzor is a part of the federal executive body that performs the functions of developing state policy and legal regulation in the established field of telecommunications, media, and the post.

In contrast, in each EU Member State there are data protection authorities (DPA). They are 'independent public authorities that monitor and supervise, through investigative and corrective powers, the application of the data protection law. They provide expert advice on data protection issues and handle complaints that may have breached the law'.[4] For instance, the Commission Nationale de l'Informatique et des Libertés (CNIL) is the independent public authority in France responsible for overseeing the application of data protection laws, including the EU General Data Protection Regulation (GDPR) and the French Data Protection Act.

When comparing Russia's data protection regulatory framework to those in other BRICS countries, notable differences arise in terms of the independence and scope of authority of the data protection agencies. In China, the

[4] <https://commission.europa.eu/>.

data protection authority operates within a framework that is not fully independent. The Chinese government maintains significant control over the regulatory processes related to data privacy and cybersecurity, evident in the close relationship between the data protection agency and the government. This centralized control allows the government to maintain a strong influence over how personal data is handled and monitored, often with a focus on state security and surveillance.

In contrast, Brazil and South Africa have regulatory bodies that operate with a greater degree of independence. Brazil's data protection authority, the National Data Protection Authority (ANPD) was established under the General Data Protection Law (LGPD), and although it is still subject to some oversight by the Executive, operates autonomously from the government. The ANPD has the power to issue guidelines, monitor compliance, and impose fines for noncompliance, allowing it to act independently when it comes to enforcing data protection regulations.

Similarly, in South Africa, the Information Regulator is an independent authority tasked with enforcing the Protection of Personal Information Act (POPIA). The Information Regulator has significant powers, including authority to investigate data breaches, monitor compliance with the law, and issue fines. Its independence from the government ensures that data protection issues are handled impartially, with a focus on safeguarding the privacy of individuals and upholding their rights.

Thus, while Russia's data protection regulator, Roskomnadzor, reports directly to the Ministry of Digital Development, Communications, and Mass Media, making it more government-controlled, Brazil and South Africa have created more autonomous frameworks for data protection enforcement.

Until 2014, data privacy had not been a topic of significant discussion or enforcement, and no significant changes were made to the existing order of personal data regulation.

The most essential updates that have crucially influenced the current Russian data protection framework are touched upon below. The overview will briefly cover the enforcement provisions, which will be discussed in more detail in the next chapter.

The Russian government has taken several large-scale measures to regulate relations involving the use of the Internet. The state's first response to the socially and politically significant use of the Internet was the introduction of severe prohibitions and restrictions to ensure the state's security, which will be covered below in more detail.

3.2.1. Data Localization Law

In 2014, the Russian parliament adopted amendments[5] to the Personal Data Law. These amendments are known as the Data Localization Law, and they came into force on 1 September 2015. Data operators that collect personal data of Russian citizens are required to store and process such personal data using databases located in Russia as a 'primary' database. Data can be transferred for further processing abroad (subject to compliance with the requirements for data transfers). Businesses and the media were highly critical of these amendments. Supporters of the amendments argue that they created significant opportunities for profit for Russian data centres. At the same time, opponents confirm that it raised operational costs for ordinary businesses that were required to redesign their data storage infrastructure. However, not all companies strive to comply with this law. For example, LinkedIn refused to comply with localization requirements.[6] As a result, the company's website and access to the social network were blocked in the territory of Russia, so ordinary residents do not have the opportunity to freely use this social network.

The trend towards internet sovereignty is not confined to Russia; it is also evident in several other BRICS countries, including China and India. These countries are increasingly seeking to assert control over information flows within their national segments of the internet. Notably, China's data localization laws serve as a key example of this movement, mandating that data generated within its borders be stored and processed locally, further reinforcing national control over digital infrastructure and information.

Both Russia's and China's data localization laws reflect a strong desire to control the flow of information within their borders, ensuring that data related to their citizens, businesses, and national security remains under domestic jurisdiction.

India has also taken steps toward data localization, particularly with the Personal Data Protection Bill (PDPB), which proposes that critical personal data must be stored in India. While some categories of data can be transferred abroad under specific conditions, the bill emphasizes that certain types of data should remain within the country to enhance privacy and security.

[5] Federal Law No 242-FZ making amendments to the Data Protection Act was approved by the upper chamber of the Russian parliament on 9 July 2014 and signed by the President on 21 July 2014.

[6] <https://iapp.org/news/a/why-linkedin-was-banned-in-russia/>.

In contrast, Brazil and South Africa do not have strict data localization requirements. Instead, they focus more on ensuring adequate protection of personal data, regardless of where the data is stored. Brazil's LGPD and South Africa's POPIA allow for cross-border data transfers, provided that the destination country has an adequate level of protection in place or appropriate safeguards are provided.

Thus, while Russia, India, and China emphasize data localization, Brazil and South Africa have adopted more flexible frameworks that allow international data transfers under certain conditions.

3.2.2. Yarovaya Law

A set of amendments to various laws that aimed to implement measures against terrorist activity was implemented in 2016.[7] They became known by the name of one of its authors—Irina Yarovaya. A part of the initiative was to amend the Data Protection Act. The amendments introduced the concept of the 'organizer of dissemination of information'. An organizer of the dissemination of information on the Internet is a person carrying out activities to ensure the functioning of information systems and (or) programs for electronic computers that are intended and (or) used for receiving, transmitting, delivering and (or) processing electronic messages of network users on the Internet. Such companies have to store communications data (images, video, voice, and text messages) for six months and provide these to the security services in the case of a court order, with decryption keys if the messages are encrypted. They also have to register with Roskomnadzor via a designated website. Several messaging apps were blocked in Russia (eg, Zello, WeChat,[8] and Telegram, which was blocked from 2018 to 2020[9]) as a consequence of this law.

[7] Federal Law 'On Amendments to the Criminal Code of the Russian Federation and the Code of Criminal Procedure of the Russian Federation in terms of establishing additional measures to counter terrorism and ensure public security' dated 7 June 2016 N 375-FZ and Federal Law 'On Amendments to the Federal Law "On Countering Terrorism" and Certain Legislative Acts of the Russian Federation Regarding the Establishment of Additional Measures to Counter Terrorism and Ensuring Public Security' dated 7 June 2016 N 374-FZ.

[8] It was blocked for about one week and then unblocked when the company decided to comply with the law.

[9] In 2020 Roskomnadzor announced a waiver of the requirement to restrict access to the Telegram messenger. It explained its decision by the willingness of the founder of Telegram to 'counter terrorism and extremism'.

3.2.3. Sovereign Internet

In 2019 a set of amendments was enacted related to the functioning of the Internet in Russia. They become known as the Sovereign Internet Law.[10] The explanatory note to the Sovereign Internet Law states that its goal is to protect the country from cyberattacks and ensure the Internet's performance in Russia via Runet, if it were to be disconnected from the global Internet.[11] In order to ensure the independent functioning of the Internet in Russia, the following new requirements were established: databases and programs associated with the provision of public government services must be located in Russia, and Roskomnadzor was given the right to block traffic in the event of Internet attacks. Many argue that the proposed measures are beneficial only to Roskomnadzor, which has even more power to block traffic on the Internet, and which may be seen as a new form of censorship.[12]

Digital sovereignty, in the context of BRICS, refers to the ability to control digital infrastructure, data, and policies, promoting national interests, data security, and privacy. It emphasizes autonomy in digital governance, allowing each nation to set its own regulations for data protection, cybersecurity, and digital trade. The aim is to reduce dependence on foreign technologies and to create a more balanced global digital landscape, as well as to assert control over the country's digital infrastructure, safeguard national security, and protect citizens' data.

While China, Russia, and to some extent India have implemented stringent measures like data localization and sovereign internet laws, Brazil and South Africa are advancing data protection laws and initiatives that strengthen local governance while fostering global cooperation. These countries are balancing national interests with the need for global interconnectedness, ensuring that digital sovereignty is a central part of their future technological strategies.

For example, Brazil issued Decree No 11.856 on 27 December 2023, establishing the National Cybersecurity Policy and creating the National Cybersecurity Committee. This policy focuses on enhancing national cybersecurity, safeguarding data, combating cybercrime, and boosting

[10] The Sovereign Internet Law is the informal name for a set of 2019 amendments to existing Russian legislation that mandate internet surveillance and grant the Russian government powers to separate Russia from the rest of the Internet: Federal Law No 90-FZ of 1 May 2019 'On Amendments to the Federal Law "On Communications" and the Data Protection Act'.

[11] Dr Andrey Shcherbovich, 'Sovereign Internet Law signed by the President of Russia' (*CyberBRICS*, 8 May 2019) <https://cyberbrics.info/sovereign-internet-law-signed-by-the-president-of-russia/>.

[12] Luca Belli, 'Cybersecurity Convergence in the BRICS Countries' (*CyberBRICS*, 20 September 2021) <https://cyberbrics.info/cybersecurity-convergence-in-the-brics-countries/>.

organizational resilience, with the committee responsible for updating the policy, assessing cybersecurity measures, and promoting international cooperation.

3.2.4. New Requirement for Localization of Major Internet Companies in Russia

On 1 July 2021, Federal Law No 236-FZ on the Internet Activities of Foreign Entities in the Russian Federation came into force, requiring foreign Internet companies whose information resource is accessed by 500,000 or more Russian users daily to establish and maintain a local presence, such as a branch, a representative office, or a subsidiary, effective 1 January 2022.

Establishing a local presence means that such companies have to open representative offices in Russia, cooperate with Roskomnadzor (in particularly responding to their notices) and place a feedback form on their websites for receiving messages from Russian citizens. Opening a representative office in Russian territory means that companies have to comply with local requirements, prohibitions, and restrictions, and it will be easier for Roskomnadzor to enforce data protection requirements against such companies.

Roskomnadzor has the power to investigate whether foreign companies are following the conditions that require them to establish a presence in Russia. The regulator shall maintain a list of such companies on one of its websites.[13]

Legislators have adopted many enforcement measures that allow the regulator to take action against the violator. Most of them are intended to restrict the online presence of the website. Among these measures are excluding websites from web-search results, completely blocking access to the website, etc. The most discussed one is slowing down the Internet speed in relation to a website (throttling). Such a measure requires targeted action on specific sites, and it is important to ensure that other websites will not be affected. Slowing down a particular website became possible after the realization of a set of amendments that require data operators to install special equipment to their network as an implementation of the Sovereign Internet Law. One of the best-known examples is the throttling of Twitter.[14]

[13] <236-fz.rkn.gov.ru>, accessed 5 January 2022.
[14] <https://www.rbc.ru/technology_and_media/10/03/2021/6048ca449a7947480d4791de>, as of 15 January 2022.

3.2.5. Current Trend: Digitalization of Russian Society and Economy, Use of AI

Digital transformation encompasses the strategic use of digital technologies to revolutionize and enhance multiple facets of society, the economy, and governance. This process involves incorporating advanced technologies like artificial intelligence, machine learning, the Internet of Things (IoT), and data analytics to foster innovation, streamline operations, and stimulate growth across various industries and public services.

In 2017, the President of Russia approved the Strategy for the Development of the Information Society in the Russian Federation for 2017–30,[15] setting out priority areas for the use of digitalization. The strategy is designed to contribute to the implementation of such national interests as the information security of citizens and the state, improving the efficiency of public administration, developing the economy and the social sphere, and ensuring law and order. The strategy is supported by measures taken at the federal and regional levels to adapt legislation to new technological conditions in various fields of activity.[16]

Russia has been working on several initiatives related to the development and deployment of digital technologies, including AI and facial recognition. These initiatives are part of a broader strategy to modernize the country's technological infrastructure, improve public services, and ensure that AI technologies are integrated into society in a controlled and regulated manner.

At the federal level, the several documents, initiatives, and laws were connected with the government's national 'Digital Economy of the Russian Federation' programme must be taken into account.[17] One of the associated projects was the experiment in the creation and use of a citizen 'Digital Profile'. The participants in the experiment are credit, insurance, and microfinance organizations and operators of financial platforms. The legal basis for the experiment is a Government Decree of 3 June 2019, No 710 'On conducting an experiment to improve the quality and connectivity of data contained in state information resources'.

Appendix 2 to Decree No 710 lists information that forms the Digital Profile (it includes about forty items). Mainly, these items are personal data (passport

[15] Decree of the President of the Russian Federation of 9 May 2017 N 203 'On the Strategy for the Development of the Information Society in the Russian Federation for 2017–2030' SZ RF. 2017. N 20. Art 2901.

[16] MA Fedotov and others (eds) *Information Law: a Textbook for Universities* (Yurayt 2020) 122.

[17] Passport of the National Program, 'Digital Economy of the Russian Federation' <http://government.ru/info/35568/>, accessed 15 January 2022.

data, residential address, taxpayer identification number, etc.) and information from public registers (for instance, about owned real estate). But it also contains information that is usually considered more 'sensitive', such as work records/labour books[18] in an electronic format, information on income and taxes paid, etc.

With the help of the Digital Profile infrastructure, for example, the following can be provided: 1. identification and authentication of specified persons; 2. access to the digital profile and provision of information included in the digital profile in electronic form; 3. provision and updating, at the request of the relevant authorized bodies, of information about the person contained in the digital profile; 4. obtaining and withdrawal of consent to the processing of personal data of citizens in cases involving the receipt of information about a person using the digital profile infrastructure; 5. providing information for the formation of requests for state and municipal services; 6. storage of information and results of the provision of the above services in electronic form.

Mochalov[19] notes that based on the analysis of Decree No 710, it can be concluded that a digital profile is not just a simple collection of information, but an ordered array of official data about a citizen or legal entity, the reliability of which is confirmed by the competent authorities of the state.

Undoubtedly, the Digital Profile system will help citizens quickly access services for which confirmation of various information is required. In turn, this will also simplify interaction between the state and the citizen, allowing citizens and foreigners to get certain services faster.

However, consolidating such a large amount of data in one place raises questions about data security. It is important that access to such data should only be provided on a need-to-know basis and when strictly necessary. Data subjects should be informed as to what part of their Digital Profile will have access to various systems. Data subjects should decide freely whether to provide their data or not.

In addition to reforms at the Federal level, larger cities have also seen some emerging technologies. In October 2021 the Moscow metro launched a new facial-recognition payment system, as the first mass-scale use of a technology that is aimed at bringing greater convenience to people's everyday lives. At the same time, it has raised reasonable concerns about the system's possible misuse for surveillance purposes. A facial recognition system will scan the face and

[18] These serve as confirmation of employment in the Russian Federation and contain the history of the places of work of an individual.

[19] AN Mochalov, 'Digital Profile: Main Risks for Constitutional Human Rights in the Context of Legal Uncertainty' (2021) 74(9) Lex Russica 90.

check it against its database.[20] A required step is to upload biometric data (face image) into the database of the system and provide consent for its use. A passenger will only need to register in a mobile application, upload a photo of his/her face and link a bank card or *Troika* (a contactless reusable card that is designed to pay for public transport in Moscow). The system then compares the face with its data bank and lets a person enter the metro, and money is debited from the card automatically. Thus, the system facilitates easy payment without the need to carry cash or phone/bank cards.

Before facial recognition was introduced for payments, similar system was already operating in the Moscow metro. Its purpose was to find wanted offenders as well as missing people (including children). The system's use in law enforcement ensures safety and security for passengers. It significantly helps to detain wanted criminals and suspects. The system is used by responsible state bodies and law enforcement officers engaged in the investigation and prevention of crimes.

However, privacy professionals and activists have expressed concerns in regard to the privacy of individuals. One can argue that the system should be more transparent and accountable, with guarantees of protection against abuse by the authorities and third parties. Another potential issues is the mass surveillance of all visitors of the metro. The creation of such systems and their operation may present some benefits in large cities such as Moscow. At the same time, it is necessary to observe and guarantee the fundamental rights and freedoms of citizens.

Another initiative of the Russian government that falls within the scope of digitalization of services is the creation of the Unified Biometric System ('UBS'). The UBS is a state digital platform that enables confirmation of a person's identity based on their biometric characteristics. Through biometrics and the UBS, government and commercial services can be accessed remotely or in person, conveniently and securely. Use of the system and processing of personal data is regulated by the Federal Law 'On the Identification and/or Authentication of Individuals Using Biometric Personal Data, Amending Certain Legislative Acts of the Russian Federation, and Repealing Certain Provisions of Legislative Acts of the Russian Federation' dated 29 December 2022, No 572-FZ ('Federal Law on the Use of Biometric Data').

[20] <https://ict.moscow/en/projects/smartcitymoscow/case/face-pay-biometric-payment-system/>, accessed 25 June 2023.

According to article 3 of the Federal Law on the Use of Biometric Data, the UBS is to be used for the identification and/or authentication of individuals by various entities, including, but not limited to:

1. Government bodies and local authorities.
2. The Central Bank of the Russian Federation.
3. Banks
4. Entities that are part of the national payment system.
5. Individuals providing professional services in the financial market (eg, lawyers, notaries).
6. Other organizations, individual entrepreneurs, and notaries.

Additionally, the UBS may be used in other legal relationships as stipulated by the laws of the Russian Federation.

The primary objective behind the implementation of the UBS is to enhance the accessibility of services that necessitate confirmation of identity, fostering a more streamlined and secure user experience.

Providing biometric personal data is a right of citizens but not an obligation. Biometrics streamline interactions when accessing services but do not exclude other methods of identification and authentication. Refusal of an individual to undergo identification and/or authentication using their biometric personal data cannot be grounds for denying them the provision of state, municipal, or other services, the performance of state or municipal functions, the sale of goods, the execution of work, or refusal of service.

Individuals have the right to request the deletion of their biometric data from the UBS, and one method to initiate this process is by submitting a request through multifunctional centres for the provision of public services. These centres are government-run facilities designed to provide a wide range of public services to citizens in a convenient and accessible manner, serving as one-stop shops where individuals can apply for various government services, access information, and carry out bureaucratic procedures, without needing to visit multiple government offices. They form part of Russia's efforts to modernize and simplify its public administration, improve service delivery, and create more transparent and efficient government interaction.

While centralizing data does raise legitimate privacy concerns, it is crucial to highlight that such trends are an integral part of the technological progress that can significantly enhance efficiency and improve public services. Access to unified data can streamline governmental processes, optimize decision-making, and improve the provision of services, including the timeline. Transparency, accountability, and robust safeguards at every stage are components of successful operation of the system. By carefully addressing the associated risks, governments can create an environment where innovation and privacy are balanced, ultimately benefiting both individuals and society as a whole.

To enhance the protection of biometric personal data and deter both individuals and organizations from violating biometric personal data laws, on 5 December 2023 members of the State Duma approved a law on tightening penalties for violations of requirements in the field of placement of citizens' biometric personal data.[21] According to the document, a new article 13.11.3 of the Code of the Russian Federation on Administrative Offences introduces independent administrative liability for violations of requirements regarding the placement of citizens' biometric personal data.

Thus, fines for unauthorized placement, updating of such data and collection without consent are introduced: for officials, ranging from 100,000 to 300,000 rubles (approximately USD 1,350 to USD 4,050), and for organizations, from 500,000 to 1 million rubles (approximately USD 6,750 to USD 13,500). Upon a repeated commission of this offence, officials will be held accountable with fines ranging from 300,000 to 500,000 rubles, individual entrepreneurs from 500,000 to 1 million rubles, and organizations from 1 million to 1.5 million rubles (approximately USD 20,250).

According to the amendments, in cases where protocols are issued by officials of Roskomnadzor, courts will be responsible for considering cases of violations related to the placement and updating of biometric information. Additionally, within their authority, the Central Bank of the Russian Federation will also have the ability to adjudicate such cases.

Moreover, Russia has established an evolving AI regulatory framework that addresses legal, technical, and ethical considerations. The legal framework includes laws like the Federal Law on Personal Data (No 152-FZ), which governs the processing of personal data for AI systems, and the Law on Experimental Legal Regimes in Digital Innovation (No. 258-FZ, 2020), which allows AI to be tested in flexible regulatory environments. To support the development of AI, the government has created the AI.gov.ru portal (available in English), providing a centralized hub for legal documents, guidelines, and resources for businesses and researchers. These efforts help Russia foster AI innovation while ensuring safety, privacy, and ethical standards in its applications.

In recent years, biometric technologies and digital profiles have been increasingly adopted across several BRICS nations, each integrating them into

[21] <http://duma.gov.ru/news/58432/>, accessed 5 December 2023.

various sectors to improve public services, enhance security, and streamline everyday activities, all in pursuit of broader goals like economic growth, digital inclusion, and cybersecurity.

In Russia, facial recognition systems are becoming more common in public spaces such as transportation, retail, and law enforcement. This is part of Russia's broader strategy to improve digital infrastructure, enhance security, and foster economic development by leveraging technology.

Similarly, India has made significant strides through its Digital India initiative, launched in 2015. A cornerstone of this initiative is Aadhaar, one of the world's largest biometric identification systems. Aadhaar uses data to verify identities for accessing government services and subsidies. Managed by the Unique Identification Authority of India (UIDAI), Aadhaar has become a key driver of digital inclusion, providing millions of Indians with access to essential services and promoting digital literacy across the nation. These efforts also contribute to India's goal of improving digital access and reducing inequality.

Meanwhile, China also has been integrating facial recognition technologies into everyday life, utilizing them in various sectors like public transportation, law enforcement, banking, and consumer services. While China's approach to biometric surveillance is among the most extensive, it highlights a global trend of using biometrics to improve efficiency, security, and innovation across sectors. This global trend also reflects a shared goal of economic growth within the BRICS countries, as digital technologies play a vital role in boosting productivity and enhancing services.

3.2.6. Latest Developments in Privacy Legislation

Several amendments were introduced into Law No 152-FZ 'On Personal Data' and other laws governing personal data processing in Russia. These changes will briefly be described. There are several changes that came into effect from 1 September 2022. For example, the response time to requests has been lowered to ten working days, and the personal data subject now has the right to obtain information on the operator's compliance with Law No 152-FZ responsibilities. Also, requirements for personal data subjects' consent increased. Consent must be specific and unambiguous. This change forces businesses to adapt and amend their standard consent form. Incident notification requirements have become more comprehensive. New obligations related to reporting obligations for security incidents were introduced which contain two steps. In case a data incident resulted in the unlawful transfer (provision, distribution, access) of personal data, an operator must notify Roskomnadzor within twenty-four hours of the discovery of the incident. The report must include the following details: the causes of the data breach, the potential harm caused, the security measures taken in response, and the contact information of the authorized representative from the data controller responsible for addressing the breach. The report should be submitted within seventy-two hours of concluding the internal investigation. However, data controllers are not obliged to notify affected individuals. Also, Law No 152-FZ becomes applicable to foreign legal entities and individuals if they process personal data of citizens of the Russian Federation on the basis of a contract or other agreement to which citizens of the Russian Federation are parties, or on the basis of the consent of a citizen of the Russian Federation to process their personal data. These amendments have confirmed the extra-territorial application of the law. Additionally, some form of obligatory registry of the record of processing activities was introduced. Such registry should include: the categories and types of personal data; categories of personal data subjects; data retention and types of processing, as well as how personal data are deleted. Another amendment came into force from 1 March 2023. Companies who want to perform the cross-border transfer of personal data must notify Roskomnadzor of their intention, and obtain permission if the recipient country does not belong to the list of countries that provide adequate protection of data subjects.

There remains huge interest in and further development for the use of the UBS. Related acts may be found on the system's webpage.[22] One of the main goals it to collect biometric personal data in one place to allow further use by public and private organizations. Collecting biometric personal data in one place for use by public and private organizations raises several important ethical, legal, and privacy concerns. While there can be legitimate reasons for collecting biometric data, such as for security or identification purposes, it must be done with great care and in accordance with established legal and ethical principles. There are some key considerations, such as informed consent, data security, and retention, as well as purpose limitation, transparency, and others.

Several amendments have been introduced into Federal Law No 149-FZ 'On information, information technologies and data protection'. In particular, hosting providers must register with Roskomnadzor and must meet several requirements such as reporting the initiation of their operations to Roskomnadzor; ensuring the stable, secure, and seamless functioning of the internet within Russia's borders; offering hosting services only following user

[22] <https://ebs.ru/>.

identification procedures as determined by the government, and guaranteeing compliance with information security requirements. Starting from 1 February 2024, hosting providers not included in the registry are not allowed to operate.

Identification procedures are currently allowed by means of the following mechanisms: use of telecommunications operator for identification purpose; use of biometric identifiers by available systems; or use of other information systems that meet the legal requirements for information security, owned by Russian citizens without citizenship in another state, or by Russian legal entities. 'Other information systems' for example includes mail service providers like mail.ru. Foreign email addresses may not be used for registration purposes in such information systems.

Such changes arouse concerns, since they pose technical challenges for users, necessitating the conversion of international addresses to Russian addresses, among other things. In principle, these amendments seek to gradually replace foreign servers and systems with Russian ones, which is consistent with the recent trend toward the localization of personal data and the formation of a sovereign Internet.

3.2.7. Human Rights and the Rule of Law Context

In recent years, there has been a notable surge in the global discussion on human rights and the rule of law, with particular emphasis on the protection of personal data. This topic becomes particularly pronounced when considered in the framework of data transfers governed by the General Data Protection Regulation (GDPR). The scope of data transfer involves the various actions of sharing, sending, or facilitating access to personal data, all of which may involve diverse entities or systems situated in various countries or regions. The GDPR imposes specific requirements and safeguards to ensure that such data transfers comply with the regulation's principles for the protection of individuals' rights and privacy. When personal data is transferred outside the European Economic Area (EEA), organizations must follow certain mechanisms and safeguards to ensure that the data continues to be adequately protected. Execution of the EU Standard Contractual Clauses (SCCs) is one mechanism that allows data transfer. The Court of Justice of the European Union (CJEU), when deciding Case C-311/18 initiated by Max Schrems, affirmed the validity of SCCs, providing that they include effective mechanisms to ensure compliance in practice with the 'essentially equivalent' level of protection guaranteed by the GDPR to EU citizens. Transfer Impact Assessment

(TIA) serves as a tool for performing such assessment. TIA is an individual case-by-case assessment to determine whether the recipient country affords an essentially equivalent level of data protection and whether the safeguards of the transfer in question would be effective.

TIA, among its various aspects, necessitates the examination of the legal framework in the third country. The TIA should comprehensively evaluate relevant laws and practices governing third-party access, with a specific focus on government or intelligence agency surveillance.

Key considerations entail scrutinizing the third country's commitment to human rights protection, adherence to data security standards, and the alignment of its legal system with that of the EU, among other crucial factors. In essence, providing a thorough and detailed account of the applicable legal prerequisites in the third country is imperative for a comprehensive TIA.

Hence, considerations related to human rights and the rule of law are pivotal in the context of a TIA. This section delves into some aspects of these critical topics in Russia.

Over the years, Russia has undertaken substantial efforts to bring its legislative landscape into harmony with international norms, as described earlier. At the same time, questions persist regarding the practical implementation and enforcement of these regulations. Despite adhering to international human rights standards, particularly the Universal Declaration of Human Rights, it is important to ensure that it should not only be well-established on paper but shall be effectively put into practice through enforcement measures.

One of the primary challenges is the potential tension between national security interests and individual privacy rights. The deployment of surveillance practices in public spaces has become a focal point of concern for human rights advocates, emphasizing the intricate task of striking a balance between ensuring the safety of citizens and upholding their fundamental right to privacy. Balancing these rights remains a delicate and evolving aspect of the rule of law in Russia.

Moreover, the increasing digitalization of society introduces an array of challenges pertaining to issues such as consent, data breaches, and the cross-border transfer of personal data.

Navigating these issues requires a nuanced approach that safeguards individual rights without hindering the technological advancements that underpin societal development.

In response to these challenges, recent developments in Russia include amendments to the Federal Law on Personal Data. These revisions underscore the government's commitment to remaining at the forefront of technological progress and adapting the legal framework to effectively address emerging challenges. This proactive stance reflects an awareness of the evolving landscape of technology and data processing, aligning legislative efforts with the dynamic technological developments.

The Personal Data Law imposes several limitations on the rights of data subjects and the processing of sensitive categories of personal data. Article 14 of the Personal Data Law specifically governs the data subject's right to access their personal data, detailing (at section 8) the limitations on these rights.

These restrictions, as outlined in article 14, are subject to federal laws, and include the following scenarios:

1. Processing for National Defence and Security:
   When personal data processing, including information acquired through operational, counterintelligence, and intelligence activities, serves national defence, state security, and law enforcement purposes.[23]
2. Detention or Criminal Accusation:
   In cases where authorities detain the data subject on suspicion of a crime or accuse them in a criminal case, or apply preventive measures before filing charges, restricting access to personal data. Exceptions may apply under the criminal procedural legislation of the Russian Federation.[24]
3. Legal Compliance for Crime Prevention:
   When the personal data are processed in accordance with the legislation on countering the legalization of incomes received through crime (money laundering) and the financing of terrorism.
4. Protection of Third-Party Rights:
   When the data subject's access to their personal data would infringe upon the rights and legitimate interests of third parties.
5. Transport Security Legislation:

In cases outlined by the legislation of the Russian Federation on transport security, where personal data processing is essential for ensuring the sustainable

[23] Art 14, s 8 of the Federal law On Personal Data 'The processing of the personal data, including the personal data obtained as the result of operative-search operations, counter-intelligence and intelligence activities takes place for the purposes of national defence, state security and law and order'.

[24] 'The personal data are processed by the bodies which have detained the personal data subject on suspicions of having committed a crime or which have presented criminal-case charges to the personal data subject or have imposed a measure of restraint on the personal data subject before presenting charges, except for the cases envisaged by the criminal procedural legislation of the Russian Federation when the suspect or accused is allowed to get acquainted with such personal data'.

and safe functioning of the transport complex and protecting the interests of individuals, society, and the state from unlawful interference.

Article 10 of the Personal Data Law explicitly prohibits the processing of special categories of personal data, such as race, nationality, political views, religious or philosophical beliefs, health status, and intimate life. Exceptions are allowed under specific circumstances detailed in sections 2 and 2.1 of article 10, permitting the processing of special categories of personal data by Russian authorities for purposes such as security, counterterrorism, transport security, and anti-corruption efforts.

It is interesting to observe limitations to the right or privacy in other BRICS countries. For example, in India, public bodies are granted certain exemptions from fully complying with personal data protection laws. These exemptions are designed to strike a balance between robust data protection and the practical needs of governmental functions, particularly in areas like national security, law enforcement, and public welfare. Under India's Digital Personal Data Protection Act 2023 (DPD Act), public bodies and government entities are permitted to process personal data without strictly adhering to the law's provisions in cases related to national security, law enforcement, or public order. This ensures that the government can effectively carry out its essential duties in these critical areas, without being overly constrained by data protection requirements.

3.3. Introduction to the Key Features of the Personal Data Law

3.3.1. Scope and Key Definitions

The Personal Data Law defines the terms 'personal data' and 'data processing', establishing a comprehensive framework governing the rights of data subjects. It outlines the responsibilities of data controllers, including guidelines on consent, policies for data localization, and regulations concerning cross-border data transfers. This legislation predominantly addresses personal data operators functioning within the territorial bounds of the Russian Federation.

In contrast to the broad territorial scope of the GDPR,[25] which safeguards the personal data of any EU citizen regardless of the company's geographical or jurisdictional location, the Personal Data Law is geographically more circumscribed. Specifically, it applies to personal data operators registered and functioning within the Russian Federation. Importantly, foreign data operators situated

[25] <https://eur-lex.europa.eu/eli/reg/2016/679/oj>.

outside Russia are mandated to comply with data localization rules when collecting personal data from Russian residents. This underscores an extraterritorial dimension in ensuring robust data protection for individuals in Russia.

The Russian definition of personal data is generally consistent with the European framework. The Personal Data Law defines personal data as any information referring directly or indirectly to an identified or identifiable individual, known as a personal data subject or data subject.[26] Encompassing a wide variety of information, personal data may also include data collected by cookies, information about geolocation, IP address, or subscriber traffic. The Personal Data Law also sets forth special categories of personal data (also known as sensitive personal data), which are subject to a higher level of protection and can be processed in certain scenarios. Sensitive personal data include a person's racial or ethnic origin, religious or political beliefs, medical data, and criminal record. In addition, the processing of personal biometric data, which a data operator may only do with the data subject's consent or under other exceptions, is also regulated by the Personal Data Law.

The Personal Data Law defines the processing of personal data rather broadly as any action or combination of actions involving personal data, carried out with or without computer equipment, including collection, recording, systematization, accumulation, storage, clarification (updating and modification), retrieval, use, transfer (dissemination, disclosure and access), depersonalization, blocking, deletion, and destruction of personal data.[27] The Personal Data Law regulates both the manual and automated data processing of personal data.

3.3.2. Key Requirements for Data Processing

The Personal Data Law requires data controllers to have a lawful basis for processing personal data. Typically, this means that the personal data controller must process personal data on the basis of consent. For example, consent may be given by data subjects in any verifiable form, including in writing, electronically or by means of implied consent.

There are certain types of processing[28] to which the Personal Data Law does not apply—for example, personal data processing by individuals solely for personal and family needs, provided that processing does not infringe the data

[26] Federal Law No 152-FZ 'On Personal Data' art 3(1).
[27] Federal Law No 152-FZ 'On Personal Data' art 3(3).
[28] ibid art 1(2).

subject's rights; processing personal data for archival purposes; and personal data processing that includes state secrets.

In the legislative framework of the Russian Federation, there is no formal notion of 'anonymized data', though it is a well-recognized concept within the domain of information security specialists. Legislation does, however, incorporate the term 'depersonalization'. Depersonalization of personal data is identified as a method of processing personal data where, upon completion, it becomes practically impossible, without the aid of supplementary information, to identify the specific individual to whom the personal data belongs. The guidelines and methodologies for anonymizing personal data are outlined in Roskomnadzor Order No 99639, issued on 5 September 2013.

While the terms 'anonymization' and 'depersonalization' may appear similar, they imply distinct techniques for handling personal data. The concept of depersonalization bears a resemblance to the GDPR's pseudonymization, although each involves different approaches to safeguarding personal data.

The classification of depersonalized data as personal remains a subject of debate. Generally, it is presumed that personal data laws do not apply to anonymized data, a stance supported by case law.[29] Conversely, Roskomnadzor contends that personal data obtained as a result of depersonalization is still personal data and remains subject to the relevant legislation.[30]

Recent statements from Roskomnadzor indicate plans to regulate and process depersonalized data in line with the Personal Data Law, with legislative amendments anticipated within a year.[31]

Certain data protection operations, such as marketing, require prior opt-in consent. For instance, processing of personal data for direct marketing purposes requires each individual's explicit opt-in consent. Every marketing communication must contain a link enabling individuals to revoke their consent (unsubscribe) at any time, or otherwise contain specific guidelines as to how this consent may be revoked. Once an individual revokes their consent, the data controller must immediately terminate direct marketing communications and related data processing—the applicable laws do not provide any grace period in this instance.

Data operators may transfer data to third parties (including affiliated companies[32]) under the following conditions:

[29] Decision of the Supreme Court of the Russian Federation dated 26 January 2011 No GKPI10-1510.
[30] <https://pravo.ru/lf/story/231731/>, accessed 15 December 2021.
[31] <https://www.pnp.ru/social/obezlichennye-dannye-mogut-nachat-obrabatyvat-kak-personalnye.html>, accessed 21 January 2022.
[32] According to art 4 of the Law 'On Protection of Competition' dated 26 July 2006 No 135-FZ, affiliates are those companies or employees (as well as representatives of the 'same group', including related

- with the data subject's consent or based on other legal bases from the closed list established by the Personal Data Law[33] (eg, when the processing of personal data is necessary for the performance of a contract to which the data subject is a party or beneficiary or guarantor; the processing of personal data is necessary to protect the life, health or other vital interests of the data subject, if obtaining the consent of the data subject is impossible);
- pursuant to a separate data transfer agreement or based on a contractual clause that includes confidentiality provisions imposed on the recipient.

Additional obligatory provisions must be included if the recipient acts in the capacity of a data processor pursuant to the operator's instructions: (i) purposes of data processing (must be consistent with the purpose that was initially mentioned during data collection); (ii) allowed actions that may be performed on personal data; and (iii) organizational and technical data protection measures.

Data may be transferred outside Russia in one of the following cases:

- transfer is made to the jurisdictions that ensure adequate protection of personal data subjects' rights (the country is considered adequate by default if it has ratified the Convention for the Protection of Individuals with Regard to Automatic Processing of Personal Data);
- subject to the written consent of a data subject;
- for the purpose of performing a contract to which the data subject is a party;
- subject to an international treaty to which Russia is a signatory;
- the transfer is required pursuant to federal laws for the protection of the Constitution, state defence, security, and transport system;
- it is necessary to protect the data subject's vital interests (if it is not possible to get the written consent of the data subject).

Russian laws permit the transfer of data to countries that are parties to the Council of Europe's Convention for the Protection of Individuals with regard to Automatic Processing of Personal Data, and to a number of non-signatory

ones) that can influence the activities of the organization and adopt its management team strategic decisions.

[33] The closed list of grounds for transferring data to a third party without the consent of the data subject is established by art 6 of the Personal Data Law.

countries deemed by Roskomnadzor to have adequate data privacy protections policies in place.[34] Roskomnadzor's most recent Order came into force on 1 March 2023. It is interesting to note that prior to that date, India and China (BRICS members) were not considered to be countries providing adequate protection of the rights of personal data subjects. The United States, not being a signatory to the Convention and not listed by Roskomnadzor as having adequate privacy protection policies, is not authorized for the transfer of personal data from Russia.

3.3.3. Data Localization Requirement

The data localization requirement mandates that entities acting as data controllers, responsible for the collection of personal data, must adhere to the stipulation that the recording, systematization, accumulation, storage, verification, and extraction of personal data belonging to Russian citizens should occur exclusively within data centres located within the borders of Russia. This regulation is applicable to both domestic and foreign data controllers, thereby affecting a great number of major international companies operating in Russia. Notable examples include Uber, Booking.com, Facebook, AliExpress, eBay, and PayPal, all of which have had to adjust their data management practices in order to comply with this legislation. To align with the mandate, corporations had to either establish new data centres in Russia or relocate existing ones, reflecting the considerable impact of this regulatory framework on the operational dynamics of these entities.

An illustrative instance of the regulatory consequences is LinkedIn, whose network activities within Russia were officially blocked in 2016 due to non-compliance with the data localization requirement. This high-profile case serves as a potent reminder of the strict enforcement of this regulation, emphasizing that not even major players in the tech industry are exempt from the legal ramifications of failing to adhere to data localization guidelines.

It is noteworthy that this legislative provision not only affects the current landscape but also has implications for potential market entrants. Any foreign websites or applications entering the Russian market must adhere

[34] Roskomnadzor Order No 128 dated 5 August 2022, 'On Approval of the List of Foreign States Providing Adequate Protection of the Rights of Personal Data Subjects'. Prior to this, Order No 274 of 15 March 2013 'On Endorsement of the List of the Foreign States Which are Not Parties to the EC Convention for the Protection of Individuals With Regard to Automatic Processing of Personal Data' was in force.

meticulously to these data localization laws to avoid the risk of being blocked. In essence, the requirement serves as a pivotal factor influencing the operational and strategic decisions of companies operating within the digital ecosystem in Russia.

3.3.4. Essential Steps to Manage Data Risks and Sustain Regulatory Compliance

The Personal Data Law requires companies to implement a range of measures designed to ensure and demonstrate that they are in compliance with the regulation. Data controllers must take appropriate technical and organizational measures against unauthorized or unlawful processing and accidental loss, changing, blocking or destruction of personal data.

In order to manage possible risks and maintain regulatory compliance, companies must consider the following steps:

- create data mapping, data flows and identify relevant data categories;
- appoint a local data protection officer who will be in charge of the compliance procedures;
- adopt local data protection policies and other required privacy documents;
- implement appropriate security measures;
- meet specific requirements including data localization laws.

It is important to carry out regular data protection audits to help ensure ongoing data privacy compliance with national data protection requirements and regulations.

Also, it is obligatory for data controllers to file a notice with Roskomnadzor prior to the commencement of data processing. This notice must contain the details of the data controller and data processor, the purposes of data processing, categories of personal data processed and categories of data subjects whose personal data is processed, the period of data processing, the legal grounds for data processing, a list of security measures undertaken by the data controller (including encryption tools), and certain other details. This notice shall be filed once and with respect to all data processing activities of the particular data controller and may be submitted online or alternatively by post. All changes in the data processing activities must be notified to Roskomnadzor within ten business days.

There are certain exemptions from this notification obligation. For instance, no notice is necessary when data processing is conducted for the purpose of executing a contract with the data subject.

Under the Personal Data Law, legal entities are required to appoint a Data Protection Officer, who is responsible for evaluating the existing data protection framework and ensuring the company's policy is in accordance with the relevant laws and codes of practice, providing data protection advice and support for staff members who are involved in processing data, and carrying out regular compliance audits. The Data Protection Officer also serves as the key point of contact between the company and the data protection authority. The role is mandatory for all organizations that process or collect personal data. Failure to appoint a Data Protection Officer is a violation of the data protection policy and may result in the imposition of fines and enforcement protocols.

3.3.5. Liability for Non-Compliance with Data Protection Laws

The broad material and personal scope of Russian data protection laws means that data protection law applies to nearly anyone processing any information at any time, and the threat of certain sanctions is omnipresent.

A data controller may face civil, administrative, or criminal liability if there is a violation of the Personal Data Law. Data protection officers responsible for the offence may also face disciplinary action.

The fines for violation of data protection laws may vary depending on the nature and severity of the breach. Administrative fines vary according to the type of violation. In some cases, more than one fine may be imposed for a single breach (eg, each affected data subject may result in an imposed fine). Fines start from RUB 75,000 (approximately USD 800) and go higher—for instance, RUB 500,000 (approximately USD 5,500) for violation of direct marketing requirements, RUB 6,000,000 (approximately USD 66,200) for a first offence of data localization violation, and up to RUB 18,000,000 (approximately USD 198,050) for a repeat offence.

In addition to fines, there may be other administrative penalties for non-compliance, including warnings, suspension of data processing activities, or even a complete ban on processing personal data. Individuals affected by a data breach may also have the right to seek compensation for damages resulting from the violation.

Moreover, unlawful data processing practices may entail forced termination of respective data processing activities and blockage of a website and/

or app, where they relate to personal data processing on such website and/or app.

3.4. A Brief Overview of the Enforcement of Data Protection Law in Russia

Data subjects in Russia have the right to directly assert their data protection rights by initiating legal action against data operators, seeking monetary damages, or claiming compensation for moral harm. Criminal liability may be incurred for illegal access, modification of computer information (including personal data), and the unauthorized disclosure of personal data related to an individual's private life. Alternatively, individuals can file complaints with Roskomnadzor, the regulatory authority overseeing data protection.

Roskomnadzor has several key enforcement mechanisms under the Government Decree issued in 2019.[35] It can investigate and rectify data protection infringements, imposing administrative fines in line with the Code of the Russian Federation on Administrative Offences. The regulator may initiate investigations independently or respond to private individuals' requests, with the authority to represent individuals in court or act in the public interest.

In the investigation process, the regulator may conduct on-site inspections at data operators' premises, or monitor their activities remotely, or perform unscheduled visits. New rules introduced in 2019 prioritize scrutiny of companies processing sensitive or biometric data on behalf of data controllers having no presence in Russia or those transferring data to countries deemed inadequate in data protection under Russian law. Unscheduled inspections may also be triggered based on online monitoring, public domain information, or data subject requests.

As a part of its corrective powers, Roskomnadzor can block websites or specific internet pages found to contain prohibited information or violate data localization laws. Based on a court decision,[36] Roskomnadzor added LinkedIn to the database on the Register of Infringers of Rights of Personal Data Subjects and required telecommunications companies to block access to LinkedIn in Russia.[37] Additionally, there were several cases that involved significant

[35] Decree of the Government 'On Adopting the Regulations on Organizing and Performing State Control and Supervision over Personal Data Processing' No 146 dated 13 February 2019.

[36] Decision of the Moscow City Court of 10 November 2016 Case No 33-38783/16 on the restriction of the access to LinkedIn Corporation from Russia.

[37] <https://iapp.org/news/a/why-linkedin-was-banned-in-russia/>, accessed 20 January 2022.

fines that were imposed on well-known messenger companies. For example, Facebook and Twitter were fined multiple times for breaching data localization laws. More recently, in August 2021, both platforms were fined RUB 15 million (approximately USD 165,500) and RUB 17 million (approximately USD 187,500) for violations of data localization laws.[38]

Also, in 2021, Roskomnadzor imposed fines on Facebook for its refusal to remove content that violated Russian legislation.[39] A Roskomnadzor spokesperson reported that in 2021, the regulatory body initiated twenty-three protocols against the owner of Facebook. As per court decisions, Facebook was directed to pay fines amounting to RUB 83 million (approximately USD 915,000).[40]

While some argue that these fines may be insignificant to tech giants like Google and Facebook, questions arise about Roskomnadzor's authority to enforce court orders and collect fines from foreign companies. The recent trend of requiring foreign companies to establish a presence in Russia may strengthen the regulator's ability to enforce measures against violations by such entities.

3.5. Conclusion

Since the early 1990s Russia has taken notable strides in acknowledging and upholding the right to privacy, demonstrating a commitment to safeguarding the personal information of its citizens. The country has actively participated in key international treaties, translating these commitments into practical implementations. Notably, Russia has embraced modern technologies integral to processing personal data, including the incorporation of personal biometric information. The introduction of the Digital Profile has streamlined interactions between citizens and the state, facilitating the swift delivery of services.

However, despite these advances, there remains a need for further refinement to make these technologies more appealing to the public, with a particular emphasis on addressing privacy concerns. A pivotal issue is the centralized storage of data, which raises apprehensions about the security of such information and the potential ulterior motives behind its utilization. The fact that Roskomnadzor is inherently a part of the Russian government, rather

[38] <https://www.rbc.ru/business/30/09/2021/6154e0d69a79473e0a35e6d1>, accessed 20 January 2022.

[39] Art 13.41 Code of Administrative Offences.

[40] <https://www.vedomosti.ru/media/articles/2021/12/24/902582-facebook-oshtrafovali>, accessed January 2022.

than an independent regulatory body, adds to individuals' unease, as there is a lingering fear that collected data may be exploited for surveillance or other government purposes.

Several other factors add to concerns regarding individual privacy. The concentration of power within the realm of information control can lead to the isolation of the Russian information society and the potential for abuse by surveillance structures. Strident data localization laws have already resulted in the prohibition of certain popular social networks in Russia. LinkedIn, for instance, opted not to comply with data localization requirements, leading to its subsequent blocking within the country. Proponents of data localization argue that this strategy is designed to protect the information of Russian citizens while simultaneously fostering commercial benefits and creating opportunities for Russian data centres.

The present scenario underscores the need for substantial improvements in Russia's data privacy legislation, with a specific focus on enhancing transparency and fostering collaboration with the public. It is evident that further efforts are required to fortify the protection of personal data and information. This entails comprehensive development from both technical and legal standpoints, making the prioritization of personal data regulation a key focus area for Russia's overall development.

Looking ahead, it will be crucial to prioritize the ongoing improvement and evolution of personal data regulation in Russia. This imperative extends beyond mere refinement of existing legal frameworks; it requires a proactive embracing of technological innovations that align with international standards for privacy protection. Transparency and collaboration should be at the forefront of these endeavours, ensuring that the public is not only informed but actively involved in shaping the trajectory of personal data governance. By designating the protection of personal data as a priority, Russia can contribute significantly to the global discourse on privacy rights while fostering a more secure and trusted digital environment for its citizens.

Globally, looking at the regulatory frameworks of BRICS countries, it is clear that while there are variations in how each nation approaches privacy, data protection, and AI development, there is a common goal among them. Russia, China, and India are among the leading BRICS nations striving to become pioneers in the use of modern technologies, particularly AI and biometrics. These countries are actively working to develop cutting-edge technologies and build infrastructure to enhance their digital economies and improve their global standing in innovation.

The BRICS countries' approaches to key data protection issues, such as data localization, data transfers, and the powers and independence of data protection authorities, highlight their various strategies towards achieving digital sovereignty. While data localization laws are increasingly being enforced, as seen in Russia and China, other countries are working towards ensuring that data is processed within their borders, but with a focus on international co-operation. In terms of data transfers, countries are balancing national interests with global trade and digital flow requirements, with mechanisms to ensure secure cross-border data movement.

The powers and remit of data protection authorities in the BRICS nations differ in scope and independence. China and Russia maintain more centralized control over their data protection agencies, while Brazil and South Africa's agencies operate with greater autonomy. The enforcement of data protection laws varies as well, with some countries relying solely on the data protection authority for enforcement, while others, like India (with its Cyber Appellate Tribunal), integrate tribunals and other agencies for more comprehensive action.

Regarding the automated processing of personal data, BRICS countries are increasingly focusing on setting clear guidelines and obligations to protect citizens from the risks of automation and AI, while still fostering technological development.

These varied approaches highlight the complex and evolving landscape of data protection and digital sovereignty within the BRICS countries, as they seek to balance individual rights, national security, and economic interests in the digital age.

4
AWAITING THE DAWN OF DATA PROTECTION REGULATION IN INDIA

Smriti Parsheera

4.1. Introduction

India is one of the world's most rapidly growing digital markets. It has the world's second largest Internet user base, is a well-known hub of information technology services, and has a vibrant digital market characterized by the co-existence of global technology players and domestic businesses. The Indian government has, in tandem, been working towards building a more digitally connected society through initiatives such as the biometric digital identity project, Aadhaar, improved broadband connectivity, digital payments, and e-governance reforms. It has also been promoting a home-grown model of digital public infrastructure development under the 'India Stack' brand. India Stack refers to a collection of state-backed digital interventions designed to promote interoperability among public and private actors in areas like digital identity, digital payments, digital records management, and personal data sharing.[1] This is reflective of the broader trend towards promoting technological autonomy and local innovation as a pathway to national development, which can be observed among other BRICS nations as well.[2]

Several of the developments pointed to above, across the public and private sectors, concern the collection, processing, and sharing of the personal data of individuals. Yet, despite the prevalence of so many data-centric activities, until very recently, India had no comprehensive data protection law to govern such practices. This situation is now expected to change, pursuant to India's

[1] Smriti Parsheera, 'Stack is the New Black: Evolution and Outcomes of the "India-Stackification" Process' (2024) 52 Computer Law & Security Review <https://doi.org/10.1016/j.clsr.2024.105947> accessed 1 April 2025.

[2] Luca Belli and Larissa Galdino de Magalhaes, 'Editorial: Toward a BRICS Stack? Leveraging Digital Transformation to Construct Digital Sovereignty in the BRICS countries' (2024) 55 Computer Law & Security Review <https://doi.org/10.1016/j.clsr.2024.106064> accessed 1 April 2025.

Smriti Parsheera, *Awaiting the Dawn of Data Protection Regulation in India* In: *Personal Data Architectures in the BRICS Countries*. Edited by: Luca Belli and Walter Britto Gaspar, Oxford University Press. © Luca Belli and Walter B. Gaspar 2025. DOI: 10.1093/9780198974468.003.0004

adoption of the Digital Personal Data Protection Act 2023 (DPD Act) on 11 August 2023.[3] However, this law is yet to be brought into effect. Until that happens, individuals continue to remain only partially protected by a patchwork of laws and directives, leaving them vulnerable to the widespread collection, processing, and misuse of personal data.

The Indian experience stands out from the other BRICS nations both in term of its stage of adoption of the data protection law—the other four countries in the original BRICS grouping already have functional data protection frameworks—and the scope and terminology that it adopts. Unlike most other data protection laws that cover personal data in all its forms (digital and physical), the DPD Act is designed specifically for the protection of 'digital data'—data that was either collected in a digital form or was digitized after being collected through other means.[4] The Act defines the persons who determine the purpose and means of processing of personal data as 'data fiduciaries', a term that is meant to signify the high level of responsibility that they must bear towards the individual. However, as the discussions that follow will reveal, this does not necessarily translate to offering a higher standard of protection under the law. In addition to the obligations of data fiduciaries, the DPD Act sets out the rights and duties of data principals, which is the term used to refer to individuals whose personal data is being protected. Further, the DPD Act lays the foundation for the establishment of a new agency, the Data Protection Board of India (DP Board). This body is yet to be constituted by the Indian government. Some preliminary steps in that direction were initiated with the release of the Draft Digital Personal Data Protection Rules 2025 (Draft Rules) that were published in January 2025 and were open for public comments until the beginning of March 2025.[5] Among other things, the Draft Rules outline the process for appointment of the DP Board's chair and members and their terms of service.

The enactment of the DPD Act followed a series of events and discussions that have been going on for well over a decade. One of these events was the 2017 landmark decision by the Indian Supreme Court affirming that privacy constitutes a fundamental right under the Indian Constitution.[6] In the years that followed, five different versions of a Data Protection Bill were put out in the public domain. This process began with the setting up in 2018 of a committee

[3] Digital Personal Data Protection Act 2023 <https://www.meity.gov.in/writereaddata/files/Digital%20Personal%20Data%20Protection%20Act%202023.pdf> accessed 21 August 2023.
[4] DPD Act 2023 s 3(a).
[5] Draft Digital Personal Data Protection Rules 2025 <https://static.mygov.in/innovateindia/2025/01/03/mygov-999999999568142946.pdf> accessed 1 April 2025.
[6] *Justice KS Puttaswamy v Union of India* (2017) 10 SCC 1.

of experts chaired by former Supreme Court judge, Justice BN Srikrishna, that recommended a draft Data Protection Bill for the consideration of the government.[7] Following this, the Indian government introduced a bill titled the Personal Data Protection Bill 2019 (PDP Bill 2019) in Parliament, signalling a clear legislative intent to regulate this area.[8] The 2019 Bill went through several rounds of public consultation, including in the course of its review by a Joint Parliamentary Committee. However, despite these efforts, in August 2022, the Ministry of Information Technology and Electronics (MeitY), the ministry in charge of the subject, unexpectedly announced the government's decision to withdraw the PDP Bill 2019.[9]

The MeitY then put out a new draft called the Digital Personal Data Protection Bill 2022 (DPD Bill 2022) for public comments in December 2022.[10] In a move that deterred an open and transparent debate, the government announced that the submissions received on this draft would not be disclosed publicly.[11] In the months that followed, the MeitY reworked this version of the draft bill and introduced the Digital Personal Data Protection Bill 2023 in the Lok Sabha, the lower house of the Indian Parliament, on 3 August 2023.[12] Just four days after its introduction, the Bill was passed by the Lok Sabha and subsequently by the Rajya Sabha, the upper house of the Indian Parliament, on 9 August. The Bill then received the President's assent and was notified as the DPD Act on 11 August. While India is not alone in terms of its long-drawn process of developing a data protection law, the lack of consistency and clarity of direction in the effort is worth noting. For example, the negotiation of the Brazilian data protection law also spanned across a similar duration, but with relatively better coherence between the different stages of the process.

Set against the background of these developments, this chapter offers a brief history of India's journey in formulating its data protection law. It focuses, in

[7] BN Srikrishna and others, 'A Free and Fair Digital Economy Protecting Privacy, Empowering Indians' (Ministry of Information Technology and Electronics, July 2018) <https://www.meity.gov.in/writereaddata/files/Data_Protection_Committee_Report.pdf> accessed 19 April 2023.

[8] Personal Data Protection Bill (PDP Bill) 2019 (Lok Sabha, 2019) <http://164.100.47.4/BillsTexts/LSBillTexts/Asintroduced/373_2019_LS_Eng.pdf> accessed 19 April 2023.

[9] 'Union Government Rolls Back Data Protection Bill' *The Hindu* (3 August 2022) <https://www.thehindu.com/news/national/union-government-rolls-back-data-protection-bill/article65721160.ece> accessed 19 April 2023.

[10] Draft Digital Personal Data Protection Bill 2022 (Ministry of Electronics & Information Technology, December 2022) <https://www.meity.gov.in/writereaddata/files/The%20Digital%20Personal%20Data%20Protection%20Bill%2C%202022.pdf> accessed 19 April 2023.

[11] Ministry of Electronics and Information Technology, 'MeitY Invites Feedback on the Draft "Digital Personal Data Protection Bill 2022"' (Press Information Bureau, 18 November 2023) <https://www.pib.gov.in/PressReleasePage.aspx?PRID = 1877030> accessed 19 April 2023.

[12] Digital Personal Data Protection Bill 2023, Bill No 113 of 2023 <https://sansad.in/getFile/BillsTexts/LSBillTexts/Asintroduced/113_2023_LS_Eng83202330313PM.pdf?source = legislation>.

particular, on the latest phase of this process involving the introduction and adoption of the DPD Act 2023. As the discussions in this chapter will reveal, the DPD Act is substantially different from the earlier bills that came out in 2018 and 2019 and had been under discussion for about half a decade. The chapter describes the context in which the proposals for a law evolved over the years and the significant ways in which the DPD Act differs from the versions that preceded it. While doing so it highlights some of the key substantive provisions of the law as well as issues that remain with it. The limited scope of rights and protections offered by the 2023 Act, broad-brush exemptions and a diluted regulatory structure being some areas of concern.

The discussions that follow would benefit from a brief overview of the legal system and rule of law context in the country. India is a parliamentary democracy with legislative functions divided between the union and state governments. At the union level, the Constitution of India allows a legislative proposal in the form of a bill to be introduced in either house of Parliament. These houses are the Lok Sabha, consisting of members elected through direct elections, and the Rajya Sabha, consisting of representatives of various Indian states and nominated members.[13] The bill then needs to be approved by both houses and receive the president's assent, following which it is notified as a law.[14] The Constitution also guarantees a spectrum of fundamental rights and provides for the judicial review of legislative and administrative actions that may infringe upon those rights.

In 2023, the Freedom in the World report, which assesses levels of political rights and civil liberties across jurisdictions, classified India under the 'partly free' category.[15] The report observed that although India's Constitution guarantees various civil liberties, there had been instances of harassment of non-governmental organizations and government critics, which diminished these freedoms in practice. The Freedom on the Net report produced by the same organization similarly gave India a partly free rating, with a score of 13/25 for obstacles to access, 20/35 for limits on content, and 17/40 for violations of user rights.[16] Another study by a UK-based website called Comparitech examined the state of surveillance in forty-seven countries and found India to be

[13] Rajya Sabha Secretariat, *The Law Making Process* (Parliament of India 2020) <https://rajyasabha.nic.in/rsnew/information_booklet/Law_Making.pdf> accessed 19 April 2023.

[14] The process differs for Money Bills, on which the Lok Sabha enjoys exclusive legislative powers and the Rajya Sabha only exercises recommendatory functions.

[15] 'Freedom in the World 2023' (Freedom House, 2023) <https://freedomhouse.org/country/india/freedom-world/2023#PR> accessed 29 November 2023.

[16] 'Freedom on the Net 2023' (Freedom House, 2023) <https://freedomhouse.org/country/india/freedom-net/2023> accessed 29 November 2023.

the third-worst performer, classifying it as having 'systemic failure to maintain safeguards'.[17] However, to put this in context, the study did not find any of the examined countries to be upholding privacy standards on a consistent basis nor as having significant safeguards and protections. Furthermore, India's assessment was conducted prior to the enactment of the DPD Act, which may lead to some improvement in its performance in future.

4.2. A Decade of Legislative Attempts

Prior to enactment of the DPD Act, the debate around the introduction of data protection legislation in India had been under progress for over a decade. Much of this was closely intertwined with developments around the government's digital identity programme, Aadhaar. The Aadhaar project, which now covers over 1.4 billion individuals, was designed to provide a verifiable, unique, and foundational digital ID to all of India's residents. The project relies on the collection of biometric and demographic data of individuals as the basis for the issuing of digital identities to them and the subsequent use of this information for authentication purposes. Aadhaar was launched in 2009 through an executive order and without any legislative backing. A Parliamentary Standing Committee that reviewed a proposed bill on the subject observed that the adoption of a data protection law had to be a prerequisite for the unique biometric identity project.[18] Alongside the Aadhaar project, the interaction between privacy and disclosure requirements under the country's public transparency law, called the Right to Information (RTI) Act 2005, also fed into the need for a discussion on privacy regulation.[19] This need was intensified by the announcement of the National Intelligence Grid (NATGRID) project,

[17] Paul Bischoff, 'Data Privacy Laws and Government Surveillance by Country: Which Countries Best Protect Their Citizens?' (*Comparitech*, 26 March 2022) <https://www.comparitech.com/blog/vpn-privacy/surveillance-states/> accessed 29 November 2023.

[18] Department-related Parliamentary Standing Committee on Finance, *Forty-Second Report on National Identification Authority of India Bill, 2010* (Lok Sabha Secretariat 2011) 33 <https://uidai.gov.in/images/report_of_the_departmental_standing_committee_on_finance_on_the_bill_13012017.pdf> accessed 19 April 2023.

[19] The creation of NATGRID was announced in 2009 as a response to the terrorist attacks in Mumbai, but the project saw a series of delays until the opening of a new NATGRID campus in the city of Bengaluru in May 2022. See Amit Chaturvedi, 'Delayed by Covid, NATGRID likely to be implemented soon' Hindustan Times (14 September 2021) <https://www.hindustantimes.com/india-news/delayed-by-covid-natgrid-likely-to-be-implemented-soon-check-details-101631609979429.html> accessed 19 April 2023; Ministry of Home Affairs, 'The Union Minister for Home and Cooperation, Shri Amit Shah Inaugurated the National Intelligence Grid (NATGRID) Bengaluru Campus Today' (*Press Information Bureau*, 3 May 2022) <https://www.pib.gov.in/PressReleasePage.aspx?PRID = 1822356> accessed 19 April 2023.

which was meant to facilitate information-sharing between domestic intelligence agencies for counter-terrorism measures, sparking concerns of a centralized surveillance apparatus being built by the government.

All of these factors served as an impetus for the government to set up a Group of Experts on Privacy in 2011. The expert group was asked to make suggestions for a proposed draft bill on privacy.[20] This was to be informed by a review of similar laws adopted by other countries and an analysis of the privacy impact of various government programmes in India. In its recommendations submitted to the government in October 2012, the expert group suggested nine principles and five salient features of the data privacy framework for India.[21] These features were technological neutrality and interoperability with international standards, a multi-dimensional understanding of privacy, horizontal applicability, conformity with privacy principles, and a co-regulatory enforcement regime. However, these recommendations and efforts at the formulation of a draft data privacy bill did not translate into legislative action, although several 'leaked' versions of a draft bill emerged between 2011 and 2014.[22]

While the process of formulating a law on data privacy effectively came to a standstill, the Aadhaar project was scaled up and continued to function for several years without the backing of a statutory framework. The sensitive nature of Aadhaar data and its extensive adoption in the public and private spheres, in many cases on a mandatory basis, led to challenges being filed before courts questioning the constitutional validity of Aadhaar. In the context of these challenges, the Indian Supreme Court constituted a nine-judge bench to look into the question of whether privacy can be regarded as a fundamental right under the Indian Constitution.[23] In what is popularly referred to as the *Puttaswamy* privacy verdict, the judges of the Supreme Court unanimously answered this in the affirmative. By doing so, this judgment laid the groundwork for the subsequent verification of Aadhaar's compliance with the fundamental right to privacy by a different bench of the Supreme Court.[24]

[20] Planning Commission, Government of India, 'Group of Experts on Privacy Submit Report' (*Press Information Bureau*, 18 October 2012) <https://pib.gov.in/newsite/PrintRelease.aspx?relid = 88503> accessed 19 April 2023.

[21] AP Shah and others, 'Report of the Group of Experts on Privacy' (Planning Commission 2012) <https://cis-india.org/internet-governance/blog/report-of-group-of-experts-on-privacy.pdf> accessed 19 April 2019.

[22] Malavika Raghavan, 'Are We There Yet?: The Long Road to Nowhere, the Demise of India's Data Protection Bill' (*Future of Privacy Forum*, 11 October 2022) <https://fpf.org/blog/are-we-there-yet-the-long-road-to-nowhere-the-demise-of-indias-draft-data-protection-bill/> accessed 19 April 2019.

[23] *Justice KS Puttaswamy v Union of India* (n 6).

[24] *Justice KS Puttaswamy v Union of India* (2019) 1 SCC 1.

The *Puttaswamy* privacy verdict emphasized that privacy has both positive and negative dimensions. On behalf of four of the judges, Justice Chandrachud noted that, 'the negative content restrains the state from committing an intrusion upon the life and personal liberty of a citizen. Its positive content imposes an obligation on the state to take all necessary measures to protect the privacy of the individual'.[25] The judges then went on to highlight the need for a robust regime for data protection that would strike a careful balance between individual interests and legitimate concerns of the state. In a bid to demonstrate this positive commitment to privacy, the MeitY constituted the Justice BN Srikrishna-led committee of experts on data protection while hearings were still going on in the *Puttaswamy* privacy case. This nine-member Committee was requested to study issues relating to data protection in India and make suggestions on the key principles along with the formulation of a draft Data Protection Bill.

The committee submitted a report titled 'A Free and Fair Digital Economy Protecting Privacy, Empowering Indians' to the government in July 2018.[26] This was accompanied by a draft of the proposed PDP Bill 2018[27] that led to the introduction of the PDP Bill 2019 in Parliament in December, 2019.[28] This bill was referred to a thirty-member Joint Parliamentary Committee (JPC) consisting of representatives from both houses of Parliament. Following a two-year-long process of internal deliberations, written comments from the public, and selective in-person hearings, the JPC submitted its report along with a revised draft of the 2019 Bill.[29]

However, soon after that the Union Minister of MeitY announced that the government had decided to withdraw the PDP Bill 2019. The explanation given was that since the JPC had suggested several changes to the 2019 Bill, the Ministry was in the process of developing a revised and comprehensive draft law.[30] Aside from the officially stated reason it is known that the previous bill met significant resistance from the private sector on the grounds of the compliance costs that would be imposed upon them. Reports suggested that the

[25] *Justice KS Puttaswamy v Union of India* (n 6), part T, para 3(I).

[26] BN Srikrishna and others (n 7).

[27] The (Draft) Personal Data Protection Bill 2018 (Ministry of Electronics and Information Technology, 2018) <https://www.meity.gov.in/writereaddata/files/Personal_Data_Protection_Bill,2018.pdf> accessed 19 April, 2023.

[28] PDP Bill 2019 (n 8).

[29] PP Chaudhary and others, 'Report of the Joint Committee on Personal Data Protection Bill, 2019' (Lok Sabha Secretariat, 2021) <http://164.100.47.193/lsscommittee/Joint%20Committee%20on%20the%20Personal%20Data%20Protection%20Bill,%202019/pr_files/Press%20Release%20on%20the%20presentation%20Report.pdf> accessed 19 April 2023.

[30] 'Union Government Rolls Back Data Protection Bill' *The Hindu* (n 9).

US tech industry had also approached Indian government agencies with a proposal to form a new working group to discuss issues with the previous bill.[31]

These pressures are likely to have played a role in shaping the DPD Act, with some describing the 2022 draft bill as a 'more tech friendly data protection bill'.[32] Section 4.4 of this chapter demonstrates some of the ways in which the DPD Act presents a significantly stripped-down version of the previous legislative proposals. This is reflected in the dilution of the compliance obligations imposed on the industry, widened government exemptions, and a weakened regulatory structure for the implementation of the law.

4.3. Data Protection under Existing Instruments

Pending the adoption of a comprehensive law on data protection, limited protections for safeguarding personal data were available under the Information Technology Act 2000 (IT Act), the rules framed under it, and certain sectoral laws.[33] The IT Act contains only two sections engaging with the subject of data privacy—sections 43A and 72A—both of which were inserted through an amendment to the law in 2008. Section 43A of the IT Act imposes an obligation to pay compensation on a body corporate that fails to maintain reasonable security practices in respect of sensitive personal data resulting in a wrongful gain or loss to an individual. Upon the implementation of the DPD Act, this section will be omitted from the IT Act.[34] Section 72A, the other relevant provision in the IT Act, is a penalty provision that imposes a punishment for unauthorized disclosure of personal information obtained under a contract. It lays down a punishment in the form of imprisonment of up to three years and/or a fine up to 500,000 rupees.

In addition to these statutory provisions, the government has notified a set of rules on the protection of sensitive personal data under section 43A, known as the IT (Reasonable Security Practices and Procedures and Sensitive

[31] Soumyarendra Barik and Aashish Aryan, 'US Bodies Push Back on Data Protection Bill, Seek New Working Group' *The Indian Express* (3 March 2022) <https://indianexpress.com/article/india/us-bodies-push-back-on-data-protection-bill-seek-new-working-group-7798193/> accessed 1 April 2025.

[32] John Reed, 'India Releases More Tech Friendly Data Protection Bill After Backlash' *Financial Times* (21 November 2022) <https://www.ft.com/content/0a72f522-2bfe-4da5-a831-2c96c8ce52ff> accessed 19 April 2023.

[33] Information Technology Act 2000 <https://www.indiacode.nic.in/bitstream/123456789/13116/1/it_act_2000_updated.pdf> accessed 19 April 2023; Information Technology (Reasonable Security Practices and Procedures and Sensitive Personal Data or Information) Rules 2011 <https://www.meity.gov.in/writereaddata/files/GSR313E_10511%281%29_0.pdf> accessed 19 April 2023.

[34] DPD Act, s 44(2)(a).

Personal Data or Information) Rules 2011 (IT Rules). The IT Rules reflect several of the safeguards that are typically seen in data protection laws, such as requirements of notice and consent, permission for disclosure, and limitations on cross-border transfers. While on paper this may have seemed like a passable framework for data protection, in reality the protections offered by the IT Act and Rules were fraught with several limitations.

The first set of issues relate to the scope of section 43A, which focused only on requirements of 'reasonable security practices' involving 'sensitive personal data' by 'body corporates'. The provision was, therefore, limiting in terms of the types of personal data covered, the exclusion of protections over and beyond data security and safety, and the exclusion of government entities that did not fall within the provided definition of body corporates. The available information on cases under section 43A points to the provision having been used mainly for claims on issues such as fraudulent transfer of funds from a person's bank account, unauthorized access to financial information, and information breaches related to falsely procured SIM cards.[35] Further, while the IT Rules adopted a broader view of data protection, as noted above, they did so by exceeding the ambit of the parent provision, that is, section 43A of the IT Act, that focused only on reasonable security safeguards.

It may appear that the early attention to reasonable security practices under section 43A, which preceded the broader law on data protection, bears some resemblance to the Chinese approach where data security has been the first and foremost consideration. However, the driving force behind India's approach at that time was very different. The call for data security protections in the IT Act was prompted by the Indian IT services industry, which found that outsourcing arrangements with foreign firms were suffering due to the lack of data protection provisions in the domestic law. In the words of a government official, the aim was 'to bring in data privacy norms without increasing compliance costs for companies while allowing some leeway for contracts to address data security concerns'.[36]

Besides concerns of permissible scope, and a business-centric (rather than citizen-centric) intent, the protections offered under the IT Act and Rules also suffered from problems of implementation, partly due to the limitations in

[35] Divij Joshi, 'A Review of the Functioning of the Cyber Appellate Tribunal and Adjudicatory Officers under the IT Act' (Centre for Internet and Society, 6 June, 2014) <https://cis-india.org/internet-governance/blog/review-of-functioning-of-cyber-appellate-tribunal-and-adjudicatory-officers-under-it-act> accessed 19 April 2023.

[36] , 'BPO Will Soon Have Some Privacy' *The Times of India* (10 August 2004) <https://timesofindia.indiatimes.com/BPOs-will-soon-have-some-privacy/articleshow/806387.cms> accessed 1 April 2025.

the functioning of the adjudicatory mechanisms under the IT Act.[37] Taking account of all these factors, the Justice Srikrishna Committee acknowledged the insufficiency of the protections available under the IT Act and rules while recommending a new and comprehensive law on data protection.[38] Various other policy actors have echoed the need for an overarching data protection law, including through private member bills introduced in the Parliament and civil society led initiatives to propose the draft text of a privacy law.[39] These factors added to the momentum for the emergence of the new DPD Act, which once notified will replace section 43A and the rules framed under it with a new framework for data protection.

In addition, there are some sector-specific norms that govern the confidentiality and protection of personal data in areas such as finance, telecommunications, and in the health sector.[40] These norms flow through a range of instruments that include legislation, rules, licence conditions and directives and are generally specific to particular types of data or use cases. To give a few examples, the Credit Information Companies (Regulation) Act 2005 contains provisions for accuracy, security, governing privacy principles, and prevention of unauthorized access of credit information.[41] The Aadhaar digital identity project, described earlier, is now governed by the Aadhaar (Targeted Delivery of Financial and other Subsidies, Benefits and Services) Act 2016, which lays down the requirements for the collection, use, and sharing of personal data for its implementation.[42]

In the health space, statutory confidentiality protections are available for specific population groups under laws such as the Mental Healthcare Act 2017 and the HIV and AIDS (Prevention and Control) Act 2017.[43] Further, there are some non-statutory frameworks that apply to personal data protection in the digital health context. The Ayushman Bharat Digital Mission, a programme for

[37] BN Srikrishna and others (n 7), 7

[38] ibid.

[39] Amber Sinha, 'As India is Set to Implement its Data Protection Law. What to Make of It?' (*Tech Policy Press*, 28 March 2025) <https://www.techpolicy.press/as-india-is-set-to-implement-its-data-protection-law-what-to-make-of-it/> accessed 1 April 2025.

[40] BN Srikrishna and others, 'White Paper of the Committee of Experts on Data Protection' <https://www.meity.gov.in/writereaddata/files/white_paper_on_data_protection_in_india_171127_final_v2.pdf> accessed 19 April 2023.

[41] Credit Information Companies (Regulation) Act 2005 <https://www.indiacode.nic.in/bitstream/123456789/2057/2/A200530.pdf> accessed 1 April 2025.

[42] Aadhaar (Targeted Delivery of Financial and other Subsidies, Benefits and Services) Act 2016 <https://uidai.gov.in/images/targeted_delivery_of_financial_and_other_subsidies_benefits_and_services_13072016.pdf> accessed 19 April 2023.

[43] Smriti Parsheera and BN Srikrishna, 'India's Legal Framework on Public Health and Privacy' in Smriti Parsheera (ed), *Private and Controversial: When Privacy and Public Health Meet in India* (Harper Collins India 2023).

the digitization of health data in the country, has a Health Data Management Policy that sets out the standards of data protection to be followed by entities involved in the collection and sharing of health data.[44] In another example, during the Covid-19 pandemic the government launched a self-screening and contact tracing app called Aarogya Setu that involved the use of demographic data, patient health records, and location data for Covid management purposes. Responding to the public outcry over the lack of data privacy protection in this intervention, a committee set up by the government introduced a time-bound framework called the Aarogya Setu Data Access and Knowledge Sharing Protocol 2020.[45] One of the main problems with such policies and protocols is the ease with which such protections can be withdrawn or altered. Their lack of statutory legitimacy also means a lack of effective enforcement structures to implement the protections.

4.4. Overview and Analysis of the DPD Act 2023

This section provides an overview of the DPD Act, drawing comparisons with previous versions of the bills and highlighting some key issues. The DPD Act 2023 contains forty-four sections and is divided into nine chapters. The broad scheme of the law is that it lays down the scope of the law, obligations of data fiduciaries, rights of data principals, and the framework for enforcement through the creation of a DP Board. Unlike its predecessor bills from 2018 and 2019, the scope of the DPD Act is restricted to 'digital personal data' that is collected in a digital format or non-digital information that has subsequently been digitized.[46] This means that the law applies only to digitized data and excludes personal data that may be collected and stored using other means, such as in physical records. This is different from the practice followed in many other countries that apply more broadly to all types of processing of personal data, regardless of the means being used (for example, in Brazil).[47] Another way in which the Indian laws differs from other BRICS countries (and from its

[44] National Health Authority, 'National Digital Health Mission: Health Data Management Policy' (Ministry of Health and Family Welfare, April 2022) <https://abdm.gov.in/publications/policies_regulations/health_data_management_policy> accessed 19 April 2023.

[45] Empowered Group on Technology and Data Management, 'Aarogya Setu Data Access and Knowledge Sharing Protocol, 2020' (Ministry of Electronics and Information Technology, 11 May 2020) <https://www.meity.gov.in/writereaddata/files/Aarogya_Setu_data_access_knowledge_Protocol.pdf> accessed 19 April 2023.

[46] DPD Act s 3(a).

[47] Art 3, General Law on the Protection of Personal Data (LGPD) 2018 <https://www.planalto.gov.br/ccivil_03/_ato2015-2018/2018/lei/L13709.htm> accessed 1 April 2025.

own precedent under section 43A of the IT Act) is by avoiding any separate categorization of sensitive personal data. The Act, however, follows the common practice of extending extraterritorial scope over the processing of digital data that takes place outside the country but relates to offering goods or services to persons in India.[48]

As discussed in the introductory text, all versions of India's data protection bills have used the term 'data fiduciary' to describe the entities that determine the purpose and means of processing of personal data, and 'data principal' to define the individual whose personal data is involved.[49] As explained by the Srikrishna Committee, this terminology is meant to clarify the role of the individual as the 'focal actor in the digital economy' and to establish a duty of care and expectations of trust on the part of the entities processing the personal data.[50] While this approach stands apart from other BRICS counterparts that use terms like 'responsible party' (South Africa) and 'data controller' (Brazil) in their laws, the obligations being placed on Indian data fiduciaries and rights available to individuals are actually narrower in some respects. This will be illustrated in the discussions that follow.

Among its main obligations, the DPD Act contains requirements relating to notice to individuals about the collection and processing of data and obtaining their consent,[51] to keep data accurate and complete,[52] and to implement appropriate technical and organizational measures to comply with the law.[53] The law also contains certain limitations on continuing retention of the data[54] and requires fiduciaries to maintain a mechanism for grievance redress.[55]

Further, the DPD requires data fiduciaries to undertake reasonable security safeguards to prevent the breach of personal data.[56] In an attempt to add some clarity to the meaning of 'reasonable security practices', the Draft Rules suggest that at a minimum, such measures should include data security measures (use of encryption, obfuscation or masking techniques, etc.), access controls and logs to monitor unauthorized access, and contractual arrangements with data processors to ensure security safeguards.[57] The exact design and scope of such

[48] DPD Act s 3(b).
[49] DPD Act 2023, ss 2(i) and 2(j).
[50] Srikrishna and others (n 7), 8.
[51] DPD Act 2023, ss 5 and 6.
[52] ibid s 8(3)(b).
[53] ibid s 8(4).
[54] ibid s 8(7).
[55] ibid s 8(10).
[56] ibid s 8(5).
[57] Draft Rules, r 6.

practices, however, is left to be determined by the regulated entities, with the DP Board having the power to impose a penalties for any observed failures in maintaining such safeguards.

In an improvement over the 2019 Bill, the enacted law requires information about a breach to be conveyed to the DP Board as well as the affected data principals, in accordance with the rules to be made by the government.[58] In contrast, the previous draft suggested allowing the regulator to determine if and when individual breach notices should be given to the affected persons. The revised requirement of notice in all cases helps in granting individuals the agency to make their own decisions on how to deal with a breach situation in addition to any regulatory action. This may include personal risk mitigation strategies or the decision to discontinue transacting with a particular data fiduciary.

Like the versions before it, the DPD Act maintains a two-tier system of regulatory obligations, consisting of certain basic requirements for all covered actors and an enhanced set of obligations for significant data fiduciaries. The significance of such entities will be determined by the government based on factors like volume and sensitivity of data processed, risk of harm to individuals, sovereignty of the country, electoral democracy, security of the state, and public order.[59] This is similar to China's practice of specifying additional principles to govern large Internet platform services and requirements of having data protection officers and independent oversight for entities that meet certain thresholds.[60]

Under the DPD Act, the additional requirements applicable to significant data fiduciaries include the conduct of data protection impact assessment, independent data audits and appointing a data protection officer.[61] As per the Draft Rules put out by the government, the DP Board would also need to be informed of any significant observations from the impact assessment or audit exercises. Further, the rules propose a new requirement of observance of due diligence by the significant data fiduciary while deploying any algorithmic software for the processing of personal data, which might pose a risk to the rights of data principals.[62]

[58] DPD Act 2023, s 8(6).
[59] ibid s 10(1).
[60] Zhao Xinhua and others, 'China Issues New Rules on Personal Information Compliance Audit' (King and Wood Mallesons, 20 February 2025) <https://www.kwm.com/cn/en/insights/latest-thinking/china-Issues-new-rules-on-personal-Information-compliance-audit.html> accessed 1 April 2025.
[61] DPD Act 2023, s 10(2).
[62] Draft Rules, r 12(3).

In addition to the consent of the user, the DPD Act recognizes several other legitimate uses for data processing. The 2022 draft of the bill had introduced a new term called 'deemed consent' to capture all such situations, a list that seemed to consolidate the diffused list of exceptions under the previous versions of the draft law. The DPD Act does away with this specific term, while retaining its concept. Its list of legitimate uses that can take place without consent begins with a 'reasonable expectation' clause to cover cases where an individual voluntarily furnishes their data to an entity and does not indicate the absence of consent for its processing.[63] The other grounds for legitimate processing include legally authorized state functions, grant of subsidies, benefits, certificates and licences, compliance with court orders, medical emergencies, public health and disasters, and purposes related to employment.[64]

Further, there are four specific rights made available to data principals—right to information about the processing of personal data, erasure and correction of information, access to grievance redress, and right to appoint a nominee to take decisions in the event of death or incapacity of the individual.[65] Alongside these rights, the DPD Act introduces certain obligations for data principles. These obligations relate to compliance with applicable laws, not registering false or frivolous grievances, not furnishing any false particulars or suppressing material information, and providing verifiably authentic information while seeking the correction or erasure of their data.[66] While it seems reasonable to expect that individuals should act in good faith while exercising their rights under the law, it is problematic to find that the law also allows for regulatory action to be taken against individuals for any violation of their duties.[67] This may result in a penalty of up to 10,000 rupees being imposed on the individual, which can be a deterrent in the exercise of their rights under the law.

Finally, the last few chapters of the law deal with the compliance and enforcement framework for data protection. The Act provides that compliance with the law will be administered by a new statutory board called the DP Board.[68] The main function of the DP Board is to determine non-compliance with provisions of the law and impose penalties for any violation by data fiduciaries.[69] The law lays down the procedure to be followed

[63] DPD Act 2023, s 7(a).
[64] ibid s 7(b to i).
[65] ibid ss 11 to 14.
[66] ibid s 15.
[67] ibid s 33(1) and the Schedule.
[68] ibid s 18.
[69] ibid s 27.

by the DP Board and lists the penalties that may be imposed for different types of violation. The highest penalty, which may extend up to two and a half billion rupees, has been indicated for a failure to take reasonable security safeguards to prevent a personal data breach.[70] An order made by the DP Board may be challenged in appeal before an Appellate Tribunal. The DPD Act 2023 designates the Telecom Disputes Settlement and Appellate Tribunal (TDSAT) as the appropriate body for this purpose.[71] The TDSAT is an existing appellate authority with jurisdiction over matters relating to telecommunications, broadcasting, cyber appeals and airport tariffs.[72]

Having laid out the broad contours of the DPD Act, the next part of this section highlights some of the key issues with it. This discussion draws upon several concerns that the author has brought up (working alongside other collaborators) in response to various rounds of public consultation on the draft law.[73] The chapter focuses on a subset of these issues, which have been selected taking into account factors like the contested nature of those provisions (for example, scope of government powers), the sweeping impact on human rights (for example, broad exemptions for state agencies) and the importance for functioning and effectiveness of the proposed law (for example, independence and accountability of the DP Board). However, this is by no means meant to serve as an exhaustive list of issues, many of which have been highlighted by other commentators.[74]

[70] ibid schedule.

[71] ibid ss 29 and 2(a).

[72] Telecom Disputes Settlement and Appellate Tribunal, 'Introduction about TDSAT' <https://tdsat.gov.in/writereaddata/Delhi/docs/introduction.php?y = 1> accessed 3 August 2023.

[73] Vrinda Bhandari and others, 'Response to the White Paper on a Data Protection Framework for India' (NIPFP, 2018) <https://macrofinance.nipfp.org.in/PDF/BKPRS2018WhitePaperResponse.pdf> accessed 19 April 2023; Rishab Bailey and others, 'Comments on the (Draft) Personal Data Protection Bill, 2018' (SSRN, 18 November 2018) <https://papers.ssrn.com/sol3/papers.cfm?abstract_id = 3269735>; Rishab Bailey and others, 'Comments on the (draft) Personal Data Protection Bill, 2019' (SSRN, 2021) <https://papers.ssrn.com/sol3/papers.cfm?abstract_id = 4051127> accessed 19 April 2023.

[74] Software Freedom Law Center, India, 'Recommendations By SFLC in On The Digital Personal Data Protection Bill 2022' (*SFLC.in*, 6 January 2023) <https://sflc.in/recommendations-sflcin-digital-personal-data-protection-bill-2022/> accessed 20 April 2023; Shailesh Gandhi, 'RTI Act Does Not Need Any Covert Amendment; it Needs Implementation' (*News Click*, 28 December 2022) <https://www.newsclick.in/RTI-act-need-covert-amendment-needs-implementation> accessed 20 April 2023; Akshit Chawla, 'Seven Issues With How The Data Protection Bill Safeguards Children's Data' (*Medianama*, 17 December 2022) <https://www.medianama.com/2022/12/223-seven-issues-data-protection-bill-childrens-data/> accessed 20 April 2023; Global Network Initiative, 'GNI Comments to the Draft India Digital Personal Data Protection Bill, 2022' (*GNI*, 4 February 2023) <https://globalnetworkinitiative.org/gni-comments-tothe-draft-india-digital-personal-data-protection-bill-2022/> accessed 20 April 2023.

4.4.1. Diminished Rights and Protections

The DPD Act 2023 stands at forty-four sections, significantly shorter than the ninety-eight sections seen in the 2019 Bill. While the number of sections does not in itself indicate the robustness of a law, in the present case the shortened length does happen to correlate with the reduced scope of protection.

First, the DPD Act 2023 has done away with several of the rights and protections that were seen in PDP Bill 2019 and were in line with internationally accepted norms of data protection. This includes the absence of provisions on collection limitation,[75] the right to portability of data,[76] and the right to be forgotten,[77] which are found in the laws of many other BRICS countries. It has also significantly diluted the standalone and explicit provision on purpose limitation seen in the earlier bill.[78] Instead, the DPD Act 2023 merges the purpose limitation requirement with the provision on consent.[79] The provision states that the consent given by the individual would be for the specified purpose and 'limited to such personal data as is necessary for such specified purpose'. This implies that the purpose limitation would apply only to those circumstances where it is necessary to obtain the individual's consent prior to processing their data. Similarly, the notice requirement under the law has also been diluted and intermeshed with the provision on consent. Section 5 of the DPD Act 2023 provides that a data fiduciary has to give an individual notice about the purpose of data collection and their legal rights while requesting consent. This excludes the fairly large array of other 'legitimate uses'[80] that would be exempted from the purpose limitation and notice requirements under the DPD Act. It may be noted that the term 'legitimate uses' captures multiple use cases like data processing based on voluntary provision of data by an individual, processing for provision of subsidies, benefits and services by state agencies, and employment-related data processing. This is, however, different from the concept of 'legitimate interests' that appears as a standalone ground for data processing in the laws of some jurisdictions, such as Brazil.[81]

[75] PDP Bill 2019, s 6.
[76] ibid s 19.
[77] ibid.
[78] ibid s 4.
[79] DPD Act 2023, s 6(1).
[80] ibid s 7.
[81] Bruno Ricardo Bioni, Mariana Rielli, and Marina Kitayama, *Legitimate Interests Under the Brazilian General Data Protection Law: General Framework and Concrete Examples* (Data Privacy Brazil Research, 2021) <https://fpf.org/wp-content/uploads/2021/07/LI-under-LGPD_Data-Privacy-Brasil-Research-Association-1.pdf> accessed 1 April 2025.

Second, the threshold of compliance being demanded from data fiduciaries has been diluted in many cases. For instance, the 2019 Bill required that the fiduciary 'shall take necessary steps' that the personal data being processed by it is accurate and complete.[82] The draft put out for consultation in 2022, however, diminished this to a requirement to make 'reasonable efforts' at ensuring accuracy.[83] This has been fixed by the DPD Act 2023 to a requirement of ensuring completeness and accuracy, but at the cost of limiting the protection to only two circumstances—where the processing is likely to make a decision that affects the individual, or while disclosing data to another fiduciary.[84] In the same vein, the requirement of 'necessary' security safeguards has been replaced with the standard of 'reasonable' safeguards.[85] The dilution in the expectations from data fiduciaries is accompanied by a new set of requirements on the duties expected to be followed by data principals; an interesting contrast, given the goals of data protection.

The diluted scope of rights and protections is also accompanied by broad brush provisions that allow the government to exempt specified entities from the application of the DPD Act. Notably, section 17(5) of the law enables the government to issue a notification within five years of its commencement to exempt 'such Data Fiduciary or classes of Data Fiduciaries' from any provision. The provision is silent on the grounds on which this provision may be triggered and open-ended as to the period for which such exemption can remain in effect. There is yet another provision that allows for a more limited exemption to be granted to notified entities, including startups, based on 'the volume and nature of personal data processed' by them.[86] The scope of this exemption extends to the requirements relating to notice, completeness, accuracy and retention of data, right to information access, and obligations for significant data fiduciaries.

4.4.2. Exemptions for State Agencies

In addition to the exceptions mentioned above, which may apply to both public and private entities, there is another controversial provision that extends specifically to notified government agencies. It enables the government to declare

[82] PDP Bill 2019, s 8(1).
[83] DPD Bill 2022, s 9(2).
[84] DPD Act 2023, s 8(3).
[85] PDP Bill 2019, s 24(1) and DPD Act 2023, s 8(5).
[86] DPD Act 2023, s 17(3).

that the provisions of the law will not apply to any 'instrumentality of the state' that may be identified by the government on certain grounds. These grounds are the sovereignty and integrity of India, security of the state, friendly relations with foreign state, public order, or for preventing incitement to the commission of a serious offence relating to the above. A provision of this nature has existed in all the versions of India's data protection bills since 2019 and, for the reasons explained below, its problematic nature has only been enhanced by the text adopted in the 2023 Act.[87]

The existence of such a provision heightens the asymmetric relationship between the citizen and the state. Particularly so in light of the fact that law enforcement agencies in India already have very wide powers to access and intercept data without the protection of judicial oversight and other accountability and transparency measures.[88] The appropriate role of the data protection law should, therefore, have been to curb rather than strengthen these unchecked powers. While reviewing the 2019 Bill, several members of the JPC had also objected to the contents of this provision in their dissent notes on similar grounds.[89]

Our submissions on the 2019 version of the PDP Bill recommended that if such a provision is to be retained in the draft it should be modified to specify the provisions of the data protection law that would continue to apply to exempted entities.[90] For instance, there seems to be little reason why requirements relating to clear and lawful purposes of processing, collection and retention limitations, and data security safeguards should not be applicable to entities that are exempted for national security and public order-related purposes. In addition, the exempted entity should be bound to put in place internal structures, such as the appointment of a retired judge as a judicial expert within the organization, to approve any actions involving the processing of personal data by that agency.

[87] See PDP Bill 2019, s 35, draft DPD Bill 2022, s 18(2), and DPD Act 2023, s 17(2)(a).

[88] Software Freedom Law Center, India, 'India's Surveillance State: Communications Surveillance in India' (*SFLC.in and World Wide Web Foundation*, 3 September 2014) <https://sflc.in/wp-content/uploads/2014/09/SFLC-FINAL-SURVEILLANCE-REPORT.pdf> accessed 20 April 2023; Rishab Bailey and others, 'Use of Personal Data by Intelligence and Law Enforcement Agencies' (SSRN, 1 August 2018) <https://macrofinance.nipfp.org.in/PDF/BBPR2018-Use-of-personal-data.pdf> accessed 19 April 2023; Smriti Parsheera and Prateek Jha, 'Cross-Border Data Access for Law Enforcement: What Are India's Strategic Options?' (*Carnegie India*, 2020) <https://carnegieindia.org/2020/11/23/cross-border-data-access-for-law-enforcement-what-are-india-s-strategic-options-pub-83197> accessed 19 April 2023.

[89] Dissent notes by Manish Tewari and others, in PP Chaudhary and others, 'Report of the Joint Committee' (n 29).

[90] Rishab Bailey and others, 'Comments on the (Draft) Personal Data Protection Bill, 2019' (n 73).

Pending progress on the much-needed project of broader surveillance reforms in India, safeguards of the nature suggested above could have helped bring in some degree of checks on the personal data-related actions of exempted government agencies. A similar proposal was put forward by JPC member Manish Tewari in his dissent note. He proposed that any exemption under the provision should only be granted pursuant to a judicial approval from the appellate tribunal that was suggested under the 2019 version of the bill.[91] The DPD Bill 2023 designates an existing body, the TDSAT, as the appellate tribunal for the purposes of the data protection law. While this body may not be the most suitable to consider data privacy-related exemptions it would still be preferable to having the executive making these decisions without any independent oversight.

The DPD Act, however, incorporates no such safeguards. Indeed, it fares worse than the previous versions on two main counts. First, it takes away some of the minimal safeguards that were suggested in the 2019 Bill, which had said that the government may specify certain procedures, safeguards, and oversight mechanisms to be followed by the exempted agency. The JPC had suggested a further clarification that any procedure laid down by the government for the exempted agency should be a 'just, fair, reasonable and proportionate procedure'.[92] Second, the DPD Act 2023 enables onward sharing of the personal data gathered by the exempted agency with the central government, with no limitation on the purposes for which it may be used by the government. It therefore expands the scope of the exemption much beyond the grounds stated earlier.

4.4.3. Impact on Right to Information

The DPD Act has diminished the scope of public transparency under the country's right to information law. The RTI Act is a transparency enhancing law that enables citizens to gain access to information that is under the control of public authorities. Public authorities are bound to respond to such information requests but this obligation is subject to certain exceptions, which includes respect for the privacy rights of the concerned individuals. As per this exception, public authorities would not be compelled to disclose any

[91] Dissent note by Manish Tewari in PP Chaudhary and others, 'Report of the Joint Committee' (n 29), 216.

[92] PP Chaudhary and others, 'Report of the Joint Committee' (n 29), 120–21.

personal information that has no relationship to a public activity or interest or would cause unwarranted invasion of the privacy of the individual.[93] For instance, courts have observed that records pertaining to the performance of an employee/officer generally fall under the ambit of personal information and cannot be made available to members of the public as a matter of right.[94]

The aim of the exemption under the RTI Act was to maintain a balance between the right to public transparency and privacy of individuals. It did so by providing that the privacy exemption would not be absolute in nature, and authorities under the RTI could require a disclosure of such information to be made if it served the larger public interest. The DPD Act has, however, done away with this balancing provision.[95] It amended the RTI Act to provide a blanket exception for any 'information which relates to personal information'. The sweeping nature of this exemption will significantly diminish the scope of the right to information under the RTI Act as any information that relates to an identifiable person could be denied on the grounds of violating their privacy.

4.4.4. Concerns with the Regulatory Structure

The success of any data protection law depends, in large part, on effective implementation, which in turn depends on the functioning of the regulatory body created under it. In India's case this would include the balancing of the data protection body's independence from the government, which will comprise a large segment of the regulated entities, and its accountability to stakeholders, the government and the public. However, every successive draft of India's Data Protection Bill has seen a weakening of the proposed regulatory framework and institutional mechanisms for data protection.

The 2019 bill proposed the creation of a new regulatory agency called the Data Protection Authority (DPA) that would consist of up to seven full-time members. The powers of the DPA would have included making regulations to operationalize various aspects of the law and undertaking enforcement actions to ensure compliance with the statute and regulations. The selection of the DPA's members was to be done through a completely executive-led selection process (a committee of three senior officials from the government). Responding to the significant criticisms of this proposal, the JPC put forth a

[93] RTI Act 1995, s 8(1)(j).
[94] *Girish Ramchandra Deshpande v Central Information Commissioner* (2013) 1 SCC 212.
[95] DPD Act 2023, s 44(3).

revised formulation including the following additional members: the Attorney General of India (the country's senior legal officer), an independent expert nominated by the government, and one director each from the Indian Institutes of Technology and Indian Institutes of Management.[96] This formulation, while marginally better, also did not go far enough in terms of ensuring the independence of the selection process from government control.

The DPD Act 2023, however, does away with the earlier formulations while opting for a weakened regulatory structure. First, it replaces the concept of the DPA with a DP Board where the number of members on the board, their process of selection, process of functioning will all be prescribed later by the government.[97] The Draft Rules put out in January 2025 have introduced the proposed provisions in this regard. By refusing to address these provisions in the primary law (as opposed to the rules) the statute errs in achieving the independence of this body from the government. This is because unlike the statue, which can be amended only through a legislative process, the rules can be modified more easily by the executive at any point of time. The 2023 Act, however, did make an improvements over its 2022 draft which suggested that even things like the qualifications of board members would be left to be determined by the government.[98]

Second, the role of the DP Board has also been curtailed, mainly to deal with data breaches and determining non-compliance with provisions of the law.[99] Unlike the previously imagined DPA, the DP Board will not have any regulation-making powers. This distinguishes the Indian DP Board from the authorities created under the data protection laws of other BRICS countries that have the power to frame regulations on different aspects of the law. The DPD Act's institutional design effectively enhances the powers that will be available in the hands of the government, allowing it to issue clarifications, restrictions, and rules on the interpretation and scope of the data protection law. For instance, the law states that the government will make rules on issues as varied as deciding upon the suitable time period for data retention,[100] designation of significant data fiduciaries,[101] and notification of restricted countries for cross-border data flows.[102] Each of these constitutes a significant power that can substantially reshape the obligations of regulated entities and the scope of

96 PP Chaudhary and others, 'Report of the Joint Committee' (n 29), 128–29.
97 DPD Act 2023, s 19(1) and (2) and s 23(1).
98 DPD Bill 2022, s 19(2).
99 DPD Act 2023, s 27.
100 ibid s 8(8).
101 ibid s 10.
102 ibid s 16.

individual rights. But the DPD Act does not cast any obligations of public consultation, cost-benefit analysis, or other forms of due process in the actions of the government while making such decisions.

4.4.5. Cross-border Data Flows

The topic of cross-border data flows has been one of the most contested aspects of the Indian data protection debate. The initial drafts of the bill began with the suggestion of imposing fairly strict localization requirements for certain types of data, which compulsorily would have to be stored on local Indian servers, and conditional data transfer models for the rest. However, these proposals were eventually relaxed in favour of the current position under section 16 of the DPD Act. The provision allows personal data to be freely transferred, except to any restricted countries that may be notified by the government. Popularly referred to as the 'blacklisting' approach, India's final approach is more liberal compared to that of any of the other BRICS countries that have provisions on prior consent, adequacy of the other country's laws, standard contractual clauses, and certification as available mechanisms for the transfer personal data outside the country.

The DPD Act's seemingly liberal position, however, comes with an important caveat. The law clarifies that its open position on cross-border flows will not restrict the operation of any other laws that may contain 'a higher degree of protection for or restriction on transfer of personal data by a Data Fiduciary outside India in relation to any personal data or Data Fiduciary or class thereof'.[103] This clarification is important for two reasons. First, the provision preserves the space for sector-specific localization provisions, a fairly large number of which are already in place in India in sectors like payments, telecommunications, cloud storage of government data, and books of accounts of companies.[104] Second, the Draft Rules interpret this provision, and the DPD Act more generally, to mean that government can also introduce additional restrictions on data flows through new rules.

Notably, the Draft Rules provide that any transfer of data to 'any foreign State, or to any person or entity under the control of or any agency of such

[103] ibid s 16(2).

[104] Smriti Parsheera, 'Country Deep Dive: India' in *Global Governance of Cross-Border Data Flows: Operationalising Practical Solutions: A Compendium of Research Papers* (Centre on Regulation in Europe 2024) <https://cerre.eu/wp-content/uploads/2024/09/240905_CBDT_FullBook_FINAL.pdf> accessed 1 April 2025.

a State' will be subject to the restrictions specified in any order issued by the government.[105] The rules also prescribe a separate requirement that significant data fiduciaries will be bound by any restrictions on the flow of 'personal data and the traffic data pertaining to its flow' that may be imposed by the government on the recommendations of a committee constituted by it.[106] In both these cases the Draft Rules defer the specifics of the nature of the restriction that would be applicable, hence creating ambiguity around the practical implications of the liberal provision on cross-border flows adopted by the DPD Act.

4.5. Other Developments: Architectures and Proposals on Data Governance

As the legislative proposal on personal data protection remained in a state of flux, there were at least two other relevant developments that intersected with the discussions on data protection. The first development related to the initiation of policy discussions around the regulation of 'non-personal data' in India. Non-personal data in this context refers either to personally identifiable data that has been anonymized, or data which by its nature was never personal in nature. Examples include anonymized health data of patients, land records, vehicle registration details, etc. In the 2019 version of the bill the government introduced a provision, section 91, that would allow them to direct any data fiduciary to furnish any anonymized personal data or other non-personal data to enable better targeting of delivery of services or formulation of evidence-based policies.[107]

This change was introduced even though the government had already constituted a separate expert committee headed by Kris Gopalakrishnan to make recommendations on the governance of non-personal data.[108] As per the recommendations of this committee, government and private organizations that collect and manage data should be bound by certain requirements like sharing details of the meta data collected by them and making data sets that are designated as high-value datasets available to requesting entities. The Gopalakrishnan committee recommended the creation of a separate

[105] Draft Rules, r 14.
[106] ibid r 12(4).
[107] PDP Bill 2019, s 91.
[108] Kris Gopalakrishnan and others, 'Report by the Committee of Experts on Non-Personal Data Governance Framework' (Ministry of Electronics and Information Technology, December 2020) 20 <https://static.mygov.in/rest/s3fs-public/mygov_160922880751553221.pdf> accessed 19 April 2023.

legal framework and statutory authority to oversee the governance of non-personal data.

The JPC, however, was of the opinion that not only should section 91 of the PDP Bill 2019 remain, but there should also be an overall expansion in the scope of the law so as to cover both personal and non-personal data. To support this idea the JPC pointed to the impossibility of making clear demarcations between personal and non-personal data, which would lead to regulatory uncertainty and complications. Several members of the JPC, however, opposed this idea in their dissent notes.[109] In alignment with these dissenting voices, the DPD Act limits its scope to digital personal data keeping any references to non-personal data out of its scope. With this, the intermingling of the policy conversations on personal and non-personal data can be said to have been settled for now, although there is still no clarity about how India will finally choose to regulate non-personal data.

The second important development relates to India's adoption of a technical architecture on consent management called the Data Empowerment and Protection Architecture (DEPA), which represents the consent layer of India Stack.[110] This refers to a model of electronic consent management and sharing of data based on the consent of the individual. The electronic consent under DEPA is to be collected, stored and managed by intermediaries called consent managers who are proposed to be regulated under the Data Protection Bill. The DPD Act defines consent managers as a person that enables an individual to give, manage, review and withdraw their consent through an accessible, transparent, and interoperable platform.[111] Such consent managers will have to be registered with the DP Board and be bound by the technical, operational, and financial conditions to be notified by the government.[112] The Draft Rules accordingly lay down the conditions of registration for consent managers.[113]

While the DPD Act now gives legal sanctity to the institution of consent managers and the rules governing them are in the process of being framed, the adoption of the DEPA framework is already underway in many sectors. This is notably the case in the financial sector, under the account aggregators regulations, and under the Ayushman Bharat Digital Health Mission for

[109] Dissent notes by Gaurav Gogoi, Derek O'Brien, and Mahua Moitra, in PP Chaudhary and others, 'Report of the Joint Committee' (n 29), 223–28, 219–20.

[110] NITI Aayog, 'Data Empowerment and Protection Architecture: Draft for Discussion' (2020) <https://www.niti.gov.in/sites/default/ files/2020-09/DEPA-Book.pdf> accessed 20 April 2023.

[111] DPD Act 2023, s 2(g).

[112] ibid s 6(9).

[113] Draft Rules, r 4 and First Schedule.

the sharing of digital health records.[114] The advantages of such a framework include the generation of verifiable consent logs that can bring in better accountability in the present system of consent. It can also bring in more efficiency and transparency in the sharing of data through the use of application programming interfaces (APIs).[115] At the same time the increasing footprint of this architecture also raises questions about its role in incentivizing greater collection and sharing of data without being able to address many of the structural problems with the over-reliance on consent as the basis of data processing.[116] Further, the roll-out of DEPA, which began before a data protection law was in place, illustrated the expedited policy track for the implementation of technical architectures in India while necessary legal structures continue to take a back seat.

4.6. Automated Personal Data Processing

The scope of Indian data protection law covers automated processing, which implies that all of the provisions of the law extend to automated processing. To elaborate, the term ‘data’ is defined as any ‘representation of information, facts, concepts, opinions or instructions in a manner suitable for communication, interpretation or processing by human beings or by automated means’.[117] Further, the term ‘automated’ has also been defined in the law. It refers to a ‘digital process capable of operating automatically in response to instructions given or otherwise for the purpose of processing data’.[118] Both wholly and partly automated operations involving personal data qualify as ‘processing’ under the DPD Act.[119] The law, however, does not contain any enhanced rights in the context of automated processing such as the right not to be subject to a decision based solely on automated processing, which is found

[114] Reserve Bank of India, ‘Master Direction—Non-Banking Financial Company—Account Aggregator (Reserve Bank) Directions’ (2016) <https://www.rbi.org.in/Scripts/BS_ViewMasDirections.aspx?id = 10598> accessed 20 April 2023; National Health Authority, ‘National Digital Health Mission: Health Data Management Policy’ (n 44).

[115] Tripti Jain, ‘Tech Tools to Facilitate and Manage Consent: Panacea or Predicament? A Feminist Perspective’ (Data Governance Network, December 2021) <https://internetdemocracy.in/reports/tech-tools-to-facilitate-and-manage-consent> accessed 20 April 2022; Smriti Parsheera, ‘An Analysis of India’s New Data Empowerment Architecture’ in *Emerging Trends in Data Governance* (Centre for Communication Governance, January 2023) 7-24 <https://ccgdelhi.s3.ap-south-1.amazonaws.com/uploads/ccg-edited-volume-emerging-trends-in-data-governance-343.pdf> accessed 19 April 2023.

[116] ibid.

[117] DPD Act 2023, s 2(h).

[118] ibid s 2(h).

[119] ibid s 2(x).

in the data protection laws of countries like Brazil and South Africa and in the European GDPR.

However, as per official accounts, some elements of the intersection between AI and data protection will be covered by a new law on digital governance, which is being referred to as the proposed Digital India Act. As per a presentation put out by the government in February 2023, the scope of the Digital India Act would include the definition and regulation of high-risk AI systems, AI-based ad targeting and content moderation, and protections against automated decision-making.[120] But this proposal has not seen much policy movement since then and its future remains uncertain.

Further, India has not yet adopted any specialized legal framework on the regulation of artificial intelligence (AI), although the government has issued some advisories on the subject.[121] Some of these advisories have been controversial on account of their intrusive and sweeping directions and lack of legislative backing. For instance, one such advisory, which was subsequently withdrawn in light of significant pushback from the industry and civil society, called for prior government approval for the deployment of any untested or unreliable AI models.[122]

The country has also seen a series of policy conversations on the development and deployment of responsible AI systems. These initiatives have been led by the government think tank, NITI Aayog. The list of policy documents includes a National Strategy for Artificial Intelligence released in June 2018, the Principles for Responsible AI issued in February 2021 and a document on operationalizing the principles for responsible AI that followed in August that year.[123] These developments, however, maintain the non-binding status of guidelines on AI and do not point to any movement toward the adoption of a regulatory framework on the subject. In summary, while the future of India's legal framework on AI remains unclear at this point, there remains extensive deployment of automated technologies in the private sector and surrounding the use of computer systems to support government administration.[124]

[120] Ministry of Electronics and Information Technology, Government of India, 'Proposed Digital India Act 2023' <https://www.meity.gov.in/writereaddata/files/DIA_Presentation%2009.03.2023%20Final.pdf> accessed 1 November 2024.

[121] Arjun Adrian D'Souza, 'India's Foray into Regulating AI' (*IAPP*, 24 April 2024) <https://iapp.org/news/a/indias-foray-into-regulating-ai> accessed 1 November 2024.

[122] ibid.

[123] White & Case, 'AI Watch: Global regulatory tracker—India' (13 May 2024) <https://www.whitecase.com/insight-our-thinking/ai-watch-global-regulatory-tracker-india> accessed 1 November 2024.

[124] Divij Joshi, 'The Legal, Institutional, & Technical Architecture of ADMS in India' (*AI Observatory*) <https://ai-observatory.in/> accessed 1 November 2024.

4.7. Conclusion

A modern and comprehensive data protection law has been a long-pending necessity for India. It is necessary for protecting the fundamental rights of citizens, checking the data excesses committed by state agencies and private actors, and ensuring global competitiveness. The task of translating this well-recognized need into a legislative reality has, however, taken much longer than it ought to have. This chapter has offered a brief history of India's attempts at formulating a law on data protection, a trajectory that was marred by a series of uncertainties and delays until the eventual adoption of the DPD Act in August, 2023.

The manner in which a new bill was hurriedly rushed through Parliament without effective parliamentary deliberation or public consultation on new ideas saw the undoing of a half-decade-long consultation process. As discussed in the chapter, as enacted, the law contains several limitations in the scope of rights and protections being offered and provisions for government exemptions. But, despite these limitations, the DPD Act signals a new dawn for data protection in India.

The Indian DPD Act reflects some parallels with the laws of other BRICS countries that have been studied in this collection of essays—for instance, through its differential treatment of data fiduciaries based on their size and relevance, additional requirements for significant data fiduciaries, and possible exemptions for startups and small businesses. This is similar to China's differential treatment of large Internet platform services and the direction under Brazil's law to facilitate compliance by small businesses and micro-enterprises. Similarly, the focus on data localization in Indian policy discourse is similar to the attention received by this subject in countries like China and Russia, although India's final approach on cross-border flows has turned out to be different from all the other BRICS countries.

There are several other reasons that make the Indian approach stand out from the other BRICS countries. First, as discussed in the chapter, the country is trailing behind in terms of the pace of adoption of its data protection law, which is still a work in progress while all the other jurisdictions already have a functional data protection framework in place. The institutional design of the Indian law also differs given its choice of creating a Data Protection Board with a limited set of functions, instead of a fully fledged regulatory authority as is seen in most other jurisdictions. Additionally, unlike most other data protection laws that cover all types of personal data, the scope of the DPD Act is limited only to digital data. There are also other differences in the terminology adopted by the law (using terms like data fiduciaries and principals) and the scope of rights and protections (no right to be forgotten, right to data portability, or restrictions on decisions based solely on automated processing).

Crucially, the Indian experience also stands out in terms of its 'tech-first approach' to digital governance. Over the last decade and a half, the country has seen a move towards greater reliance on state-endorsed technology solutions to achieve societal objectives in areas like digital identity, digital payments, and most recently consent management. The creation of the institution of consent managers under the DPD Act is also a part of this trend. While a technical architecture that is designed to bring greater accountability in consent-collection and data-sharing is a valuable tool, it is not sufficient to meet the overall goals of a holistic data protection framework.

The enactment of the DPD Act and its adoption of the consent management framework are, therefore, only the first steps towards the dawn of meaningful data protection in the country. This will have to be followed by the arduous process of creating the new statutory board, framing sound rules to give effect to several important aspects of the law, and building compliance capacity among stakeholders. The DPD Act makes an important start in this direction, albeit with an incomplete set of protections that will have to be refined and improved with time. It is possible that this law will be challenged, revisited, and refined in the coming years through legislative or judicial interventions. In parallel, there is much to be done in terms of institution-building and rule-making to give life to the new law.

5

ASSESSING THE CHINESE PERSONAL INFORMATION PROTECTION LAW (PIPL) AND BEYOND: THE STAKEHOLDER ARCHITECTURE OF DATA PROTECTION IN CHINA

Wayne Wei Wang, Sofia Chang Nogueira, and Larissa Chen Yi Qian

5.1. Introduction

China's pre-PIPL data protection regime was characterized by fragmentation, doctrinal incoherence, and a paucity of integrated statutory guidance, which rendered even expert legal interpretation a fraught exercise. The prevailing legal architecture—diffuse, underdeveloped, and internally inconsistent—left courts with limited capacity to produce principled adjudication, instead requiring them to navigate the interstices between codified norms and policy imperatives emanating from the central leadership.[1] Judicial discretion thus functioned not merely as a mechanism of legal interpretation but as an instrument for accommodating shifting policy orientations within the broader socialist legality framework.

Legislative authorities were acutely aware of the disjunction between codified norms and administrative practice. Widespread abuses of personal information—ranging from unauthorized collection to instances of fraud—had generated significant public disquiet.[2] In response, China's institutional

[1] Minhao Benjamin Chen and Zhiyu Li, 'Courts without Separation of Powers: The Case of Judicial Suggestion in China' (2023) 64 Harvard International Law Journal 203.

[2] Yue Lu, '一场信息保护的博弈' ['A Game of Information Protection'] (*Xinhua Net*, 2021) <http://www.xinhuanet.com/legal/2021-10/20/c_1127974932.htm> accessed 23 April 2023.

Wayne Wei Wang, Sofia Chang Nogueira, and Larissa Chen Yi Qian, *Assessing the Chinese Personal Information Protection Law (PIPL) and Beyond: The Stakeholder Architecture of Data Protection in China*
In: *Personal Data Architectures in the BRICS Countries*. Edited by: Luca Belli and Walter Britto Gaspar,
Oxford University Press. © Luca Belli and Walter B. Gaspar 2025. DOI: 10.1093/9780198974468.003.0005

system, premised on performance legitimacy,[3] demonstrated a capacity for policy recalibration in light of emergent social harms. This responsiveness intensified the imperative to formulate a dedicated legislative framework to regulate the collection and processing of personal data.

In the absence of a comprehensive data protection statute and an integrated enforcement infrastructure, the regulatory landscape was historically anchored in the Cybersecurity Law (CSL), promulgated in 2016. However, enforcement authority remained opaque and diffuse. The oft-cited metaphor of 'nine dragons governing the waters' (九龙治水) aptly captured the institutional ambiguity: either too many agencies claimed overlapping authority or none assumed responsibility, generating a regulatory vacuum in practice.[4]

The PIPL emerged through a tripartite legislative process, comprising two rounds of public consultation (in October 2020 and April 2021) and final enactment in August 2021,[5] with over fifteen years of debate over its institutional design,[6] which echoed the Brazilian and Indian experiences of data protection codification. The evolution of the statutory text across these drafts offers a window into the legislature's evolving conceptualization of stakeholder rights and obligations. These revisions also reflect a growing awareness of structural asymmetries in informational power, although preliminary groundwork had already been laid by the CSL and the 2021 Data Security Law (DSL), which began to allocate substantive authority and responsibility among data processors, state actors, and individuals.

This chapter provides a thorough evaluation of the PIPL, applying a stakeholder-centric framework—focused specifically on data actors—to analyse the statutory allocation of rights, obligations, and enforcement authority. The legislative choice to define 'personal information' (个人信息) reflects a conceptual framework that, while superficially resembling definitions found in other jurisdictions, particularly the EU's General Data Protection Regulation (GDPR), diverges markedly in both its scope and practical application. As such, this chapter compares the PIPL with analogous legal frameworks

[3] Hongxing Yang and Dingxin Zhao, 'Performance Legitimacy, State Autonomy and China's Economic Miracle' (2015) 24 Journal of Contemporary China 64.

[4] Tai Ming Cheung, 'The Rise of China as a Cybersecurity Industrial Power: Balancing National Security, Geopolitical, and Development Priorities' (2018) 3 Journal of Cyber Policy 306, 316.

[5] Fei Qiu, '个人信息保护法的立法往事' ['The Legislative History of the Personal Information Protection Law'] (法治周末 *Rule of Law Weekend*, 4 November 2021) <https://finance.sina.cn/tech/2021-11-04/detail-iktzscyy3607023.d.html> accessed 3 May 2023.

[6] Yehan Huang and Mingli Shi, 'Top Scholar Zhou Hanhua Illuminates 15+ Years of History Behind China's Personal Information Protection Law' (*DigiChina—Stanford University*, 8 June 2021) <https://digichina.stanford.edu/work/top-scholar-zhou-hanhua-illuminates-15-years-of-history-behind-chinas-personal-information-protection-law/> accessed 6 December 2022.

globally, paying particular attention to its position within the BRICS bloc, to highlight areas of both alignment and divergence in legal interpretation and cultural context.

The chapter opens with a brief overview of the rule of law and institutional legal structures in the People's Republic of China, to contextualize the PIPL within its normative and administrative environment. It then traces the antecedents of the PIPL, focusing on the institutional drivers and political logic behind its enactment. Following this, it examines the PIPL in relation to cognate legislation—particularly the CSL, DSL, and the 2020 Civil Code—to clarify the PIPL's place within the NPC's legislative hierarchy. The final section engages in a doctrinal analysis of the PIPL's core provisions, with particular attention to the asymmetrical allocation of data rights and responsibilities, the pluralistic enforcement regime, and the procedural mechanisms for redress and sanction.

Ultimately, the chapter argues that China's data protection architecture represents a distinctive amalgam of normative principles and institutional imperatives. While it draws selectively from international models, its underlying logic and operational mechanisms remain embedded in China's unique administrative, political, and legal traditions.

5.2. The Chinese Legal System: Brief Overview

As articulated in its Constitution, 'The People's Republic of China, is a socialist state under the people's democratic dictatorship led by the working class and based on the alliance of workers and peasants'.[7] This constitutional formulation, which was formally adopted at the fourteenth National Congress of the Communist Party of China (CPC), grounds the ideological articulation of 'socialism with Chinese characteristics' and reflects the CPC's constitutional and institutional centrality in the Chinese legal and political order.[8]

Within this system, the CPC occupies the position of ruling party, entrusted with the leadership of the socialist project. Other legally recognized political

[7] Constitution of the People's Republic of China 1982 art 1. The standard English translation of 人民民主专政 is 'People's Democratic Dictatorship'. See the latest constitution's English version at <https://english.www.gov.cn/archive/lawsregulations/201911/20/content_WS5ed8856ec6d0b3f0e9499913.html>. At its core, the term signifies the synthesis of democratic and authoritarian elements to preserve the people-oriented character of state power. It denotes a constitutional theory in which democratic participation is extended to the 'people' as defined by the state, while coercive measures are reserved for those deemed antagonistic to the socialist order.

[8] Xiaobo Dong and Yafang Zhang, *On Contemporary Chinese Legal System* (Springer 2023) <https://doi.org/10.1007/978-981-99-2505-6>.

parties, while nominally independent, function within a framework of what is often termed 'multi-party cooperation and political consultation under the leadership of the Communist Party', and are conventionally described as participating parties.[9] These entities explicitly affirm the CPC's leadership and engage collaboratively in pursuit of shared socialist objectives, rather than in adversarial or oppositional roles characteristic of pluralist democracies.

The Constitution further declares that all state power belongs to the people, exercised through the National People's Congress (NPC) and local people's congresses at various levels. These bodies establish and oversee the activities of administrative, judicial, and procuratorial organs, which are constitutionally accountable to the congresses and subject to their supervision.[10] This arrangement formalizes a system of indirect democratic participation, structured within a single-party framework.

With respect to individual rights, the Constitution enumerates a range of civil and socio-economic entitlements, including rights to vote and stand for election, freedom of speech, press, assembly, association, religious belief, personal dignity, and rest, among others. However, these rights are coextensive with a set of constitutionally prescribed obligations. Articles 52 to 54 impose duties on citizens to safeguard national unity and ethnic solidarity, comply with laws and social norms, maintain public order, respect collective morality, and protect the 'security, honor, and interests of the motherland'.

While these obligations are formally articulated, their normative content often relies on language that is broad and indeterminate. Terms such as 'national unity', 'social morality', and 'honor of the motherland' are open-textured and subject to evolving interpretative frameworks, which may be shaped by prevailing policy priorities and the discretion of enforcement authorities. This vagueness gives rise to a pliable legal environment, in which the balance between state interests and individual rights may shift across contexts and over time.

In the domain of cyberspace, these constitutional obligations have been operationalized through regulatory instruments that limit online anonymity and impose duties on platforms to authenticate user identities.[11] Regulations such as the Provisions on the Administration of Internet Information Services

[9] ibid.
[10] ibid.
[11] The Cybersecurity Law of the People's Republic of China, enacted in 2017, includes provisions related to real-name registration. Art 24 of the Cybersecurity Law, for example, stipulates that network operators in China are required to implement measures to verify the identity of users when they sign up for online services. This real-name registration requirement aims to enhance the management of online information and improve cybersecurity.

and accompanying enforcement guidelines mandate that service providers monitor content and implement compliance protocols. [12] Such frameworks embody the state's emphasis on public order, ideological security, and information sovereignty in digital governance.

As explored in this chapter, the Chinese legal system manifests a form of normative exceptionalism, particularly in its asymmetrical treatment of private and public power. Both Brazil's LGPD and China's PIPL exempt state security activities from general data protection requirements, but with notable differences in approach. Brazil carves out specific exceptions for 'public security, national defense, state security, or criminal investigations' while still requiring these exempted activities to observe basic data protection principles.[13] China's framework demonstrates a more pronounced asymmetry, introducing significant individual data rights in the private sector while simultaneously allowing broader interpretation for state actors, for instance, allowing facial recognition under 'public security' justifications. This reflects China's more expansive view of legitimate state power exemptions, compared to Brazil's relatively more constrained approach.

Notably, the Chinese Constitution does not contain an explicit, codified right to privacy. Instead, it codifies some related rights inferring certain elements of privacy.[14] In this respect, the PIPL operates primarily as a statutory mechanism regulating the obligations of private data processors, rather than as a constitutional guarantee enforceable against public authorities. The rights framework it constructs is thus more administrative than constitutional in nature, and its protective function is circumscribed by the institutional logic of state-centred governance.

China's model of data regulation, reflecting a broader paternalistic and developmentalist orientation, should be understood within its own legal-cultural and political-ideological context. This chapter aims to offer a comprehensive examination of the PIPL, situating it within the larger architecture of China's governance model. It highlights the distinctiveness of China's rights discourse—both in its normative structure and institutional implementation—and underscores the importance of analysing data protection not as a

[12] For instance, those protocols include the Regulations for Internet Content Management Administration Law Enforcement Procedures. See their English translation at <https://digichina.stanford.edu/work/regulations-for-internet-content-management-administration-law-enforcement-procedures/>.

[13] See Lei No 13.709, de 14 de agosto de 2018 (Lei Geral de Proteção de Dados Pessoais), art 4.

[14] Wayne Wei Wang, 'Contextualizing Personal Information: Privacy's Post-Neoliberal Constitutionalism and Its Heterogeneous Imperfections in China' (2024) 55 Computer Law & Security Review 106030.

transposable legal category, but as a function of China's particular constitutional and administrative configuration.

5.3. The Pre-history of the PIPL: A Brief Retrospective

Prior to the release of the first draft of the PIPL of the People's Republic of China in October 2020, the regulatory framework governing protection of personal information—or, more broadly, personal data—in China was characterized by fragmentation and sectoral particularism. Rather than a unified, comprehensive regime, the landscape consisted of a patchwork of sector-specific statutes, administrative regulations, judicial interpretations, and normative documents issued by an array of institutional actors, including legislative, judicial, and quasi-governmental bodies. This included, most prominently, the 2017 CSL, alongside a constellation of industry-specific guidelines and policy measures.[15]

5.3.1. Hard Law and Soft Law

For example, prior to the adoption of the first Civil Code of China in May 2020 and in force as of 1 January 2021,[16] the General Rules of the Civil Law of the People's Republic of China, from 2017, established that 'the personal information of a natural person shall be protected by law'.[17] Moreover, also published in 2017, the Personal Information Security Specification (GB/T 35273-2017—and later updated in 2020), became the most thorough standard for personal information protection in China until the enactment of the PIPL.[18] The Specification included those components that are comparable to rules established in the EU's General Data Protection Regulation (GDPR) and also transplanted in other BRICS justifications, for instance, by establishing a broad definition of personal information, including both direct and indirect personal information ('PI'),[19] setting forth principles related to PI processing/

[15] Min Jiang, 'Cybersecurity Policies in China' in Luca Belli (ed), *CyberBRICS: Cybersecurity Regulations in the BRICS Countries* (Springer 2021) 186.

[16] 中华人民共和国民法典 [Civil Code of the People's Republic of China] 2020 (Order No 45 of the President) (CCC 2020).

[17] 中华人民共和国民法总则 [General Provisions of the Civil Law of the People's Republic of China] 2017 (Order No 66 of the President), art 111.

[18] Jiang (n 15) 186.

[19] Information security technology—Personal information (PI) security specification—GB/T 35273—2020 (Replacing GB/T 35273-2017) 2020 s 3.1. In the GDPR, art 4(1) defines personal data as any type of data 'related to an identified or identifiable person'.

handling,[20] and warranting personal information rights/interests for PI subjects.[21] However, as a technical standard, it was regarded by academics as a type of 'soft law' for reference and compliance purposes, and could not be enforced with regulatory authority by administrative bodies.[22]

5.3.2. A Legislative Fragmentation

As noted above, issues relating to the protection of personal information and the preservation of confidentiality were, prior to the enactment of a unified legal framework, addressed in a piecemeal fashion through sector-specific legislation, administrative guidelines, and supplementary regulatory provisions tailored to the particularities of discrete contexts. This regulatory pattern—marked by fragmentation, normative overlap, and inconsistent enforcement—bears notable resemblance to the experience of other BRICS jurisdictions, most notably Brazil. In both China and Brazil, the move toward the adoption of comprehensive data protection legislation was driven in significant part by the deficiencies of the prevailing regulatory architecture, particularly its inefficacy in ensuring coherent and consistent personal data governance across sectors.

For instance, the Resident Identity Card Law established the duty of confidentiality for public security organs regarding citizens' personal information gained through fabricating, issuing, assessing, or collecting identity cards from residents.[23] Moreover, the 2006 Anti-Money Laundering Statute stipulated that information correlating to clients' identities and commercial transactions, amassed for anti-money laundering objectives, must remain confidential, precluding disclosure to third parties except when legally sanctioned, exclusively utilized by authorities conducting anti-money laundering inquiries and enforcement, and solely for the purpose of scrutinizing anti-money laundering or pursuing criminal prosecutions against such activities.[24] Lastly, the Telecommunications and Internet Personal User Data Protection Regulations from 2013, applicable to 'the collection and use of personal user

[20] ibid ss 4 and 5. The GDPR establishes principles for personal data processing in art 5.
[21] ibid s 8. Data subjects (the equivalent to what the Specification calls PI subjects) enjoy rights as defined by the GDPR's chapter 3.
[22] Jiang (n 15) 186.
[23] 中华人民共和国居民身份证法 [Law of the People's Republic of China on Resident Identity Cards] 2003 (Order No 4 of the President) art 6.
[24] 中华人民共和国反洗钱法 [Anti-Money Laundering Law of the People's Republic of China] 2006 (Order No 56 of the President) art 5.

data in the process of providing telecommunications services and Internet information services within the borders of the People's Republic of China',[25] and the 2019 Regulations on the Protection of Children's Personal Information on the Internet, aimed at shielding the personal information of children (minors under the age of fourteen) on the Internet.[26]

5.3.3. Agenda Enablers in the State Informatization

Over the last decade, China's regulatory architecture governing information governance has undergone a marked transformation—less an ad hoc assemblage of sectoral norms than an increasingly integrated legal order. This emergent coherence is evidenced by the enactment of the DSL, which provides a structurally tiered framework for safeguarding data deemed critical to national and economic security, and more prominently, by the promulgation of the PIPL. The PIPL—effective as of November 1, 2021—constitutes China's first comprehensive statute on personal data protection, codifying baseline obligations for the collection, processing, and transfer of personal information. More than merely legislative innovation, the PIPL represents the terminus of over fifteen years of fragmented regulatory experimentation and sustained scholarly engagement with the normative foundations of PI in the Chinese legal system.[27]

The chronicle of PIPL originates from 2001 when China instituted the National Informatization Leading Group as an integral phase in the nation's informatization trajectory.[28] A pivotal aspect of this progression entailed protecting personal information; consequently, in 2003, an assemblage of scholars from the Chinese Academy of Social Sciences was commissioned to conduct comparative and contextually congruous research on PI protection.[29] This inquiry yielded the PIPL proposition proffered by experts in 2005, accompanied by a three-volume book series expounding additional research findings in the subsequent annum. The same year, 2005, saw the drafting of the 'Scholars' Proposed Model Law of the People's Republic of China on the Protection of

[25] 电信和互联网用户个人信息保护规定 [Telecommunications and Internet Personal User Data Protection Regulations] 2013 (Order No 24 of the Ministry of Industry and Information Technology) art 2.

[26] 儿童个人信息网络保护规定 [Provisions on the Protection of Children's Personal Information on the Internet] 2019 (Order No 4 of the Cyberspace Administration of China) art 1.

[27] Huang and Shi (n 6).

[28] ibid.

[29] ibid.

Personal Information'.[30] Nevertheless, owing to administrative reconfigurations and emergent priorities, such as transitioning the informatization endeavours from the State Council Informatization Office to a bureau within the Ministry of Industry and Information Technology, the advancement of the PIPL proposal was once deferred.[31]

In this context, and in recognition of China's significant advances in its informatization course, an emerging increase of PI-based crimes, and the escalating use of data underpinning decision-making and commercial operations nationwide, a PIPL legislative proposal re-emerged on the law-making agenda. The legislative progress of the PIPL was expedited by Xu Yuyu's cardiac arrest following a PI-utilized phone fraud in 2016, stimulating social reactions and debates by arousing public awareness of PI breaches.[32] In 2018, the thirteenth National People's Congress Standing Committee unveiled its Quintennial Legislative Blueprint for 2018 to 2023, which included the compilation of the first Chinese Civil Code, as well as proposals for the PIPL and the DSL, in its list of prioritized initiatives.[33]

The first draft of the proposed PIPL during the legislative period of 2018 to 2023 was published in October 2020, the second draft in April 2021, and the final version on 20 August 2021, to come into force about four months later. The PIPL contains seventy-four articles, divided into eight chapters. But to what degree does the PIPL deviate from other entities that perform comparable roles in the realm of data governance and regulation of personal information?

5.4. The Role of the PIPL: A Synthesis of National Data Legislation

In order to regulate the processing of data both within its jurisdiction and in the context of cross-border transfers, China has instituted a comprehensive data governance architecture. Central to this framework is what may be termed the 'Troika of Data Protection'—comprising the PIPL, the DSL, and the CSL. Collectively, these statutes establish a multi-layered regime governing the

[30] Lu (n 2).
[31] Huang and Shi (n 6).
[32] Lu (n 2).
[33] Changhao Wei, 'Translation: 13th NPC Standing Committee Five-Year Legislative Plan' *NPC Observer* (7 September 2018) <https://npcobserver.com/2018/09/07/translation-13th-npc-standing-committee-five-year-legislative-plan/> accessed 20 January 2023.

collection, use, storage, and transfer of data, reflecting a coordinated legislative response to the risks posed by digitalization.

This tripartite structure invites comparative reflection with other BRICS jurisdictions, where approaches to data governance have diverged. As other chapters indicate, Brazil, for instance, has enacted sector-specific rules addressing cybersecurity, but lags in the articulation of a coherent, overarching data security framework. India, while having promulgated data security obligations in various forms for over two decades, suffers from diffuse implementation and regulatory ambiguity. Russia's regulatory emphasis lies less in formulating substantive data protection norms than in asserting sovereign control over data flows—most notably through data localization mandates and content regulation. South Africa stands apart within the BRICS context in having adopted a dedicated Cybercrimes Act, which, alongside its data protection statute (POPIA), imposes explicit obligations concerning data security and cybercrime prevention.

Thus, the emergence of legislative hierarchy and intent implies that the discourse surrounding 'data protection' in China should be understood as a 'data governance' system—an intricate model aiming to establish a 'third way' that transcends the conventional differentiation between personal and non-personal data.[34] Furthermore, it extends beyond data protection and cybersecurity, addressing cyber/digital/data sovereignty, and technical aspects of data governance such as confidentiality, integrity, and availability—the Data CIA criteria set by the International Standard Organization (ISO).[35] It reflects China's long-standing wish to achieve an imperative balance between development and security in the digital epoch. In a sense, China's data and cybersecurity governance system is evidence of a dialectic philosophy that promotes social prosperity, economic development, and the maintenance of national sovereignty,[36] as very recently advocated by its core policymakers as a 'data infrastructure system'.[37] This can be seen as a politico-economic

[34] Luca Belli, 'New Data Architectures in Brazil, China, and India: From Copycats to Innovators, Towards a Post-Western Model of Data Governance' (2022) 18 The Indian Journal of Law and Technology 1.

[35] See the standards of the ISO/IEC 27001—Information security management systems.

[36] For instance, in 2015 China released the country's strategic plan, 'Made in China 2025', aimed at reducing reliance on foreign technology and achieving economic growth and political legitimacy through the development of the digital economy. See ISDP, 'Made in China 2025' (Institute for Security & Development Policy 2018) <https://isdp.eu/content/uploads/2018/06/Made-in-China-Background.pdf>.

[37] CPC Central Committee and State Council, '关于构建数据基础制度更好发挥数据要素作用的意见' ['Opinions on Building a Better Data Infrastructure System to Fully Utilize the Role of Data Elements'] (2022) <http://www.gov.cn/zhengce/2022-12/19/content_5732695.htm> accessed 24 April 2023. It states: 'The establishment of a data infrastructure system holds significant importance in terms of both national development and security. To expedite the establishment of a data infrastructure

discourse on institutional transformation from monolithic regulation to pluralistic governance, concurrently featuring deep multi-stakeholder cooperation and diverse-scenario integration, in China's decentralization reform of the administration.[38]

5.4.1. CSL vs DSL vs PIPL

At one time, the Chinese legislative framework as regards personal information was sporadic and disjointed, with numerous provisions interspersed throughout assorted legislative texts. This fragmented approach persisted following the 2012 National People's Congress Decision on Strengthening Network Information Protection (NPC Decision),[39] and influenced subsequent statutes, including the Consumer Rights and Interests Protection Law (2013 amendment),[40] Criminal Law amendments,[41] the CSL,[42] and the E-commerce Law.[43] A considerable proportion of this dispersed legislative package comprised principle-oriented, declaratory provisions that exerted minimal practical influence—for instance, the 2012 NPC Decision, which lacks provisions outlining legal accountability and serves primarily as a symbolic pledge.[44]

This decentralized legislation engendered at least two propensities: first, a potential discord within the legal interpretative framework, evidenced by

system, it is imperative to leverage China's extensive data scale and diverse application scenarios, unlock the potential of data elements, fortify and broaden the digital economy, augment the novel impetus of economic growth, and establish a fresh national competitive edge'.

[38] Ronghua Shen, '推进"放管服"改革:内涵、作用和走向' ['Promoting the Reform of "Decentralization and Service": Connotation, Function and Direction'] [2019] 中国行政管理 [Chinese Public Administration] 15, 15.

[39] Standing Committee of the National People's Congress, '关于加强网络信息保护的决定' ['Decision on Strengthening Network Information Protection'] (2012) <http://www.gov.cn/jrzg/2012-12/28/content_2301231.htm> accessed 23 April 2023.

[40] 中华人民共和国消费者权益保护法 [Law of the People's Republic of China on the Protection of Consumer Rights and Interests] 2013 (Order No 7 of the President).

[41] In 2009, art 253 of Criminal Law Amendment (VII) made it a crime to obtain and provide citizens' personal information in specific circumstances, which was further improved in the Criminal Law Amendment (IX) in 2015.

[42] 中华人民共和国网络安全法 [Cybersecurity Law of the People's Republic of China] 2016 (Order No 53 of the President) (CSL 2016). An open-access English translation of the CSL for reference purposes can be found at <https://digichina.stanford.edu/work/translation-cybersecurity-law-of-the-peoples-republic-of-china-effective-june-1-2017/> (Stanford's Digital China Project).

[43] 中华人民共和国电子商务法 [E-Commerce Law of the People's Republic of China] 2018 (Order No 7 of the President).

[44] Rong Wang, '我国《个人信息保护法》立法前路' ['China's Personal Information Protection Law Legislative Road Ahead'] (互联网前沿 *Internet Frontiers*, 2017) <https://www.tisi.org/16113> accessed 24 April 2023.

the markedly divergent definitions of personal information across multiple legislative enactments,[45] culminating in disparities in law enforcement rules and compliance system ambiguities for law-abiding entities. Secondly, the protective regime concerning personal information was increasingly characterized by administrative oversight and criminalization.[46] For instance, the Criminal Law Amendment (IX) considerably expanded the sentencing scope for the crime of infringing upon citizens' personal information—the unlawful action of obtaining, selling, or distributing someone else's personal information without their consent, elevating the maximum sentence from three to seven years.[47] Additionally, in 2017, the Ministry of Public Security publicly sought input on amending the Public Security Administrative Punishment Law, which would also introduce 'detention' penalties, thereby curtailing the personal liberties of individuals who breach their user information protection obligations.[48]

China's CSL was formally promulgated in 2016,[49] following a structured legislative process that included public consultation and iterative drafting. The initial draft was released by the Standing Committee of the National People's Congress in June 2015,[50] with a revised version circulated in 2016 to solicit public and institutional feedback.[51] The law was subsequently adopted by the National People's Congress in November 2016 and came into force in June 2017.[52]

However, the multifaceted nature of cybersecurity in China transcends conventional notions encompassing cybercrime, cyberwar, cyber defence, and safeguarding personal data,[53] simultaneously integrating economic and societal advancement policies within its development-security discourse,[54] by

[45] See the discussions in section 4.1.

[46] Wang (n 44).

[47] 中华人民共和国刑法(2015修正) [Criminal Law of the People's Republic of China (2015 Amendment)] 2015 (National People's Congress), art 253.1.

[48] See art 57, proposed by Ministry of Public Security, 'Public Security Administrative Punishments Law (Draft Revisions for Solicitation of Public Comments)' (*China Law Translate*, 18 January 2017) <https://www.chinalawtranslate.com/治安管理处罚法-（修订公开征求意见稿/> accessed 24 April 2023.

[49] See the final version of the CSL at <http://www.gov.cn/xinwen/2016-11/07/content_5129723.htm>.

[50] NPC, '网络安全法（草案）全文' ['The Full Text of the Cyber Security Law (Draft)'] (*The National People's Congress of the People's Republic of China*, 7 June 2015) <http://www.npc.gov.cn/npc/c1481/201507/82ce4cb5549c4f56be8a6744cf2b3273.shtml> accessed 23 April 2023.

[51] NPC, '网络安全法（草案二次审议稿）全文' ['Full Text of the Cybersecurity Law (Draft for Second Deliberation)'] (*The National People's Congress of the People's Republic of China*, 2016) <http://www.npc.gov.cn/zgrdw/npc/lfzt/rlyw/2016-07/05/content_1993588.htm> accessed 23 April 2023.

[52] CSL 2016.

[53] Jiang (n 15).

[54] Institute of Cybersecurity of China Academy of Cyberspace, '筑牢国家网络安全屏障—我国网络安全工作发展成就与变革' ['Building a Strong National Cybersecurity Barrier—the

shifting the ideological focus from technological issues to international geo-political concerns (focusing on the period from 1994 to 2016),[55] and to those persistently changing concepts, such as content security and data security (from 2016 forward).[56] Indeed, the conceptualization of cybersecurity on technology, infrastructure, content, and data, upgraded to the level of national security,[57] featured the data regulatory model with Chinese characteristics.[58]

What distinguishes China's regulatory trajectory, however, is not simply the formal consolidation of its data governance regime, but the extent to which cybersecurity has been conceptualized as a multidimensional project—entwining technical regulation with ideological, economic, and geopolitical imperatives. In this regard, China's approach finds few analogues among its BRICS counterparts. Only India has articulated a similarly integrated vision of digital sovereignty and developmental transformation, as evidenced by initiatives such as India Stack and Digital India.[59] By contrast, other BRICS states have tended to adopt more compartmentalized or rhetorically driven approaches. South Africa, for instance, has made technical strides through the implementation of Zero Trust architectures and engagement in cross-border cybersecurity cooperation,[60] while Brazil—under the current Lula administration—has advanced ambitious proposals for institutional reform, including the creation of new cybersecurity bodies.[61] At the multilateral level, BRICS as a bloc has begun to exhibit modest regulatory convergence in areas

Achievements and Changes in China's Cybersecurity Work Development'] (2022) <https://www.secrss.com/articles/50447> accessed 25 April 2023.

[55] Weishan Miao, Jian Xu, and Hongjun Zhu, 'From Technological Issue to Military-Diplomatic Affairs: Analysis of China's Official Cybersecurity Discourse (1994–2016)' in Jeremy Hunsinger, Matthew M Allen, and Lisbeth Klastrup (eds), *Second International Handbook of Internet Research* (Springer Netherlands 2020).

[56] Rogier Creemers, 'The Chinese Conception of Cybersecurity: A Conceptual, Institutional and Regulatory Genealogy' [2023] Journal of Contemporary China 1, 12.

[57] '没有网络安全就没有国家安全，没有信息化就没有现代化.' ['Without cybersecurity, there is no national security; without informatization, there is no modernization']—President Xi Jinping, see his Speech at the first meeting of the Central Leading Group for Cyber Security and Informatization on 27 February 2014.

[58] Henry S Gao, 'Data Regulation with Chinese Characteristics' in Mira Burri (ed), *Big Data and Global Trade Law* (CUP 2021).

[59] Ingrid Schneider and Krishna Ravi Srinivas, 'A Chance for India to Shape a Data Governance Regime' *The Hindu* (14 March 2023) <https://www.thehindu.com/opinion/lead/a-chance-for-india-to-shape-a-data-governance-regime/article66615759.ece> accessed 5 April 2025.

[60] BCX, 'Cybersecurity Trends and Adoption in Africa: a Comprehensive Overview for 2025' (*BCX*, 15 January 2025) <https://www.bcx.co.za/technology-insights/cybersecurity-trends-and-adoption-in-africa-a-comprehensive-overview-for-2025/> accessed 5 April 2025.

[61] Joe Devanny and Russell Buchan, 'Brazil's Cyber Strategy Under Lula: Not a Priority, but Progress Is Possible' (Carnegie Endowment for International Peace, 8 August 2023) <https://carnegieendowment.org/2023/08/08/brazil-s-cyber-strategy-under-lula-not-priority-but-progress-is-possible-pub-90339> accessed 5 April 2025

such as data protection, content governance, and cybercrime,[62] though the depth and coherence of such efforts remain uneven.

In essence, the DSL and the PIPL are perceived by policy architects as constituents of an overarching cybersecurity regulatory framework. Consequently, a degree of both synergy and discord exists amidst the trio concerning normative explication and scrutiny. As an illustration, the CSL inaugurated a particular emphasis on preserving critical information infrastructure (CII)[63]—subject to the Multi-Level Protection System[64]—encompassing public communicative and informational utilities possessing the capacity to considerably imperil national security and interests.[65] This culminates in the Data Grading and Classification System under the DSL.[66] Pertaining to personal data, the CSL prescribes the principle of data localization for personal information and important data amassed and produced by CII operators, necessitating storage within China's borders, save for instances where security assessments by the Cyberspace Administration of China (CAC) and additional State Council departments permit otherwise.[67]

Such regulatory stringency—especially the integration of cybersecurity considerations into the treatment of both infrastructural and personal data—has no close analogue among other BRICS jurisdictions. While Russia and South Africa have prioritized cybersecurity within their respective national strategies, they have not articulated a comparably comprehensive or securitized framework for data governance. In this respect, the Chinese model stands apart in its synthesis of cyber, data, and national security regulation within a single, coherent legislative architecture.

[62] Luca Belli, 'Cybersecurity Convergence in the BRICS Countries' (*CyberBRICS*, 20 September 2021) <https://cyberbrics.info/cybersecurity-convergence-in-the-brics-countries/> accessed 4 April 2025.

[63] The Critical Information Infrastructure Security Protection Regulations were enacted on 1 September 2021, subsequent to their approval at the thirteenth Standing Committee meeting of the State Council on 27 April 2021. The objective is to safeguard the security of critical infrastructure and defend against cyber threats, in accordance with the Cybersecurity Law. Critical information infrastructure is defined by regulations as comprising of significant network infrastructure and information systems in crucial industries, including but not limited to telecommunications, energy, transportation, finance, and e-government. The destruction, loss of functionality, or data leakage of critical infrastructure could have a substantial impact on national security, the economy, public interest, and people's livelihood. See 关键信息基础设施安全保护条例 [Critical Information Infrastructure Security Protection Regulations] 2021 (Order No 745 of the State Council) art 2.

[64] CSL 2016, art 21.

[65] ibid art 31.

[66] 中华人民共和国数据安全法 [Data Security Law of the People's Republic of China] 2021 (Order No 84 of the President) (DSL 2021) art 21. An open-access English translation of the DSL for reference purposes can be found at <https://digichina.stanford.edu/work/translation-data-security-law-of-the-peoples-republic-of-china/> (Stanford Digital China Project).

[67] CSL 2016, art 37.

Moreover, the DSL, ratified in June 2021 during the twenty-ninth session of the Standing Thirteenth National People's Congress,[68] a brief interval after the promulgation of the PIPL, further fortified China's data governance paradigm, encompassing provisions for transnational data transfer and delineating regulations that interconnect with both the PIPL and the CSL of China. The DSL accentuates the protection of national security by augmenting the stipulations of the CSL and expanding China's extraterritorial jurisdiction over specific data categories.[69] Concurrently, it advocates for open data endeavours,[70] as well as incentives for 'soft law'—inclusive of enhancing societal cognizance of data security,[71] fostering self-regulatory measures,[72] devising ancillary technological standards,[73] and endorsing security certification.[74] In pursuit of this objective, the DSL inaugurates a data grading and classification system that categorizes data predicated on various factors, including significance to economic and social development, potential detriment to national security, public interests, lawful rights and interests of individuals or organizations, and the likelihood of alteration, destruction, disclosure, or illicit procurement or utilization of information.[75] Notably, the DSL introduces a novel classification of 'core national data' that subsumes domains such as national security, vital components of the national economy, significant facets of citizens' lives, and major public interests.[76]

The DSL distinctly bolsters institutional mechanisms for national data security by allocating the National Security Council,[77] in collaboration with vertical departments under the Ministry of Public Security, Ministry of State Security, and the CAC,[78] the responsibility of supervising its implementation. Furthermore, the DSL stipulates that each administrative region and department is accountable for data acquisition and security within their respective domains.[79] As the DSL emphasizes national security, it enforces more rigorous regulations on data localization and transfer,[80] as well as imposes stringent

[68] DSL 2021.
[69] CAC, '专家解读｜《数据安全法》为全球数据安全治理贡献中国智慧和中国方案' ['Expert Interpretation | "Data Security Law" Contributes Chinese Wisdom and Chinese Solutions to Global Data Security Governance'] (*Cyberspace Administration of China*, 2021) <http://www.cac.gov.cn/2021-06/15/c_1625341228851523.htm> accessed 25 April 2023.
[70] DSL 2021, ch V.
[71] ibid art 9.
[72] ibid art 10.
[73] ibid art 17.
[74] ibid art 18.
[75] ibid art 21.
[76] ibid.
[77] ibid art 5.
[78] ibid art 6.
[79] ibid.
[80] ibid ch IV.

penalties for failure to comply.[81] For example, it elucidates the prerequisites for accessing data to preserve national security or probe criminal activities,[82] as well as mandates prior authorization for foreign judicial or law enforcement agencies' data requisitions.[83] In addition, any transfer overseas of important China-originated data imposes a security assessment in accordance with the CAC's guidelines.[84]

The interrelation between the CSL, DSL, and PIPL was further underscored by the 2022 amendments to the CSL. In September 2022, the CAC resolved to modify the CSL, with the aim of harmonizing its provisions with recently enacted legislation, such as the Administrative Punishment Law, DSL, and PIPL.[85] For instance, the revised draft of the CSL refined the legal liability provisions concerning violations of personal information rights and interests by invoking the application of the PIPL. The monetary penalty has also been increased from 1 million yuan to 50 million yuan, or 5 per cent of the previous year's turnover.[86] The amendment inaugurates more stringent penalties for breaches of the CSL,[87] endowing authorities with grander legal authority to address violations and safeguard users' rights.[88]

5.4.2. The Conflicting Role? The PIPL vs the Chinese Civil Code (CCC)

China's data protection regime beyond the PIPL exhibits institutional coherence through the troika of the data governance framework. This framework enhances the extent of China's PI protection under its administrative law or public law system. However, the explanatory guidelines of the individual rights

[81] ibid ch VI.
[82] ibid art 35.
[83] ibid art 36.
[84] ibid art 31.
[85] CAC, '关于公开征求《关于修改〈中华人民共和国网络安全法〉的决定（征求意见稿）》意见的通知' ['Notice on Public Solicitation of Opinions on the "Decision on Amending the Cybersecurity Law of the People's Republic of China" (Draft for Comments)'] (*GOV.CN*, 2022) <http://www.gov.cn/xinwen/2022-09/14/content_5709805.htm> accessed 2 May 2023.
[86] ibid.
[87] This was highlighted in the Didi Chuxing case, in which the ride-hailing company received a record fine of US$1.2 billion for contravening China's cybersecurity, data security, and personal information protection regulations including the CSL. 'China Ride-Hailing Giant Didi Fined $1.2bn after Probe' *BBC News* (21 July 2022) <https://www.bbc.com/news/business-62248513> accessed 23 April 2023.
[88] Arendse Huld, 'China Cybersecurity Law: CAC Solicits Opinions on Amendment' (*China Briefing News*, 20 September 2022) <https://www.china-briefing.com/news/china-cybersecurity-law-cac-solicits-opinions-on-amendment/> accessed 23 April 2023.

protection established in the Chinese Civil Code (CCC) represent another significant aspect of comprehending the PIPL.

China attempted to formulate civil laws on four separate occasions after 1949, but external circumstances impeded success until the Fourth Plenary Session of the Eighteenth Central Committee of the Communist Party of China that marked the beginning of the codification.[89] In 2014, the Fourth Plenary Session of the Eighteenth Central Committee of the Communist Party of China decided to codify the Civil Code.[90] A 'two-step process' was later established to elaborate on the General Provisions followed by the compilation of sub-sections of the Civil Code, ultimately leading to a unified Civil Code.[91] The compilation began in 2015, with the General Provisions passed in 2017 and subsequent subsections integrated in December 2019.[92] After further refinement by the Standing Committee, the Civil Code was deliberated upon during the Third Session of the thirteenth National People's Congress in 2020,[93] and ultimately took effect in January 2021.[94]

Once perceived as the foundational legislation governing the market economy, the Civil Code emerged in part as a redressal mechanism for reputation and privacy infringements amidst the digital revolution characterized by pervasive information dissemination.[95] Central to this notion is the distinct delineation of personality rights, encapsulated within chapter 6 of Book IV, which concurrently establishes personal information protection and the civil right to privacy.[96] In this context of juxtaposed enumeration, personal information is construed as a legal interest rather than an aspect of personality

[89] Xinhua News Agency, 'China Drafting Civil Code: Spokeswoman' (*The State Council of the People's Republic of China*, 2 April 2016) <http://english.www.gov.cn/news/top_news/2016/03/04/content_281475301143367.htm> accessed 23 April 2023.

[90] Xinhua News Agency, '新时代的人民法典—《中华人民共和国民法典》诞生记' ['The People's Code of the New Era—The Birth of the "Civil Code of the People's Republic of China"'] (*Central's People Government of the People's Republic of China*, 2020) <http://www.gov.cn/xinwen/2020-05/28/content_5515766.htm> accessed 25 April 2023.

[91] ibid.

[92] ibid.

[93] ibid.

[94] CCC 2020.

[95] Central's People Government of the People's Republic of China, '人民美好生活的法治保障—写在《中华人民共和国民法典》诞生之际' ['Guarantee of the Rule of Law for a Better Life for the People—Written on the Occasion of the Birth of the "Civil Code of the People's Republic of China"'] *People's Daily* (28 May 2020) <http://www.gov.cn/xinwen/2020-05/31/content_5516270.htm> accessed 25 April 2023.

[96] Art 1032 of the CCC defined privacy as 'the tranquility of the private life of a natural person, and the private space, private activities, and private information that he is unwilling to be known to others'. In contrast, art 1034 defined personal information as 'various information recorded electronically or in other forms that can identify a specific natural person separately or in combination with other information, including a natural person's name, date of birth, identity card number, biological recognition information, address, telephone number, e-mail address, health information, and whereabouts information, among others'.

rights.[97] This metamorphosis from a singular privacy paradigm in the pre-Civil Code era to a dualistic framework inclusive of both privacy and personal information protection has engendered a more inconsistent judicial implementation of privacy-vs-personal-information terminology.[98] Despite article 1034, which elucidates the distinction between personal information and the right to privacy by employing the phrase 'personal information of privacy nature', these discrepancies persist.[99]

5.5. The Characteristics of the PIPL: a Multidimensional Perspective

The Chinese PIPL legislative intent, as stated in the official public statement made by its legislator in October 2020,[100] precisely prior to the publication of the first draft, is to remedy the lack of regulation of the widespread collection and use of personal information by different parties, as well as institutionally reaching an interest-coordinating trade-off between frequent infringements of personal information and the development of the digital economy. Although some claim a considerable degree of comparability between the PIPL and the GDPR,[101] a significant portion of the PIPL rules features their normative heterogeneity from the established ones.

5.5.1. What is (Sensitive) Personal Information?

The PIPL featured an intentional normative trade-off between regulation and growth. On the one hand, article 4 of the PIPL initiated and expanded the scope of personal information, as well as excluding anonymization from the PI definitive scope, notably from a compliance perspective. Prior

[97] Personal information defined in the CCC is classified as encompassing 'other personality interests arising from personal freedom and personal dignity'. See CCC 2020, art 990.

[98] Lu Zhang, '"Personal Information of Privacy Nature" under Chinese Civil Code' (2021) 43 Computer Law & Security Review 105637, 2–3.

[99] ibid 5.

[100] Junchen Liu, '关于《中华人民共和国个人信息保护法（草案）》的说明' ['Explanation on the Personal Information Protection Law of the People's Republic of China (Draft)'] (*National People's Congress*, 2020) <http://www.npc.gov.cn/npc/c30834/202108/fbc9ba044c2449c9bc6b6317b94694be.shtml> accessed 26 January 2023.

[101] Xu Ke and others, 'Analyzing China's PIPL and How It Compares to the EU's GDPR' (2021) <https://iapp.org/news/a/analyzing-chinas-pipl-and-how-it-compares-to-the-eus-gdpr/> accessed 11 January 2023.

to the PIPL, personal information was defined in the then-existing laws for practitioners' reference, such as the CSL[102] and the Chinese Civil Code.[103] In both contexts, there was a narrow interpretation of PI in the context of identifiability, in which the term 'identifiability' implied only the requirement of 'identification' but not the requirement of 'relating-to'. The National Standard GB/T 35273 in between, short for Information Security Technology—Personal Information Security Specification, for the first time, broadened the concept of 'personal information' to include 'any type of information recorded electronically or by other means that, by itself or in combination with other information, can identify a specific natural person or reflect the activities of a specific natural person'.[104] In Annex A (GB/T 35273-2020), it indicated the two criteria for determining PI, namely 'identification + relating to'.[105] The former focuses on the inherent attributes of an individual that are identifiable. In contrast, the latter focuses on the information generated by a particular natural person in the course of his or her activities (eg, location data, phone call history, web browsing history, etc).

On the other hand, the PIPL diverges from the GDPR in its approach to sensitive personal information (PI). Article 28 of the PIPL provides a flexible 'generalization + enumeration' definition of sensitive PI, likely offering room for interpretation and compliance in emerging technologies. Categories of sensitive PI in the PIPL include biometrics, religious beliefs, specific identity, medical and health, financial accounts, trajectory/location data, and information of minors under fourteen years old.[106] Meanwhile, the PIPL imposes more stringent handling prerequisites for sensitive PI, with extra procedural

[102] As art 76(5) of the Cybersecurity Law states, 'Personal information means all kinds of information recorded in electronic or other forms, which can be used, independently or in combination with other information, to identify a natural person's personal identity, including but not limited to the natural person's name, date of birth, identity certificate number, biometric information, address, and telephone number'.

[103] CCC 2020, art 1034: 'Personal information is information recorded electronically or in other ways that can be used, by itself or in combination with other information, to identify a natural person, including the name, date of birth, identification number, and biometric information, residential address, telephone number, email address, health information, whereabouts, and the like, of the person'.

[104] Information security technology—Personal information (PI) security specification—GB/T 35273—2020 (Replacing GB/T 35273-2017) (n 19), s 3.1.

[105] ibid Annex A.

[106] 中华人民共和国个人信息保护法 [Personal Information Protection Law of the People's Republic of China] 2021 (Order No 91 of the President) (PIPL 2021) art 28. An open-access English translation of the PIPL for reference purposes can be found at <https://digichina.stanford.edu/work/translation-personal-information-protection-law-of-the-peoples-republic-of-china-effective-nov-1-2021/> (Stanford's Digital China Project).

obligations to PI handlers. Sensitive PI handling is influenced by factors such as purpose specificity, data handling necessity, and security measure stringency.[107] The PIPL requires separate consent mechanisms for sensitive PI handling,[108] disallowing general consent, authorization, or bundling tactics. Additionally, the PIPL mandates not only informing the individual but also notifying them of the necessity and impact of handling sensitive PI on their rights and interests.[109]

Among the BRICS countries, China's PIPL defines sensitive personal information broadly as data that, if misused, could endanger individual dignity or security. Brazil's LGPD enumerates specific sensitive data categories—such as race, religion, political views, health, sex life, and biometric or genetic identifiers—requiring explicit consent for processing, subject to narrow exceptions.[110] India's DPDPA (2023) does not define sensitive data per se but adopts a risk-based model, imposing heightened obligations on Significant Data Fiduciaries based on factors like data volume, sensitivity, and potential national impact.[111] Russia's Federal Law No 152-FZ similarly designates special categories, including biometric, health, and criminal data, which are strictly regulated and generally require explicit consent, with safeguards commensurate to data sensitivity.[112]

The final conceptual expansion is on the PI of the deceased. Article 49 of the PIPL provides a comprehensive approach to addressing the issue of posthumous management of personal information in the era of big data. It is institutionally rooted in the provisions of article 994 of the Civil Code regarding the protection of the personality rights of the deceased.[113] It offers a framework for the inheritance of personal data, enabling individuals to exercise their autonomy and testamentary freedom. Thus, the PIPL, to some extent, allows for priority to be given to the deceased's own arrangements for their personal information.[114]

[107] ibid.
[108] ibid art 29.
[109] ibid art 30.
[110] See Lei No 13.709, de 14 de agosto de 2018 (Lei Geral de Proteção de Dados Pessoais) arts 5(II), 11.
[111] See Digital Personal Data Protection Act 2023 (India) s 10.
[112] See Federal Law No 152-FZ on Personal Data (27 July 2006, Russia) arts 6, 10, 19, 22.
[113] As art 994 of the Chinese Civil Code states, 'Where the name, likeness, reputation, honour, privacy, or body of a deceased person is infringed upon, his spouse, children, and parents have the right to request the actor to assume the civil liability according to the law . . .'.
[114] As art 49 of the PIPL states, ' . . . except as otherwise arranged by the deceased before his or her death'.

5.5.2. Rights Bundle of Data Subjects: Intensifying Individual Control over Data

In essence, the PIPL's conceptual basis, rooted in the self-determination of personal information, seeks to supplement the bundle of rights (权利束), as prescribed by the Civil Code and viewed as an expandable normative concept concerning the positive rights formulation for personal information—namely, instrumental rights granted to individuals by the state through institutional safeguards in order to fulfil its obligation to protect personal information.[115] To address the exorbitant power asymmetry between individuals and information handlers, characterized by disparities in technical, economic, and information prowess, the PIPL confers rights upon individuals and imposes obligations upon information handlers, like most data protection legislation, to rectify this imbalance, entailing, for example, judicious access to and control of data.

The architecture of data control is initially manifested through article 44, establishing the right to know, the right to decide, and the right to restrict/refuse—individuals possess an overarching privilege to dictate the management of their PI. Nevertheless, this provision, as a more eminent stratum of jurisprudence, omits the delineation of the scope and demarcations pertaining to an individual's right to know. Concurrently, article 44 stipulates, as an 'exception clause', that exclusions apply 'unless otherwise dictated by legislation and administrative regulations'. This suggests that under exceptional circumstances—such as when personal data is processed in pursuit of demonstrable public interest objectives or for the prevention and investigation of unlawful or criminal conduct—the data subject's rights above may be lawfully limited or derogated from, subject to proportionality and necessity constraints as recognized in statutory and administrative practice.

The PIPL also serves to enhance individuals' control over their personal data by delineating rights to access, duplication, rectification, and deletion, as likewise but abstractly stipulated in the Civil Code.[116] Article 45 of the PIPL strengthens an individual's right to know and decide the treatment of their personal data, in tandem with its article 44, while article 107 of the CCC safeguards access and duplication rights, and grants the

115 Wang Xixin, '重思个人信息权利束的保障机制：行政监管还是民事诉讼' ['Reflecting upon the Protection Mechanism of Personal Information Rights Bundle: Administrative Supervision or Civil Litigation'] (2022) 44 法学研究 Chinese Journal of Law 3.

116 CCC 2020, art 1037.

right to contest and rectify inaccuracies. Furthermore, articles 46 and 47 elucidate rights to rectify, supplement, and delete personal information, building upon the Civil Code and CSL.[117] The PIPL broadens the circumstances for deletion requests,[118] integrates exemptions to article 1037 of the Civil Code, and necessitates the creation of mechanisms for receiving and processing applications to exercise individual rights. Lastly, the PIPL final draft commendably incorporates specificity into article 47(1)(a) by clarifying the conditions for deletion applicability, although further clarification on 'deletion of personal information that is technically unattainable' remains necessary.

The intensification of individual data control, as manifested through article 45 of the PIPL, aims to dismantle data silos and monopolies by instituting the right to data portability, aligning with policy trajectories that emphasize internet governance, anti-competitive practices, and antitrust constraints, while fostering data interoperability and common prosperity.[119] However, the actualization of data portability necessitates further clarification on legitimate grounds for personal information transfer, technical milieu, and third-party rights and interests balancing, like those in article 20 of the GDPR and article 18 of the LGPD, lest enterprises face augmented compliance burdens and unbridled competition. Article 48 of the PIPL also endows users with a claimable right to request clarification in accordance with standard clause contracting rules of the CCC,[120] compelling private entities to solicit informed consent upon initial application engagement.[121]

Despite these provisions, the PIPL's scope remains indeterminate, encompassing limitations and ambiguities surrounding binary choices, data collection indispensability, and the distinction between fundamental and augmented commercial functions,[122] rendering the efficacy of discourse between individual users and personal information handlers in a transitional phase, as will be discussed in the following.

[117] ibid; CSL 2016, art 43.

[118] PIPL 2021, art 47.

[119] Nathaniel Taplin and Jacky Wong, 'Common Prosperity: Decoding China's New Populism' *Wall Street Journal* (28 August 2021) <https://www.wsj.com/articles/common-prosperity-decoding-chinas-new-populism-11630159381> accessed 4 May 2023.

[120] CCC 2020, art 496(2).

[121] Konrad Kollnig and others, 'Before and after China's New Data Laws: Privacy in Apps' (*arXiv*, 2 March 2023) 5–6 <http://arxiv.org/abs/2302.13585> accessed 11 April 2023.

[122] ibid 5.

5.5.3. General and Special Obligations of Data Handlers

While endowing data subjects with enhanced autonomy over their personal information, the PIPL concurrently delineates fundamental tenets, encompassing 'Explicit Purpose + Minimal Scope' and 'Informed-Consent' processing rules, alongside provisions for security breach disclosure and rectification, as well as distinct responsibilities for prominent, platform-based personal information handlers. Nevertheless, these imposed duties exhibit a pronounced emphasis on security discourses and reactive strategies in response to societal and public perceptions, such as debates surrounding automated decision-making and facial recognition technology.

5.5.3.1. The principle of 'explicit purpose + minimal scope' (purposefulness + necessity) (article 6)

The principle of purposiveness, articulated in Article 6 of the PIPL, requires that the processing of personal data be directed toward a specific, legitimate, and reasonably ascertainable purpose. It further demands a demonstrable nexus between that purpose and the functional offerings of the data-handling entity. Closely related is the principle of necessity, which operates as a foundational constraint on data collection practices. Under this standard, only data strictly relevant and proportionate to the fulfilment of an organization's operational objectives may be lawfully collected, thereby precluding the accumulation of superfluous or tangential information.

The application of these principles is neither formalistic nor uniform; rather, it is contingent upon the structure and logic of divergent business models and must be interpreted in conjunction with pre-existing regulatory instruments that anticipate and inform the PIPL's normative framework. For instance, mobile application operators are required to assess whether the scope of personal information they collect exceeds what is deemed 'necessary' under the Provisions on the Scope of Necessary Personal Information for Common Types of Mobile Internet Applications,[123] which delineate baseline requirements across thirty-nine app categories. This regulatory apparatus thus operationalizes the necessity principle through sector-specific guidance, introducing a functionalist calibration between legal standards and industry practice.

[123] 常见类型移动互联网应用程序必要个人信息范围规定 [Provisions on the Scope of Necessary Personal Information for Common Types of Mobile Internet Applications] 2021 (No 14 of the Secretary Bureau of Cyberspace Administration of China).

5.5.3.2. The principle of 'informed consent' (articles 13, 14, 15, 16, and 17)

The PIPL marks a significant departure from the CSL's unitary legislative foundation, which is principally anchored in the monolithic 'informed consent' paradigm. It carefully refines and amplifies the scope of the exception 'otherwise mandated by law or administrative regulations', as articulated in article 1035 of the Civil Code. To explicate with greater doctrinal precision, this clause—prior to the PIPL's enactment—had broader applicability under article 42, paragraph 1 of the CSL, wherein consent functioned as the central normative basis for personal information processing, subject only to limited exceptions such as anonymization.

For instance, the Personal Information Security Specification enumerates eleven exemptions from the consent requirement, notwithstanding the fact that not all are undergirded by formal legal authority.[124] Concurrently, article 1036 of the Civil Code delineates three specific circumstances under which personal information may be processed without the data subject's consent. Against this background, the seven lawful bases for processing personal information set forth in article 13 of the PIPL represent a more comprehensive and normatively robust articulation of the 'informed consent' principle, one that is marked by heightened legal determinacy. This evolution may, in turn, contribute to greater efficiency in the circulation and handling of personal information.

Fundamentally, the 'Informed Consent' doctrine, extrapolated from the 13th, 14th, 15th, 16th, and 17th provisions of the PIPL, can be construed as follows: the acts of 'informing' and 'consenting' form the bedrock tenets in the domain of PI handling. Acquiescence should be elicited premised upon the provision of exhaustive prior disclosure, eschewing deceptive, duplicitous, or intimidatory stratagems.[125] Providers must not, under any circumstance, withhold products or services contingent upon a person's declining to consent.[126] Entities involved in data management ought to offer an expedient mechanism for the retraction of consent.[127] Contrasting with the preliminary draft, the ratified version incorporates an ancillary stipulation in the legitimate reasons for the PI handling, specifically the 'imperative administration of human resources'.[128] This provision functions as an equipoise to redress the predicament

[124] Information security technology—Personal information (PI) security specification—GB/T 35273—2020 (Replacing GB/T 35273-2017) (n 19).
[125] PIPL 2021, art 14.
[126] ibid art 16.
[127] ibid art 15.
[128] ibid art 13(2).

wherein the breadth of employee personal data garnered on the foundation of an employment contract is markedly circumscribed, and its application is confined.[129]

Notably, within the parameters of article 14 in the PIPL, the notions of 'separate consent' and 'written consent' are expounded, and ensuing clauses lay down the mandate for separate consent in particular circumstances pertaining to the PI handling: 1) the relaying of processed PI to a third-party entity;[130] 2) the public exhibition of processed PI;[131] 3) the deployment of personal visual and identity data (eg facial recognition) accrued in public domains for objectives transcending the preservation of public safety;[132] 4) the handling of sensitive PI;[133] 5) the outbound PI transfer.[134]

5.5.3.3. Security obligations: measures, audits, and assessments

The PIPL, meanwhile, outlines the security obligations of entities handling personal information in safeguarding the confidentiality and integrity of such data. The law integrates provisions from the CSL,[135] mandating the maturity of a comprehensive executive framework for the stratified stewardship of personal information. Handlers must employ sophisticated technical measures, including encryption and de-identification for instance, to ensure the security, autonomy, and controllability of personal information.[136] Furthermore, the integration of instructional mechanisms for training practitioners and devising emergency plans into routine operations is required.[137] The PIPL also obliges the designation of a personal information protection officer (PIPO) contingent upon reaching a predetermined threshold for personal information handling.[138] That said, Brazil's LGPD broadly requires 'technical and administrative measures' without prescribing specific implementations,[139] and India's DPDP Act similarly employs a principles-based approach with 'reasonable security measures',[140] giving organizations flexibility in implementation while being

[129] 'The employment contract shall contain the basic information of the worker, including the worker's name, address, and resident ID card or other valid ID card numbers, etc.' See 中华人民共和国劳动合同法 (2012修正) [Labor Contract Law of the People's Republic of China (2012 Amendment)] 2012 (Order No 73 of the President) art 17.
[130] PIPL 2021, art 23.
[131] ibid art 25.
[132] ibid art 26.
[133] ibid art 29.
[134] ibid art 39.
[135] CSL 2016, arts 25, 26, 39, and 40.
[136] PIPL 2021, art 51.
[137] ibid.
[138] ibid art 52.
[139] See Lei No 13.709, de 14 de agosto de 2018 (Lei Geral de Proteção de Dados Pessoais) art 46.
[140] See Digital Personal Data Protection Act 2023 (India) s 8(5).

less prescriptive than China's regulation, reflecting different regulatory philosophies that balance compliance clarity against implementation flexibility.

The PIPL evidently addresses the regulatory gap for foreign organizations by stipulating that foreign personal information handlers subject to the legislation must institute specialized domestic entities or designate domestic representatives.[141] These handlers are obliged to submit their commitments to the department overseeing personal information protection (eg CAC and its subordinate agencies).[142] This provision parallels the extraterritorial jurisdiction expansion of the PIPL, aligning it with similar mechanisms in the EU's General Data Protection Regulation (GDPR),[143] as well as other extraterritorial counterparts globally. Consequently, foreign personal information handlers potentially subject to the PIPL are required to establish institutions within China or appoint representatives for submission.

The PIPL mandates that personal information handlers undertake a personal information protection impact assessment (PIPA) prior to engaging in specific handling activities.[144] This evaluation is consistent with the 'personal information security impact assessment' notion portrayed in the Chinese national standard, GB/T 39335-2020.[145] The EU's GDPR encompasses a comparable legal framework, the Data Protection Impact Assessment (DPIA), which data controllers must fulfil when processing activities pose a heightened risk to the rights and freedoms of personal data subjects.[146] India's 2023 DPDP Act adopts a targeted approach where only government-designated 'significant data fiduciaries' (based on data volume, sensitivity, and risk) must conduct periodic impact assessments;[147] while Brazil's LGPD employs the most flexible framework, allowing its data protection authority discretionary power to request assessments rather than mandating them for specific processing activities, giving organizations greater implementation flexibility at the cost of less prescriptive guidance.[148] By elevating DPIA prerequisites to obligatory legal responsibilities, the PIPL may thus impose more rigorous stipulations on corporate internal compliance system development, streamlining compliance

[141] PIPL 2021, art 53.
[142] ibid.
[143] General Data Protection Regulation (GDPR) 2016 (2016/679) art 3.
[144] PIPL 2021, art 55.
[145] Information security technology—Guidance for personal information security impact assessment—GB/T 39335-2020 2020.
[146] GDPR 2016, art 35.
[147] See Digital Personal Data Protection Act 2023 (India) ss 10(1), 10(2)(c)(i). See also Anirudh Burman, 'Understanding India's New Data Protection Law' (Carnegie Endowment for International Peace, 3 October 2023) https://carnegieendowment.org/research/2023/10/understanding-indias-new-data-protection-law?lang = en accessed 4 April 2025.
[148] Lei No 13.709, de 14 de agosto de 2018 (Lei Geral de Proteção de Dados Pessoais) art 38.

and execution for handlers while diminishing internal decision-making intricacy and uncertainty risk.

5.5.3.4. 'Taming' platforms: gatekeeping and automated decision-making

Substantial internet platforms, characterized by vast user populations and complex business structures,[149] wield significant power over transactions and personal data processing within their purview, thereby incurring heightened legal responsibilities for personal information (PI) protection. The PIPL defines a 'gatekeeper' based on three criteria: providing essential internet platform services, having a substantial user base, and operating a complex business model, all of which are required. Regulations further specify that a 'substantial user base' means over 50 million registered users or more than 10 million monthly active users, while 'essential internet platform services' involve data processing with significant effects on national security, economic operations, or international livelihood.[150] However, there is no specific explanation for what constitutes a 'complex business model'. Therefore, an entity qualifies as a 'gatekeeper' if it is a 'personal information handler' with over 50 million registered users or 10 million monthly active users, operates a complex business, and has activities that exert significant influence.

In accordance with article 58, enhanced oversight of 'gatekeeper' corporations can be achieved by implementing four measures regarding these prominent digital platforms: establishing autonomous organizations comprising external members for PI protection supervision, formulating platform obligatory rules for PI handling and security, managing non-compliant behaviour within the platform, and disseminating social responsibility reports for public scrutiny.[151] Conversely, the PIPL recognizes that smaller PI handlers do not pose systemic risks and, as stated in article 62(2), prescribes tailored PI protection protocols and standards to be separately introduced for these entities, as well as for emerging technologies like facial recognition and artificial intelligence.[152]

Pursuant to article 24 of the PIPL, PI handlers employing automated decision-making instruments are mandated to ascertain transparency in the decision-making process and maintain equitable and impartial outcomes.[153]

[149] PIPL 2021, art 58.
[150] 网络数据安全管理条例 [Online Data Security Management Regulations] 2024 (Order No 790 of the State Council) (ODSMR 2024) art 62(8).
[151] PIPL 2021, art 58.
[152] ibid art 62(2).
[153] ibid art 24.

Differential treatment in aspects such as pricing or other transactional terms that lack reasonable justification, exemplified by the prevalent phenomenon of 'Big Data Shashu'—a business tactic of using behavioural data to manipulate price discrimination—is prohibited,[154] which is analogous to article 22 of the GDPR.[155] Furthermore, congruent provisions are present in the Personal Information Security Specification and the E-Commerce Law.[156] In instances where automated decision-making mechanisms are utilized for disseminating information or engaging in commercial promotion towards individuals, PI handlers ought to furnish alternative choices devoid of personalized targeting or facilitate convenient refusal methods for the recipients.[157] In circumstances where automated decision-making significantly impinges on an individual's rights and interests, the individual reserves the right to solicit elucidation and to reject decisions derived solely from automated processes.[158]

5.5.4. Limited Constraints upon the Public Sector

Indeed, the PIPL imposes regulatory constraints on the public sector, albeit to a limited extent in section 3 of chapter 2. The legislature necessitates conformity to the aforesaid section regarding its legitimate enactment while abiding by both general and specific stipulations pertaining to the PI handling, including the inform/notice obligations.[159] Exceptions exist wherein legal and administrative regulations necessitate confidentiality or exempt the need for disclosure under specific circumstances, as well as instances where notifying state organs would impede the execution of statutory obligations.[160] Moreover, the statute obliges data localization for public institutions, and when transferring data across borders is indispensable, a security assessment must be undertaken.[161]

Further elucidated within section 3 are discrete guidelines for public institutions handling PI. Article 33 unambiguously asserts that, concomitant with the exclusive guidelines of this section, the endeavours of public institutions in

[154] Yaling Jiang, 'China's Personal Information Protection Law Is Here. What's Changing?' (*SixthTone*, 2021) <https://www.sixthtone.com/news/1008846> accessed 8 May 2023.

[155] GDPR 2016, art 22.

[156] See Information security technology—Personal information (PI) security specification—GB/T 35273—2020 (Replacing GB/T 35273-2017) (n 19), s 7.5(b); E-Commerce Law of the People's Republic of China 2018, art 18.

[157] PIPL 2021, art 24.

[158] ibid.

[159] ibid art 35.

[160] ibid.

[161] ibid art 36.

relation to PI handling are additionally subject to other provisions delineated within the PIPL.[162] Simultaneously, article 37 incorporates 'bodies authorized by legal statutes and regulations to oversee public affairs' within the horizon of provisions applicable to public institutions handling PI while performing their legislatively mandated responsibilities.[163] It substantively broadens the ambit of applicability for this section, establishing a benchmark for 'public affairs functions' that extends beyond the narrowly circumscribed purview of state organs.

5.5.5. Cross-Border Personal Information Flow with Chinese Characteristics

The PIPL introduces an intricate regulatory framework for data localization and transference, which ought to be, however, in part concretized through legal interoperability.[164] Central to this framework is the stipulation that handlers of personal information adhere to protection criteria delineated by the law, in addition to relevant international treaties and conventions China has concluded or acceded to,[165] serving as bilateral and multilateral approaches to reaching adequacy across jurisdictions. That said, the statute espouses the unobstructed flow of personal information across borders, concomitantly ensuring the deployment of rigorous security measures to achieve offshore recipients' jurisdictional protective adequacy.[166]

In general, the definitive draft amalgamates and systematizes the indispensable prerequisites for cross-border PI transfers by embracing obtaining the explicit consent of the individuals concerned and notifying them of the imminent transference.[167] Article 38 of the PIPL elucidates the stipulations for the provision of personal information to global recipients, which entail ascertaining that the activities of foreign recipients are congruent with the protection standards mandated by the legislation. This universal obligation establishes an overarching mechanism for transnational data transfer, attainable via three primary modalities: a Personal Information Security Assessment (PISA) supervised by the cyberspace departments, Personal Information

[162] ibid art 33.
[163] ibid art 37.
[164] Luca Belli and Danilo Doneda, 'Data Protection in the BRICS Countries: Legal Interoperability through Innovative Practices and Convergence' (2023) 13 International Data Privacy Law 1.
[165] PIPL 2021, art 38.
[166] ibid.
[167] ibid art 39.

Protection Certification (PIPC) conferred by specialized institutions, or the enactment of Standard Contractual Clauses (SCCs).[168] This multifarious approach to PI protection exemplifies China's dedication to upholding protection and security amidst an increasingly interconnected global setting.

Comparatively, BRICS countries exhibit divergent approaches to transnational data transfers: China implements the most prescriptive framework with three government-overseen pathways (Security Assessment, Certification, or Standard Contractual Clauses); Brazil recently aligned closer to the EU model with its August 2024 ANPD Resolution establishing adequacy decisions, SCCs, and binding corporate rules;[169] Russia employs a notification-and-approval system requiring companies to inform Roskomnadzor before transfers and obtain approval for non-adequate countries;[170] India takes a unique 'negative list' approach, allowing transfers to all countries except those specifically restricted by the government;[171] while South Africa permits transfers when recipients are subject to adequate protective laws or binding agreements,[172] with each framework reflecting varying degrees of government intervention versus business flexibility and different underlying philosophies about data sovereignty versus free data flows.

Specifically, the tripartite avenues for the transfer of personal information (PI) beyond national boundaries adhere to a hierarchical order of applicability, in accordance with the Chinese paradigm for data security: 1) primarily, the PISA criteria serve as a fundamental consideration for data exportation;[173] 2) subsequent to ascertaining the inapplicability of security assessment classification, the selection between PIPC[174] and SCCs[175] may be exercised.

[168] ibid art 38.

[169] Fernando Bousso and Matheus Botsman Kasputis, 'Brazil's New Regulation on International Data Transfers' (*IAPP*, 4 September 2024) <https://iapp.org/news/a/brazil-s-new-regulation-on-international-data-transfers> accessed 4 April 2025.

[170] DLA Piper, 'Transfer in Russia—Data Protection Laws of the World' <https://www.dlapiperdataprotection.com/index.html?t = transfer&c = RU&c2 => accessed 4 April 2025.

[171] See DPDPA 2023, s 17.

[172] See POPIA, s 72.

[173] In 2022, the China Administration of Cybersecurity (CAC) introduced the 'Measures for the Security Assessment of Outbound Data Transfer', which provided comprehensive guidelines for the transfer of important data and data managed by Critical Information Infrastructure Operators (CIIOs), or data exceeding the threshold established by the CAC. See 数据出境安全评估办法 [Measures for the Security Assessment of Outbound Data Transfer] 2022 (Order No 11 of the Cyberspace Administration of China).

[174] In 2022, the TC260, short for National Information Security Standardization Technical Committee, released the Version 2.0 of the standard documentation, namely Cybersecurity Standards Practice Guide—Security Certification Specifications for Cross-Border Processing Activities of Personal Information. See 网络安全标准实践指南—个人信息跨境处理活动安全认证规范V2.0 [Cybersecurity Standards Practice Guide—Security Certification Specifications for Cross-Border Processing Activities of Personal Information V2.0] 2022 (TC260-PG-20222A).

[175] In 2023, the CAC eventually issued the 'Measures for the Standard Contract for the Outbound Transfer of Personal Information'. See 个人信息出境标准合同办法 [Measures for the Standard

For instance, article 40 of the PIPL decrees that operators of critical information infrastructure and PI handlers who process personal information up to the threshold specified by the CAC and its subordinate agencies, must store domestically collected data within the borders of China in order to address concerns regarding data localization.[176] In circumstances mandating the provision of data beyond national borders, the exclusive prerequisite of security assessment (PISA) is applicable,[177] in lieu of the stipulations delineated in article 38 pertaining to the PIPC and SCCs.[178] This post-security-assessment exception supplements and details the constraints imposed by the CSL.[179] This methodology is intended to ensure uniform adherence to data protection measures while expediting reasonable PI cross-border flow within a fortified infrastructure.

Meanwhile, on 22 March 2024, nearly six months after the release of the Draft Regulations on Regulating and Promoting Cross-Border Data Flows, the CAC officially promulgated the 'Regulations on Promoting and Regulating Cross-Border Data Flows' (hereinafter referred to as the 'New Cross-Border Data Regulations'), which took effect immediately upon publication.[180] This marked the establishment of a uniquely Chinese 'dynamic adjustment mechanism for cross-border data regulation'. The 'New Cross-Border Data Regulations' provide regulatory exemptions for data transfers abroad by enumerating specific scenarios and aligning with practical needs, thereby reducing compliance burdens for businesses in common business contexts. However, while the regulations relax requirements for certain data transfers, they impose stricter oversight on the export of sensitive personal information. Compared to the more rigid, prohibitive measures adopted in other jurisdictions, these regulations offer a more flexible and clear compliance framework, supporting safe and orderly cross-border data flows in diverse business scenarios. Additionally, the regulations reference the negative list mechanism within free trade zones, which facilitates cross-border data flows by specifying restricted or prohibited data types, thereby allowing data not on the list to move more freely and simplifying the compliance process for businesses.[181]

Contract for the Outbound Transfer of Personal Information] 2023 (Order No 13 of the Cyberspace Administration of China).

[176] PIPL 2021, art 40.
[177] ibid.
[178] ibid art 38.
[179] CSL 2016, art 37.
[180] 促进和规范数据跨境流动规定 [Provisions on Promoting and Regulating Cross-border Data Flow] 2024 (Order No 16 of the Cyberspace Administration of China).
[181] ibid art 6.

5.6. The Enforcement of the PIPL: The CAC and Others

Diverging from certain legal frameworks, such as that of the EU, China has yet to institute a singular data protection authority. Instead, a multifaceted enforcement climate persists, with the CAC assuming a supervisory and coordinating capacity, and specialized agencies shouldering discrete responsibilities. The PIPL stipulates that the national cyberspace departments shall orchestrate and harmonize PI protection efforts, as well as the relevant supervision and administration tasks.[182] Furthermore, the legislation allocates the obligations of various State Council departments (including public security, market supervision, industrial information and technology, and sectoral regulatory bodies) within their respective purviews, collectively referred to as 'departments responsible for PI protection'.[183] As for the grassroots enforcement, the PIPL also delegates responsibility for its execution to pertinent departments at the county level or above, under the authority of local people's governments.[184] Concurrently, the inception of the National Data Administration (NDA) transpired in the early months of 2023, tasked with the mandate of synchronizing the progression of Digital China, the digital economy, and the digital societal landscape, among other pertinent areas. The NDA is poised to operate as a central-level entity under the auspices of the National Development and Reform Commission, while simultaneously sharing designated functions with the CAC.[185]

Actually, the BRICS countries exhibit distinct approaches to data protection authorities: China uniquely employs a multi-agency regulatory framework with the CAC coordinating among specialized agencies, while the other BRICS nations have adopted more centralized models similar to the EU's approach—Brazil with its National Data Protection Authority (ANPD), India with the Data Protection Authority of India (DPAI), Russia with Roskomnadzor (Federal Service for Supervision of Communications, Information Technology and Mass Media), and South Africa with its Information Regulator established under POPIA; this divergence highlights China's preference for distributed regulatory authority versus the single-authority approach adopted by other BRICS members, creating different enforcement dynamics where China gains

[182] PIPL 2021, art 60.
[183] ibid.
[184] ibid.
[185] Yan Luo and others, 'China Reveals Plan to Establish a National Data Bureau' (*Global Policy Watch*, 8 March 2023) <https://www.globalpolicywatch.com/2023/03/china-reveals-plan-to-establish-a-national-data-bureau/> accessed 23 April 2023.

flexibility but potentially sacrifices consistency, while other BRICS countries benefit from unified oversight but may lack China's regulatory specialization across different sectors and technological domains.

Essentially, the PIPL delineates the distribution of authority and responsibility within a complex regulatory framework, incorporating supervisory bodies endowed with extensive interpretive discretion and robust safeguards. Consequently, in relation to the PIPL, their status transcends that of a basic regulator, establishing those bodies as co-governance adjudicators. This role involves not only the traditional regulatory sphere but also spearheads initiatives in consciousness-raising, education, and guidance;[186] it is additionally entrusted with the evaluation of PI protection in mobile apps,[187] as well as the refinement of supplementary regulations and benchmarks,[188] the advancement of identity verification technologies,[189] and the facilitation of PI protection assessment and accreditation services for the entities concerned.[190]

Chapter 7 of the PIPL addresses the legal liability of enterprises neglecting their responsibilities—three classifications: administrative, civil, and criminal, in conjunction with public interest litigation. Initially, the legislation substantially augments the penalty standard for administrative liability. Beyond the million-penalty standard established by the preceding CSL,[191] the statute introduces a novel penalty criterion for 'grave circumstances', escalating the unit fine.[192] The new penalty threshold for 'grave circumstances' has been elevated to no more than 50 million yuan, or up to 5 per cent of the prior year's turnover, potentially resulting in business suspension or even revocation of pertinent business permits or licenses.[193] Fines imposed on those directly accountable and other responsible parties have increased to at least 100,000 yuan and up to one million yuan.[194] Furthermore, the newly designated department responsible for PI protection at the provincial level or higher may elect to prohibit them from serving as directors, supervisors, senior managers, and PI protection officers within relevant enterprises for a specified duration.[195] In instances where PI handling does not yet constitute a severe violation defined as 'grave circumstances' above-mentioned, mobile apps can still be instructed

[186] PIPL 2021, art 61(1).
[187] ibid art 61(3).
[188] ibid art 62(1).
[189] ibid art 62(3).
[190] ibid art 62(4).
[191] CSL 2016, art 64.
[192] PIPL 2021, art 66.
[193] ibid.
[194] ibid.
[195] ibid.

to suspend or terminate service.[196] Meanwhile, article 69 of the PIPL stipulates the principle of presumed fault in cases of PI infringement, signifying that PI handlers must present exculpatory evidence in pertinent lawsuits.[197] Lastly, the PIPL re-emphasizes the circumstances of PI-related crimes,[198] and links to the system of breach-of-credit files.[199]

One of the most innovative approaches in the PIPL is to lay out grounds for public interest litigation. Three types of organizations—people's procuratorates, consumer organizations as established by law, and entities recognized by the CAC—can initiate public interest litigation pertaining to personal information violations.[200] Another Notice by the Supreme People's Procuratorate clarifies that procuratorial organs at all levels should prioritize the following aspects when executing their duties in public interest litigation: strict protection of sensitive PI; specialized protection of vulnerable groups' PI; focused protection of PI managed in key sectors (such as education, healthcare, employment, social security, consumption), and large-scale personal information involving over one million people; and precise protection of personal information of specific subjects formed by temporal, spatial, and other connections.[201]

5.7. Conclusion

The evolution of China's personal data protection legislation has been a progressive gaming process, particularly with regard to how the Chinese institution intervenes and responds to the public's concerns. Concurrently, the intellectual participation of the academic community in structuring China's data protection system via, for instance, Expert Legislative Proposal Drafts, manifests prominently an endeavour forged through studying multiple jurisdictions, including the EU, from a comparative perspective, all while adapting them in consonance with domestic socio-political and economic institutional considerations.

196 ibid.
197 ibid art 69.
198 ibid art 71.
199 ibid art 67.
200 ibid art 70.
201 Jingjing Yan, '最高检下发通知明确个人信息保护公益诉讼办案重点' ['The Supreme People's Procuratorate Issued a Notice to Clarify the Key Points of Handling Public Interest Litigation Cases for Personal Information Protection'] (*Supreme People's Procuratorate*, 2021) <https://www.spp.gov.cn/spp/zdgz/202108/t20210822_527281.shtml> accessed 9 May 2023.

China's data protection framework, thus, ought to be comprehended along two distinct trajectories. Initially, the primary impetus for its data protection legislation was geared towards mitigating personal information-associated illicit activities and fortifying the cybersecurity—both at a system and infrastructure echelon—of state informatization. Although these original drivers embraced some rights protection provisions, it was not until the enactment of the PIPL that the fundamental rights/interests framework for data protection was carved out in a relatively complete, clear, and predictable manner. Secondly, it is imperative to recognize that China's data protection architecture extends beyond the PIPL and is more accurately depicted as a fusion of data governance mechanisms. This incorporates, at a minimum, the data governance troika—CSL, DSL, and PIPL, in addition to their respective derivatives. This interconnected mixture/fusion has also materialized in the recent Online Data Security Management Regulations.

In this context, the Chinese data protection framework should not be regarded as an absolute parallel to the prevailing international system; it cannot be directly 'aligned, or right-sizing' demanding a substantial delineation of key legal transposition terms—such as the characterization of personal information or the definition of a handler/processor, which requires a considerable degree of differentiation.

After delineating and advocating for the principal dichotomies, this chapter discerns that, analogously to the previously mentioned comparative legal legislative procedure, the PIPL indeed advances in a significant leap, empowering data subjects with rights while simultaneously crystallizing the responsibilities of data handlers. Furthermore, it inaugurates a poly-sectorial and interdepartmental collaborative regulatory system, with the CAC presiding as the chief agency.

Notably, it deploys anonymization as a pivotal stipulation to stimulate the circulation of personal information. It has designed a comprehensive rights framework for data subjects, which is largely commensurate with the General Data Protection Regulation (GDPR), albeit with constraints imposed on the right to data portability, as well as the asymmetrical decisive power among different stakeholders due to the normative uncertainty between general principles and exceptional measures. In terms of obligations incumbent upon data handlers, the PIPL underscores overarching principles and orchestrates a specialized system of security responsibilities. This framework includes creating a gatekeeper role for large-scale platforms, along with mechanisms to deny automated decision-making. Finally, China's transnational PI transfer paradigm is strikingly multifaceted, endeavouring to harmonize security concerns with the free flow of PI through a stratified data classification mechanism. The practical implications and repercussions of the 'data sovereignty' clauses within the PIPL,[202] which makes a complex element of cross-jurisdictional data protection adequacy, are yet to be fully discerned and understood.

[202] PIPL 2021, arts 42 and 43.

6
PERSONAL DATA ARCHITECTURES IN SOUTH AFRICA

Sizwe Snail ka Mtuze and Melody Musoni

6.1. Introduction

The South African government, like many around the world, is transitioning into the digital industrial revolution, popularly known as the Fourth Industrial Revolution (4IR). This transition is characterized by the adoption of information and communication technologies (ICTs) to drive digital transformation of both the public and private sectors. The Covid-19 pandemic accelerated this shift, boosting the uptake of technology to achieve the objectives of e-government,[1] e-learning, and mobile health. According to the thirteenth United Nations E-Government Survey of 2024, the United Nations E-government index (EGDI) for South Africa has a value of 0.8616 and ranks at 40 (fortieth) in the world.[2] Central to this digital transformation is the strategic use of data and growing reliance on proper data infrastructures like cloud computing, being a reflection of the advances achieved in digital government skills, services, and infrastructure.[3] This data-driven shift underscores the importance of comprehensive data strategies and data governance frameworks to manage, protect, and secure vast amounts of information.[4] Given the increased generation and processing of personal data as part of the 4IR, the need

[1] There are four different types of e-government services, namely e-services, e-democracy, e-commerce, and e-management. E-services is where government services, programmes, and information are delivered online. E-democracy is where the internet or digital communications are used for voting or improving participatory government. E-commerce is where goods and services are paid for digitally, and e-management is where government sectors and businesses can share information, maintain records, and improve data flow. Toni GLA van der Meer, Dave Gelders, and Sabine Rotthier, 'E-democracy: Exploring the Current Stage of E-government' (2014) 4 Journal of Information Policy 489; Abid Thyab Al Ajeeli and Yousif A Latif Al-Bastaki, *Handbook of research on e-services in the public sector: E-government strategies and advancements* (Information Science Reference 2010).
[2] United Nations E-Government Survey (2024) Chapter 3, p 96.
[3] ibid.
[4] State Information Technology Agency Digital Transformation 2020–2024 Strategic Plan, p 26.

Sizwe Snail ka Mtuze and Melody Musoni, *Personal Data Architectures in South Africa*
In: *Personal Data Architectures in the BRICS Countries*. Edited by: Luca Belli and Walter Britto Gaspar,
Oxford University Press. © Luca Belli and Walter B. Gaspar 2025. DOI: 10.1093/9780198974468.003.0006

to protect such data has become more critical than ever. In South Africa, several laws and policies have been established to regulate, govern, or provide guidance on, among others, the use, processing, security, confidentiality, availability, integrity, residency, and privacy of data.

This chapter discusses the existing laws which shape personal data governance in South Africa. It examines existing laws and regulations that outline the rights of individuals and obligations of entities handling personal data. It explains the legal tools and measures that have been introduced and implemented to directly and indirectly secure and protect personal data. The chapter further assesses the effectiveness of such measures and tools. Considering that data governance is still a new area of law, the chapter discusses the current developments in this area, as well as providing recommendations on how to improve the proper governance of data architectures in South Africa.

6.2. Protection of Personal Information and the Right to Privacy as Contained in the Constitution

The right to privacy is explicitly protected in South Africa by the common law in conformity with the *boni mores*[5] and section 16 of the 1996 Constitution of the Republic of South Africa (hereafter the Constitution),[6] which is the trend in most BRICS countries. Brazil also has had since 2022 an explicit right to data privacy and right to privacy, Russia has an explicit right to privacy in its Constitution, followed by India and China which respectively have the right to privacy as stated by India's Constitution as well as confirmed by jurisprudence and certain elements in the respective Chinese laws. Case law has interpreted the extent of this right and has asserted privacy rights for both individuals and juristic persons.[7] In South Africa the *boni mores* (legal convictions of the community or public policy) are informed by the Constitution and its values, which include human dignity, equality, and the promotion of human rights and freedoms. These values are used as both a tool of interpretation, with the courts having to favour an approach which protects the constitutional values and as an objective standard against which conduct can be measured.[8] The

[5] AE Strode, '*Boni Mores* and Consent for Child Research in South Africa' (2015) 8(1) South African Journal of Bioethics and Law 22 for a discussion of the *boni mores* principle in the context of bioethics and consent.

[6] The Constitution of South Africa, Act 108 of 1996.

[7] A Makulilo (ed), *African Data Privacy Laws* (Springer 2016) 189.

[8] *United Democratic Movement v President of the Republic of South Africa and Others (African Christian Democratic Party and Others Intervening; Institute for Democracy in South Africa and Another as amici curiae) (No 2)* 2003 (1) SA 495 (CC) para 19.

courts have held that the concept of *boni mores* is 'now deeply rooted in the Constitution and its underlying values'.[9] These values coincide with some key values of *ubuntu* such as human dignity itself, respect, inclusivity, compassion, concern for others, honesty and conformity.[10] In confirming the inclusion of public policy or *boni mores,* the Constitutional Court held in *Barkhuizen v Napier*:[11]

> Public policy represents the legal convictions of the community; it represents those values that are held most dear by the society . . . public policy is now deeply rooted in our Constitution and the values which underlie it . . . And the Bill of Rights, as the Constitution proclaims, 'is a cornerstone' of that democracy . . . What public policy is . . . must now be determined by reference to the values that underlie our constitutional democracy as given expression by the provisions of the Bill of Rights.

At common law the right to privacy is recognized as a personality right which is protected by the law of delict.[12] In respect of the content of the right to privacy it has been said that 'the individual's right to privacy safeguards an undisturbed private life and offers the individual control from intrusion into one's private sphere'.[13] The broad right of all to privacy is broken down into a non-exhaustive list of facets of this right, which include the right to have your personal information lawfully, securely processed, and stored by a responsible party. The right to privacy is included in section 14 of the Constitution[14] (and was also included and protected in section 13 of the Interim Constitution).[15] In the case of *Mistry v Interim National Medical and Dental Council and Others,*[16] the Court held that:

> information communicated from one health inspector to another to carry out an inspection was not within the scope of a person's constitutional right to

[9] *African Dawn Property Finance 2 (Pty) Ltd v Dreams Travel and Tours CC and Others* 2011 (3) SA 511 (SCA) para 22.

[10] JY Mokgoro 'Ubuntu and the law in South Africa' (1998) 1(1) Potchefstroom Electronic Review 17.

[11] 2007 (5) SA 322 (CC) paras 28–29.

[12] Makulilo (n 7) 189.

[13] C Cuijpers, 'A Private Law Approach to Privacy: Mandatory Law Obliged?' (2002) Scripted Volume 4 Issue 4 312, in which she quotes P Block, 'Het Recht op privacy. Een ondersoek naar de betekenis van het Nederlandse en het Amerikaanse recht' (2002) oom Jurisdische Uitgevers 323.

[14] Act 108 of 1996.

[15] Act 200 of 1993. It encompasses the rights of persons to the protection of personal information; not to have their person or home searched; their property searched; their possessions seized; or the privacy of their communications infringed.

[16] (CCT13/97) 1998 (4) SA 1127.

> information privacy... information was not obtained in an intrusive manner ... the information obtained was not about the person's personal life ... the information was not used for a purpose other than what is was obtained for and lastly how and who the information had been disseminated.

The issue of data privacy as a subset of the right to privacy was also answered in the case of *Blacksash Trust v Minister of Social Development and others*[17] wherein its third party-appointed service provider NET 1 and CPS had misused personal information of grant beneficiaries. The Court held that:

> the contract must contain adequate safeguards to protect various aspects of the personal dignity and autonomy of grant benefits.... the payment method it determines should contain adequate safeguards to ensure that personal data obtained payment process remains private and may not be used for any other [purpose].[18]

The Constitutional Court in the various cases mentioned above confirmed that the Constitution does indeed protect personal information, as a facet of the right to privacy which is contained in the Constitution.

6.3. The Personal Data Protection Architecture

Personal data or personal information of data subjects in South Africa is protected by the Protection of Personal Information Act[19] (POPIA). POPIA was passed as a law on 19 November 2013, but different sections of the Act came into operation on different dates. For example, the date of commencement of section 1 on definitions and chapter 5 on supervision or establishment of the office of the Information Regulator[20] was 1 December 2016. Other sections of POPIA came into full effect on 1 July 2020 and responsible parties were given a grace period until 1 July 2021 to comply.[21] POPIA was closely modelled

[17] (CCT 48/17) 2017 (5) BCLR 543(CC) para 53.
[18] ibid at 76.
[19] Protection of Personal Information Act 4 of 2013.
[20] The Information Regulator is an independent Data Protection and Access to Information Authority of South Africa as mandated by the POPIA in terms of section 39.
[21] Sizwe Snail ka Mtuze, 'The Convergence of Legislation on Cybercrime in South Africa: A Practical Approach to the Cybercrimes Act 19 of 2020 and the Protection of Personal Information Act 4 of 2013' (2022) 43(3) Obiter Law Journal 536, 563.

after Directive 95/46/EC of the European Parliament and of the Council (EUDPD),[22] which was replaced by the EU's GDPR.[23]

Section 2 of POPIA sets out four main objectives of the Act. First, the purpose of the Act is to give effect to the constitutional right to privacy, by safeguarding personal information when processed by a responsible party, subject to justifiable limitations that are aimed at balancing the right to privacy against other rights, particularly the right of access to information and protecting important interests, including the free flow of information within the Republic and across international borders. Secondly, the Act establishes minimum threshold requirements for the lawful processing of personal information. Thirdly, the Act provides persons with rights and remedies to protect their personal information from processing that is not in accordance with the Act. Lastly, the Act establishes voluntary and compulsory measures to ensure respect for and to promote, enforce, and fulfil the rights protected by the Act.

POPIA established the office of the Information Regulator, which is an independent body that is only accountable to Parliament and subject to the Constitution and laws of South Africa.[24] This arrangement is similar to other BRICS countries such as Brazil and Russia, but unlike China where there is co-governance by regulators and total exemptions of the state from the Data Protection Board. POPIA's further mandate is to protect individuals' personal information as well as regulate circumstances when it would be lawful to give access to information in terms of the Promotion to Access of Information Act[25] (PAIA). POPIA applies to any (all) processing activity involving personal information of a data subject.[26]

POPIA defines a 'responsible party' as a public or private body or any other person which, alone or in conjunction with others, determines the purpose of and means for processing personal information. The term 'responsible party' is the entity that is usually referred to as a 'controller' in data protection frameworks, taking inspiration from the European model. In terms of section 4 of POPIA, there are eight conditions for lawful processing of personal information. These conditions are found in sections 8 to 25 of POPIA and are the following: (a) accountability (section 8); (b) processing limitation (sections 9 to 12); (c) purpose specification (sections 13 and 14); (d) further processing

[22] Directive 95/46/EC of the European Parliament and of the Council of 24 October 1995 on the protection of individuals with regard to the processing of personal data and on the free movement of such data (EUDPD).

[23] General Data Protection Regulation of the European Union 2016/679.

[24] POPIA s 39.

[25] Promotion to Access of Information Act 2 of 2000.

[26] POPIA s 3(1).

limitation (section 15); (e) information quality (section 16); (f) openness (section 17 and 18); (g) security safeguards (section 19 to 22); and (h) data subject participation (section 23 to 25).

6.3.1. How Personal Data is Protected—the Conditions for the Lawful Processing of Personal Information

Unlike India, where there are no fundamental data protection principles, South Africa has similar data protection principles to other BRICS countries, but as previously mentioned the POPIA was closely modelled after Directive 95/46/EC of the European Parliament and of the Council (EUDPD). As a result the POPIA does not contain all the new and novel data protection provisions that were introduced by the GDPR such as 'data protection by design' as well as data portability or those which are contained in the Brazilian Law on data protection such as 'non-discrimination'.[27]

Section 4 of POPIA lists eight conditions for lawful processing of personal information.[28] 'Accountability' is the first condition. In general terms this entails the accountability principle and aims to ensure that the obligation imposed by a particular data-privacy law is given teeth and effect.[29] The accountability condition means ensuring that obligations under POPIA are honoured and observed.[30] In practice, this entails appointing an Information Officer, and deputies if need be, putting in place relevant governance documents to assist with proper compliance with POPIA, providing POPIA training and awareness, as well as managing the relationships with service providers and vendors.

'Processing limitation', the second condition, emphasizes that for processing to be lawful, there should be limits to the reason why personal information is processed, the type of personal information, and the subjects from whom personal information is collected.[31] 'Lawfulness of processing' requires that processing of personal information must always be lawful, in accordance with the law and in a reasonable manner that does not infringe the privacy of a data subject.[32] The 'minimality principle' is a part of the second condition. It provides that personal information can only be processed given that the purpose

[27] Article 6 (IX) of the Brazilian General Data Protection Law (LGPD).
[28] S Papadopoulos and S Snail ka Mtuze (ed) *Cyberlaw @SA* (2021) 355, Van Schaik.
[29] ibid 442.
[30] Section 8 of the POPIA.
[31] Makulilo (n 7) 207; POPIA s 9.
[32] POPIA s 9.

for which it is processed is adequate, relevant, and not excessive.[33] Information is adequate if it is of acceptable quality and quantity.[34]

'Consent', 'justification', and 'objection' are also part of the second condition. There are six grounds for lawful processing of personal information. First, processing of personal information can take place when such a consent, or in the case of a child the consent of a competent person, has been duly obtained.[35] The onus is on the responsible party to show that consent was indeed given. Such consent may also be withdrawn at any time by the data subject, but that will not affect the processing prior to notice of the withdrawal.[36] Processing may also take place if it is necessary to carry out actions for the conclusion or performance of a contract to which the data subject is party.[37] Personal information may also be processed if processing complies with a legal obligation imposed on the responsible party,[38] or to protect the legitimate interest of the data subject.[39] This legal justification is appropriate in instances where a responsible party is processing personal information at a small scale.[40]

It has been argued that POPIA's concept of 'legitimate interest' is much broader than the GDPR's concept of 'vital interest'.[41] Legitimate interest is much broader than vital interest and can include instances where there is a financial benefit to a data subject or making products or services more accessible to a data subject.[42] Section 11(1)(e) of POPIA also permits the processing of personal information if it is for the proper performance of a public law duty by a public body. Finally, the other legal ground to process personal information is if processing is necessary for pursuing the legitimate interests of the responsible party or of a third party recipient of information.[43] De Stadler and others correctly argue that just because a responsible party or third party has a legitimate interest does not automatically mean the processing is lawful.[44] It is still important for them to demonstrate that the limitation of a data subject's right to privacy is reasonable in line with the Constitution.[45] The data subject

[33] See s 10 and the explanation of the 'minimality principle' by Elizabeth de Stadler and Paul Esselaar, *A Guide to the Protection of Personal Information Act* (Juta 2017) 22.
[34] Elizabeth de Stadler, *Over-thinking the Protection of Personal Information Act: The last POPIA book you will ever need* (Juta 2021) 258.
[35] POPIA s 11(1)(a).
[36] POPIA, s 11(2)(a)–(b).
[37] POPIA s 11(1)(b).
[38] POPIA s 11(1)(c).
[39] POPIA s 11(1)(d).
[40] De Stadler and others (n 33) 195.
[41] De Stadler and others (n 33) 58–59.
[42] De Stadler and others (n 33) 59.
[43] POPIA s 11(1)(e).
[44] De Stadler and others (n 33) 60.
[45] Section 36 of the Constitution of the Republic of South Africa, 1996.

may object to processing, unless legislation allows for processing.[46] A data subject may also object to the processing of personal information for direct marketing, which is different from unsolicited electronic communications (spam), which are regulated by section 69.[47]

'Direct collection from data subject' is also a part of the second condition. It requires that a responsible party should collect personal information directly from the data subject.[48] However, this strict requirement has exceptions,[49] such as the impracticality of obtaining the personal information from the data subject; that the information is contained in a public record; was made public by the data subject; the fact that consent was given that one's information may be used for other purposes; that it prejudices the legitimate interest of the data subject; or that it is necessary to use processed information in the interests of national security or to comply with an obligation imposed by law.[50]

'Purpose specification', the third condition, expressly requires that personal information must be collected for a purpose that is specific, explicitly defined, and lawful.[51] The importance of this requirement must be emphasized, as failure to comply with it may expose a responsible party to civil claims for damages. The personal information must be destroyed after the purpose for which it was collected has been accomplished[52] or has ended. The personal information may only be further kept for statistical, historical, and research purposes provided there are proper safeguards in place to protect the personal information.[53]

'Further processing limitation', the fourth condition, means that information may not be further processed in a manner that is incompatible with its original purpose.[54] Compatibility is determined by referring[55] to the relationship between the purpose of the intended further processing and the purpose for which the information has been collected, the nature of the information concerned, the consequences of the intended further processing for the data subject, the manner in which the information has been collected, and any contractual rights and obligations between the parties.[56] The further processing of

46 POPIA s 11(3)(a).
47 POPIA s 11(3)(b).
48 POPIA s 12(1).
49 Makulilo (n 7) 208.
50 POPIA s 12(2).
51 POPIA s 13(1).
52 POPIA s 13(2).
53 POPIA s 14(1) and (2).
54 POPIA s 15(1).
55 Makulilo (n7) 209.
56 POPIA s 15(2).

personal information is not incompatible with the purpose of collection if the data subject or a competent person where the data subject is a child has consented to the further processing of the information; if the information is available in or derived from a public record or has deliberately been made public by the data subject; or if further processing is necessary to avoid prejudice to the maintenance of the law by any public body, including the prevention, detection, investigation, prosecution, and punishment of offences.[57] Furthermore, the further processing of personal information is not incompatible with the purpose of collection if it has to comply with an obligation imposed by law or to enforce legislation concerning the collection of revenue as defined in section 1 of the South African Revenue Service Act, 34 of 1997; for conducting proceedings in any court or tribunal that have commenced or are reasonably contemplated; in the interests of national security; the further processing of the information is necessary to prevent or mitigate a serious and imminent threat to public health or public safety or the life or health of the data subject or another individual; the information is used for historical, statistical, or research purposes; and the responsible party ensures that the further processing is carried out solely for such purposes and will not be published in an identifiable form, or the further processing of the information is in accordance with an exemption granted under section 37.[58]

'Information quality', the fifth condition, means that a responsible party must take reasonably practicable steps to ensure that the personal information is complete, accurate, not misleading, and updated where necessary. In taking such steps, the responsible party must have regard to the purpose for which personal information is collected or further processed. [59]

The measures regulating 'openness', the sixth condition, correspond to the principle of transparency and prescribe that responsible parties must maintain the documentation of all processing operations under its responsibility as referred to in sections 14 or 51 of PAIA.[60] To comply with this condition, responsible parties must maintain information manuals of their processing activities to make such data available upon request.[61] Sections 14 and 51 of PAIA require public bodies and private bodies, respectively, issue a manual which contains a description of the body's structure, contact details, a guide on how a data subject can exercise their right of access to a record, the types of records that a

[57] POPIA s 15(3); also see Papadopoulos and Snail (n 28) 359.
[58] ibid.
[59] POPIA s 16.
[60] POPIA s 17.
[61] Snail at page 566.

body holds, the description of the services available to members of the public from the body and how to gain access to those services, and a description of all remedies available in respect of an act or failure to act by the body. The Information Regulator has developed guidelines and template manuals which can be used by private and public bodies to develop their own PAIA manuals.[62] The data subject must always be informed when personal information is collected, the purpose of its collection, the name and address of the responsible party, whether it is mandatory or not to give the information, the consequences of a failure to provide information, whether the collection is in terms of a legal obligation, whether the responsible party intends to transfer the information outside Republic of South Africa, and any other relevant information.[63]

'Security safeguards', the seventh condition, entail that responsible parties must also observe data security by applying appropriate and reasonable technical and organizational steps as envisaged by section 19(1) of POPIA. Thus the concept of data security as such is incorporated in the POPIA at a high level, unlike most BRICS countries that only require that reasonable measures be in place to secure data. In determining which security measures to adopt or implement, a responsible party must have due regard to generally accepted information security practices and procedures which may apply to it or be required in terms of specific industry or professional rules and regulations.[64] Although the security of personal information is usually associated with technical ICT measures, the security of physical records should not be ignored. As much as electronic communications and records are accommodated within modern legal discourse, the effect that organizational measures will have on documents as known in the bricks-and-mortar world should not be forgotten.[65] Achieving an adequate degree of security can be divided into four steps to be completed for compliance with section 19(2), namely: risk identification; establishment and maintenance of appropriate safeguards; verification of effective implementation; and updating safeguards.[66] The above-mentioned requirements are however not to be compared with the multilayered approach to data security management in China.

In the event of a security breach as envisaged by section 21, a responsible party must report to the Information Regulator a data breach of personal information or, where a reasonable belief that this has occurred exists, where

[62] Available at https://inforegulator.org.za/paia-guidelines/ accessed 1 November 2022.
[63] POPIA s 18.
[64] POPIA, s 19(3).
[65] De Stadler and Esselaar (n 33) 35.
[66] ibid.

an unauthorized person has acquired or accessed personal information regarding the data subject. In terms of section 21(1) a responsible party and the processor of personal information on behalf of a responsible party must conclude a written agreement stipulating the manner in which the processing will be done; the obligation is on the processor to implement security measures.[67] When a security breach occurs, the responsible party has a legal duty to report the breach to the Information Regulator[68] and in certain instances to the data subject.[69] Section 22 requires that such notification needs to be made within a reasonable period after a reasonable discovery of the compromise, taking into account the needs of law enforcement which may be reasonably required to determine the extent of the breach and to restore the integrity of the responsible party's information system. The notification must provide sufficient information to the data subject to allow it to take protective measures as a result of the breach.[70] The Information Regulator recently published its Guidelines on Section 22 Notification of Security Compromises.[71] These guidelines do not prescribe a specific time period for reporting a security compromise but emphasize that the security compromise must be reported as soon as possible. POPIA is different from article 33 of the GDPR, where there is a requirement to report a data breach within seventy-two hours. Other BRICS countries such as Brazil also specify a reasonable period as three days.

If the data breach affects the general public, the Information Regulator may direct how notifications may be publicized. On the one hand, emphasis must be placed on the importance of security measures when processing personal information and the notification must also state that, when implementing these measures, a responsible party must take into account generally accepted practices and procedures.[72] On the other hand, appropriate security measures must be taken by a responsible party when processing personal information and the measures taken should warrant a level of security that is commensurate with the risks inherent in the type of personal information being processed.[73]

The principle of 'data subject participation', the eighth condition, gives data subjects two core rights, namely the right of access to personal information and the right to correction of personal information. First, the right of access to personal information gives data subjects three entitlements, namely the right

[67] Makulilo (n 7) 210.
[68] POPIA s 22(1).
[69] POPIA s 22(3).
[70] POPIA s 22(5).
[71] Available at https://inforegulator.org.za/popia-forms/ accessed on 30 October 2022.
[72] Papadopoulos and Snail (n 28) 362.
[73] ibid.

to know from the responsible party what personal information is held by the responsible party, the right to the production of proof of the consent to process the data subject's personal information, and the right to be advised about the entitlement to have incorrect personal information to be corrected by the responsible party.[74] The right of access to information may be limited in certain instances. A responsible party may refuse a request for access to information if certain grounds exist as provided for under PAIA.[75] Secondly, as much as data subjects have the right to have their personal information corrected by a responsible party, data subjects also have the right to request the responsible party to destroy and or delete their personal information once the purpose it was collected for has ceased.[76]

Failure to comply with any of the eight above-mentioned conditions for lawful processing of personal information may amount to an interference with the right to protection in terms of section 73 and may expose the transgressor to be issued with an infringement notice and administrative fine under the terms of section 104 of POPIA.[77]

Apart from the eight conditions for lawful processing of personal information, POPIA also provides for certain instances where a responsible party needs to obtain prior authorization from the Information Regulator. Section 57 of POPIA requires that if a responsible party wishes to link personal information connected to a unique identifier for another purpose other than that for which it was collected and for further processing, the responsible party must seek authorization from the Information Regulator.[78] Additional instances when prior authorization is required are when a data subject's unlawful or questionable conduct is processed, criminal conviction information is being processed, information is processed for credit reporting or special personal information, or personal information of children is being processed in another country that does not have adequate levels of protection.[79] The Information Regulator also issued a Guidance Note on Application for Prior Authorization[80] which provides additional clarification on processing activities subject to prior authorization. Recently the Information Regulator has also issued a Guidance Note in respect of Direct Marketing,[81] as well as a Guidance Note on The Processing

[74] POPIA s 23.
[75] POPIA s 23(4).
[76] POPIA s 24.
[77] Papadopoulos and Snail (n 28) 373.
[78] POPIA s 57.
[79] Makulilo (n 7) 211 and also see POPIA s 107(b).
[80] Available at <https://inforegulator.org.za/prior-authorisation/> accessed 1 November 2022.
[81] Information Regulator, Guidenacne note on Direct Marketing (acccessed at guidance-note-on-direct-marketing-in-terms-of-the-protection-of-personal-information-act-4-of-2013-popia.pdf).

Of Personal Information of Voters and The Countering of Misinformation and Disinformation During Elections.[82]

Section 105 of POPIA specifically defines account numbers and provides that responsible parties need to obtain prior authorization if they intend to process the account number. An account number for the purposes of sections 105 and 106 of POPIA means a unique identifier that has been assigned to one data subject only or jointly to more than one data subject, by a financial or other institution which enables the data subject to access funds or credit facilities, or to access joint funds or joint credit facilities. Examples of unique identifiers include a bank account number, policy number, identity number, employee number, student number, telephone number, mobile phone number, or reference number.[83] Any unlawful processing thereof would be criminal and subject to criminal prosecution and sanctions. In addition, section 72 prescribes that personal information about a data subject may not be transferred to a third party in a foreign country, unless the recipient of the data in the foreign country is subject to a law, binding corporate rules, or a binding agreement that provides an adequate level of protection of personal information. The principles in that country should be substantially similar to the conditions for lawful processing of personal information that apply in South Africa.[84]

Laws which protect consumers in South Africa also protect their personal data. The Consumer Protection Act[85] (CPA) protects the consumer's right to privacy by regulating how suppliers and service providers process consumers' contact details for the purposes of direct marketing. Section 11 of the CPA provides that the right of every person to privacy includes the right to refuse to accept, require another person to discontinue, or in the case of an approach other than in person, to pre-emptively block, any approach or communication to that person, if the approach or communication is primarily for the purpose of direct marketing. With the entry into full effect of POPIA, the CPA provisions on direct marketing can be read in line with section 69 of POPIA.

[82] Information Regulator, Guidenacne note on Guidance Note on The Processing Of Personal Information of Voters and The Countering Of Misinformation And Disinformation During Elections (acccessed inforegulator.org.za/wp-content/uploads/2020/07/final-guidance-note-on-the-processing-of-personal-information-of-voters-and-the-countering-of-misinformation-and-disinformation-during-elections.pdf).

[83] Guidance Note on Prior Authorisation, p 5.

[84] Makulilo (n 7) 179.

[85] Consumer Protection Act 68 of 2008.

6.3.2. The Rights of a Data Subject

POPIA has put in place a set of rights which protect data subjects as well as their personal information. POPIA defines a 'data subject' as the person to whom personal information relates. It defines 'personal information' as information relating to an identifiable, living, natural person, and where it is applicable, an identifiable, existing 'juristic' or legal person. This definition for personal information is unique to South Africa as it extends to juristic persons (companies, partnerships, joint ventures, close corporations, etc.). Since POPIA is relatively new, it remains to be seen how juristic persons will be able to rely on its provisions to protect their personal information.

The rights of a data subject are clearly set out in section 5 of POPIA and are considered as the consequences of the broader right to privacy. These rights include the right to be notified of the processing of their personal information, the right to access, correct, or delete records of their personal information, the right to object to the processing of their personal information, including for direct marketing purposes, and the right to submit complaints to the Information Regulator. In terms of section 5, a data subject has the right to have his, her, or its personal information processed in accordance with the conditions for the lawful processing of personal information as referred to in chapter 3 of POPIA. Section 5(a)(i) and (ii) provide that a data subject has the right to be notified that personal information about him, her, or it is being collected as well as the right to know when his or her or its personal information has been accessed or acquired by an unauthorized person as provided for in terms of sections 18 and 23. Section 5(b) goes further in affording the data subject the right to establish whether a responsible party holds personal information of that data subject and to request the responsible party access to his, her or its personal information as provided for in terms of section 23.[86]

Section 5(c) and (d) guarantee the data subject the right to request, where necessary, the correction, destruction or deletion of his, her, or its personal information as provided for in terms of section 24 and also confer upon a data subject the right to object, on reasonable grounds relating to his, her, or its particular situation, to the processing of his, her, or its personal information as provided for in terms of section 11(3)(a).[87] In addition to the above, a data subject has the right to object to the processing of his, her, or its personal information

[86] Papadopoulos and Snail, *Cyberlaw @ SA IV: The Law of the Internet in South Africa* (3rd edn, 2021) 355.
[87] ibid.

at any time for the purposes of direct marketing, in terms of section 11(3)(b) or, alternatively, in terms of section 69(3)(c). The latter section provides that a data subject has the right to object to having his, her or its personal information processed for purposes of direct marketing by means of unsolicited electronic communications, except as referred to in section 69(1) as provided for by section 5(e) and (f).[88] The Information Regulator has prepared several forms which can be completed and submitted by data subjects to exercise their rights, such as the right to objection to processing of personal information or the right to correct or delete personal information.[89]

Lastly, a data subject has the right to submit a complaint to the Information Regulator regarding the alleged interference with the protection of the personal information of any data subject, or to submit a complaint to the Information Regulator in respect of a determination of an adjudicator as provided in terms of section 74 of POPIA. According to the Information Regulator Annual Report 2021–22, its POPIA Division investigated and finalized 229 out of 544 complaints received.[90] Moreover, a data subject may institute civil proceedings regarding the alleged interference with the protection of his, her or its personal information as provided for in sections 9 and 5(h) and (i).

6.3.3. Exclusions and Exemptions to the Application of POPIA

POPIA completely excluded certain information from its scope and most of the exclusions are like those found in the EUDPD and GDPR.[91] The first exclusion relates to personal information that has been de-identified to the extent that it cannot relate to any person.[92] De-identification can be difficult to achieve, and 'in order to meet a sufficient standard of de-identification there must be no "reasonably foreseeable" method to re-identify the data subject'.[93] The second exclusion relates to processing of personal information in the course of a purely personal or household activity.[94] The third exclusion applies to processing of personal information by or on behalf of a public body if the processing involves national security, identifying financing for terrorism,

[88] Van der Merwe and others, *Information Communication Technology Laws* (Lexis Nexis 2016) 465.
[89] The forms can be accessed at <https://inforegulator.org.za/popia-forms/>.
[90] Information Regulator Annual Report 2021–22, pp 23–24. The full report is available at <https://www.inforegulator.org.za/wp-content/uploads/2022/10/Info%20Regulator%20Annual%20Report%202021-22-compressed.pdf>.
[91] Makulilo (n 7) 205.
[92] POPIA s 6(1)(b).
[93] De Stadler and others (n 17) 90.
[94] POPIA s 6(1)(a).

defence, or public safety, or if the processes involve crime prevention and detection thereof, money laundering, and other criminal investigations and prosecutions.[95] Fourthly, cabinet, its committees and the executive council of a province, as well as a court when performing its judicial functions, are excluded from the scope of POPIA.[96]

The final exclusion refers to journalistic, literary, or artistic expression as contained in section 7, which inter alia states that 'this Act does not apply to the processing of personal information solely for the purpose of journalistic, literary, or artistic expression to the extent that such an exclusion is necessary to reconcile, as a matter of public interest, the right to privacy with the right to freedom of expression'. In clarifying the provision regarding journalistic exclusion, the recent case of *Els and Another v eMedia Investments (Pty) Ltd*,[97] which dealt with an application to interdict a TV show based on infringements of POPIA, the court held that:

> The test in section 7 is similar to that for considering an ordinary claim for a right to privacy . . . the balancing exercise required under section 7 of POPIA between the respective rights of privacy and freedom of expression appears to be the same under POPIA as it would for an ordinary claim of a right to privacy . . . It might be assumed that these competing rights weigh evenly on the scale.

Journalists in South Africa are bound by a Code of Ethics.[98] Section 4 of this code requires the media to take reasonable steps to ensure that the personal information under their control is protected from misuse, loss, and unauthorized access[99] and to ensure that personal information they gather is accurate and reasonably complete and up to date.[100] The media are also required to take steps to verify the accuracy of their information and, if necessary, to amend it where a person requests a correction to be made to his or her personal information.[101] Further, the media shall only disclose sufficient personal information to identify the person being reported on[102] and to inform the affected person and take reasonable steps to mitigate any prejudicial effects where it

95 POPIA s 6(1)(c).
96 POPIA s 6(1)(d)–(e).
97 (25902/2021) [2024] ZAGPJHC 1164 (19 November 2024).
98 Code of Ethics and Conduct for South African Print and Online Media.
99 ibid section 4.1.
100 ibid section 4.2.
101 ibid section 4.3.
102 ibid section 4.4.

is reasonably suspected that an unauthorized person may have obtained access to personal information held by the media.[103] The provisions of the Code of Ethics cover some of the POPIA conditions for lawful processing of personal information. However, it remains to be seen if the Code of Ethics is adequate.[104] It is submitted that public interest should not override the lawful processing of personal information.

6.3.4. Protection of Personal Data Beyond Borders

It is important to distinguish between simply routing electronic information through one country on its way to another (which is usually the case for e-mail as it transitions across servers) and actual transfer of information so that it can be processed in another country. The GDPR provides that 'A transfer of personal data to a third country or an international organisation may take place where the Commission has decided that the third country, a territory or one or more specified sectors within that third country, or the international organisation in question ensures an adequate level of protection. Such a transfer shall not require any specific authorisation'.[105] Section 72 of POPIA was specifically included in view of these requirements and, to a large extent, mirrors the language of the GDPR. Section 72 states that a responsible party may not transfer personal information about a data subject to a third party who is in a foreign country unless the third party who is the recipient of the information is subject to a law, binding corporate rules, or binding agreement which provide an adequate level of protection. Such law or binding rules must also in terms of section 72(1) of POPIA effectively uphold the principles for reasonable processing of the information that are substantially similar to the conditions for the lawful processing of personal information relating to a data subject. In addition, in terms of section 72(2) of POPIA such responsible party and or operator/controller must also adhere to the laws in that foreign country that are substantially similar to the POPIA which relate to cross-border sharing of personal information.

Although the provision itself is rather brief, it is submitted that it remains one of the most important provisions in POPIA, in that the advent of information brokerage and operators within the meaning of POPIA being a global

[103] ibid section 4.4.
[104] De Stadler and others (n 33) 97.
[105] GDPR art 45(1).

phenomenon, the protection of the personal information of persons within the South African jurisdiction is pertinent.[106]

Transfer of personal information outside of South Africa is permitted under five grounds. First, a responsible party in the Republic may not transfer personal information about a data subject to a third party who is in a foreign country unless the third party who is the recipient of the information is subject to a law, binding corporate rules or binding agreement which provide an adequate level of protection that (i) effectively upholds principles for reasonable processing of information that are substantially similar to the conditions for the lawful processing of personal information and (ii) includes provisions, that are substantially similar to this section, relating to the further transfer of personal information from the recipient to third parties who are in a foreign country.[107] The key to allowing the flow of personal information across borders is in taking cognizance of and keeping within the bounds of the eight conditions for lawful processing of personal information.[108] Unlike the GDPR, which empowers the European Commission to make 'adequacy decisions', POPIA does not empower the Information Regulator with similar powers.[109] It has been argued that it is up to a responsible party to make such an assessment.[110]

Secondly, transborder flows of personal data may also be permitted if the data subject consents to the transfer of his or her personal information to a third party within a foreign country.[111]

Thirdly, if the transfer would be necessary for the performance of a contract that exists between the responsible party and that particular data subject or for the implementation of pre-contractual measures taken in response to the data subject's request, it would be permitted.[112]

Transfer is also permitted if it is necessary for the conclusion or performance of a contract concluded in the interest of the data subject between the responsible party and a third party.[113]

Finally, transborder flow of personal information is permitted if the transfer is for the benefit of the data subject and it is not reasonably practicable to obtain consent of the data subject to that transfer, but if it were reasonably practicable to obtain such consent, the data subject would be likely to give it.[114]

106 Papadopoulos and Snail (n 28) 369.
107 POPIA s 72(1)(a).
108 POPIA s 72(1)(a)(i).
109 De Stadler and others (n 33) 429.
110 De Stadler and others (n 33) 429.
111 POPIA s 72(1)(b).
112 Makulilo (n 7) 216; POPIA s 72(1)(c).
113 POPIA s 72(1)(d).
114 POPIA s 72(1)(e).

By implication, South Africa has such requirements applicable to data processing within the country, and POPIA is the embodiment of those requirements. It focuses on the transfer of personal information beyond the borders of South Africa as it will be the duty of information processors within the compliant data processing regime that will exist in South Africa to comply when transferring personal information outside South Africa.[115] This process is ultimately a mandate of the Information Regulator, and this will likely take place in a cooperative rather than coercive spirit. It is submitted, however, that the Regulator will have coercive tools to compel compliance if necessary. The long title of POPIA specifies as part of its purpose that it is 'to regulate the flow of personal information across borders of the Republic; and to provide for matters connected therewith'.

Section 72 of POPIA, unlike the EU requirements, does not spell out and call for the rule of law, independence, respect for human rights and fundamental freedoms. The Constitution, however, being the supreme law of the land against which all legislation, including POPIA, is tried, certainly addresses this shortfall.[116] As many of the member states of the European Union perhaps do not have reasonably modern constitutions that explicitly traverse such issues, these would have had to be included in the GDPR to cover them. Within the South African context, a simple and correct reading of section 72 reveals that the flow of personal information is subject to adequate data privacy protection rules in the foreign country.[117]

6.3.5. Protection of Personal Data in the Age of AI

The twenty-first century presents challenges to human liberties in the form of automated decision-making as well as well as profiling technologies.[118] The POPIA addresses ADM and profiling techniques in section 71 under the heading 'Automated Decision Making'. A data subject has the right not to be subject, under certain circumstances, to any decision which is based solely on

[115] D Van Der Merwe and others, *Information and Communications Technology Law* (Lexis Nexis 2nd edn, 2016) 477.

[116] S 172(2)(a) of the Constitution; *Graham Robert Herbert NO and Others v Senqu Municipality and Others* [2019] ZACC 31 at 21.

[117] Van Der Merwe and others (n 115) 478.

[118] AL Alkalay, 'The Regulation of Automated Decision Making and Profiling in an era of Big Data and Ambient Intelligence: A European and South African Perspective' in Abdulraf and Dube (eds), *Data Privacy Law in Africa – Emerging Perspectives* (University of Pretoria 2024) 344.

the basis of the automated processing of his, her or its personal information intended to provide a profile of such person as provided for in terms of sections 71 and 5(g).[119] Alkalay is of the view that scholars such as Roos and Naude have misconstrued and equated 'decisions relating to automated decision making' to 'profiling', which are two distinct processes.[120] Some of the examples of profiling include profiles created to assess a data subject's performance at work, creditworthiness, reliability, location, health, personal preferences or conduct (section 71(1)).

De Stadler and others gave a good example on the application of section 71. If an organization decides to interview certain people based solely on the results achieved in an online aptitude test, that decision is an automated decision with 'legal consequence' or 'substantial degree' on a data subject.[121] Similarly, section 71 applies to a website loan application which uses algorithms and automated credit-searching to provide an immediate decision on a loan application.[122]

Section 71(1) unfortunately does not explain 'legal consequences' and 'substantial degree', nor has the Information Regulator made any decisions or issued any guidance note on the matter.[123] Section 71(2) provides an exception in the instances where a decision is taken in light of the conclusion or execution of a contract where a data subject's request has been met or where a data subject's request in terms of a contract has been met,[124] or where the matter is governed by a law or code of conduct.[125] It must be mentioned that POPIA has a deficiency when it comes to regulating Artificial Intelligence (AI) in the context of 'profiling', in that it does not define this in the context of automated decision-making, unlike the GDPR which actually defines the word profiling to include 'any form of automated processing of personal data consisting of the use of personal data to evaluate certain aspects relating to a natural person, in particular to analyse or predict aspects concerning that natural persons performance at work, economic situation, health, personal preference, interests, reliability, behaviour, location or movement' (article 4(4) of the GDPR).

119 Papadopoulos and Snail (n 28) 355.
120 Alkalay (n 118) 345.
121 De Stadler and others (n 33) 448.
122 ibid 450.
123 Alkalay (n 118) 346.
124 POPIA s 71(2)(a)(i).
125 POPIA s 71(2)(b).

6.3.6. Independence of DPA and Enforcement Mechanisms

Enforcement of POPIA falls mainly within the ambit of the powers of the Information Regulator. As mentioned above, the office of the Information Regulator is an independent body that is only accountable to Parliament and subject to the Constitution and the law of the land. Part of the independence enjoyed by the Information Regulator is to be impartial and to perform its functions and exercise its powers without fear, favour, or prejudice.[126] The rigid stance of the Information Regulator issuing Enforcement Notices and Fines against both government institutions and private institutions since 2023 is an indication of its independence similar to that of Data Protection Authorities (DPAs) of fellow BRICS countries Russia and Brazil, which have also recently issued fines. The Information Regulator enjoys financial independence by having an allocated budget for it to carry out its functions.[127] A lot of DPAs on the African continent do not have such independence as the Information Regulator. The administrative structures of the DPAs, lack of financial independence, and political influence may inhibit them from acting independently.[128] During the 2021/22 financial year, the budget allocation for the Information Regulator was increased from R 45.4 million to over R 87 million. This enabled the Regulator to recruit employees to perform core business and requisite support services.[129] In its Strategic Plan, however, the Information Regulator also indicated that the increase in the country's national debt could lead to budget cuts which will have implications for the budget of the Regulator.[130] The Information Regulator also has a body called the 'Enforcement Committee'[131] which assist the Members in considering, assessing, and investigating as well as deciding upon complaints and issuing of Enforcement Notices. The Enforcement Committee may also assist with making recommendation on fines as well as other in instances of non-compliance with the Enforcement Notice.[132] The Enforcement Committee is composed of at least 3 (three Members but not more than five members). The

[126] POPIA s 39(b).
[127] POPIA s 52.
[128] Mercy King'ori and Hunter Dorwart, 'A Look into DPA Strategies in the African Continent' (2022) 1 The Future of Privacy Forum 5–6.
[129] Information Regulator Annual Report 2021–22, p 10.
[130] Information Regulator Strategic Plan 2022/23–2026/27, p 12. Available at <https://inforegulator.org.za/strategic-reports/> accessed 1 November 2022.
[131] The terms of reference for the Enforcement Committee are available at <https://inforegulator.org.za/wp-content/uploads/2020/07/TERMS-OF-REFERENCE-FOR-THE-ENFORCEMENT-COMMITTEE.pdf> accessed on 31 October 2022.
[132] POPIA s Section 93 of POPIA.

main positions are chairperson or alternative chairperson, one member of the Regulator and three ordinary members appointed by the Regulator.

Some of the powers, duties, and functions of the Information Regulator include monitoring and enforcing compliance by public and private bodies with POPIA, handling complaints regarding the unlawful processing of personal information, etc.[133] The Information Regulator has been actively involved in keeping members of the public updated in instances of major data breaches and cyberattacks. Media statements were issued by the Information Regulator following the TransUnion data breach,[134] the Experian data breach,[135] and the Department of Justice and Constitutional Development ransomware attack.[136] More recently the Information Regulator also issued a R 5 million (USD 800,000) fine against the Department of Justice and Constitutional Development[137] and issued enforcement notices against the Dischem and its operator Grapevine,[138] the State Security Agency, IEC,[139] as well as TikTok[140] and Meta (WhatsApp).[141]

The Information Regulator has also issued several guidance notes to assist responsible parties to understand their obligations in terms of POPIA. Issued guidance notes include ones covering the processing of special personal information, the processing of personal information of children, the processing of personal information in the management and containment of Covid-19 pandemic, etc.[142]

Sections 73 to 99 of POPIA deal with possible interference with personal information and the mandatory refusal of disclosure of information in terms of PAIA. Further sections deal with complaints,[143] assessments,[144]

[133] POPIA s 40.

[134] Media statement available at <https://inforegulator.org.za/wp-content/uploads/2020/07/MEDIA-STATEMENT-The-Regulator-instructs-TransUnion-to-report-in-greater-detail-regarding-their-security-compromise.pdf> accessed 31 October 2022.

[135] Media statement available at <https://inforegulator.org.za/wp-content/uploads/2020/07/ms-20211027-Experian.pdf> accessed 31 October 2022.

[136] Media statement available at <https://inforegulator.org.za/wp-content/uploads/2020/07/ms-20210913-ITsystems.pdf> accessed 31 October 2022.

[137] Media statement available at <https://inforegulator.org.za/wp-content/uploads/2020/07/media-statement-infringement-notice-issued-to-the-department-of-justice-and-constitutional.pdf> accessed 6 November 2024.

[138] Media statement available at <https://inforegulator.org.za/wp-content/uploads/2020/07/final-media-statement-enforcement-notice-issued-to-dischem-pharmacies-ltd.pdf> accessed 6 November 2024.

[139] Media statement available at <https://inforegulator.org.za/wp-content/uploads/2020/07/Media-Invite-for-Media-Briefing-PAIA-high-profile-cases-POPIA-progress.pdf> accessed 6 November 2024.

[140] ibid.

[141] ibid.

[142] Available at <https://inforegulator.org.za/guidance-notes/> accessed 31 October 2022.

[143] POPIA ss 74–76.

[144] POPIA s 89.

the Information Regulator's powers,[145] referrals to a regulatory body,[146] pre-investigation and the settlements of complaints,[147] investigation(s) proceedings by the Information Regulator,[148] warrants,[149] legal advice communicated to clients exempted from search and seizure,[150] search and seizure,[151] information notices (decisions),[152] read together with section 94, the enforcement committee,[153] right of appeal,[154] and civil remedies.[155] A reading of the available written authorities on POPIA shows that instituting proceedings through the courts against responsible parties is an option that remains available to data subjects and that a heavy burden is placed on responsible parties to refrain from contravening the provisions of the Act through the imposition of strict liability.[156] Section 99(1) of POPIA provides that 'a data subject or, at the request of the data subject, the Regulator, may institute a civil action for damages in a court having jurisdiction against a responsible party for breach of any provision of this Act as referred to in section 73, whether or not there is intent or negligence on the part of the responsible party'. Another important consideration from this section 99 is the fact that the Information Regulator's powers and functions are extended in terms of POPIA in that it is empowered to institute action on behalf of a data subject.[157]

6.3.7. Offences, Penalties and Administrative Fines

Chapter 11 of POPIA propounds the punitive action that may be instituted on persons who violate the provisions of the Act. POPIA thus provides for an idiosyncratic manner of dealing with perpetrators, should there be an unlawful interference with protected personal information. Any person who hinders, obstructs, or unlawfully influences the Information Regulator, or any person acting on behalf of or under the direction of the Information Regulator in the

[145] POPIA s 77.
[146] POPIA s 78.
[147] POPIA ss 79–80.
[148] POPIA s 81.
[149] POPIA ss 82–85.
[150] POPIA s 86.
[151] POPIA ss 87–88.
[152] POPIA ss 90–91.
[153] POPIA ss 93–96.
[154] POPIA ss 97–98.
[155] POPIA s 99.
[156] Makulilo (n 7) 220.
[157] ibid; POPIA s 99(1).

performance of the Regulator's duties and functions under the Act, is guilty of an offence.[158]

Chapter 11 deals with offences and penalties and administrative fines against persons who hinder the functions of the Information Regulator. It deals in particular with breach of confidentiality,[159] obstruction of the execution of a warrant,[160] failure to comply with enforcement or information notices,[161] offences committed by a witness,[162] unlawful acts by a responsible party in connection with an account number,[163] and unlawful acts committed by third parties in connection with an account number.[164] POPIA thereafter specifies the penalties, the jurisdiction of the courts and administrative fines.[165] The sections contained in chapter 11 can therefore be distilled under two headings, namely offences and penalties and, secondly, administrative fines.[166] There are a number of offences specified in POPIA, which carry sanctions of the imposition of a fine or imprisonment. The Information Regulator has the autonomy in terms of section 109(1) to decide which form of sanction is appropriate given the particular circumstances of the infringement.[167] Once criminal charges have been laid against a responsible party, the Information Regulator may not impose administrative fines.[168]

6.4. Other Measures to Protect Personal Data

6.4.1. Data Localization

Unlike other BRICS countries such as Brazil, Russia, and China, South Africa has no explicit laws on data localization. The protection of the security and privacy of local personal data seems to be a reason preferred by those in support of data localization which justifies placing restrictions on the free flow of information. Some of the BRICS countries, such as South Africa and Brazil, which have being exposed to egregious cyberattacks seem to be in support of this.[169]

158 POPIA s 100.
159 POPIA s 101.
160 POPIA s 102.
161 POPIA s 103.
162 POPIA s 104.
163 POPIA s 105.
164 POPIA s 106.
165 In POPIA ss 107–109.
166 Papadopoulos and Snail (n 28) 373.
167 ibid.
168 Sizwe Snail ka Mtuze, 'The Convergence of Legislation on Cybercrime in South Africa: A Practical Approach to the Cybercrimes Act 19 of 2020 and the Protection of Personal Information Act 4 of 2013' (2022) 43(3) Obiter Law Journal 569.
169 Shanelle van der Berg, 'Data Protection in South Africa' (2021) Wits Policy Brief 2, p 6.

Some authors are of the view that data localization, like most protectionist measures, results in marginal gains for few local entrepreneurs as well as employees, as it causes significant economic harm on the other hand to small and medium and large businesses which will suffer the negative consequences of limited or lack of access to data.[170].

In 2024 the Department of Communications and Digital Technologies by way of Notice 2533 of 2024, in line with the Electronic Communications Act,[171] developed the National Data and Cloud Policy (the Data and Cloud Policy). The Data and Cloud Policy seeks to enable a pathway for citizens to derive social economic value out of data so that they can participate in an inclusive digital economy.[172] The policy also sets out certain benefits that South Africa as a country will experience from such as enhanced data security as required by POPIA, including digital transformation, improved public service delivery, and economic growth collaboration.[173] The Data and Cloud Policy also makes important policy interventions on matters relating to digital infrastructure, access to data and cloud services, creating a digital trust environment, cross-border data transfers and data sovereignty, capacity development, competition in the data and cloud market, as well as research and development.[174]

6.4.2. Protection of Critical Infrastructure and Critical Data

Beyond the legal frameworks directly focused on protecting personal information, there are other architectures in South Africa which indirectly contribute to the protection of personal data. These architectures are mainly targeted at ensuring that government entities, particularly ministries, departments, and agencies (MDAs) (like social security, healthcare, identification, law enforcement) which are responsible for processing large amounts of personal data have additional security safeguards in place to protect personal data. For example, the objective of the recently adopted Critical Infrastructure Protection Act[175] (CIP Act) is to secure critical infrastructure against threats,[176] ensure that information pertaining to security measures applicable to critical infrastructure

[170] Kholofelo Kruger, 'The Impact of Data Localization Laws on Trade in Africa' (2022) Wits Policy Brief 8, p 3.
[171] Act No 36 of 2005.
[172] Data and Cloud Policy (2024) 9.
[173] ibid 11.
[174] ibid 18–31.
[175] The Critical Infrastructure Protection Act 8 of 2019.
[176] CIP Act s 2(a).

remains confidential, subject to PAIA or any other Act of Parliament that provides for the lawful disclosure of information.[177]

The CIP Act does not define critical infrastructure, but instead it gives a guideline on how to classify infrastructure as critical infrastructure. Section 16(2) of the CIP Act provides that infrastructure qualifies as critical infrastructure if the functioning of such infrastructure is essential for the economy, national security, public safety, and the provision of basic public services; and the loss, damage, disruption, or immobilization of such infrastructure may severely prejudice the functioning or stability of the Republic, the public interest with regard to safety, and the maintenance of law and order and national security. Section 16(2) of the CIP Act further provides other factors that can be considered to determine if an infrastructure qualifies as critical infrastructure. Some of the factors are that the infrastructure must be of significant economic, public, social, or strategic importance, and the interruption of a service rendered by the infrastructure will have a significant effect on the health or safety of the public. Government departments such as the Department of Health or the Department of Home Affairs process vast amounts of personal information and sensitive personal information. These departments benefit from additional protection afforded under the CIP which is aimed at securing critical infrastructure against threats.

Data infrastructures that have been declared as critical infrastructure are required to have in place security measures, including cybersecurity measures, which secure the infrastructures. Adoption of risk management tools to identify vulnerabilities, and to assess, mitigate, and resolve these vulnerabilities should be central to the effective protection of critical infrastructures.

6.5. Protection of Data from Cybercriminals

It is not a surprise that South Africa is among the top African countries that have been the target of cyberattacks in recent years. Between 1994 and 2016, more than fifty-four cyberincidents were reported, with some incidents involving hacking of the South African Police Service (SAPS), the state's Government Communication and Information System, and major telecommunications providers.[178] These cyberattacks can cripple businesses and the economy. In addition the Cybercrime Act, South Africa is seen as one of the

177 CIP Act s 2(b).
178 Snail (n 21) 537.

BRICS countries that has proactive data security legislation. Brazil has seemingly made better progress than South Africa. India, although one of the first BRICS countries to pass legislation criminalizing cybercrime, has unfortunately lagged behind in recent time when it comes to aspects of data security and cyber security laws. Unlike China, South Africa does not have an advanced and multilayered approach to the cybercrimes and cybersecurity regulation with the aim of securing personal data and national security.

To respond to the growing spectre of cyber threats, the South African government has promulgated laws which provide certain protections to data and data infrastructures by criminalizing those who may try to access data unlawfully. Most of these laws carry heavy criminal sanctions against any unlawful access or interference with data, which may act as a deterrent to cybercriminals. These laws also promote cooperation between the private sector and law enforcement as well as cybersecurity training as ways to equip those who will be responsible for implementing these laws.

In addition to laws regulating personal data and critical data, the law also criminalizes any unlawful access, interference, or interception of data, computer programs, computer systems, and computer data storage medium. The recently passed Cybercrimes Act criminalizes all forms of cybercrime and cyber-related offences on data and data architectures.

Some of the objectives of the Cybercrimes Act include creating offences which have a bearing on cybercrime, to criminalize the disclosure of data messages which are harmful, to provide for interim protection orders, etc.[179] Part I of chapter 2 of the Cybercrimes Act criminalizes cybercrimes such as unlawful access, unlawful interception of data, unlawful acts in respect of software or hardware tools, unlawful interference with computer data storage media or computer systems, unlawful acquisition, possession, provision, receipt, or use of passwords, access codes or similar data or devices, cyber fraud, cyber forgery and uttering, cyber extortion, and theft of incorporeal property.[180] Part II of the Act criminalizes malicious communications such as data messages which incite damage to property or violence, data messages which threaten persons with damage to property or violence, and disclosure of data messages of intimate images.[181] The crime of disclosure of a data message of intimate image is popularly known as revenge pornography.[182] Part III of

[179] Cybercrimes Act, Preamble.
[180] Cybercrimes Act ss 2–12.
[181] Cybercrimes Act ss 14–16.
[182] The term 'revenge porn', also known as non-consensual pornography/involuntary pornography, involves the distribution of sexually graphic images of an individual where at least one of the individuals

the Act criminalizes any attempting, conspiring, aiding, abetting, inducing, inciting, instigating, instructing, commanding, or procuring to commit an offence.[183]

The prevalence of cybercrimes such as hacking[184] poses a threat to personal data, government data, business data, and critical data. Hacking is becoming increasingly sophisticated and user-friendly due to the affordability and easy access of hacking tools. With the increase in the use of various botnets for hacking,[185] data and data infrastructures are constantly under threat. The growth of botnet hacking is troublesome for both government and business due to the unlimited number of cyberattacks which can be launched.[186]

Cybercrimes which target the DNS infrastructure, websites, and data infrastructures are also criminalized in South Africa. Ransomware attacks, denial of service attacks and distributed denial of service (DDoS) attacks are also cyberattacks which threaten data and data architectures. Ransomware attacks pose a great security threat because they can incapacitate the core business functions of a system.[187] As the name suggests, a ransomware attack is an attack motivated by money, as the criminals are interested in extorting money from their victims. Recently South Africa's major city of Johannesburg was subjected to a ransomware attack. The criminals managed to access public-facing data which resulted in the city suspending its online services.[188] There are other emerging cybercrimes which can immobilize computers

depicted did not consent to the dissemination. Melody Musoni, 'The Criminalization of "Revenge Porn" in South Africa' (2019) 41 Obiter Law Journal 61, 62.

[183] Cybercrimes Act s 17.

[184] Hacking is defined as gaining unauthorized access to a computer system, programs, or data. Fernando M Pinguelo and Bradford W Muller, 'Virtual Crimes, Real Damages: a Primer on Cybercrimes in the United States and Efforts to Combat Cybercriminals' (2011) 16 Virginia Journal of Law and Technology 116, 132.

[185] Botnets are collections of software agents that run automatically to commandeer massive numbers of computers to allow cybercriminals to conduct large-scale malicious activity including spreading spam, stealing log-in credentials and personal information, or distributing malware to others. Ibid.

[186] Pinguelo and Muller (n 184) 133.

[187] Aaron Zimba and Mumbi Chishimba, 'On the Economic Impact of Crypto-Ransomware Attacks: the State of the Art on Enterprise Systems' (2019) 4 European Journal for Security Research 3.

[188] Shortly after the city of Johannesburg was subjected to ransomware attacks, most South African banks were also subjected to a similar attack: South African Banking Risk Information Centre (SABRIC) report. The Johannesburg attacks started with a ransom note which was delivered via email to both unattended as well as staff e-mail addresses, all of which were publicly available: Malibongwe Dayimani, Soyiso Maliti, and Genevieve Quintal, 'SA Now Hostage to Cyber Ransom' *Sunday Dispatch* (26 October 2019) 5. In July 2019, City Power came under a ransomware attack that prevented thousands of prepaid customers from buying electricity. Shaun Smillie, 'Hackers Hold City, Banks to "Ransom"' *Saturday Star* (26 October 2019).

and computer networks. One good example is the crime of crypto-jacking, which presented itself when more people started cryptocurrency trading and crypto-mining. Crypto-jacking is the unauthorized use of someone else's computer to mine cryptocurrency. Due to the high computing power required for crypto-mining, hackers employ different tactics to launch the crypto-mining code on unsuspecting victims. The result of crypto-jacking is the victim's computing power slows down and they are unable to effectively carry out their own activities.

Considering some of the above-mentioned cybercrime activities, the Cybercrimes Act has defined criminal acts broadly, potentially covering all types of cybercrime activity relating to data and data infrastructure. Section 2 of the Cybercrimes Act provides that:

(a) Any person who unlawfully and intentionally access a computer system or a computer data storage medium, is guilty of an offence.
(b) For purposes of paragraph (a)—
  (i) A person accesses a computer data storage medium, if the person—
    (aa) uses data or a computer program stored on a computer data storage medium; or
    (bb) stored data or a computer program on a computer data storage medium; and
  (ii) a person accesses a computer system, if the person—
    (aa) uses data or a computer program held in a computer system;
    (bb) stores data or a computer program on a computer data storage medium forming a part of the computer system; or
    (cc) instructs, communicates with, or otherwise uses, the computer system.[189]

Section 3 of the Cybercrimes Act criminalizes the unlawful and intentional interception of data including electromagnetic emissions from a computer system carrying such data, within or which is transmitted to or from a computer system.[190] It is an offence for any person to unlawfully and intentionally possess data or the output of data, with the knowledge that such data was intercepted unlawfully as contemplated in section 3(1) of the Cybercrimes Act.[191]

189 Cybercrimes Act s 2.
190 Cybercrimes Act s 3(1).
191 Cybercrimes Act s 3(2).

The Cybercrimes Act defines 'interception of data' as the acquisition, viewing, capturing, or copying of data of a non-public nature through the use of a hardware or software tool or any other means, so as to make some or all of the data available to a person, other than the lawful owner or holder of the data, the sender or the recipient or the intended recipient of that data and includes the examination or inspection of the contents of the data and diversion of the data or any part thereof from its intended destination to any other destination.[192]

Similar provisions on unlawful access to data are contained in the Council of Europe Convention on Cybercrime (the Budapest Convention). Article 2 of the Budapest Convention provides that 'Each party shall adopt such legislative and other measures as may be necessary to establish as criminal offences under its domestic law, when committed intentionally, the access to the whole or any part of a computer system without right. A party may require that the offence be committed by infringing security measures, with the intent of obtaining data or other dishonest intent, or in relation to a computer system that is connected to another system'. The Budapest Convention also criminalizes the illegal interception of computer data under article 3.[193]

Any unlawful and intentional interference with data or a computer program is an offence.[194] Interference with data or a computer program means to permanently or temporarily delete data or a computer program, alter data or a computer program, render vulnerable, damage or deteriorate data or a computer program, render data or a computer program meaningless, useless or ineffective, obstruct, interrupt or interfere with the lawful use of data or a computer program, or deny access to data or a computer program held in a computer data storage medium or a computer system'.[195] Similarly, section 6 of the Cybercrimes Act criminalizes the unlawful and intentional interference with a computer data storage medium or a computer system. Interference with a computer data storage medium or a computer system means to permanently or temporarily alter any resource, or interrupt or impair the functioning, the confidentiality, the integrity and availability of a computer data storage medium or a computer system.[196] It has been noted that the wider definition

[192] Cybercrimes Act s 3(4).

[193] 'Each party shall adopt such legislative and other measures as may be necessary to establish as criminal offences under its domestic law, when committed intentionally, the interception without right, made by technical means, of non-public transmissions of computer data to, from or within a computer system, including electromagnetic emissions from a computer system carrying such computer data. A party may require that the offence be committed with dishonest intent, or in relation to a computer system that is connected to another computer system'. Art 3 of the Cybercrime Convention.

[194] Cybercrimes Act s 5(1).

[195] Cybercrimes Act s 5(2).

[196] Cybercrimes Act s 6(2).

of interference will ensure legal certainty for the courts when dealing with cyberinterferences of various nature.[197]

In order to unlawfully access any data, criminals usually make use of hacking tools which can be software tools, hardware tools, and passwords and access codes. The Cybercrimes Act criminalizes the intentional use and possession of any software or hardware tools for the purposes of unlawfully accessing, intercepting, and interfering with data.[198] It also criminalizes the unlawful acquisition, possession, provision, receipt or use of passwords, access codes, or similar data or device.[199] Most hackers either possess or use hacking tools to unlawfully access computer systems and networks without authorization. Closely related to possession of hacking tools is the offence of unlawfully and intentionally acquiring, possessing, providing to another person, or using a password, an access code, or similar data or device for purposes of contravening the provisions of sections 2(1) or (2), 3(1), 5(1), 6(1), 8, or 9(1).[200] Password, access code, or similar data or device includes a secret code or pin, an image, a security token, an access card, any device, biometric data, or a word or a string of characters or numbers used for financial transactions or user authentication in order to access or use data, a computer program, a computer data storage medium or a computer system.[201] Any person using digital technologies needs to be careful as it is prima facie immaterial whether unlawful software or hardware tools in one's possession are subject to unlawful use by another.[202]

Apart from the Cybercrimes Act, hacking is also criminalized under the Regulation of Interception of Communications and Provision of Communication-Related Information Act (RICA Act).[203] Section 2 of the RICA Act provides that no person may intentionally intercept or attempt to intercept or authorize, or procure any other person to intercept or to attempt, at any place in the Republic, any communication in the course of its occurrence or transmission. Snail argues that attempting to intercept or monitor a data communication unlawfully is as sanctionable as actually doing it.[204] However lawful grounds of justification do apply, such as necessity, private defence, lawful interception, consent, court order, or interception directive.[205]

[197] Snail (n 28) 549.
[198] Cybercrimes Act s 4.
[199] Cybercrimes Act s 7.
[200] Cybercrimes Act s 7(1).
[201] Cybercrimes Act s 7(3).
[202] Snail (n 6) 548.
[203] Regulation of Interception of Communications and Provision of Communication-Related Information Act 70 of 2002.
[204] Sizwe Snail, 'Cybercrime in the Context of the ECT Act' (2008) JBL 63.
[205] ibid.

Ransomware attacks are criminalized under the Cybercrimes Act. Cyberextortion is a crime under South African law. Cyberextortion happens when a person commits or threatens to commit any offence contemplated in sections 3(1), 5(1), 6(1), or 7(1)(a) or (d) of the Cybercrimes Act for the purpose of obtaining any advantage from another person or compelling another person to perform or to abstain from performing any act.[206] Section 3(1) of the Cybercrimes Act provides that any person who unlawfully and intentionally intercepts data is guilty of an offence. Section 5(1) of the Cybercrimes Act provides any person who unlawfully and intentionally interferes with data or a computer program is guilty of an offence. It is also an offence to unlawfully and intentionally interfere with a computer data storage medium or a computer system.[207]

6.5.1. How Effective are these Cybersecurity Measures?

Whilst the CIP Act creates an enabling environment for effective protection of critical data infrastructures, the challenge with this act is one of implementation. The CIP Act establishes the Critical Infrastructure Council, which consists of the Secretary of Police Service together with officials from the Department of Defence, Department of Home Affairs, Department of Public Works, National Disaster Management Centre, South African Local Government Association, SAPS, and State Security Agency.[208] The Council's expenses and remuneration are defrayed from the budget allocation of the Civilian Secretariat for the Police Service.[209] This can potentially create budgetary constraints which may affect the proper execution of the duties of the Council. South Africa's criminal justice system is already under immense pressure due to a plethora of reasons, including a lack of financial resources to investigate crimes. To defray a budget from the police will likely worsen the current situation. The result may be that crimes committed against critical infrastructure may not be properly investigated or prosecuted.

Some of the goals of the NCPF are to coordinate the promotion of cybersecurity measures by all role players in relation to cybersecurity threats, through interaction with and in conjunction with the Cybersecurity Hub, and strengthening intelligence collection, investigation, prosecution, and judicial

[206] Cybercrimes Act s 10.
[207] Cybercrimes Act s 6.
[208] CIP Act s 4(2).
[209] CIP Act s 6.

processes, in respect of preventing and addressing cybercrime, cyberterrorism and cyber warfare, and establishing public–private partnerships for national and action plans in line with the NCPF.[210] Whilst this solution is commendable, one should note that it is a long-term goal which is likely to take a considerable time for upskilling all police officers to enable them to deal with cybercrime cases.

The ratification and implementation of the African Union Convention on Cyber Security and Protection of Data (Malabo Convention) heralds a significant potential for bolstering intra-continental collaboration concerning cybersecurity. The Malabo Convention, in its article 28, strongly advocates for State Parties to establish specialized institutions, like Computer Emergency Response Teams (CERTs and CSIRTs), fostering the exchange of crucial information on cyber threats and vulnerability assessments. In concurrence with this, the Lome Declaration of 2022 reinforces this imperative, advocating for the establishment and effective operation of dedicated agencies, governance structures, teams, and networks, aimed at combatting cybercrime and fortifying cybersecurity. Furthermore, it emphasizes the urgency of capacity building in cybersecurity through these measures.

A pivotal advance advocated by the African Union is the formulation of an AU Cyber Security Strategy, accompanied by the establishment of Operational Cybersecurity Centres. This strategic approach aims to mitigate the manifold risks associated with cyberattacks, data breaches, and the misuse of sensitive information within the continent. In addition to the AU's initiatives, external entities like Smart Africa have launched the Network of African Cyber Security Authorities (NACSA), geared towards fostering the exchange of knowledge, experience, and best practices in cybersecurity across African nations. Further augmenting these efforts are pan-African initiatives such as the Network of African Women in Cybersecurity, focusing on bolstering cyber capacity among women in this domain. These collective endeavours signify a concerted effort to fortify cybersecurity across the African continent.

At a more global level, the International Telecommunications Union's (ITU) Global Cybersecurity Agenda High-Level Expert Group (HLEG) also emphasized the importance of collaborative work to enhance security procedures and technical measures. The ITU was identified as a global centre of excellence for the collection and distribution of timely telecommunications/ICT cybersecurity-related information, including a publicly available institutional

[210] NCPF p 71.

ecosystem of sources to enhance cybersecurity capabilities worldwide.[211] Part of this cooperation includes collaborating in the development of materials for establishing national CSIRTs and for effectively communicating with CSIRT authorities. The Global Forum on Cyber Expertise (GFCE) has collaborated with AUDA-NEPAD to enhance cyber capacity building and improving cyber resilience within AU member states. A GFCE Africa Hub was founded and it is a platform that is bringing together different stakeholders to build local capacity, promote cybersecurity awareness, and develop solutions to counter cyber threats.

Cybersecurity measures adopted in South Africa under both the Cybercrimes Act and the CIP Act face the challenge of implementation. The SAPS lacks digital expertise to identify, investigate and gather electronic evidence relating to cyberattacks and cybercrimes. What is commendable about the CIP Act is the encouragement and promotion of cooperation between the SAPS and the private sector. Similarly, section 34 of the Cybercrimes Act requires electronic communications service providers and financial institutions to provide technical assistance or any other assistance as may be reasonably necessary to a police official or an investigator. The NCPF[212] also noted the importance of capacity-building through upskilling the police with relevant skillsets to deal with cybercrime.[213] Despite South Africa's engagement in numerous national, regional, continental, and international capacity-building initiatives, these endeavours are still in their infancy. While the recent implementation of the Malabo Convention is a significant milestone, many nations have yet to establish robust cybersecurity strategies and enact essential cybercrime legislation. The absence of a comprehensive legal framework poses substantial hurdles in cultivating a cybersecurity culture and ensuring the safeguarding of critical infrastructure. Moreover, the uneven adoption and execution of data protection laws in specific regions contribute to the overall underdeveloped state of cybersecurity.

Looking ahead, South Africa must intensify its collaborative efforts with both international and local stakeholders to enhance capacity-building

[211] Report of the Chairman of HLEG, ITU Global Cybersecurity Agenda (GCA) High-Level Expert Group (HLEG).

[212] The NCPF provides that 'a cybercrime strategy would nevertheless need to ensure that the forensic capabilities be created that are necessary to analyse electronic evidence in relation to any crime, or that all law enforcement officers, prosecutors and judges are provided at least with basic skills in this respect'. NCPF GN 39475 4 December 2015, 71.

[213] Lack of skilled LEA is not only common in South Africa but is prevalent in other countries. Research study conducted in Nigeria pointed out that the Nigerian government is not well equipped with sophisticated hardware to track down cybercriminals. AC Onuora and others, 'The Challenges of Cybercrime in Nigeria: An Overview' (2017) AIPFU Journal of School of Sciences 1, 4.

programmes. This entails the development of more extensive outreach initiatives and community-level engagements or partnerships. Efforts should also be directed towards bolstering support for civil society organizations engaged in cybersecurity and capacity-building while encouraging the private sector to actively participate in supporting initiatives aimed at enhancing cybersecurity capacity.

6.6. Conclusion

South Africa's legislative environment provides stringent protection of different types of data and data architectures. POPIA is an important piece of legislation which provides a reasonably effective framework for the protection of personal information processed by private and public bodies. POPIA has in place minimum conditions which must be met before the processing of personal information to ensure that personal information is processed lawfully. This protects the privacy and interests of the data subjects. The enforcement mechanisms put in place under the POPIA are aimed at ensuring that the personal information of data subjects is lawfully processed, and non-compliance carries penalties.

The Information Regulator, as the data protection regulatory body, plays a significant role in monitoring and enforcing compliance with POPIA. The Information Regulator has been actively involved in notifying members of the public about actions taken by responsible parties during major cyberattacks and data breaches that have recently happened. Actions taken against public entities like the SAPS demonstrate the commitment and independence of the Information Regulator. However, due to budget constraints and limited human resources,[214] it remains to be seen if the Information Regulator will be able to effectively and sufficiently provide protection to all data subjects whose personal information may be unlawfully processed. The recent appointment of the Enforcement Committee is an indication that the Information Regulator is taking data protection matters seriously. Further, the inclusion of South Africa on the adequacy list from Botswana[215] is also significant in demonstrating that foreign states view POPIA as an adequate law.

[214] Melody Musoni, 'Challenges to POPIA Compliance and Enforcement' (2021) <https://www.ppmattorneys.co.za/popia-compliance/> accessed 31 October 2022.

[215] Melody Musoni, 'Africa: The State of Cross-Border Transfer of Personal Data in the SADC Region' (2022) Data Guidance < https://www.dataguidance.com/opinion/africa-state-cross-border-transfer-personal-data> accessed 31 October 2022.

South African laws also protects personal data, non-personal data, and data infrastructure from cybercriminality. The Cybercrimes Act, though a relatively new law, plays a central role in criminalizing any unlawful access, unlawful interception, and unlawful interference with data, computer networks, and computer storage media. By criminalizing various activities involving data, there are assurances and public trust that personal data and non-personal data will be protected and any unlawful activities involving such data will be met with criminal sanctions.

Similarly, the Critical Infrastructure Protection Act is another important law which protects data and data infrastructure. The CIP Act criminalizes the unauthorized access to critical infrastructure. Where data or data infrastructure is classified as critical infrastructure, such data enjoys additional protections provided for in terms of the CIP Act. The heavy criminal sanctions in terms of the Cybercrimes Act and the CIP Act will likely deter criminals from committing such crimes. However, due to a lack of skilled police officers and cybercrime investigators to conduct investigations and lawfully obtain electronic evidence, which is admissible in a court of law, these criminal laws may not be effective.

Finally, recent developments on data policy frameworks need to be explored in detail. Examples of these frameworks include South Africa's National Cloud and Data Policy or the African Union Data Policy Framework. It is imperative that as rules and guidance on data governance are developed, data protection principles as set out in data protection laws should be promoted.

7
FOSTERING SUSTAINABLE DATA FLOWS IN THE BRICS COUNTRIES: TOWARDS A GLOBAL FRAMEWORK FOR DATA GOVERNANCE

Luca Belli, Walter Britto Gaspar, and Pablo Andres Palazzi

7.1. Introduction

This book has explored a wide range of issues regarding the emerging data architectures of the BRICS members. Each of these countries has built or considerably restructured its national data protection framework over the past five years, taking inspiration from similar models and engaging in several types of legal transplants, but also introducing important elements of innovation. Particularly, Russia and South Africa, having been the first two BRICS countries to legislate on the matter, have drawn strong inspiration from the 'classic' European model, while Brazil, China, and India can be seen as latecomers, thus having had the time to introduce more original and novel elements in their systems.[1]

China and India, particularly, have introduced the highest level of innovation in their regulatory models, which are amongst the most recent and the most original in the realm of data protection laws, as will be discussed in the forthcoming sections. Possible hypotheses for their willingness to develop an

[1] Luca Belli, 'New Data Architectures in Brazil, China, and India: From Copycats to Innovators, towards a Post-Western Model of Data Governance' (2022) 18 Indian Journal of Law and Technology 1 <https://www.ijlt.in/journal/new-data-architectures-in-brazil%2C-china%2C-and-india%3A-from-copycats-to-innovators%2C-towards-a-post-western-model-of-data-governance> accessed 7 March 2023.

Luca Belli, Walter Britto Gaspar, and Pablo Andres Palazzi, *Fostering Sustainable Data Flows in the BRICS Countries: Towards a Global Framework for Data Governance* In: *Personal Data Architectures in the BRICS Countries*. Edited by: Luca Belli and Walter Britto Gaspar, Oxford University Press. © Luca Belli and Walter B. Gaspar 2025. DOI: 10.1093/9780198974468.003.0007

original model are intrinsic characteristics of these two countries, besides the specific traditions and characteristics of their legal systems. For instance, their size might exempt these countries from being guided by external pressures and demands regarding their data protection choices, thus allowing them to enjoy greater leeway to craft their regulations more independently. Hence, the main preoccupations of China and India may be meeting their internal demands and adopting their own pace, rather than regulating to keep pace with Europe. Social and political circumstances are also to be considered, such as the greater flexibility with which state actors can move and the greater coordination they enjoy, including regarding the implementation of data protection legislation.

This concluding chapter focuses on the possibilities of BRICS countries' cooperating, to foster convergence and legal interoperability regarding the regulation of personal data flows. It builds on the previous chapters' descriptions and analysis of BRICS data protection frameworks to highlight converging and diverging points, as well as innovative normative developments in BRICS jurisdictions. This is showcased in the image of a shared data protection skeleton on top of which BRICS countries can build efforts of legal interoperability, with particular focus on fostering sustainable transborder data exchanges, digital trade, and cooperation, while guaranteeing that data subjects' rights are respected and information security is fully enforced. Importantly, the chapter also considers the data protection frameworks recently adopted by the 'new' BRICS members ie Egypt, Ethiopia, Indonesia, Saudi Arabia, the United Arab Emirates, and the still emerging framework of Iran.

As it emerged in the chapters of this volume, besides convergences and space for cooperation, there are also significant gaps and divergences between the data governance models adopted by these countries. The following sections will first highlight some key points of convergence that give rise to a shared data protection skeleton that can support legal interoperability ambitions of the grouping. Subsequently the chapter examines the most innovative elements of the BRICS frameworks and to what extent they diverge. As will be stressed, the BRICS countries foresee large exceptions for governmental access to personal data, an element that should be considered carefully when crafting strategies aimed at enhancing legal interoperability. Moreover, the entry of new countries to the BRICS grouping adds a new layer of complexity, as a larger number of national idiosyncrasies needs to be considered. The careful consideration of these elements is particularly relevant to avoid that existing divergences hinder the BRICS ambitions of developing 'a global framework for data governance, including cross-border data flows, to . . . ensure the interoperability of data regulatory frameworks at all levels'.[2]

Importantly, as anticipated in Chapter 1 of this volume, the promotion of legal interoperability in data governance can be seen as a form of collective exercise of data sovereignty,[3] through the joint definition of shared regulatory strategies which can promote secure international data flows while respecting national legislation. Data sovereignty is a concept that can be defined as 'the capacity to understand how and why (personal) data are processed and by whom, develop data processing capabilities, and effectively regulate data processing, thus retaining self-determination and control'.[4] From this perspective, the elaboration of shared data governance arrangements, particularly as regards data transfers, aims at allowing multiple parties—spanning from the BRICS members to potentially all UN members—to agree upon common solutions, building meaningful transparency, enhancing accountability, and strengthening security of data processing, thus constructing a multilateral approach to data sovereignty. In fact, the establishment of shared data governance mechanisms is instrumental to extending the reach of data subjects' rights and increasing legal certainty for data controllers as well as for regulators, while promoting cooperation as regards research, development, and trade.

As will be argued in this chapter, there are multiple paths to foster legal interoperability. These span from the adoption of binding international agreements, negotiated at the international level, which can establish shared data protection standards and facilitate institutional cooperation; to the adoption of mutual adequacy decisions by national regulatory authorities, recognizing the respective frameworks of the BRICS members as equally protective; or the use of standard contractual clauses, that can be approved by regulators and incorporated in contracts to bind contractual parties to the respect of shared data governance requirements; or the mutual recognition of binding corporate rules that multinational companies generally include in their internal policies to frame data governance.

These options are not mutually exclusive and can be combined. However, the former two strategies mentioned above are considerably more complex

[2] BRICS, XVI BRICS Summit, Kazan Declaration 'Strengthening Multilateralism for Just Global Development and Security' (Kazan, Russia, 23 October 2024), para 71 <https://dirco.gov.za/xvi-brics-summit-kazan-declaration-strengthening-multilateralism-for-just-global-development-and-security-kazan-russian-federation-23-october-2024/>.

[3] See L Belli, WB Gaspar, and S Singh, 'Data Sovereignty and Data Transfers as Fundamental Elements of Digital Transformation: Lessons From the BRICS Countries (2024) 54 Computer Law & Security Review..

[4] ibid.

due to their bureaucratic nature, while the latter two may be much easier to implement as they rely on contractual tools, thus making them inherently more agile and easier to adopt. Aware of the existing heterogeneities and similarities amongst BRICS data protection frameworks, this chapter will provide some concrete suggestions of potential paths to be pursued to promote legal interoperability, after having discussed the main convergences and divergences of the BRICS data protection regimes.

Notably, the final part of this chapter adopts a proactive approach, distilling a set of shared principles that can be seen as the conceptual basis of both BRICS and global data governance frameworks and will emphasize that model contractual clauses are likely the most palatable and realistic option to foster a shared BRICS data governance solution. In this perspective, the final Annex to this chapter will provide a concrete proposal of Model Contractual Clauses for Data Transfers in the BRICS countries, explaining how such clauses may look. Importantly, the BRICS countries should be seen as a laboratory for data governance. Indeed, given their heterogeneity, it can be argued that the approaches that can work at the BRICS level may likely be scaled up at the global level.

7.2. A Shared Data Protection Skeleton

Based on the analysis of the BRICS frameworks, a non-exhaustive but telling list of policy elements can be identified around which the data protection regimes of the group members are converging.[5] Due to the relatively recent development of the BRICS data protection framework, decision-makers in these countries have enjoyed the privilege of constructing their legal frameworks based on existing best practices and, as will be highlighted, with a view to finding creative solutions for problems that other legislators have been unable to tackle properly.

A patent example of convergence is the definition of personal data itself, which all BRICS countries consider as information related to an identified or identifiable natural person, although, interestingly, the South African framework extends the protection further, encompassing data related to legal persons also, as will be discussed in the next section.[6] A similar approach also

[5] See L Belli, 'Data Protection in the BRICS Countries: Enhanced Cooperation and Convergence towards Legal Interoperability' (2021) 3 New Media Journal. Chinese Academy of Cyberspace Studies 73–77.

[6] See CyberBRICS Project, 'BRICS Data Protection Map' (*CyberBRICS*, 2021) Policy Question 7 <https://cyberbrics.info/data-protection-across-brics-countries/> accessed 8 October 2021.

underpins the definitions of sensitive data, data subject, and data controller, although the terminology utilized may vary slightly.[7]

The core principles upon which the data protection architecture is erected are also commonly shared. The principles included in BRICS frameworks may be found in virtually all data protection regulations and allow identifying a globally applicable principle core that is usually common beyond BRICS, at least as regards the first four principles. The BRICS data protection principles[8] include consent, purpose limitation, fair and lawful processing, necessity, data minimization, and accountability. Furthermore, BRICS legislators have included a similar spectrum of rights, although with different flavours.[9] All BRICS frameworks embrace provisions establishing the individual rights of access to data, correction of incomplete, inaccurate, or outdated data, elimination of personal data processed with the consent of the data subject, and revocation of consent.

BRICS data protection frameworks also present a very comparable set of obligations for data controllers and processors.[10] Interestingly, the data controller concept has different contours in the five frameworks. The South African framework uses the term 'responsible party' rather than 'controller'. The new Chinese Personal Information Law refers to a 'personal information handler', meaning 'organizations and individuals that, in personal information handling activities, autonomously decide handling purposes and handling methods' (art 73.1). This would be roughly synonymous with the Brazilian and Russian (or EU) data controller, while the PIPL's 'entrusted party' (art 21) would reflect the data processor acting according to the controller's instructions.[11]

Meanwhile, the Indian Digital Personal Data Protection Act uses the concept of 'data fiduciary', which the Justice Srikrishna Committee claimed marked a conscious decision to depart from the narrative of a 'controller' and 'subject', thus stressing the importance of the duty of care that underpins the relationship between a principal and a fiduciary.[12] The core obligations for data controllers in the BRICS include abiding by data protection principles, obtaining free and informed consent in order to process data, duly communicating

[7] ibid 'Definitions'.
[8] ibid Policy Question 9.
[9] ibid Policy Question 13.
[10] ibid Policy Question 14.
[11] See n 51.
[12] See Rishab Bailey and Trishee Goyal, 'Fiduciary Relationships as a Means to Protect Privacy: Examining the Use of the Fiduciary Concept in the Draft Personal Data Protection Bill, 2019' (*The Leap Blog*, 13 January 2020) <https://blog.theleapjournal.org/2020/01/fiduciary-relationships-as-means-to.html> accessed 8 October 2021.

information on the data processing, and ensuring the security of all personal data under their responsibility.

The normative elements enshrined in the Indian Act demonstrate concrete potential to adopt innovative approaches that can inspire BRICS countries and other countries globally. Perhaps the most relevant example is the trend to move the regulatory approach itself from an exclusive focus on legislation to one aimed at leveraging digital public infrastructures, such as the "consent managers" tools based on 'accessible, transparent and interoperable platforms' (art 2.g) enabling data regulation for consent management purposes.

Importantly, all BRICS countries have considered the essential role of international data transfers for the (digital) economy. All BRICS allow for international data transfers, whenever foreign third parties are deemed as providing an acceptable level of protection, but some of them have explicit data localization provisions (Russia and China) or sector-specific data localization regimes (India). Hence, there has been both a convergence and divergence regarding key international issues such as data localization and transfer restrictions. India is a particularly interesting case, prescribing both localization of specific types of personal data, such as financial, payment, and insurance data,[13] but simultaneously allowing unrestricted transfers of personal data as a general rule (art 16). The Brazilian and South African frameworks include no requirement to store any types of personal data within national jurisdictions, but define requirements for data transfers to be legal. Russia was the first country since 2015 to enshrine a data localization obligation in its national framework.

The same applies to China, where the PIPL prescribes that all personal data must be stored within the country, unless the Cyberspace Administration of China (CAC) determines differently. The Indian approach has evolved considerably from the draft Personal Data Protection Bill 2021, which proposed to require every data fiduciary to ensure that at least one serving copy of personal data to which the framework applies had to be stored on a server or in a data centre located in the country, to the much more liberal approach enshrined in the DPDP Act 2023. Indeed, the current general rule is no restriction, but exceptions can be defined with specific regulation, as happens for the Indian banking and insurance sectors.

[13] Notably, s 94 of the Indian Companies Act 2013, read with ss 88 and 92 of the Companies Accounts Rules 2014, mandates storage of financial information at the registered office of the company. In 2018, the Reserve Bank of India ordered all payment system providers to store information relating to payment systems in servers located under India's territorial control, according to a circular titled 'Storage of Payment System Data'. Section 3(9) of the Insurance Regulatory and Development Authority of India's Maintenance of Insurance Records Regulation 2015 requires covered organizations to store insurance data within India.

In case of international data transfers, the evaluation of a sufficient level of protection is performed through quite heterogeneous mechanisms, spanning from the adoption of adequacy decisions on foreign legal frameworks, as foreseen in the GDPR, to specific administrative authorizations to transfer data for national service providers, or yet to the use of corporate rules or binding agreements admitted by national authorities.[14] Given the large number of criteria and the variety of mechanisms that BRICS countries adopt to regulate international data transfers, and considering how crucial this issue is to facilitate BRICS digital cooperation, especially regarding intra-BRICS free flows of information, this topic will be explored in this concluding chapter of the book, so that the reader will be able to fully appreciate its relevance after having delved into the data protection system of each specific BRICS country.

Importantly, all data protection frameworks in BRICS countries have an extraterritorial reach, except for South African law, which only applies when either the responsible party is domiciled in the country or is using means in South Africa, but does not extend to foreign entities providing services, goods, or collecting data about South African nationals from abroad. Perhaps surprisingly, all BRICS data protection laws apply also to the government. However, a lot of exceptions exist, such as the Brazilian legal exemption of any activity related to national security, national defence, or criminal enquiry to the application of the law, or the Indian Digital Data Protection Act 2023's highly criticized clauses attributing sweeping powers to the Federal Government to exempt any governmental agency from the scope of the law.

As for situations where social and cultural traits have a broader importance, major differences between BRICS data protection frameworks may be observed. Such is the case, for example, of the measures protecting children's data. Brazil has chosen a system akin to the European one, considering children as any person under twelve years old. In 2019, prior to China's data protection law, the Cyberspace Administration of China (CAC) released a data privacy regulation related to children, the 'Provisions on Cyber Protection of Personal Information of Children', which is sometimes compared to COPPA (the US Children Online Privacy Protection Act), requiring parental consent for children under fourteen.

Finally, all BRICS countries seem to envisage a benefit in having a specific authority overseeing the implementation of the law, although the ways they design their national authorities differ considerably and may be seen as a reflection of their legal and institutional frameworks. In 2020, Brazil established a

[14] See (n 49) Policy Question 22.

new Data Protection Authority (DPA), the National Data Protection Authority (ANPD), complemented by a very innovative multistakeholder body acting as a Privacy and Data Protection Council (CNPD). Recently, the ANPD became an independent body after the promulgation of a decree[15] by the Federal Government, later confirmed by Brazilian Parliament, but the ANPD is not fully independent as its budget is still defined—rather discretionarily—by the Ministry of Justice.

In Russia, data protection is overseen by the Federal Service for Supervision of Communications, Information Technologies, and Mass Communications (Roskomnadzor), while in China the responsible body is the Cyberspace Administration of China (CAC). Importantly, both the Russian and Chinese regulators are not independent bodies but are incorporated as parts of the respective federal governments. Besides data protection, both organs have extremely large remits, encompassing several designations that, in other countries, are typically attributed to different regulators, such as cybersecurity, content regulation, or telecommunications regulation. Crucially, their lack of independence has been criticized and identified by scholars and observers alike as one of the core reasons why the Russian and Chinese frameworks cannot be deemed as providing substantially equivalent protections to data protection systems whose regulators' independence is guaranteed.[16]

However, one must acknowledge that, despite being open to criticism for lack of independence, the Russian and Chinese models of super-regulators present a clear advantage of having a unique and centralized authority for digital matters to which new departments can be easily added, every time that a new technological challenge emerges, and new laws are adopted, such as artificial intelligence or platform governance, with no need to establish new ad hoc regulators. Indeed, as shown by the South African and Brazilian experience, the need to establish a new regulator, rather than expand an existing super regulator, is frequently one of the most visible vulnerabilities of a new regulatory systems, whose effectiveness ends up being considerably jeopardized by political gridlock regarding funding, staff, independence, and many other administrative details, which may seem negligible but *de facto* lead to enormous delays and dysfunctional regulatory systems that are not taken seriously by the regulated.

[15] See n 58.

[16] See for instance Jan Czarnocki and others, 'Government Access to Data in Third Countries' (2019). Study prepared by Milieu under Contract No EDPS/2019/02-13 for the benefit of the European Data Protection Board (EDPB).

Lastly, the Indian Digital Personal Data Protection Act 2023 provides for the establishment of the Data Protection Board of India, although this regulatory body has not been established at the time of this writing. South Africa was the only BRICS country to have a genuinely independent Information Regulator, subject only to the Constitution and to the law, and accountable to the National Assembly. However, it is worth mentioning that it took exactly ten years from the approval of POPIA for the regulatory system to start being effective, and such an enormous delay has inevitably undermined the credibility of the regulator.

7.3. Innovative BRICS Data Protection Practices

While BRICS countries are taking relevant inspiration from existing frameworks to develop their own national data protection regimes, it is essential to acknowledge that they are also introducing considerable innovations. This section offers a selection of the most innovative features of the BRICS data protection frameworks. While these elements have only recently been introduced, they should be considered carefully as they offer some interesting and innovative approaches that are likely to be replicated by other countries in the future.

7.3.1. Brazil and the LGPD Implementation: the National Council of Data Protection and Privacy and the Influence of the Consumer Protection Framework

The Brazilian data protection framework,[17] even if only very recently enacted and still lacking several steps to be fully implemented, clearly presents some very particular characteristics. Importantly, such features mainly stem from typical experiences and practices present in other fields of the country's legal system.

The framing and drafting of the LGPD took at least eight years since its first official draft was released[18] until its enactment. In fact, this first official draft is the development from unofficial drafts produced during the series of

[17] Parts of this section are based on L Belli and D Doneda, 'Data Protection in the BRICS Countries: Legal Interoperability through Innovative Practices and Convergence' (2023) 13(1) International Data Privacy Law 1–24 <https://doi.org/10.1093/idpl/ipac019>.

[18] A record of the original draft submitted for public consultation, as well as the contributions received, are available at <http://www.doneda.net/2020/03/08/consultas-publicas-protecao-de-dados/>.

debates in a Mercosur (the economic area binding together Argentina, Brazil, Paraguay, and Uruguay) working group on electronic commerce which, since 2004, evaluated a proposal made by Argentina of a data protection model law for the economic area.[19] As Brazil did not have such a law nor a bill, some drafts began to circulate within Federal Government's boundaries at that time[20], which developed into a draft bill submitted to public consultation in 2010 by the Brazilian Ministry of Justice.[21]

This first draft resembled, in its structure and fundamental concepts, the data protection framework in Convention 108 of the Council of Europe and Directive 95/46/CE of the European Union. At the same time, it presented some typical traits of the Brazilian law system, such as the explicit reference to Brazilian consumer law pillars and to the Public Civil Action Law. The final text of the LGPD, even if based on this initial draft, changed enormously, due to the relevant number of contributions received in the public consultations organized by the Brazilian Ministry of Justice, and the intense legislative process, from 2016 to 2018, which included a series of public hearings, consultations and calls for suggestions and meetings with stakeholders.

The result of this participatory process was the engagement of several actors in the discussion but also the introduction of Brazilian legal system views and instruments into the texts as a way of absorbing the views of the various stakeholders. Moreover, as will be highlighted, the participatory multistakeholder process, which led to the elaboration of the law, has been incorporated in the governance system designed by the law. The final text of what later became the LGPD is the result of an intense debate among diverse sectors of Brazilian society which not merely legitimized data protection tools and concepts transplanted from foreign legislations, but rather shaped them in a way they could best fit Brazilian legal tradition, introducing regulatory and participatory structures which became key characteristics of the Brazilian data protection framework in comparison with international standards.

These remarks on the LGPD's formative process are brought into consideration to give context on some specific characteristics of the LGPD which were identified as innovative practices. This context is also different from the one

[19] Mercosur, 'XII Reunión ordinaria del subgrupo de trabajo nº13—Comércio Electrónico' (15 June 2004) <https://documentos.mercosur.int/simfiles/docreuniones/23116_SGT13_2004_ACTA02_ES.pdf> accessed 8 October 2021

[20] For a description of the development of Brazilian General Data Protection Law since its first drafts, see Danilo Doneda, 'Panorama histórico da proteção de dados pessoais' in Laura Schertel Mendes and others (eds), *Tratado de Proteção de Dados Pessoais* (Forense 2020) 3–20. The original draft law is available at <http://culturadigital.br/dadospessoais/>.

[21] This consultation is still available at <http://pensando.mj.gov.br/dadospessoais2011/> (April 2021)

found in other non-European countries, which typically debated their own data protection bills for a shorter time and, typically, considered the need to include into their legal system the rules that could facilitate international data transfers, thus fostering digital trade with Europe.

In Brazil, pressure to shape domestic legislation to better accommodate international data flows has never been one of the major guiding forces for the elaboration of a data protection framework. In fact, one of the few elements of external pressure was the commitment of the Federal Government to join the OECD as a member country[22], which would require the integration of several OECD Recommendations in the Brazilian legal system, including the establishment of a data protection framework. Nevertheless, this urge was important to motivate some of the Federal Government bodies, which were traditionally silent if not sceptical about the LGPD, to endorse the proposal.

Such multistakeholder endorsement from the Brazilian private sector, academia, and civil society, together with the consensus reached in the National Congress, played a relevant role in facilitating the LGPD's approval and enactment. Considering this background, it is not surprising that the resulting law would reflect (i) the presence of a multistakeholder consultative council as an auxiliary body to the Brazilian Data Protection Authority, and (ii) a strong connection to the Brazilian consumer protection framework, noticeable in both procedural and substantial material aspects of the LGPD.

The LGPD created as its Data Protection Authority the National Data Protection Authority (ANPD, *Autoridade Nacional de Proteção de Dados*), together with a consultative multistakeholder body, the National Data Protection and Privacy Council (*Conselho Nacional de Proteção de Dados e Privacidade*). The Council has strictly consultative functions and does not make decisions, nor does it have any supervision or administrative tasks. Its competences are listed in article 58-B of LGPD and include providing ANPD with suggestions, proposals, and support for its actions and, particularly, for the development of the National Data Protection Policy; drafting annual reports on the actions performed by ANPD; drafting studies and promoting debates and public hearings; and, generally, promoting data protection knowledge and culture among Brazilian people.

[22] The OECD's Guidelines on the Protection of Privacy and Transborder Dataflows of Personal Data was a pivotal document in the development of international data protection standards when it came out in 1980, and maintains its importance. Compliance with these guidelines is one of the requirements if Brazil is eventually to join OECD as a member country. See 'Personal Data Protection at the OECD' (OECD, 2021) <https://www.oecd.org/general/data-protection.htm> accessed 8 October 2021.

The Council presents a multistakeholder composition: of its twenty-three members, five are appointed by the Federal Government, one by the Federal Senate, one by the House of Representatives, one by the National Justice Council, one by the Public Ministry National Council, one by the Brazilian Internet Steering Committee, three chosen amongst representatives of non-governmental organizations, three from science and technology institutions, three from national confederations from the productive sector, two from the private sector, and two from trades unions and worker organizations. The nomination process for each counsellor is defined by the institutions themselves. The stakeholder groups mentioned generically will have the possibility to suggest candidates and the board of directors of ANPD will choose the most adequate representatives of each group, and subsequently submit those names to the Presidency of Republic, which will have a final say on the list and nominate the counsellors.

The presence of a sound multistakeholder element in the Council pays tribute to at least two driving factors. First, the noticeable multistakeholder experience of the Brazilian Internet governance ecosystem, where CGI.br—the Brazilian Internet Steering Committee (*Comitê Gestor da Internet*)—has played a pivotal role in the development of the Internet in the country since its early days, frequently characterized as a 'multistakeholder model' that became a global benchmark.

The second factor was the concrete dialogue between several sectors by the time LGPD had become a bill and was being debated in the National Congress. The resonance among diverse stakeholders gave birth even to a coalition of institutions, enterprises, and organizations from several areas to support the approval and enactment of LGPD. One of the by-products of these discussions was indeed the need to create a governance structure in the Brazilian data protection framework, to accommodate and give a voice to these stakeholders in the process of implementation of data protection.

It is important however, to stress that while the Brazilian framework may be seen as a hallmark of multistakeholder participation in policy suggestion, it performs much less as regards policy implementation.

7.3.2. Freely Shareable Personal Data, Opt-out, and Data Localization in Russia

In Russia, personal data protection is regulated by Federal Law No 152-FZ, which was adopted in 2006 and subsequently amended in December 2017 and in December 2020.[23] As emphasized above, the Russian data protection framework is implemented by Roskomnadzor, a super regulator with particularly large competence and powers, which has frequently been criticized for its lack of independence, being administratively subordinated to the Russian Ministry for Media and ICTs. The latest amendments to the Russian framework entered in force partly in March 2021 and partly in July 2021. As discussed by Zanfir-Fortuna and Iminova,[24] these amendments aim at tackling four areas.

First, the amended provisions introduce a new category of personal data that can be freely shared, defined as 'personal data allowed by the data subject to be disseminated'. Second, the Russian legislation now includes rules allowing personal data to become freely sharable with an unlimited number of persons. To do so, the law establishes the obligation to collect specific, affirmative, and separately collected consent from the data subject. The rationale behind the creation of this new category of personal data resembles that behind GDPR article 9(2)(e), a largely under-appreciated norm,[25] which allows the processing of sensitive data when 'processing relates to personal data which are manifestly made public by the data subject'.

According to the amended Russian data protection framework, personal data allowed by the data subject to be disseminated can only be processed when an organization or individual processing them can prove that the data subject expressed consent according to the modalities specified by the law. Third, the law introduces the possibility for Roskomnadzor—the Russian Communications, Information Technologies, and Mass Communications Regulator—to create a centralized database of all the expressions of consent regarding the unlimited dissemination of personal data. Lastly, the law establishes a new absolute right to opt out of the dissemination of personal data, which can be exercised 'at any time'.

Conspicuously, consent is the only legal basis for the processing and dissemination of 'freely' shareable personal data. Such data is defined by a new paragraph 1.1, in article 3 of the law, as 'personal data to which an unlimited

[23] See Russian Federal Law No 519-FZ of 30 December 2020 'On Amendments to the Federal Law "On Personal Data"' <http://publication.pravo.gov.ru/Document/View/0001202012300044> accessed 8 October 2021.

[24] Gabriela Zanfir-Fortuna and Regina Iminova, 'Russia: New Law Requires Express Consent For Making Personal Data Available To The Public And For Any Subsequent Dissemination' (*CyberBRICS*, 2 March 2021) <https://cyberbrics.info/russia-new-law-requires-express-consent-for-making-personal-data-available-to-the-public-and-for-any-subsequent-dissemination/> accessed 8 October 2021.

[25] For a rare analysis of this norm, see Edward S Dove and Jiahong Chen, 'What Does it Mean for a Data Subject to Make their Personal Data 'Manifestly Public'? An Analysis of GDPR Article 9(2)(e)' (2021) 11(2) International Data Privacy Law <https://academic.oup.com/idpl/article/11/2/107/6146670> accessed 8 October 2021.

number of persons have access to, and which is provided by the data subject by giving specific consent for the dissemination of such data, in accordance with the conditions in the Personal Data Law'. According to the new article 10.1, personal data can be freely shared only after the granting of specific, express, unambiguous, and separate consent. Under Law 152-FZ, the natural or legal person that determines the purposes of personal data processing, the composition of personal data to be processed, and the operations performed with personal data, is defined as the 'data operator'.[26] Article 10.1(1) creates a new obligation for the operator to obtain the data subject's separate, specific, and express consent to disseminate personal data, on top of the regular consent to process data.

Silence or inaction cannot configure the consent needed for free dissemination of data, and the data subject must also enjoy the possibility to choose specific categories of personal data that can be freely disseminated. Furthermore, any operator, be it the first one collecting the freely shareable data or anyone else processing freely shareable personal data, bears the onus to 'provide evidence of the legality of subsequent dissemination or other processing', under article 10.1(2).

The establishment of the aforementioned obligation has also led the Russian legislator to introduce the possibility for Roskomnadzor to create a centralized consent management system to collect all the expressions of consent. Indeed, according to article 10.1(6), consent to turn personal data into freely shareable data can be collected by the operator or via a dedicated 'information system' which may be envisaged as a digital public infrastructure established by Roskomnadzor.[27] This system may resemble the Data Empowerment and Protection Architecture implemented by India and discussed in the next section.

Another innovative practice introduced by the recent amendments of the Russian law is the new absolute right to opt-out of dissemination of freely shareable personal data. Indeed, article 12.1(12) prescribes that the free dissemination of personal data can be halted at any time, on request from an

[26] This term refers to both roles of controller and processor, which are split in other BRICS frameworks such as the Brazilian LGPD or the South African POPIA. See CyberBRICS Project (n 6).

[27] This information system is intended as a consent-management or consent-registry platform through which individuals can issue, track, and later revoke (if desired) their express consent for their personal data to be made accessible/disseminated to an unlimited group. Recent reporting suggests the Russian government is planning to establish by 2028 a central register of consents of processing personal data on the Gosuslugi portal (public services state portal) so that individuals can see who has permissions over their data and possibly revoke them. S Lantyukhov 'The correct permission: a register of consents to the processing of personal data will be created at Gosuslugi' Izvestia (online, 26 August 2025) <https://en.iz.ru/en/node/1942775>.

individual. The right to opt out from dissemination can be exercised to withdraw previously expressed consent, by specifically identifying the personal data to which the request refers, the diffusion of which should be terminated. Interestingly, the opt-out request can also be used as a tool to stop the dissemination of data for which consent has not been lawfully collected. In this latter case, the data subject can address the request either to the operator that is illegally disseminating the personal data or to a court of law.

The timeframe for stopping the dissemination will depend on the modalities of the request. In the case of lawful collection of consent, article 10.1(13) establishes that sharing must terminate as soon as the request is received. In the case of illegal sharing, article 10.1(14) prescribes that sharing must stop within three business days from the reception of the request, or within a different timeframe established by a court order.

Lastly, it is important to mention that, Russian 'data localization' policies are not particularly recent; indeed, Russia can be considered a 'trailblazer' in this peculiar field, as the normative provisions it adopted as early as September 2015, have inspired many other countries,[28] including BRICS neighbours, such as China and India. In particular, article 18 of Federal Law No 152-FZ enshrines the obligation of the operator to ensure localization within Russian servers of processing activities related to all personal data collected from Russian citizens.

Data localization came into force on 1 September 2015 and includes the possibility of blocking the operator's online resources, whenever personal data of Russian citizens are processed in violation of localization requirements. Clearly, Russia's invasion of Ukraine and the consequent Western sanctions have exacerbated the already prevailing tendency towards data localization and 'Internet sovereignty', deemed by Russia a top priority of national security, justifying the implementation of a wide array of restrictive measures.[29]

To illustrate this tendency, several scholars have highlighted the initiatives that Russia has introduced, over recent years, with the aim to expand control

[28] For up-to-date details on how widespread the adoption of data localization norms is, see N Cory and L Dascoli, 'How Barriers to Cross-Border Data Flows Are Spreading Globally, What They Cost, and How to Address Them' (*Information Technology & Innovation Foundation*, 2021) <https://itif.org/publications/2021/07/19/how-barriers-cross-border-data-flows-are-spreading-globally-what-they-cost/>.

[29] See A Shcherbovich, 'Data Protection and Cybersecurity Legislation of the Russian Federation in the Context of the "Sovereignization" of the Internet in Russia' in L Belli (ed), *CyberBRICS: Cybersecurity Regulations in the BRICS Countries* (Springer 2021) 67–131 <https://link.springer.com/chapter/10.1007/978-3-030-56405-6_3>; F Daucé and F Musiani (eds), 'Infrastructure-embedded control, circumvention and sovereignty in the Russian Internet' (*First Monday*, May 2021) <https://firstmonday.org/ojs/index.php/fm/issue/view/693>.

over data flows and regulate Internet users' behaviour, for instance blocking access to a large amount of content labelled as 'extremist information', while also building considerable cyberdefence capabilities.[30] As such, data localization has become one of the fundamental tussles—although not the only one—of the Russian strategy for the assertion of digital sovereignty, based on a blend of data-related policies and 'infrastructure-embedded control'.[31] It is important to recognize that this Russian blend of digital sovereignty is increasingly inspiring governments and legislators globally.[32]

7.3.3. Indian Data Empowerment and Protection Architecture

In July 2015, the government of India launched the Digital India[33] programme, an ambitious plan aimed at fostering the digital transformation of the country. While Digital India has very strong connectivity and eGovernment components, another key component, which is based on the establishment of a Digital Public Infrastructure, is a set of APIs[34] commonly referred to as the 'India Stack'[35] that is particularly relevant to explain the evolutions of the Indian data protection framework since the inception of Digital India. Indeed, the India Stack is deemed by the Indian government as instrumental to achieving the Digital India vision, consisting in a substantial digital transformation fostering inclusive growth in highly strategic areas, such as digital products and services and automated manufacturing, thus unleashing job opportunities.[36] While the expansion of connectivity is instrumental in supporting this vision, two elements of the India Stack are key to our analysis: Aadhaar and DEPA.

Aadhaar means 'foundation' in Hindi and is the national digital identity system that by 2021 had been extended to more than 94 per cent of the Indian population, making it 'one of the most successful rollouts of any tech product

[30] ibid.
[31] See Daucé and Musiani (n 29).
[32] See Cory and Dascoli (n 28).
[33] Digital India, available at <https://www.digitalindia.gov.in/> accessed 8 October 2021.
[34] An API, or application programming interface, is a piece of software that allows different software applications to interact and exchange data, according to the specifications established by the API.
[35] See <https://www.indiastack.org/>.
[36] Importantly, this vision is not exempted from critique, notably considering that the India Stack has been essentially designed by iSpirt (the Indian Software Products Industry Round Table), a think tank for the Indian software products industry which has been criticized for its close ties with both government and large corporations, raising concerns related to conflict of interests, transparency, and accountability. See <https://privacyinternational.org/sites/default/files/2017-12/Fintech%20report.pdf>.

anywhere'.[37] As noted by Kak, Parsheera, and Kotwal, Aadhaar's ability to uniquely identify individuals based on their biometric/demographic information has led the Indian government to make 'mandatory, the use of Aadhaar numbers for various welfare schemes like the transfer of direct cash benefits under public distribution of food grains, employment guarantee benefits, midday meals in schools, subsidies, etc'. While Aadhaar can be made mandatory for government benefits and welfare, it continues to be extensively used on a 'voluntary basis' as an ID proof for all these other purposes.

Due to Aadhaar's potential for privacy abuse, the constitutionality of the programme was challenged before the Indian Supreme Court. As discussed in this volume's chapter dedicated to India, with the landmark *Puttaswamy* case,[38] the Supreme Court seized the occasion to pronounce the existence of a fundamental right to privacy in India, which can only be limited through fair, just, and reasonable procedures, clearly foreseen by the law. At the same time, the Court's decision opened the path to the elaboration of the first draft of the Indian Data Protection Bill, which later became the Digital Personal Data Protection Act 2023.

One of the most compelling features of the Indian approach to data governance is the use of digital public infrastructures (DPIs) as techno-regulatory tools, embedding normative values in technical architectures. In August 2020, the Indian government's policy think tank Niti Aayog issued a draft paper aimed at fostering discussion on a new Data Empowerment and Protection Architecture (DEPA) framework.[39] The paper builds upon previous development of the 'electronic consent framework' which was adopted in 2017,[40] as well on the existing implementations of the concept through the account aggregators framework, already adopted by the Indian financial sector.[41] DEPA is presented as a 'secure consent-based data sharing framework to accelerate financial inclusion'.

[37] Aaryaman Vir and Rahul Sanghi, 'The Internet Country: How India created a digital blueprint for the economies of the future' (*Tigerfeathers*, 14 January 2021) <https://tigerfeathers.substack.com/p/the-internet-country> accessed 13 October 2021.

[38] For an analysis of the case, see Vrinda Bhandari and others, 'An Analysis of Puttaswamy: The Supreme Court's Privacy Verdict' (2017) 11 IndraStra Global <https://nbn-resolving.org/urn:nbn:de:0168-ssoar-54766-2> accessed 13 October 2021.

[39] See Niti Aayog, 'Data Empowerment And Protection Architecture: Draft for Discussion' (2020) <https://niti.gov.in/sites/default/files/2020-09/DEPA-Book_0.pdf> accessed 13 October 2021.

[40] See iSPIRT, 'Electronic Consent Framework' (*ProductNation*, 5 May 2019) <https://pn.ispirt.in/tag/electronic-consent-framework/> accessed 13 October 2021.

[41] See George Mathew, 'Account Aggregators: New Framework to Access, Share Financial Data' *The Indian Express* (8 September 2021) <https://indianexpress.com/article/explained/account-aggregators-new-framework-to-access-share-financial-data-7490966/> accessed 13 October 2021.

While the Indian concept of consent managers may resemble pre-existing Personal Data Stores (PDSs) or Personal Information Management System (PIMSs) such as CitizenMe and Solid, it is important to stress that previous PDS and PIMS examples are relatively niche initiatives.[42] The Indian experiment of electronic consent management frameworks within the DEPA, is the first nation-wide initiative stemming from the Indian digital transformation 'India Stack' plan and has become a new hallmark of the Indian data architecture.

Through the establishment of DEPA, Niti Aayog aims at creating 'an evolvable regulatory, institutional, and technology design for secure data sharing' that can 'empower individuals with control over their personal data'.[43] The elaboration of DEPA is particularly relevant, as it has been conceived to create a software architecture, based on shared public protocols, allowing all Indians to regulate and somehow 'customize' the flow of personal information that third parties may collect and process.

In practice, DEPA acts as a system of digital consent management. The system will be based on the development of technical specifications to allow individuals to give consent to processing of personal data, defined by Ministry of Electronics and Information Technology,[44] and the introduction of 'consent managers' that will act as a new category of intermediaries. Such a framework has already been adopted in the financial sector, through the Account Aggregator system, established by the Reserve Bank of India. This latter system is grounded on the specification of technical standards and the establishment of a category of regulated intermediaries, named 'account aggregators', which act as consent managers within the financial sector.[45]

In this perspective, the goal of the DEPA consent managers is to facilitate the flow of personal data from information providers to the users of the information, based on the consent of the individual. Thus, consent managers are supposed to act as data fiduciaries, which enable a data principal to gain, withdraw, review, and manage his consent through an accessible, transparent, and interoperable platform. They are not supposed to exploit personal data, but rather to be 'data blind' and merely serve as a 'conduit for encrypted data flows'.[46]

[42] See S Abiteboul, B André, and D Kaplan, 'Managing your Digital Life with a Personal Information Management System' (2015) 58(5) Communications of the ACM 32–35; G Brochot and others, 'Personal Data Stores' (2015) Cambridge Judge Business School.

[43] See Niti Aayog (n 39) 26–27.

[44] See Ministry of Electronics and Information Technology, Electronic Consent Framework—Technology Specifications Version 1.1 (2016) <http://dla.gov.in/sites/default/files/pdf/MeitY-Consent-Tech-Framework%20v1.1.pdf> accessed 13 October 2021.

[45] See Reserve Bank of India, 'Account Aggregator Ecosystem API Specifications' (8 November 2019) <https://api.rebit.org.in/> accessed 14 October 2021.

[46] See Niti Aayog (n 39) 15.

Importantly, DEPA is also presented by Niti Aayog as the final layer of the India Stack, aimed at providing secure digital data sharing through consent. To understand DEPA, is indeed necessary to take a step back and remind that DEPA is a key 'layer' of the India Stack, which aims at allowing all interested stakeholders—be they public bodies, businesses, start-ups, or non- profits—to use the Indian public digital infrastructure to deliver services.

However, one common concern with the DEPA model is that it could lead to the over-simplification of consent. Indeed, the 'consent manager' proposed under DEPA has the potential to become an element for both enhancement or reduction of data control from the individual, depending on how the DEPA structure is designed and its degree of synergy with the implementation of the Digital Personal Data Protection Act by the Data Protection Board of India that, at the moment of this writing has not been established yet. As emphasized by Reddy and others, one must keep in mind that the primary objective of the DEPA framework shall be to grant individual control over personal data through the establishment of a secure and well-functioning protocol to share data across institutions, ultimately leading to individual empowerment and well-being.[47]

Lastly, it is important to note that the Indian legislator seems to have taken inspiration from China as regards the need to couple its normative framework with a didactic approach, introducing 'illustrations' aimed at exemplifying concepts that might be new for Indian stakeholders. This is indeed a very useful technique explored by the Chinese legislator by annexing examples to the regulatory standards, such as the Personal Information Security Specification, which proves to be extremely useful to facilitate compliance.

7.3.4. China's Facilitative Regulation, Institutional Coordination, Data Security Approach, and the Normative Innovation of the Personal Information Protection Law (PIPL)

China's approach has been innovative in terms of facilitative regulation, institutional coordination, relevance of cybersecurity, and normative updates. One of the most relevant features of the Chinese approach is its understanding of regulation as a technique that does not solely yield restrictive outcomes.[48]

[47] S Reddy and others, The Centre for Internet and Society's Comments and Recommendations to the Data Empowerment and Protection Architecture (The Centre for Internet and Society 2020).

[48] A Ma, *China as a Double-Bind Regulatory State: How Internet Regulators' Predicament Produces Regulatees' Autonomy* (Palgrave Macmillan 2024).

Indeed, regulation can also aim at generating facilitative effects, thereby expanding the operational latitude of regulated firms. Both facilitative and restrictive regulations encompass the formal and informal rules, practices, and norms designed to respectively broaden and constrain the freedom of action of regulated entities.

Facilitative regulations can significantly enhance the operational capabilities of regulated entities. For instance, industrial policy articulated at multiple governmental levels may offer tax credits or grants to companies investing in research and development, thereby fostering innovation and technological advancement that aligns with normative goals.[49] In this perspective, China's administrations compete among each other to offer the best conditions for start-ups and enterprises to develop their (digital) products and services. Conversely, most data protection frameworks are based on restrictive regulations, imposing obligations and prohibiting certain types of data processing operations, rather than incentivizing the desired types.

As noted by Belli, in 2015 China adopted a set of ambitious policy and investment strategies, including the 'Internet Plus' and 'Made in China 2025', which focused on facilitating digital transformation through the expansion of Internet connectivity, the Internet of Things (IoT) and its enablers, followed by a National Plan for Artificial Intelligence Development and the AI Governance Principles, to reap the benefits of connectivity and datafication.[50] These plans complemented the adopted legal documents, such as the Cybersecurity Law, the Personal Information Security Specification, the E-Commerce Law, and PIPL, with facilitative regulation instruments, promoting the development of domestic industries.[51] In this perspective China's focused industrial policy on key sectors where the government has strongly backed domestic players including via huge public investments and facilitating the export of Chinese digital products and services.[52]

Moreover, having realized the complexity of digitization processes and of the regulation of data processing, starting from 2014 China has redesigned its cyber-related institutions to facilitate the elaboration and implementation of policies regarding information governance and cybersecurity. In this

[49] L Belli, 'New Data Architectures in Brazil, China, and India: From Copycats to Innovators, towards a post-Western Model of Data Governance' (2022) 18(3) Indian Journal of Law and Technology 1–59.
[50] ibid.
[51] US Chamber of Commerce, 'Made in China 2025: Global Ambitions Built on Local Protections' (2017) <https://www.uschamber.com/assets/archived/images/final_made_in_china_2025_report_full.pdf>.
[52] United Nations Conference on Trade and Development, 'Cross-Border Data Flows and Development: For Whom the Data Flow', Digital Economy Report 2021, UNCTAD/DER/2021.

perspective, China established a new Cybersecurity and Informatization (CI) '*xitong*', created the new Cyberspace Administration of China (CAC) as a new cyber regulator, and organized the new Central Commission for Cybersecurity and Informatization (CCCI).[53] A *xitong* is a peculiar Chinese administrative structure,[54] aimed at providing a dedicated 'policy system', involving all the public sector stakeholders affected by a specific policy area.

The goal of the *xitong* is to deal with the complexity of a multi-layer administration in a gigantic state, thus being able to coordinate and regulate efficiently specific sectors. This systemic approach should be studied and considered carefully as it can facilitate stakeholder communication, cooperation, and coordination, well beyond the policy suggestion, promoted by the Brazilian multistakeholder approach. Interestingly, Brazil also adopts a similar type of administrative configuration, also called system, in some policy areas such as the National Consumer Protection System and the Brazilian Military Cyber Defence System.[55]

Furthermore, China has openly stated its willingness to leverage data governance to assert sovereignty over cyberspace, exerting control, and protecting from foreign threats its national digital assets, while developing solid cybersecurity. It is important to emphasize that the expansion and control over digital infrastructures as well as the use of technology to maintain social stability and detect potential threats are high priorities for the Chinese government and have historically been considered as complementary dimensions and pursued jointly. The high relevance of these goals and their interdependence have been tellingly highlighted by President Xi Jinping himself, stressing that 'cybersecurity and informatization are two wings of one bird, two wheels of one cart, we must uniformly plan, uniformly deploy, uniformly move forward, and uniformly implement matters'.[56]

The strong cybersecurity component is indeed a key feature of the Chinese data architecture, emphasized since the 2012 decision of the National People's Congress to consider data protection and information security as necessary

[53] See R Creemers, *China's Cyber Governance Institutions* (Leiden Asia Centre 2021).

[54] See D Barnett, *Cadres, Bureaucracy, and Political Power in Communist China* (Columbia University Press 1967).

[55] National Consumer Protection System (Sistema Nacional de Defesa do Consumidor—SNDC) <https://www.consumidor.gov.br/pages/conteudo/publico/6>; Ordinance No 3.781/GM-MD. (17 November 2020). Military Cyber Defence System (SMDC) <https://www.in.gov.br/web/dou/-/portaria-n-3.781/gm-md-de-17-de-novembro-de-2020-289248860>.

[56] See R Creemers, 'Central Leading Group for Internet Security and Informatization Established' (*China Copyright and Media*, 1 March 2014) <https://chinacopyrightandmedia.wordpress.com/2014/03/01/central-leading-group-for-internet-security-and-informatization-established/>.

extensions of public order and national security.[57] In this perspective, the Cybersecurity Law prescribes that the state is responsible for establishing and improving a system of cybersecurity standards,[58] including rules for a 'graded protection of cybersecurity'.[59]

Building on the bases set by the Cybersecurity Law, the Personal Information Security Specification of 2018 established that it is obligatory to 'disclose the scope, purpose, and rules for processing personal information in a clear and comprehensible manner and accept external oversight'.[60] The elaboration of the Specification was considered necessary to fill many normative gaps, providing guidance on how to improve data subject awareness, corporate compliance, national oversight, and business good practices, setting new guidelines for personal data processing.

It is also important to stress that, despite the non-binding status of specifications in the Chinese legal system, the Personal Information Security Specification must be seen as a cornerstone of the Chinese data architecture. Indeed, the Specification plays an essential role translating normative elements easily understandable for lawyers into technical commands easily understandable for developers, thus critically supplementing legislation with technical standards that can be easily updated. In this perspective, shortly after the adoption of the Specification, the Chinese National Information Security Standardization Technical Committee, a key standard-setting body typically referred to as 'TC260',[61] started to update the specification to amend

[57] ibid; Z Wang, 'Systematic Government Access to Private-Sector Data in China' (2012) 2(4) International Data Privacy Law 220, 221–24.

[58] Cybersecurity Law of China art 15.

[59] Cybersecurity Law of China art 21. The 'graded protection of cybersecurity' refers to the Multi-Level Protection Scheme (MLPS), a concept which can be dated back to administrative rules from 1994 and 2007, and turned into a statutory obligation with the Cybersecurity Law's art 21, and reinforced by the 2022 Data Security Law's art 27 ('in data processing by making use of the internet or any other information networks, the abovementioned data security obligations shall be fulfilled on the basis of the **classified protection system for cyber security**'). According to the MLPS scheme, information systems need to be graded on a range from 1 to 5, and network operators must apply the cybersecurity measures according to the system's grade. PricewaterhouseCoopers, 'Cyber Security Law—Addressing the Compliance Complexities' (*PwC*, 30 November 2022) <https://www.pwc.de/en/international-markets/german-business-groups/china-business-group/cyber-security-law-addressing-the-compliance-complexities.html>. Furthermore, in May 2019, three national standards were issued by Chinese regulators: Information Security Technology—Baseline for Cybersecurity Classification Protection (GB/T 22239-2019), known as the 'MLPS 2.0 Baseline'; Information Security Technology—Technical Requirements of Security Design for Cybersecurity Classification Protection (GB/T 25070-2019); and Information Security Technology—Evaluation Requirements for Cybersecurity Classification Protection (GB/T 28448-2019). Together, they provide detailed and technical and administrative requirements on how to implement the MLPS. B Li, 'China: MLPS 2.0—Baseline Requirements and Practical Takeaways for Businesses' (*DataGuidance*, 22 August 2022) <https://www.dataguidance.com/opinion/china-mlps-20-baseline-requirements-and-practical>.

[60] Personal Information Security Specification, 2018, art 4e.

[61] See <https://www.tc260.org.cn/>.

several requirements for personal information controllers to make them clearer and more easily implementable. On 6 March 2020, TC260 and the State Administration for Market Regulation issued the 2020 amended version GB/T 35273-2020, which took effect on 1 October 2020.

The Specification provides guidance on the i) scope, ii) normative references, iii) terms and definitions, iv) basic principles of personal information security, v) personal information collection, vi) personal information retention, vii) use of personal information, viii) rights of personal information subjects, ix) entrusted processing, sharing, transfer, and public disclosure of personal information, x) handling of personal information security incident, and xi) personal information security management requirements for organizations.

Critically, the Specification adopts a remarkably didactic approach, offering detailed instructions and concrete examples—especially in its appendix—illustrating how to comply with normative provisions. Notably, the Specification Annexes provide examples of what is to be considered personal information (Annex A); a guide on how to identify sensitive personal information (Annex B); methods to safeguard independent choice of personal information subject (Annex C); and a model explaining how to draft a personal information protection policy (Annex D).[62] This approach is a particularly relevant feature of the Chinese systems, which understands the difficulty of complying with a new and highly technical law, regulating a matter with which much of the population is highly unfamiliar, and cannot be successful without explicit guidance.

Lastly one of PIPL's major innovations consist in going beyond existing standards including some last-generation norms yet to be considered in other major data protection legislations, such as the provision on its article 58 that commands big platform internet services to establish an independent supervision board with external members. This is a relevant accountability measure which can have very positive effects and is not found in any other data protection framework. The same article 58 also mentions the obligation of internet platforms to release reports on their data processing activities and to accept what is described as 'society's supervision'.

PIPL, in fact, provides for a set of provisions which are entirely new to data protection frameworks, such as the ban on automated decision-making for price discrimination (article 24) or the provisions for handling people's data of deceased individuals (article 49). This latter type of provisions usually depends not only on data protection standards but on other aspects of a country's legal

[62] Personal Information Security Specification, 2020, Annexes A, B, C, D.

system regarding the protection of personality and family law, among others, but, in PIPL, this issue has been regulated by the data protection framework. It is important to stress this element of innovation as it is already deploying an international influence, as it is visible in article 14 of the Indian Digital Personal Data Protection Act 2023, which regulates data protection in the event of death, clearly taking inspiration from its Asian neighbour.

7.3.5. The South African Framework: POPIA's Scope and the Nature of the DPA and of the DPO

POPIA, South Africa's data protection law, was established in November 2013 to bring transparency and accountability to entities processing personal data, aiming at providing individuals with control over their personal information. POPIA applies to any organization processing personal data within South Africa and to foreign organizations processing personal information in the country. However, the territorial scope defined by section 3 of POPIA can be seen as narrower than the GDPR or LGPD, as the South African law only applies when the responsible party (ie, the controller) is either domiciled in South Africa or is 'using means' in South Africa, hence avoiding the more overarching reference to the offering of goods or services, or monitoring of individuals from abroad.

While its most distinctive features are not unique in the world, they deserve to be mentioned as they make the South African framework unique within the BRICS context and may serve as useful experiences to be studied by other BRICS nations. First, POPIA applies not only to personal data relating to living individuals, but also to personal data relating to existing legal persons, such as companies and non-profits. Second, POPIA establishes the Information Regulator as the independent data protection authority within the South African jurisdiction, but also empowering the body to monitor and enforce compliance with the Promotion of Access to Information Act 2000 (PAIA Act 2 of 2000). In this sense, the data protection officer has a broader function than the one usually attributed by other frameworks. For this reason, the DPO is defined by POPIA and PAIA as an 'information officer', which plays an instrumental role to fulfil obligations related to both the protection of personal data and the due regulation of access to records held by public or private entities.

One of the main peculiarities of POPIA is that its section 1 considers as a 'data subject' the individual or the 'juristic person' to whom personal information relate. In the same spirit, personal information is any information relating to an identifiable, living, natural person, and where it is applicable an identifiable, existing 'juristic person'. In the South African legal framework, there are two categories of legal subjects: natural persons and juristic persons (usually defined as 'legal persons' in other frameworks). All human beings are considered as natural persons and legal subjects. Juristic persons are certain types of associations of natural persons, such as companies or non-profits. Hence, a major peculiarity of POPIA is that it includes juristic persons under its scope of application.

All responsible parties must appoint an Information Officer (IO). If no appointment is made, the head of the organization (for example, the chief executive officer or managing director) is automatically considered as the organization's IO. Importantly, the details of each organization's IO must be registered with the Information Regulator of South Africa or InfoReg (the national DPA), which has established a dedicated online portal to facilitate this task.[63] IOs are also allowed to delegate their duties to deputy information officers.

Lastly, an important procedural element is the appointment of the Board of InfoReg, as it is both a testament to the highly democratic and open tradition that South Africa has endeavoured to incorporate into all governance processes since the Mandela era, and a good practice that other countries could very easily copy. To identify members of the InfoReg, with appropriate qualifications and a sufficient degree of diversity—at least one member must have experience as a practising advocate or attorney, or a professor of law at a university, while the remaining members must be appointed on account of any other qualifications, expertise and experience relating to the objectives of the regulator—the South African Parliament issues an open Call for Applications or Nominations.[64]

7.4. Governmental Access to Personal Data in the BRICS

Having highlighted some of the main elements of innovation in the BRICS framework, this section will discuss how the countries regulate governmental access to personal data. Indeed, conditions surrounding governmental access and processing of personal data in the BRICS countries may prove a crucial point of tension regarding legal interoperability of data protection systems.

[63] Online Portal—Registration of Information Officers, available at <https://www.justice.gov.za/inforeg/portal.html> accessed 14 October 2021.
[64] The most recent Call is available at <https://www.parliament.gov.za/press-releases/media-statement-justice-and-correctional-services-committee-calls-nominations-information-regulator> accessed 14 October 2021.

Table 7.1 summarizes the treatment given to government processing of such data in the Brazilian, Russian, Indian, Chinese, and South African data protection laws, while the frameworks of the newly added members of the grouping—Egypt, Ethiopia, Indonesia, Iran, Saudi Arabia, and the UEA—will be analysed in the following section. The table showcases different approaches—some more detailed, others less so—toward the matter. However, it is important to emphasize that data protection legislation alone does not provide a full picture of the data protection architecture in this regard, since there are areas of government use of personal data, such as police investigations and intelligence activities, which may not be covered by personal data protection laws or that may be further specified in other laws, as demonstrated in following.

Chinese data protection law does not provide much specification of government access and processing of personal data. Data processors are generally defined to arguably include government actors. Legal bases do not include a specific hypothesis for government use, although some could be used by government actors to access and process personal data in specific situations. The most specific terms in this regard are given in section 3 (articles 33 to 37), concerning 'Special provisions on the processing of personal information by state organs'. Of note are article 36, which establishes a data localization requirement when data is processed by state organs, and article 37, which extends that section's provisions to organizations managing public affairs by force of law or regulation.

Although the treatment of government access to personal data in the PIPL is limited, there is a wider legal context that affects this matter. The Chinese framework on criminal investigations, the Cybersecurity Law, the National Security Law, the National Intelligence Law and the Counter-Espionage Law are some of the main normative documents influencing the status of government access to personal data in China. In general, the authors highlight shortcomings in these laws that may lead to undue or arbitrary government access to personal data, due to use of undefined or broadly defined legal terms and processes. That is to say, the lack of a definition of, for example, 'strict formalities' in the Counter-espionage Law article 12 may lead to access to personal data under insufficient restrictions. Similarly, the use of terms like 'public security' and 'societal interests' in these laws are broad and grant extensive leeway for data access. This problem is compounded by insufficient independent oversight mechanisms and pathways to the realization of data subjects' rights, especially in the face of security, intelligence, or criminal investigation activities.[65]

[65] Jan Czarnocki and others, 'Government Access to Data in Third Countries' (European Data Protection Board 2021) EDPS/2019/02-13.

Table 7.1 Government processing of personal data in BRICS countries

Country	Definition of processing agents include State agents	Specific legal basis for State processing	Specific requirements for data processing by the State	Special exceptions for data processing by the State	Shared use between Public and Private agents
Brazil (law n 13, 709 / 18)	Art 5, VI and VII, include natural or legal persons governed by 'public or private law'.	Art 7, III and 11, II, b contain specific legal bases for processing by the Public Administration.	Chapter IV (arts 23 to 32) contains specifications regarding processing of personal data by Public Authorities.	Art 4 exempts data processing for public safety, national defence, state security or activities of investigation and prosecution of criminal offenses from the LGPD's provisions.	Art 26 regulates the shared use of personal data between public entities and private entities for the execution of public policies, requiring transparency and adherence to data protection principles.
Russia (Federal Law n 152-FZ)	Art 1 expressly mentions various governmental bodies. Art 3(2) defines operator to include 'a state authority, municipal authority'.	Art 6(4) contains a legal basis for data processing necessary to the execution of various executive powers by state authorities.	Art 13 covers data processing in the context of state or municipal information systems.		
India	The definition of Data Fiduciary and Processor mention 'any person', without specific mention of State actors. The definition of "person" includes the State (art. 2, (i) and (s)(vi)).	Art 7(b) and (c) contain specific authorizations for state processing of data for the State to provide certain services to the Data Principal or to perform instrumentalities or functions or, finally, in the interest of the country's sovereignty and integrity.	In the hypothesis of art. 7(b), previous consent is required, that the data be held in digital form,.and that standards be followed in "accordance with the policy issued by the Central Government or any law for the time being in force for governance of personal data". For art. 7(c), no such requirements are instituted.	Art 17 exempts government from application of the law when processing is necessary 'in the interests of sovereignty and integrity of India, security of the State, friendly relations with foreign States, maintenance of public order'.	No explicit mention of Public-Private sharing or shared use, although legitimate uses (art. 7) could be interpreted to include such cases.

(continued)

Table 7.1 Continued

Country	Definition of processing agents include State agents	Specific legal basis for State processing	Specific requirements for data processing by the State	Special exceptions for data processing by the State	Shared use between Public and Private agents
China (PIPL)	Personal data processors are not defined in specific terms to include or exclude State actors.	There is no specific legal basis, although broader bases such as Art 13 (3) or (7) may include state authorities in specific situations. There is, however, a specific section (3) of Chapter II dedicated to information processing by State Organs.	Art 36 establishes a data localization obligation for personal data, as well as a specific security assessment of these data processing activities. Art 37 extends Section 3's rules (arts 33 to 37) to organizations administering public affairs via authorization by law or regulation.		
South Africa (POPIA)	The concept of 'responsible party' explicitly includes 'public or private' bodies.			There is no legal basis per se. However, there is an exclusion for processing by a public body in limited cases, meaning the law does not apply in the hypotheses of Art 6(c).	

Regarding Russia, although there are specific provisions related to personal data processing by state authorities in the Federal Data Protection Law, there remain broad powers with minimal oversight, particularly under the Yarovaya Law (Federal Law of 6 March 2006 No 35-Fz on counterterrorism) and the Data Localization Law (Federal Law No 242-FZ), as well as the Data Protection Act (Federal Law No 149-FZ). As noted in the Chinese scenario, these laws can be used to enable extensive state access to personal data, especially for purposes related to national security and anti-terrorism, with few constraints and limited transparency. Russia's personal data law framework technically acknowledges privacy rights, but enforcement is inconsistent. Notably, the Federal Security Service (FSB), the Russian government's internal security and counterintelligence agency, has wide-ranging authority to access stored data without subject notification. The absence of independent oversight mechanisms is particularly concerning, as this leaves individuals with limited avenues for challenging or even being aware of government data access.

India's Digital Personal Data Protection Act of 2023 contains equally general language that leaves leeway for ample governmental access and processing of personal data. This is especially evident in its section 17. Section 17(1) creates exceptions to the application of chapters II (obligations of data fiduciary) and III (rights and duties of data principal), as well as section 16 (restrictions of international transfers) for law enforcement, criminal investigations and judicial activities. Section 17(2) creates an ample exception to the Act when personal data is processed by state actors when:

> 17(2) The provisions of this Act shall not apply in respect of the processing of personal data—
>
> (a) by such instrumentality of the State as the Central Government may notify, in the interests of sovereignty and integrity of India, security of the State, friendly relations with foreign States, maintenance of public order or preventing incitement to any cognizable offence relating to any of these, and the processing by the Central Government of any personal data that such instrumentality may furnish to it; and (b) necessary for research, archiving or statistical purposes if the personal data is not to be used to take any decision specific to a Data Principal and such processing is carried on in accordance with such standards as may be prescribed.

These jurisdictions share the issue of containing overly broad permissions or insufficiently defined safeguards to government access and processing of personal data, especially in activities related to security and intelligence. Brazil's LGPD, on the other hand, contains a chapter solely dedicated to personal data and processing by public authorities, besides containing specific legal bases for execution of public policies requiring personal and special category personal data processing. That chapter's contents provide specification on the conditions under which processing by public authorities may take place, such as the connection of the stated purpose to public interest objectives, transparency and accountability duties, indication of a Data Protection Officer, and the exceptional cases where data may be transferred to private entities from those public authorities.

However, article 4 of the LGPD also contains a set of broad exceptions for public security, national defence, state security, and activities for the investigation and prosecution of criminal offences. These cases should be regulated in a specific law, but as yet no such law exists, which leaves a significant legal gap in control over government access to personal data in crucial hypotheses. The LGPD principles still apply, as well as the existing safeguards in laws such as Law No 9,296/1996 (Interception of Communications), Law No 12,850/2013 (Organized Crime Law), Law No 13,344/2016 (Human Trafficking Law), and Law No 12,965/2014 (Marco Civil da Internet), where applicable, such as the need for judicial authorization for accessing personal data and judicial oversight of such activities.

Finally, South Africa is a similar case to Brazil, as POPIA creates an exception for use of personal data by a public body (section 6 c):

> (i) which involves national security, including activities that are aimed at assisting in the identification of the financing of terrorist and related activities, defence or public safety; or (ii) the purpose of which is the prevention, detection, including assistance in the identification of the proceeds of unlawful activities and the combating of money laundering activities, investigation or proof of offences, the prosecution of offenders or the execution of sentences or security measures, to the extent that adequate safeguards have been established in legislation for the protection of such personal information.

Government access and processing of personal data in these cases is regulated by other norms, such as the Regulation of Interception of Communications and Provision of Communication-Related Information Act (RICA), the National Strategic Intelligence Act, and the Cybercrimes Act. All these have faced criticism for overly broad language and a lack of safeguards, such as 'notification to the subject of surveillance, independent judicial authorization, protection for journalists and practising lawyers, and proper management of intercepted information',[66] issues that have led the country's Constitutional Court to declare RICA unconstitutional[67] and to attempts to reform it to better protect privacy.[68]

In summary, a crucial point of tension in government access to personal data is those cases where public security, national defence, and intelligence activities are involved. China, Russia, and South Africa showcase issues in existing regulation of these activities, with overly broad language which leaves space for abuses. Brazil is lacking in terms of specific regulation of government access to personal data in these exceptional cases; however, it does provide specific guidance in other situations and has pre-existing laws that provide some safeguards regarding privacy in the course of those state activities that are accepted in the general data protection law.

7.5. Data Protection in the New BRICS: Egypt, Ethiopia, Indonesia, Saudi Arabia, the United Arab Emirates, and Iran

As pointed out in Chapter 1 of this volume, the BRICS grouping has recently expanded to include four new members: Egypt, Ethiopia, the United Arab Emirates, and Iran. The first three have all approved general data protection laws in the past two years. In July 2020, Egypt adopted its Resolution No 151 of 2020 on the Protection of Personal Data; in 2021, the United Arab Emirates adopted Federal Decree-Law No 45 of 2021on the Protection of Personal Data, which entered into force in January 2022; and in July 2024, Ethiopia enacted the Personal Data Protection Proclamation No 1321/2024. Only Iran is still in the process of elaborating its framework upon the Draft Protection of Personal Data Law, proposed by the Ministry of Communications and Information Technology and announced in 2018.

Given the very recent entry of these countries in the BRICS grouping as well as their relatively limited experience of data governance, the new BRICS members' frameworks have not been analysed in detail, but some key features of

[66] Anja Hofmeyr, 'An End to Secret State Surveillance under RICA' (*Cliffe Dekker Hofmeyr*, 16 February 2021) <https://www.cliffedekkerhofmeyr.com/en/news/publications/2021/Dispute/Dispute-Resolution-Alert-16-February-2021-An-end-to-secret-state-surveillance-under-RICA.html> accessed 8 November 2024.

[67] ibid.

[68] Admire Moyo, 'Good Attempt but RICA Bill Still Flawed, Say Legal Experts' (*ITWeb*, 15 November 2023) <https://www.itweb.co.za/article/good-attempt-but-rica-bill-still-flawed-say-legal-experts/P3gQ2qGAPRG7nRD1> accessed 8 November 2024.

their data protection laws are explored in this section. Notably, the existing set of principles, data subject rights, data security obligations, and data transfer mechanisms embedded in their respective legislations are highlighted, as these elements might be particularly relevant regarding the new BRICS quest to develop 'a global framework for data governance, including cross-border data flows, to . . . ensure the interoperability of data regulatory frameworks at all levels'.[69]

7.5.1. Egypt

Egypt's Personal Data Protection Law No 151 of 2020 was published in the Official Gazette on 15 July 2020, and came into effect on 14 October 2020. Its introduction was motivated by the increasing reliance on digital technologies and the need to safeguard citizens' personal data amidst rising concerns about privacy violations and data misuse. The law mandates that personal data be collected for specific, legitimate purposes that are clearly communicated to the data subject. Article 3 also states that the data must be accurate, valid, and secured, processed legally and within the scope of its collection purposes. Retention of personal data should not exceed the necessary duration for its intended purpose. The law also requires data controllers to ensure the confidentiality and security of personal data, preventing unlawful access, breach, damage, alteration, or manipulation through illegal procedures, per article 4.[70]

Article 2 grants Egyptian citizens several rights under this law, including the right to know, review, access, and obtain their personal data; to withdraw prior consent for the retention or processing of their personal data; to rectify, edit, erase, add, or update their personal data; to limit the scope of data processing; to be informed of any personal data breach affecting their data; and to object to the processing of their personal data or its results if it conflicts with their principal rights and freedoms.

As regards data security obligations, article 7 mandates that data controllers must report personal data breaches to the Data Protection Centre within seventy-two hours. Breaches related to national security must be reported

[69] BRICS, Kazan Declaration (n 2) para 71.

[70] 'Egypt: Government Issues New Data Protection Law' (*Baker and McKenzie*, 28 September 2020) <https://insightplus.bakermckenzie.com/bm/data-technology/egypt-and-united-arab-emirates-egypt-issues-new-data-protection-law>.

immediately. Controllers also need to inform the data subject within three business days, detailing the steps taken. A Data Protection Officer (DPO) must be appointed to oversee data protection compliance (article 8).

Transferring personal data to a foreign country is prohibited unless the destination guarantees equal or higher protection levels, and a licence or permit is obtained (article 14). Indeed, article 14 of the Law mandates that any company wishing to transfer personal data outside of Egypt must first obtain a licence from the Regulator. Moreover, such transfers are permitted solely to countries that provide a level of protection for personal data equivalent to that established by Egyptian law. Article 15 outlines several exceptions to the restrictions imposed by article 14, all of which are contingent upon the prior acquisition of explicit consent from the data subject. Conditions for transfer include the conformity of the data's nature or purpose, legitimate interest in the data by controllers, processors, or subjects, and a data protection level abroad that is not below Egypt's standard (article 16).

To enforce the provisions of this law, the Egyptian government established the Personal Data Protection Centre (PDPC) as the independent regulatory authority responsible for overseeing compliance. Article 19 delineates an extensive array of duties and competencies assigned to the Regulator. Notably, it is tasked with the responsibility of issuing licences to companies for the processing of data and for facilitating cross-border data transfers. The PDPC is tasked with issuing licences for data processing activities and ensuring adherence to the law's requirements. It has the authority to impose administrative penalties for non-compliance, including fines and operational restrictions.

Despite the establishment of this regulatory body, the law has faced criticism regarding its implementation and potential shortcomings. Critics argue that the law lacks clarity in certain provisions, particularly concerning the rights of individuals and the obligations of data controllers. Additionally, some stakeholders worry that the law may not adequately protect against state surveillance practices, given Egypt's historical context of stringent governmental control over personal freedoms.

7.5.2. Ethiopia

Ethiopia's Personal Data Protection Proclamation No 1321/2024 stipulates that data collection and processing should be limited to specific purposes explained to users, ensuring legitimacy and transparency (article 6). Users must be informed about how their data is handled (article 12).

Ethiopian citizens have rights to be informed about data processing activities (article 24); to access their personal data (article 25); to correct or erase data under certain circumstances (articles 27 and 28); to restrict processing (article 30); to object to processing for specific reasons (article 29); and to receive their data in a transferable format (article 32).

The Proclamation on Personal Data Protection was enacted in May 2022 as part of broader reforms aimed at modernizing the country's legal framework in line with international standards. This law emerged from a growing recognition of the need to protect personal information amid rapid digital transformation and increased internet penetration in Ethiopia. The Proclamation seeks to establish clear guidelines for data processing activities while safeguarding individual privacy rights. Its approval marked a significant step forward in addressing concerns about data privacy in a country where such regulations were previously lacking. However, the Ethiopian government later decided to designate the Ethiopian Communications Authority (ECA) as the data protection regulator, raising significant concerns regarding impartiality and accountability of the organ.[71]

Critics argue that entrusting a government agency with such a critical role undermines the effectiveness of data protection measures, as the ECA is inherently susceptible to governmental influence, which may compromise its ability to operate independently and objectively. Furthermore, the ECA's oversight capabilities are questioned in light of its existing responsibilities to oversee the telecoms sector, leading to fears that it may prioritize governmental interests over personal data protection.

The proclamation mandates the implementation of measures like encryption and data transfer restrictions, providing safeguards against unauthorized access, disclosure, or data loss (article 17). Personal data cannot be transferred to countries lacking adequate data protection standards unless certain conditions are met (article 18). These conditions include: adequate protection abroad; data subject's informed consent; necessity of the transfer according to the Proclamation standards, which include execution of a contract; and transfer of personal data collected from a public register (article 20).

[71] Ashenafi Endale, 'Critics fear Comms Authority Personal Data Dominion, Impartiality in Legislative Wrangle' (*The Reporter*, 13 January 2024) <https://thereporterethiopia.com/38279/>.

7.5.3. Indonesia

Through the enactment of Law No 27 of 2022, Indonesia's Personal Data Protection Law (PDP Law) enables Indonesia to align closely with international standards of data privacy, modelled on the EU's General Data Protection Regulation. Following the enactment of the PDP Law, data controllers and processors were given a two-year transition period to conform, which ended on 17 October 2024. Before the PDP Law, Indonesia did not have a comprehensive law on personal data protection, instead having separate legislation which was either sector-, matter- or nature-specific that regulated general aspects of privacy and personal data protection.

Under article 20 of the PDP Law, for data processing to be lawful, an organization must either obtain express consent from the data subjects to process their data for specific purposes, or be fulfilling contractual obligations, protecting key interest of the data subjects, serving public interests, complying with legal requirements, or have a legitimate interest. The Indonesian Data Protection Authority is formally tasked with functions of policy specification, supervision, and enforcement of the PDP law, including dispute resolution, as defined by articles 58–61 of the legislation. However, the Authority has not been established yet, at the time of this writing, and the Ministry of Communication and Informatics (MOCI) is temporarily fulfilling the abovementioned responsibilities, ensuring compliance, supervising the implementation of data protections, coordinating cross-border data transfers, overseeing notifications of data breaches, and enforcing sanctions for non-compliance.

The PDP Law outlines key principles that govern the collection and processing of personal data in order to address their country-specific concerns whilst aligning Indonesia's data protection standards with international standards, thus improving the safety and trust of digital interactions within Indonesia. These principles include lawfulness and transparency (article 27), purpose limitation (article 28), data minimization (article 27), accuracy (article 29), and integrity and confidentiality (article 36). Data subjects are also afforded several rights, including the right to be informed (article 5), right to access (article 7), right to erasure (article 8), right to rectification (article 6), right to restrict processing (article 11), right to object to processing (article 8), right to data portability (article 13), right to withdraw consent (article 9), right to sue and receive compensation (article 12), and the right to object to automated decision-making (article 10).

The law requires certain organizations to appoint a Data Protection Officer (DPO) per article 53, a crucial role in ensuring data protection regulation compliance. An organization is required to appoint a DPO if processing personal data is part of their core activities or if an organization handles large quantities of sensitive personal data. Failure to appoint a DPO where required can lead to administrative sanctions such as a written warning, fine, or temporary suspension of data processing activities.

Although the PDP Law does not provide any specific technical measures or standards, article 35 specifies general measures to data controllers as they are obligated to protect and ensure the security of the personal data that they process. These obligations include the setting out and implementation of operational technical measures in order to protect personal data from any disruption whilst being processed, which is contrary to law and regulation provisions, and to determine the appropriate level of security necessary for the personal data by taking into account the nature of the data and risks. Importantly, when data breaches occur, the data controller and data processor must notify the affected data subjects and the Indonesian DPA within seventy-two hours and include the personal data involved, when and how the breach occurred, and any measures taken to mitigate harm, per article 46.

Lastly, article 56 of the PDP Law sets data transfer conditions in order to ensure that cross-border personal data transfers from Indonesia meet clear data protection standards. The recipient country must have a level of personal data protection that is equivalent to or exceeds that which is provided under the PDP Law. The yet-to-be-established Indonesian Data Protection Authority will be the entity responsible to perform such assessment. If this level of adequate protection is not met, the data exporter must ensure that binding, adequate safeguards, such as standard contractual clauses (SCCs) are in place. If neither adequacy of protection nor appropriate safeguards are in place, prior consent is required from the data subject, per article 56(4).

7.5.4. Saudi Arabia

The Kingdom of Saudi Arabia's Personal Data Protection Law (PDPL) was issued 16 September 2021 and then amended 27 March 2023. It is based on a similar set of key principles that are found in most BRICS countries, set by article 11, including lawfulness, fairness and transparency, purpose limitation, data minimization, accuracy, storage limitation, integrity and confidentiality, and accountability. According to article 5(1) PDPL, the primary legal basis for the processing of personal data is consent of the data subject. However, the PDPL also provides circumstances where consent is not required for the processing of personal data, such as compliance with a legal obligation or is necessary for the fulfilment of a contract (article 6.2), and for the purpose of legitimate interest (article 6.4).

Data controllers are obligated to comply with the PDPL, including the restriction on the use of personal (article 14) and sensitive data (article 35), and to enforce security measures (article 19) and manage data breaches (article 20). Furthermore the PDPL mentions in article 30(4)(c) the need for data controllers to register with the 'Competent Authority', the Saudi Authority for Data and Artificial Intelligence (SDAIA). Article 30(2) states that data controllers must also appoint a data protection officer in certain cases such as when the data controller is a public entity who processes personal data on a large scale, when large scale personal data processing is a primary activity or when processing sensitive data is a core activity of the data controller.

Article 4 of the PDPL also affords individuals data subject rights in order to empower their citizens and increase their level of control over their personal data. These rights include the right to be informed (article 4.1), a right to access their personal data (article 4.2), a right to request correction if their personal data is inaccurate, incomplete, or out of date (article 4.4), a right to request erasure (article 4.5), a right to withdraw consent (article 5.2), and a right to request provision of personal data in a readable and clear form (article 4.3). Whilst these rights provide a level of control to individuals, their enforcement relies upon the performance of the newly created SDAIA.

Lastly, data transfer is specifically regulated by article 29 of the PDPL. Organizations wishing to transfer Saudi personal data must ensure the receiving country has an adequate level of personal data protection, per article 29(2)(b). If the protection level falls below the PDPL standards, additional safeguards are necessary. These safeguards may include standard contractual clauses (SCCs) or binding corporate rules (BCRs). Furthermore, the law sets additional requirements for the transfer of sensitive data, including the implementation of appropriate security measures to protect the personal data when at rest and in transit, notifying the data subject about the transfer, providing them with information regarding the data protection laws of the recipient country, and obtaining a written agreement from the receiving organization which outlines the security measures that will be utilized to protect the data. Importantly, article 1(11) of the law provides an explicit definition of sensitive data, which include but are not limited to: biometric data, data on sexual orientation, ethnic origin, religious beliefs, children's data, criminal records, political opinions, and health data.

7.5.5. United Arab Emirates

The United Arab Emirates' Federal Decree-Law No 45 of 2021 prescribes lawfulness, fairness, transparency, purpose limitation, data minimization, data quality, retention, and security. Additional provisions may be detailed in the Executive Regulations (article 5). The Federal Decree-Law was enacted in September 2021 as part of a broader vision to enhance privacy protections as a strategic step to foster legal certainty within a rapidly evolving digital landscape. This law reflects a commitment from UAE authorities to align local regulations with global standards, such as GDPR and OECD Guidelines, while promoting innovation and economic growth through digital transformation initiatives.[72]

According to the new framework, UAE citizens have rights to access their data; to transfer their data; to object to data processing; to rectify and erase their data; and to have their data processed without consent in specific cases (eg, public interest, health protection, contractual performance) (article 4). The law also requires the implementation of technical and organizational measures to maintain high data security standards, such as encryption and pseudonymization. Measures must ensure the availability and testing of the effectiveness of implemented security protocols (article 20). A DPO with sufficient skills and knowledge in data protection must be appointed (article 10).

Enforcement of this law is managed by an independent regulator known as the UAE Data Office, which operates under the Ministry of Digital Economy. This office is tasked with overseeing compliance with data protection regulations, providing guidance to organizations on best practices, and handling complaints from individuals regarding potential violations of their data rights. The UAE Data Office has been empowered to issue fines for non-compliance and ensure that organizations adhere to established standards for data processing and protection.

Lastly, data transfers are restricted to approved countries or specific situations (eg, contractual necessity, public interest). There is no mechanism to use contracts to safeguard data transfers to unapproved countries, according to articles 22 and 23 of the decree-law.

Despite these advances, critics have raised concerns about certain aspects of the UAE's data protection regime. Some argue that while the law establishes important principles for personal data handling, it lacks robust mechanisms

[72] See the official website of the United Arab Emirates, dedicated to data protection issues <https://u.ae/en/about-the-uae/digital-uae/data/data-protection-laws>.

for accountability and transparency, particularly regarding government access to personal information. Additionally, there are worries about how effectively individual rights will be enforced in practice.

7.5.6. Iran

As mentioned previously, Iran has not yet enacted a comprehensive data protection framework, although the Ministry of Communications and Information Technology proposed a Draft Protection of Personal Data Law in 2018.[73] Importantly, the draft has been criticized for being 'poorly conceived and inconsistent with the international legal obligations of Iran to adequately protect the privacy rights of its citizens', including by failing to clearly define the key data protection principles that typically represent the conceptual basis of each data protection framework.[74] Furthermore, the draft also includes broad definitions of 'security' exceptions in article 12, which has been criticized for allowing data processing under vague circumstances related to national security.[75]

Oversight of the implementation of this law is to be managed by a yet-to-be-created Data Protection Commission, as proposed in article 13. The Commission would be tasked with ensuring compliance with the law and protecting individuals' rights concerning their personal data. However, concerns have been raised regarding the composition of this Commission, as it might include members associated with the security agencies. This raises questions about the effectiveness and impartiality of oversight in a context where governmental surveillance is common.

As regards regulating personal data transfers, it is important to note that article 38 of the draft law sets data localization requirements limiting 'foreign-based processing'. Indeed, the article would prescribe that Iranian citizens' personal data 'can only be stored in the data centres located in the sovereign realm of the Islamic Republic of Iran or the foreign-based data centres approved by the relevant authorities'.

[73] Mohammad Mustafa Mohiqi, 'Personal Data Protection in the Iranian Legal System' (2023) 16(3) Journal of Politics and Law < https://doi.org/10.5539/jpl.v16n3p10>.

[74] Personal Data Protection and Safeguarding Draft Act (June 2019) art 19 <https://www.article19.org/wp-content/uploads/2019/06/Legal-Analysis-of-Draft-Data-Protection-Act.pdf>.

[75] ibid.

7.6. Transborder Data Transfers in the BRICS

Normative mechanisms regulating international data transfers and including some forms of data localization present some converging paths among BRICS countries while each country has established unique mechanisms to regulate them, with varying degrees of flexibility.

The elements of convergence and divergence in the BRICS frameworks regulating data transfers reveal idiosyncrasies of each country's jurisdiction and approach to personal data regulation. Even where the rules converge amongst BRICS countries, it is interesting to observe the small differences that exist, which point to the juridical specificities of each system and the often-heterogeneous manners for implementing similar normative prescriptions through regulatory techniques.

The following sections provide an overview of the main regulatory strategies adopted by the BRICS countries to frame international data transfers, comparing these approaches to subsequently identify what could be the most promising path for cooperation in data governance. Lastly, the concluding section of this chapter dares proposing some concrete guidance regarding how such cooperation could be enacted by the BRICS grouping, leveraging the existing venues to enhance their digital cooperation.

7.6.1. Consent and Adequacy Decisions

One clear element of convergence is represented by data transfers based on the data subject's consent. This legal basis allows data processing in all jurisdictions. It comes surrounded by adjectives that give specific requirements for its validity, such as 'full knowledge, and in a voluntary and explicit statement' (China's PIPL, art 14); 'free, specific, informed, unconditional and unambiguous with a clear affirmative action' (Indian DPDP Act 2023, s 6) 'voluntary, specific and informed' (RSA's POPIA, art 1); and 'free, informed and unequivocal' (Brazilian LGPD, art 5). The Russian 2015 Data Localization Law has also required data operators to process personal data of Russian citizens within Russia as a 'primary' jurisdiction for the database, although data can be transferred abroad when complying with additional requirements.

Interestingly, in the DPDP Act, the general standard adopted by the law is based on non-restriction of data transfers, unless the Indian Government defines specific limits, such as the Reserve Bank of India's Directive 2017-18/153, whose paragraph 2(i) mandates data localization for payment system providers, that are required to store payment data within India.

Hence, in all BRICS jurisdictions, consent is one of the possible legal bases for data processing in general, which becomes particularly useful in case of data transfers. However, the qualification of consent with varying strict conditions aims at making sure that it truly represents the will of the data subject, while also maintaining more leverage in the regulators' capability to restrict transfers if needed.

In the case of international data transfers, consent is a possible legal basis in all BRICS jurisdictions, except for a significant difference in the case of China. Indeed, due to the specific structure of PIPL's article 13, consent cannot be deemed as an independent legal basis allowing data transfers, but rather as a prerequisite of almost any international data transfer, which must also observe the requirements set forth in article 38.

In other words, except under one of the six non-consent cases in article 13 of the PIPL, it is a necessary legal basis for data transfers outside of Chinese borders. Additionally, these transfers must either pass a security assessment by a state agency, undergo a personal information protection certification as regulated by a state cybersecurity and informatization department, or implement standard contractual clauses, recently adopted by China.[76] This creates a unique structure enabling the control of data transfers, whereby the state maintains important regulatory prerogatives regarding cybersecurity and data protection matters, being able to define under what conditions transfers are allowed. This approach aligns with the Chinese data architecture's close ties 'with data sovereignty, national security and increasingly personal data protection to maintain the "legal, secure and free flows" of transborder data'.[77]

Given the existence of consent as a shared legal ground for personal data processing, with some specific caveats, it is important to emphasize that the design of contractual tools based on the joint application of consent as a lawful ground for processing and the adoption of model contractual clauses as a

[76] CAC and China, 'Standard Contractual Measures for the Transmission of Personal Information [Automatic Translation]' (*Cyberspace Administration of China*, 24 February 2023) <http://www.cac.gov.cn/2023-02/24/c_1678884830036813.htm> accessed 20 June 2023.

[77] Yik-Chan Chin and Jingwu Zhao, 'Governing Cross-Border Data Flows: International Trade Agreements and Their Limits' (2022) 11 Laws 63, 6 <https://www.mdpi.com/2075-471X/11/4/63> accessed 4 July 2023.

facilitator of international data transfers may be one of the most promising strategies to foster intra-BRICS data flows. This option will be explored in further detail in the following sections, to understand the extent to which it might be feasible and under what conditions.

Another increasingly widespread regulatory basis for the international transfer of personal data is the use of the so-called 'adequacy decisions'[78] issued either by the national data protection regulator or a government branch, recognizing the substantially equal level of data protection in third countries and, therefore, allowing data transfers. Being the first BRICS country to have adopted a data protection framework, Russia offers an interesting example of the use of adequacy decisions, as it automatically extends such recognition to all signatories of the Council of Europe's Convention for the Protection of Individuals with Regard to Automatic Processing of Personal Data, more commonly known as 'Convention 108' and signed by Russia in 2006.[79] Furthermore, Roskomnadzor, the Russian ICT regulator, has also formally deemed as adequate numerous non-European countries, such as Argentina (which received adequacy also from the European Union) but also several African countries that the European Commission has never considered as adequate, such as Angola, Benin, Gabon, Mali, Morocco, South Africa, and Tunisia.[80]

Importantly, the majority of BRICS countries' data protection frameworks, except for South Africa and India, contain provisions allowing international data transfers in accordance with specific international engagements. China and Brazil share a commonality regarding this hypothesis. Both countries allow international data transfers in compliance with treaties concerning judicial or law enforcement cooperation, with an additional mention of 'intelligence' activities that justify personal data transfers in the case of Brazil.

This latter point seems particularly puzzling in the case of Brazil, since the Brazilian LGPD excludes from its scope data processing for law enforcement purposes, thus creating a remarkably wide grey area allowing the transfer of

[78] Adequacy evaluations, according to which a national regulator determines if a foreign jurisdiction's data protection law meets the national standards, have become widespread in many countries while being based on highly diverse criteria. According to a recent study, besides the European Union, sixty-five countries have already established adequacy reviews of foreign jurisdictions to ascertain if international transfers of personal data may be allowed to cross their borders. See A Chander and PM Schwartz, 'Privacy and/or Trade' (2023) 90 University Chicago Law Review 49.

[79] Council of Europe, 'Chart of Signatures and Ratifications of Treaty 181' <https://www.coe.int/en/web/conventions/full-list> accessed 20 June 2023.

[80] ibid 75.

data but exempting law enforcement from abiding to the general data protection framework.

Indeed, Brazil allows data transfer under the more general 'international agreements' category in article 33, VI—'where the transfer results in a commitment undertaken under an international cooperation agreement'. It must be acknowledged that the wording of this provision creates remarkable confusion, since, if taken at face value, it seems to enact conditional legality of a current data transfer. A less unclear formulation could have suggested the legality of transfers resulting *from* a commitment, rather than *in* a commitment. This obscure provision may lead to multiple interpretations. It could be that the legislator intended to allow for the preparatory measures for an international agreement, or that the data transfers following an international agreement are allowed. The exact sense and the solution to this legal conundrum remain open to the Data Protection Authority's guidance.

Lastly, the new BRICS countries present a similar set of options. Apart from the above-mentioned embryonic Iranian framework, which seems to propose a general data localization mandate, all the other newcomers in the BRICS grouping allow data transfers to countries deemed as adequate by the national regulators, or under other specific conditions. Article 15 of the Egyptian law allows transfers when a licence has been obtained from the DPA and where the level of protection is not less than that provided under the Law. However, the law does not specify the criteria to be followed to ascertain which national regimes can be deemed as adequate unlike other data protection laws. As such, the DPA will need to define the criteria for adequacy and licences for cross-border transfers in future policies and regulations.

Ethiopia's Proclamation presents a more ample menu of options allowing data transfers when the data controller or processor must provide evidence that the receiving jurisdiction has an appropriate level of protection for personal data, as outlined in article 18 of the Proclamation; when the data subject has given explicit consent for the transfer after being informed about the potential risks involved; when the data transfer is necessary according to the provisions of the Proclamation (article 20), such as contractual obligations or legal compliance; and when personal data is originally collected from a public register intended to provide information to the public (article 21).

Lastly, the UAE framework allows data transfers through signing agreements with foreign institutions and companies to comply with the UAE personal data protection law, and where either consent is provided, or the transfer is contractually necessary.

7.6.2. A BRICS-led Approach to International Data Transfers Rules

A BRICS-led approach to international data transfers could be seen from two perspectives. On the one hand, it could act as a framework facilitating data flows amongst BRICS members and partners, providing an alternative to established international data governance frameworks, such as the Council of Europe Convention for the Protection of Individuals with Regard to Automatic Processing of Personal Data, better known as Convention 108, or the African Union Convention on Cyber Security and Personal Data Protection, better known as Malabo Convention. From this perspective, the aim of the possible shared solutions would be to foster legal interoperability amongst leading emerging economies.

On the other hand, a BRICS-led approach may be particularly interesting as a prototype of what could be scaled up as a global framework for data governance, promoted by the 'locomotive forces of the Global South'.[81] These options are not mutually exclusive; neither are they complementary. In both cases, besides fulfilling the commitments of the Kazan Declaration, setting the bases for the elaboration of a global framework for data governance, a BRICS enhanced cooperation on these matters would contribute directly to the implementation and expansion of the 2021 BRICS Framework for Ensuring Consumer Protection in e-Commerce.[82]

This consideration is particularly relevant as talks around a multilateral framework for e-commerce, which would include aspects of cybersecurity and personal data protection, have been ongoing under the World Trade Organization's Joint Initiative on E-Commerce, which delivered a 'stabilized text' after five years of negotiations.[83] WTO efforts might prove useful to identify elements of consensus, but they might have limited effectiveness, per se, due to the current WTO paralysis. Given the recent adoption of a UN Convention against Cybercrime proposed and brokered under the relevant influence of BRICS countries, it would be interesting to utilize the BRICS as a laboratory to test the elaboration of the data governance framework to be discussed at the UN level. In this perspective a BRICS-led initiative could be built to complement and expand the UN Proposed Normative

[81] L Belli, ' BRICS: The New Digital Locomotives' (*Beijing Review*, 11 July 2022) <https://www.bjreview.com/Opinion/Voice/202207/t20220711_800300500.html>.

[82] BRICS Framework for Ensuring Consumer Protection in e-Commerce (2021) https://brics2023.gov.za/wp-content/uploads/2023/07/Framework-for-ensuring-consumer-protection-in-e-commerce-2021.pdf.

[83] WTO, Joint Statement Initiative on E-commerce INF/ECOM/87 (26 July 2024) <https://www.wto.org/english/tratop_e/ecom_e/joint_statement_e.htm>.

Foundations for International Data Governance: Goals and Principles,[84] with the aim of providing concrete proposals to support international data governance.

Moreover, as mentioned in the introduction of this volume, since the 2021 BRICS Summit, resulting in the New Delhi Declaration, BRICS leaders have not only established a formal mechanism for enhanced cooperation in e-commerce but they have also expressed the intention to:

> advance practical intra-BRICS cooperation in [cybersecurity] including through the implementation of the BRICS Roadmap of Practical Cooperation on ensuring Security in the Use of ICTs and the activities of the BRICS Working Group on Security in the use of ICTs, and underscore[d] also the importance of establishing legal frameworks of cooperation among BRICS States on this matter and acknowledge[d] the work towards consideration and elaboration of proposals, including on a BRICS intergovernmental agreement on cooperation on ensuring security in the use of ICTs and on bilateral agreements among BRICS countries.[85]

From this perspective, one of the reasons for the BRICS grouping's unusual character is that despite their highly heterogenous nature, all the countries have relevant interests in increasing both cybersecurity and trade, by leveraging data processing fostering their data sovereignty.[86] As noted by Burri, all these international developments reveal the 'intensified contestation between free data flows as an essential element of the data-driven economy and the protection of privacy as a sovereign right of states to safeguard their citizens'.[87] As such, they are ongoing processes that will determine sovereign states' policy choices—such as the ability to enact data localization legislation, to adopt policies directed at concepts such as 'data sovereignty' and to promote policies directed at promoting digital development and bridging existing divides.[88]

Data transfers are at the core of digital transformation efforts and, depending on how they are regulated, they can undermine or strengthen digital

[84] UN Chief Executives Board for Coordination. Proposed Normative Foundations for International Data Governance: Goals and Principles. United Nations system contribution to the advancement of international data governance. CEB/2024/2/Add.1 (8 November 2024) <https://unsceb.org/proposed-normative-foundations-international-data-governance-goals-and-principles>.

[85] BRICS, XIII BRICS Summit, New Delhi Declaration (9 September 2021) <https://web.archive.org/web/20231015202017/https://brics2021.gov.in/brics/public/uploads/docpdf/getdocu-51.pdf>.

[86] Belli, Gaspar, and Singh (n 3).

[87] Mira Burri (ed), *Big Data and Global Trade Law* (Cambridge University Press 2021).

[88] Chin and Zhao (n 77).

Table 7.2 BRICS international personal data transfer rules

Norm absent in this jurisdiction =	⊗
Norm present in this jurisdiction =	☑

Rule / Country	Brazil	Russia	India[a]	China	South Africa
Adequacy decision or adequate protection in destination country's law	☑	☑	⊗	☑	☑
With consent from the data subject	☑	☑	⊗	☑	☑
When related to international agreements	☑	☑	⊗	☑	⊗
Contract clauses (standard clauses or negotiated clauses)	☑	⊗	⊗	☑	☑
For the execution of a contract or its preliminary acts	☑	☑	⊗	⊗	☑
Global corporate norms	☑	⊗	⊗	⊗	☑
Certificates and codes of conduct	☑	⊗	⊗	☑	⊗
Protection of life and health	☑	☑	⊗	⊗	⊗
Authorization by the data protection authority	☑	⊗	⊗	⊗	⊗
To a person or entity engaged in the provision of health services or emergency services where such transfer is necessary for prompt action	⊗	⊗	⊗	⊗	⊗
Passing a security assessment organized by the State cybersecurity and informatization department	⊗	⊗	⊗	☑	⊗
When the transfer is necessary for the execution of public policy or legal attribution of the public service	☑	⊗	⊗	⊗	⊗
For the protection of values provided for in federal laws	⊗	☑	⊗	⊗	⊗
In the interest of the data subject	⊗	⊗	⊗	⊗	☑
To comply with a legal or regulatory obligation	☑	⊗	⊗	⊗	⊗
To exercise rights in a judicial, administrative or arbitration procedure	☑	⊗	⊗	⊗	⊗
Data localisation	⊗	☑	⊗	⊗	☑

Source: the authors, based on Belli and Doneda 2022; CyberBRICS Project 2020. A detailed table can be found at: https://is.gd/uwapus.

[a] India's Digital Personal Data Protection Act (DPDP Act) 2023 determines in section 17 that the government may restrict cross-border flows, but does not set localisation obligations or predetermined cross-border flow rules or restrictions. There are, however, sectoral regulations that prescribe data localisation for specific categories of data, and have been maintained by the Act, such as the Reserve Bank of India's localisation requirements. See Burman, 'Understanding India's New Data Protection Law' (*Carnegie Endowment for International Peace*, 3 October 2023) <https://carnegieendowment.org/research/2023/10/understanding-indias-new-data-protection-law?lang=en> accessed 7 November 2024.

sovereignty.[89] Table 7.2 provides a schematic overview of the data transfer requirements defined by the BRICS countries in their respective frameworks.

7.7. A Principle-based Approach for Data Governance Cooperation in the BRICS and Beyond

Data Protection Authorities of the BRICS countries are called to play a fundamental role in the regulation of data transfers and digital trade, ultimately having the power to facilitate or limit legal interoperability among the BRICS members and beyond. In this respect, it seems important to emphasize that continuous interactions and cooperation between DPAs would be essential to reach common understandings of, for example, what are the basic data protection principles to which all data processing activities shall abide and the minimum procedural and substantive protections for data subjects. The definition of such elements at the BRICS level, especially as regards a shared principle base, should be seen as a highly instrumental step towards the definition of a developing 'a global framework for data governance, including cross-border data flows, to . . . ensure the interoperability of data regulatory frameworks at all levels'.[90] Indeed, the agreement of a shared set of BRICS principles for data governance could help crystallize a consensus position upon which global efforts could be built.

Furthermore, it is not absurd to posit that BRICS countries can mutually recognize their pre-determined legal pathways for ensuring compliance across jurisdictions, as well as what certification schemes, contractual clauses, or binding corporate rules, that each country uses to regulate transborder data flows. This scenario could be reached by formal and informal means, via formal intergovernmental cooperation projects involving DPAs as well as through dedicated research initiatives fostering shared analysis of common problems, such as the data governance-related activities promoted by the CyberBRICS project. As suggested by Belli and Doneda,[91] the ideal and most sophisticated type of cooperation could even take the form of 'a general "BRICS Data Protection Framework" or a more specific "BRICS Data Transfers Framework" or "BRICS Data Security Framework"'. However, it is important to stress that, to date, no official coordination mechanism for BRICS Data Protection

[89] Belli, Gaspar, and Singh (n 3).
[90] BRICS, Kazan Declaration (n 2) para 71.
[91] Belli and Doneda (n 17).

Authorities has been established and, typically, this type of effort requires considerable diplomatic preparatory work that may take several years to achieve even very timid results.

From this perspective, the first step should be the establishment of a BRICS Working Group on Data Governance, facilitating information exchange and involving the regulators, ideally, creating a calendar of regular meetings of the BRICS Data Protection Authorities. Such initiative could be modelled on the best practices defined by the BRICS Working Group on the Security of ICTs and the BRICS E-commerce Working Group. Indeed, a BRICS Working Group on Data Governance would play an instrumental role in promoting digital cooperation, stimulating the joint analysis of a variety of data-related issues of mutual concern, including automated processing of personal data and artificial intelligence regulation, while also preparing the terrain for the construction of a BRICS data governance framework.

While the establishment of a joint working group facilitating discussion could be relatively easy, it is important to acknowledge that the elaboration of an intra-BRICS data governance framework may be a much more ambitious and arduous task as it would require overcoming apparent incompatibilities and grey areas. Such incompatibilities include overbroad norms (eg, the Russian mention of allowing transfers for the protection of the Constitution, national defence and state security), differing legal requirements or definitions (eg, the Chinese general consent rules and the Chinese and Russian data localization models) and very heterogeneous organizational structures (mainly, the matter of the independence of DPAs in each country's administrative structure). This list may become even longer when considering the idiosyncrasies of the new BRICS countries, as illustrated in the previous section.

Such a framework, however, should be seen as the final goal providing the necessary legal certainty for the flourishing of an open, secure, and mutually beneficial digital environment, based on shared rules facilitating digital trade and services among BRICS countries, guaranteeing equivalent protections to data subjects. Furthermore, the framework may be reached incrementally, starting by the definition of a less ambitious yet equally important set of shared data governance principles, upon which future agreements might be built. These principles would not only safeguard individual rights but also promote interoperability, enhance data security, and consider developmental aspects. This chapter identifies key data governance principles grounded in existing norms.

Importantly, such principles can be already distilled form the comparison of the BRICS frameworks exposed in this volume and their agreement at the

BRICS level could represent a positive step forward in the achievement of the goals recently set by the UN Global Digital Compact with regard to data governance at the international level, advancing 'responsible, equitable and interoperable data governance approaches' with particular emphasis on data privacy and security and cross-border data flows.[92] In this spirit, the analysis conducted along this book illustrate that BRICS countries could already agree on a shared set of principles that can be distilled from their frameworks.

Below, a set of normative and operational principles that could be agreed upon by BRICS countries in order to enhance their cooperation on data governance is proposed.

Normative principles:

- Informational self-determination. This well-established data protection principle underpins the right and capacity to decide when and to whom (personal) data is disclosed, and the extent to which data can be processed. In its individual dimension, corresponding to the right of a natural person to control and determine what others can do with data that refers to them. Its collective dimension is the sentence of data sovereignty, corresponding to the sovereign right to promote the use and regulation of data in the national interest.
- Lawfulness and good faith. This principle applies to data processing at both national and international level, emphasizing that the processing of personal data must adhere to legal standards, being conducted in good faith by all actors involved in the processing, and only when an explicitly identified legal ground allows data processing. The principle is instrumental to ensuring that individuals and regulatory authorities are informed about how their data will be used, guaranteeing that any kind of processing involving more than one entity at domestic or international level, will abide to agreed standards.
- Rights-based approach. A rights-based approach considers that data protection plays an essential role to foster the full spectrum of human rights and policy frameworks need to uphold individuals' rights of access, rectification, deletion, limitation of processing, portability, and opposition.
- Informed consent. When processing of personal data relies on consent as a legal ground, consent must be a free, informed, and unequivocal

[92] The Global Digital Compact was adopted by world leaders on 22 September 2024 at the Summit of the Future in New York. See United Nations Global Digital Compact A/79/L.2 <https://www.un.org/global-digital-compact/sites/default/files/2024-09/Global%20Digital%20Compact%20-%20English_0.pdf>.

expression of the data subject's agreement to the processing of his/her personal data for a specific purpose.

- Purpose specification. Data processing should be limited to specific, legitimate purposes that are clearly defined at the time of collection. This principle mitigates the risks of misuse by ensuring that data is not used in ways that are incompatible with its original purpose.
- Transparency. This principle mandates that information regarding the processing of personal data, including about which entities are involved in such processing and how, is communicated to the individual to which the data refers to, in a clear, precise, and easily accessible manner.
- Accountability. This principle is highly complementary to legality and good faith as clear accountability mechanisms to ensure compliance with data governance norms. Accountability typically includes a clear definition of roles and responsibilities as regards data processing, keeping track of all data processing activates, conducting regular audits, and providing remedies for individuals whose rights have been violated.
- Data security. The data security principle mandates the implementation of appropriate technical and organizational safeguards against unauthorized access, loss, or damage to personal data. Effective security measures must be implemented from the conception until the implementation phase of the data processing to protect individual rights, preserve data confidentiality, integrity, and availability, thus enhancing cybersecurity as a whole and, in turn, public trust in digital systems.
- Necessity and proportionality. This principle involves collecting only the data necessary for the specified purposes, thereby reducing the risk of exposure and misuse. The principle can be also referred to as 'data minimization'.
- Data quality and accuracy. According to this principle, processed data should be accurate and, where necessary, updated to fulfil the specified purposes. Hence, the parties responsible for processing data shall take reasonable steps to keep data up-to-date and eliminate incorrect data, particularly when decisions affecting individuals are made based on this information.
- Non-discriminatory processing. Processing of personal data cannot be carried out for unlawful or abusive discriminatory purposes.

Operational principles:

- Effective oversight and remedies. This principle requires the establishment of well-resourced regulatory bodies capable of enforcing data protection laws and promoting a culture of compliance. Hence, regulators must ensure that individuals are fully informed about their data rights and have accessible mechanisms to seek redress, while data processors are held accountable for their practices.

- Interoperability. To facilitate cooperation in data processing at both national and international level, technical and legal interoperability is essential. This principle mandates the adoption of shared and compatible technical and normative standards that enable seamless cross-border data flows while maintaining high levels of information security and trust.
- Secure and legal data transfers. This principle aims at ensuring that data subjects' rights are safeguarded and data-related obligations are respected, even when data are transferred internationally, thus preventing unauthorized access and misuse of personal data during cross-border transfers.
- Privacy by design. This principle mandates a proactive approach that integrates data protection principles into the development and operation of technologies, systems, and business practices. This principle ensures that privacy is considered at every stage of the data lifecycle, minimizing risks and enhancing the protection of personal data by default
- Promotion of Privacy Enhancing Technologies (PETs). PETs play a remarkably important role providing software and hardware solutions aimed at strengthening data protection. PETs can be developed in the form of Digital Public Infrastructures (DPIs) by leveraging digital systems built on open, secure and interoperable technologies to facilitate safe and trusted exchange of data, based on user consent management.
- Facilitative regulation. Facilitative regulation is based on the dedication of financial resources in the form of investments, tax exemptions, and grants to promote research, development and innovation that promote data processing in alignment with data protection principles. This principle encourages the funding and adoption of innovative solutions that enhance data security, privacy, and compliance, so that technological advancements contribute positively to data governance frameworks.

The abovementioned principles are interdependent and serve as a foundation for building trust in digital ecosystems crucial for economic growth and social development, being instrumental to foster a cohesive approach to data governance at the BRICS and global level. However, the next section will argue that it is important to consider how BRICS countries are already regulating cross-border data flows, to be able to increment BRICS cooperation towards the definition of shared mechanisms, beyond the identification of shared principles.

7.8. From Shared Model Contractual Clauses to a BRICS-led Data Governance Framework

The previous sections have highlighted the existence of common ground amongst the BRICS regarding the importance of consent as a shared legal basis allowing international data transfers as well as the relevant role played by data regulators in all the members of the grouping. Importantly, all BRICS countries except for Russia also deem as legal all data transfers occurring in accordance with model contractual clauses. While Russia does not explicitly recognize this option, the fact that transfers are allowed by the country in case of execution of a contract provides some room for potential use of model contractual clauses also in this country. Indeed, while such model contractual clauses would not be automatically recognized by the Russian system as a legal basis for data transfers per se, their inclusion in contractual agreements explicitly accepted by the data subject could reach the desired outcome. In this perspective, the use of BRICS model contractual clauses becomes a practical and pragmatic option for all the members of the grouping.

In terms of the actual language adopted in model contractual clauses, there are already existing references that might be indicative of a shared path in BRICS countries. Relevant references in this sense already exist, such as the Council of Europe Model Contractual Clauses for the Transfer of Personal Data, ASEAN's Model Contractual Clauses, the Ibero-American Data Protection Network's Model International Transfer of Personal Data Agreement, as well as China's Personal Information Export Standard Contract and Measures on the Standard Contract. These documents aim at providing adequate language to ensure that personal data are transferred with a corresponding level of protection in contracting parties' jurisdictions. They all draw inspiration from the EU's standard contractual clauses, but include important specificities.[93]

As indicated by Matheson and Roberts and others,[94] some topics of particular interest, due to representing relative convergence or divergence in these existing instruments, include:

[93] Linklaters, 'Comparison. EU and China's Standard Contracts for Cross-Border Data Transfers'; Alex Roberts, Roger Li, and Tiantian Ke, 'China's Standard Contract for Cross-Border Data Transfers Released: Key Implications and Comparison against the EU SCCs' (*Linklaters*, 7 March 2023) <https://www.linklaters.com/en/insights/blogs/digilinks/2023/march/chinas-standard-contract-for-cross-border-data-transfers-released> accessed 20 June 2023; Lee Matheson, 'Not-so-Standard Clauses. Examining Three Regional Contractual Frameworks for International Data Transfers' (*Future of Privacy Forum*, 2023) <chrome-extension://efaidnbmnnnibpcajpcglclefindmkaj/https://fpf.org/wp-content/uploads/2023/03/FPF-SCC-Not-So-Standard-Clauses-Report-FINAL-single-pages-1.pdf>.

[94] Matheson (n 93); Roberts, Li, and Ke (n 93).

- Subsequent processing of personal data after transfer, including government access requests and subcontracting of processing.
- Models differentiated according to the types of actors involved, ie, controller-to-controller contracts, controller-to-processor contracts etc.
- Pre- and post-transfer due diligence, audit and record-keeping obligations, including in reference to processing activities and purposes and their respective subsequent alterations.
- Choice of law and forum.
- Transferring sensitive personal data and data related to automated decision-making.

These subjects are crucial to ensuring correct processing of personal data in international data flows, as well as legal certainty in face of contracting parties and the various legal systems involved. A BRICS-oriented project of legal interoperability based on model contract clauses would have to address these issues as a unified front, allowing for a facilitated exchange of data rooted in information security, national sovereignty, informational self-determination, and protection of user rights. In this perspective, the Annex to this chapter offers a concrete blueprint that BRICS countries could follow to face these issues. Indeed, the proposed Model Contractual Clauses could be readily utilized to ensure an appropriate level of protection for the transfer of personal data within BRICS members.

As demonstrated in this volume, although most BRICS countries are at the beginning of their data protection journeys, they have made significant strides in this area, setting up their data architectures, and even proving their willingness to be creative rather than merely engaging in legal transplants. Further coordination in this area could prove beneficial and provide a pathway to the development of a 'post-western model of data governance'[95] shaping rules governing international flows from a Global South perspective. A first step towards this vision could be the definition of BRICS model contractual clauses, regulating data transfers through an agile and more easily updatable tool that could be adopted by all current and future club members, with no need for a remarkably complex—if possible, at all—alignment of multiple adequacy measures or burdensome and highly unlikely international law instruments.

[95] Luca Belli, 'New Data Architectures in Brazil, China, and India: From Copycats to Innovators, towards a Post-Western Model of Data Governance' (2022) 18(2) Indian Journal of Law and Technology 1–58.

Importantly, the BRICS alignment towards shared data protection mechanisms has the potential to be particularly beneficial, reducing transaction costs, deflating barriers to cross-border trade, and fostering similar levels of protection of individual rights. The convergence towards increasingly legally interoperable frameworks is already happening due to a phenomenon of transnational diffusion,[96] grounded on a process of adoption and reproduction of rules, procedures, and good practices that are deemed as reliable and efficient. On top of such phenomena, BRICS countries are demonstrating their willingness and capacity to be innovators and offer important contributions to the creation of a new generation of data protection policy and technology tools. The definition of BRICS model contractual clauses, or even, perhaps one day, a BRICS-led international treaty on data governance or a more institutionalized mutual adequacy system may considerably boost digital trade and digital cooperation of the bloc, as long as data transfers are regulated in a way that enable electronic commerce and services while ensuring that national sovereignty is fully respected.

Given the BRICS appetite for artificial intelligence, IoT, Smart Cities, fintech, and a variety of data-hungry technologies, and given the already relevant degree of compatibility of the existing BRICS data protection frameworks, this policy area should be a considered a suitable testbed to further cooperation enhancement. In this sense, it is important to stress the BRICS leaders' approval of the revised Terms of Reference of the BRICS Working Group on Security in the Use of Information and Communication Technologies (WGSICT), which plays a key role as regards BRICS digital policy coordination and cooperation, the BRICS Roadmap of Practical Cooperation on Ensuring Security in the Use of ICTs, and the recent establishment of the BRICS Framework for Ensuring Consumer Protection in E-Commerce.[97]

In this context the BRICS leaders have explicitly reaffirmed 'the importance of establishing legal frameworks of cooperation among BRICS member States on ensuring security in the use of ICTs and acknowledge the work of the WGSICT towards consideration and elaboration of proposals on this matter'.[98] Moreover, the 2021 BRICS Framework for Ensuring Consumer Protection in e-Commerce

[96] For a more detailed discussion on how juridical systems be interoperable, see L Belli and N Zingales, 'Interoperability to Foster Open Digital Ecosystems in the BRICS Countries' in Chinese Academy of Cyberspace Studies, Xinhua Institute, China Institute of International Studies (eds), *Shared Vision for the Digital World: Insights from Global Think Tanks on Jointly Building a Community with a Shared Future in Cyberspace* (The Commercial Press 2023).

[97] See BRICS 'Declaration of the 11th BRICS Summit' (Brasília 2019) para 19 <https://eng.brics-russia2020.ru/images/00/68/006895.pdf> accessed 14 October 2023.

[98] See <https://is.gd/fuyito>.

explicitly recognizes that '[a]dequate safeguards and measures are needed to ensure privacy and security of the consumers [and resolves] to enhance cooperation through the BRICS E-commerce Working Group',[99] thus elevating data protection to an explicit cooperation item in the BRICS digital policy agenda.

Considering the high level of compatibility of existing data protection frameworks in the BRICS and the ongoing tendency towards enhanced cooperation on digital matters, it would be interesting to see the WGSICT and the E-Commerce Working Group putting forward concrete proposals on a BRICS data cooperation framework, perhaps starting by proposing BRICS model contractual clauses for international data transfers. Both the WGSIC and E-Commerce Working Group enjoy a unique position as well as an explicit mandate to elaborate proposals in this sense, thus becoming a key vector of legal interoperability within the BRICS.

Such proposals would also allow to concretely implement a BRICS STI Architecture, offering a unique opportunity to test a cooperation mechanism that is explicitly aimed at improving the coordination of BRICS initiatives on science, technology, and innovation.

7.9. Conclusions

BRICS countries have demonstrated that, while they remain a very heterogeneous grouping, they can achieve impressive results, when coordinating joint concrete actions, spanning from the establishment of an entirely new global financial institution such as the New Development Bank, to the proposal and brokering of a new treaty, such as the UN Convention against Cybercrime. Despite their obvious diversity, the BRICS countries' perspectives over personal data protection align on many fronts, and their frameworks are already presenting a considerable level of compatibility, even in the absence of a formal international agreement.

Moreover, the BRICS countries have a relevant advantage of being a small club that continues to share an ample range of interests, although the recent expansion has brought considerable new complexity into the BRICS family. Enhancing intra-BRICS cooperation on digital matters, generally, and data governance, particularly, is not only possible, but should be seen as a strategic choice aimed at regulating international data flows in a secure and trustworthy fashion.

[99] BRICS, 'Framework for Ensuring Consumer Protection in E-Commerce' (2021) <https://brics2021.gov.in/brics/public/uploads/docpdf/getdocu-44.pdf>.

There is an increasing yearning for enhanced cooperation on digital governance amongst BRICS countries, as especially highlighted by the 2021, 2022, 2023, and 2024 BRICS Summit Declarations, as well a renewed political impetus, bringing willingness to expand the grouping and utilize it as a leading force for the Global South. Such cooperation may have a variable geometry, considering that some countries have a stronger ideological alignment than others, especially regarding the IBSA—India, Brazil and South Africa—countries, the China-Russia duo, and the new middle eastern BRICS partners. However, considering that many data protection policy elements are already remarkably compatible and converging, the enhancement of BRICS' legal interoperability looks not only feasible, but also achievable.

In their 2024 Declaration, BRICS leaders have made explicit their appetite for the development of 'a global framework for data governance' and, as argued in the introduction of this volume, BRICS policies are starting to be seen as models influencing other countries, especially in the Global Majority. The development of convergent and legally interoperable data protection frameworks should be uppermost in the list of their policy priorities as it is one of the few regulatory fields that is simultaneously key in protecting individuals, providing juridical certainty to businesses, fostering international trade, and enhancing cybersecurity.

Growing cooperation and legal interoperability amongst BRICS countries regarding digital policy is not only possible, it is already happening, and is explicitly advocated by BRICS leaders themselves. The degree of policy convergence now depends on how much BRICS will manage to synchronize their political priorities and, critically, how much they will decide to dare in the implementation of the tools that are at their disposal. The shared principles identified in the previous section and the Model Contractual Clauses included in the Annex offer a useful path to follow to enhance cooperation on data governance issues.

Indeed, as clearly demonstrated by the Kazan Declaration, BRICS are interested in seizing the opportunity to further enhance their cooperation, as the increased convergence and compatibility of their data protection frameworks may be beneficial for both individuals and businesses in the grouping. To do so, multiple venues are available and should be explored. The BRICS Roadmap of Practical Cooperation on Ensuring Security in the Use of ICTs[100] could offer a

[100] The Roadmap was proposed at the eighth BRICS Summit in Goa, India, and adopted at the ninth BRICS Summit in Xiamen, China. See <https://brics2021.gov.in/BRICSDocuments/2017/Xiamen-Declaration-2017.pdf>.

suitable framework for cooperation and implementation of the recent BRICS commitments to enhance intra-BRICS cooperation on digital policies and data governance, and to leverage the BRICS Science, Technology, and Innovation (STI) Architecture, which aims at enabling and evaluating BRICS initiatives in the STI field.

The BRICS Framework for Ensuring Consumer Protection in e-Commerce, could offer an interesting venue for experimentation of new proposals, and exchange of good practices through the BRICS E-commerce Working Group. Ideally, a new dedicated BRICS Working Group on Data Governance should be created to foster better coordination and exchange of information on the issue and, ultimately, facilitate the elaboration of BRICS Model Contractual Clauses—which can be based on the clauses offered in the annex to this chapter—and, if necessary, a more ambitious BRICS Data Governance Framework.

As discussed in this volume, the BRICS countries have many differences but also relevant incentives to deepen their cooperation and alignment, even more so considering their renewed impetus and recent expansion. The policy experimentation with the goal of establishing a new BRICS-led data governance regime should be considered seriously, beyond mere academic exercises, as it has the potential to set the basis for a new post-Western model of data governance. Only history will tell if the BRICS grouping will be able to play a major role in the development of a global data governance approach. Meanwhile, this volume offers a humble contribution to support a better understanding of where BRICS countries start from, which directions they may pursue, and which goals they may reach in their journey towards the construction of their personal data architectures, and how such architectures may contribute to their aspiration to shape global frameworks for data governance.

7.10. Annex: Model Contractual Clauses for the Transfer of Personal Data from Controller to Controller/Processor in the BRICS Countries

NOTE: These Model Contractual Clauses (hereinafter 'the Clauses') aim to ensure an appropriate level of protection for the transfer of personal data to countries that are BRICS members.

PART I—GENERAL CLAUSES

Clause 1. Purpose and Scope

1.1. The aim of these Clauses is to ensure compliance with the requirements for the Transfer(s) of Personal data to BRICS members. In this regard, these Clauses, together with their Annexes which form an integral part thereof provide an appropriate level of protection for the transfer of Personal data involved in the Transfer.

1.2. These Clauses shall apply to the Transfer(s) of Personal data as described in Annex 1.

1.3. The purpose(s) of the Transfer(s) of Personal data is described in Annex 1.

1.4. These MCC will apply, unless a more protective model or Data Protection law is available in the country of origin or the country of destination.

Clause 2. Definitions

As used in these Clauses, the following terms starting with a capital letter shall have the following specific meanings:

Applicable law: rules for the protection of Personal data applicable in the jurisdiction of the Data exporter.

Biometric data: data resulting from a specific technical processing of Personal data concerning the physical, biological or physiological characteristics of an individual, which allows the unique identification or authentication of the individual when it is precisely used to uniquely identify the data subject.

BRICS: bloc of countries formed by Brazil, Russia, India, China, and South Africa, and all members formally included in the grouping.

Controller: the natural or legal person, public authority, service, agency, or any other body which, alone or jointly with others, has decision-making powers with respect to the Processing.

Data breach: any accidental or unauthorized access to, destruction, loss, use, modification, or disclosure of Personal data due to a violation of the principle of data security.

Data exporter: the Controller, located in a country that is a Member of BRICS that transfers Personal data to a Data importer.

Data importer: the Controller to which the Data exporter transfers Personal data and that is located in a country that is a member of BRICS.

Genetic data: all Personal data relating to the genetic characteristics of an individual that have been either inherited or acquired during early prenatal development, as they result from an analysis of a biological sample from the individual concerned including chromosomal, DNA or RNA analysis, or analysis of any other element enabling equivalent information to be obtained.

MCC: These Model Contractual Clauses.

Onward transfer: the transfer of Personal data by the Data importer to another Controller or Processor located in the same or in another jurisdiction.

Party (or Parties): the Data importer and/or Data exporter signatories to these Clauses.

Personal data: any information relating to an identified or identifiable individual (hereinafter 'Data subject'), whatever his/her nationality or residence.

Processing: any operation or set of operations performed on Personal data, such as the collection, storage, preservation, alteration, retrieval, disclosure, making available, erasure, or destruction of, or the carrying out of logical and/ or arithmetical operations on such data. Where automated processing is not used, processing means an operation or set of operations performed upon Personal data within a structured set of such data which are accessible or retrievable according to specific criteria.

Processor: a natural or legal person, public authority, service, agency, or any other body that processes Personal data on behalf and under the instructions of the Controller.

Sensitive data: (i) genetic data, (ii) Personal data relating to offences, criminal proceedings and convictions, or related security measures; (iii) Biometric data processed for the purpose of uniquely identifying a person; or (iv) Personal data for the information they reveal relating to racial or ethnic origin, political opinions, trade-union membership, religious or other beliefs, health, or sexual life.

Supervisory authority/ies: one or more authorities responsible for ensuring compliance with the provisions of the Applicable law.

Third Party: a natural or legal person, public authority, service, agency, or any other body that is not a Party to these Clauses but to which the Personal data is onward transferred by the Data importer, located in the same or in a different jurisdiction as the Data importer.

Third-party beneficiary: the Data subject whose Personal data have been transferred under these Clauses.

Transfer: the disclosure or making available of Personal data to a recipient subject to the jurisdiction of a country that is a member of the BRICS.

Clause 3. Amendment of the MCC

3.1. These Clauses set out appropriate safeguards, including, obligations for Controllers, enforceable Data subject rights, and effective legal remedies, provided they are not modified, except to add or update information in the Annexes or to choose an option where it is provided for by the specific Clause. This does not prevent the Parties from including these Clauses in a wider contract and/or to add other clauses or additional safeguards, provided that they do not contradict, directly or indirectly, these Clauses, or the Applicable law.

3.2. These Clauses are without prejudice to obligations to which the Data exporter is subject by virtue of the Applicable law.

Clause 4. Interpretation and Relation with Other Agreements

4.1 These Clauses shall be read and interpreted in the light of the provisions of the Applicable law.

4.2 These Clauses shall not be interpreted in a way that conflicts with rights and obligations provided for in the Applicable law. If the meaning of the Clauses is unclear or there is more than one meaning, the meaning which most closely aligns with the Applicable law will apply.

4.3 In the event of a contradiction between these Clauses and the provisions of related agreements between the Parties, existing at the time these Clauses are agreed or entered into thereafter, these Clauses shall prevail. The exception to this is where the conflicting terms of the related agreements provide greater protection for Data subjects, in which case those terms shall prevail over these Clauses.

Clause 5. Execution of the Clauses and Notices

5.1 These Clauses may be executed in any number of counterparts, each of which when executed and delivered shall constitute a duplicate original, but all counterparts together shall constitute a single agreement. Once each Party has received a counterpart signed by the other Party (or a digital copy of that signed counterpart), those counterparts will together constitute one and the same instrument and each of which will be, and will be deemed to be, an original.

5.2 Each Party warrants that it has full corporate power and has been duly authorized by all necessary corporate action on its part, to enter into, execute, deliver and perform its obligations under these Clauses.

5.3 All notices and requests under these Clauses by a Party to another Party shall be in writing and shall be served by regular mail, or by electronic mail to the key contact indicated on the First Page, or to such different addresses as may be communicated by the Party by written notice to the other Party. If the notice or request is sent by electronic mail, it will be deemed to have been delivered at the time the electronic mail was sent, or if that time is outside of the receiving Party's normal business hours, the receiving Party's next normal business day, and provided no notice of non-delivery or bounce back is received.

Clause 6. Accession Clause

6.1 An entity that is not a Party to these Clauses may, with the agreement of the other Parties, accede to these Clauses at any time, either as a Data exporter or as a Data importer, by completing and signing Annex 2 and, if required, updating the description of the transfer in Annex 1.

6.2 Once it has completed and signed Annex 1.2, the acceding entity shall become a Party to these Clauses and shall have the rights and obligations of a Data exporter or Data importer in accordance with its designation in Annex 1.2.

6.3 The acceding entity shall have no rights or obligations arising under these Clauses from the period prior to becoming a Party.

Clause 7. Third-Party Beneficiaries

The Parties agree and acknowledge that any Data subject whose Personal data were transferred under these Clauses shall be entitled to invoke the safeguards and guarantees set out in Section II and III of these Clauses as a Third-party beneficiary with respect to any provisions of these Clauses affording a right, action, claim, benefit or privilege to such Data subject with respect to its Personal data.

SECTION II—DATA PROTECTION SAFEGUARDS: RIGHTS AND OBLIGATIONS OF THE PARTIES

Clause 8. Due Diligence and Cooperation

8.1 The Data exporter warrants that it has used reasonable efforts to determine that the Data importer is able, in particular, through the implementation of appropriate technical and organizational measures, to satisfy its obligations under these Clauses.

8.2 The Data exporter shall cooperate with and provide reasonable assistance to the Data importer, if that is necessary to enable the Data importer to comply with its obligations set out in this Section.

Clause 9. Purpose Limitation

The Data importer shall process the Personal data only for the specific purpose(s) of the Transfer, as set out in Annex 1.1. It may also process the Personal data:

(a) when this is necessary to preserve the vital interests of the Data subject;
(b) for the establishment, exercise, or defence of legal claims in the context of specific administrative, regulatory or judicial proceedings in a particular case.

Clause 10. Transparency of Processing

10.1 In order to enable Data subjects to exercise their rights effectively pursuant to these Clauses, the Data importer shall proactively inform them, free of charge, either directly or through the Data exporter of:

(a) its identity and the contact details;
(b) the legal basis and the purpose(s) of the intended Processing;
(c) the purposes and categories of Personal data processed;
(d) the Recipients or categories of Recipients of the Personal data, if any;
(e) the means of exercising the rights set out in these Clauses;
(f) any necessary additional information in order to ensure fair and transparent Processing of the Personal data such as the retention period, the logic underlying the Processing (in particular in case of the use of algorithms for automated decision making, including profiling) or information on Onward transfers (including the grounds therefor and the measures taken in order to guarantee an appropriate level of protection); and
(g) the right to obtain a copy of these Clauses.

10.2. Paragraph 1 shall not apply where the Data subject already has the relevant information.

10.3 Where the Personal data are not collected from the Data subjects, the Data importer shall not be required to provide such information to the Data subject or to the Data exporter where the processing is expressly prescribed by law, or this proves to be impossible or involves disproportionate efforts. In the latter case, the Data importer shall, to the extent possible, make the information publicly available.

Clause 11. Accuracy and Data Minimization

11.1 Each Party shall ensure that the Personal data is accurate and, where necessary, kept up to date. The Data importer shall take every reasonable step to ensure that Personal data that is inaccurate, having regard to the purpose(s) of Processing, is erased or rectified without delay.

11.2 If the Data importer is informed by the Data exporter of corrections made by the Data exporter to the Personal data, the Data importer shall promptly implement those corrections.

11.3 The Data importer shall ensure that the Personal data is adequate, relevant and not excessive in relation to the purpose(s) of Processing.

Clause 12. Limited Retention Period

The Parties agree that the Data importer shall retain the Personal data for no longer than necessary for the purpose(s) for which it is processed. It shall put in place appropriate technical and organizational measures to ensure compliance with this obligation, including erasure or anonymization of the data and all back-ups at the end of the retention period.

Clause 13. Data Security

13.1 The Data importer and, during transmission, also the Data exporter shall implement appropriate security measures, both of a technical and organizational nature, for each Processing, in particular to protect against the risk of Data breaches. In adopting such measures, they shall take into account, in particular, the nature of the Processing, the nature and volume of the Personal data processed, the degree of vulnerability of the technical architecture used for the Processing, the state of the art, and the cost of implementation. The measures should be commensurate with the seriousness and probability of the potential risks. The Parties shall consider having recourse to security techniques such as encryption or pseudonymization, including during transmission, where the purpose(s) of Processing can be achieved in that manner.

13.2 The Parties have agreed on the technical and organizational measures set out in Annex 1.3. The Data importer shall carry out regular checks to ensure that these measures continue to provide an appropriate level of security and shall update them where this is no longer the case.

13.3 If there is a substantial change in the security measures implemented and described in Annex 1.3, the Parties shall update the Annex.

13.4 In the event of a Data breach concerning Personal data processed by the Data importer under these Clauses, the Data importer shall take appropriate measures to address the Data breach, including measures to mitigate its possible adverse effects.

13.5 The Data importer shall notify—without undue delay and, where feasible, not later than 72 hours after having become aware of the Data breach—at least the Data exporter, who shall notify the competent Supervisory authority in case the Data breach may seriously interfere with the rights and fundamental freedoms of the Data subjects.

13.6 In addition, the Data importer shall notify, either directly or through the Data exporter without undue delay, the Data subjects concerned by the Data breach, where it is likely to result in a high risk to their rights and freedoms. Such notification is not required if appropriate technical and organizational measures have been applied to the Personal data affected that render it unintelligible to any person not authorized to access it, if the Data importer has taken subsequent measures which ensure that the high risk is no longer likely to materialize, or if it would involve disproportionate efforts (in which case the Data importer shall instead make a public communication or take a similar measure whereby the Data subjects are informed in an equally effective manner).

13.7 In both cases, the notification shall include adequate and meaningful information on, notably, the nature of the Data breach, the contact points where more information can be obtained and possible measures that Data subjects could take to address the Data breach, including measures to mitigate its possible adverse effects.

13.8 Where not all the relevant information related to the Data breach is available, notification may take place 'in stages', with more information to be provided as soon as it becomes available.

Clause 14. Sensitive Data

Where the Transfer involves Special categories of data, the Data importer shall apply additional safeguards that guard against and are adapted to the risks that the Processing of such data may present for the interests, rights and fundamental freedoms of the Data subject, notably the risk of discrimination.

Clause 15. Onward Transfers

15.1 The Data importer shall not onward transfer the Personal data to a Third party unless:

a) the law of the Third party's jurisdiction, including its international commitments under applicable international treaties or other agreements, ensures an appropriate level of protection or,

b) the Third party enters into a legally binding and enforceable instrument with the Data importer ensuring the same level of data protection as under these Clauses, and the Data importer provides a copy of the instrument to the Data exporter or,

c) the Onward transfer is necessary for the establishment, exercise or defence of legal claims in the context of specific administrative, regulatory or judicial proceedings in a particular case or,
d) the Onward transfer is necessary in a specific case in order to protect the vital interests of the Data subject or of another natural person; or,
e) where none of the other conditions apply, the Data importer has obtained the explicit consent of the Data subject for the specific Onward transfer, after having informed him/her of its purpose(s), the identity of the Third party and the possible risks of such transfer to him/her due to the lack of an appropriate level of data protection. In this case, the Data importer shall inform the Data exporter of the Onward transfer based on consent and, at the request of the latter, shall transmit to it a copy of the information provided to the Data subject.

15.2 Any Onward transfer is subject to compliance by the Data importer with all the other safeguards under these Clauses, in particular as regards purpose limitation.

Clause 16. Processing Under the Authority of the Data Importer

16.1 The Data importer shall ensure that any person acting under its authority, including a Processor, processes the data only on its instructions and in compliance with these Clauses.

16.2 The Data importer remains fully liable to the Data exporter, the competent Supervisory authority/ies and Data subjects for its obligations under these Clauses where it has subcontracted the processing to its Processors or authorized an employee or other person to process the data under its authority.

Clause 17. Documentation for Compliance Purposes

17.1 Each Party shall be able to demonstrate compliance with its obligations under these Clauses. To this end, it shall keep appropriate documentation of the Processing activities carried out under its responsibility.

17.2 Each Party shall make such documentation available to the competent Supervisory authority/ies on request.

17.3 The Data importer guarantees that it has carefully considered the impact the intended Processing might have on the rights and fundamental freedoms of Data subjects prior to the commencement of such Processing, according to the circumstances of the specific Transfer, and has taken the necessary and appropriate technical and organizational measures to comply with these Clauses, and to demonstrate such compliance to the competent Supervisory authority/ies.

Clause 18. Rights of Data Subjects

18.1 Without undue delay, and at the latest within one month of the receipt of the enquiry or request, the Data importer, if necessary, with the assistance of the Data exporter, shall deal with any enquiries and requests it receives from a Data subject related to the Processing of his/her Personal data, including Onward transfers, and the exercise of his/her rights under these Clauses. That period may be extended by up to two further months where necessary, taking into account the complexity and number of enquiries and requests. The Data importer shall inform the Data subject of any such extension as soon as possible, and no later than five days before the end of the maximum period indicated in the first sentence, together with the reasons for the delay.

18.2 The Data importer shall inform Data subjects in a transparent and easily accessible format, through individual notice or on its website, of a contact point competent to receive enquiries, deal with requests (including on the exercise of individual rights) and handle complaints.

18.3 The Data importer shall take appropriate measures to facilitate such enquiries, requests and the exercise of Data subject rights. Any information provided to the Data subject shall be in an intelligible and easily accessible form, using clear and plain language that should be understood by a lay person.

18.4 Data subjects shall have the following rights against the Data importer:

a) not to be subject to a decision significantly affecting them based solely on the automated processing of their Personal data without having the right to challenge such a decision, to put forward their point of view and arguments, and obtain a human review, unless the automated decision is authorized by law which provides for suitable measures to safeguard the interests, rights and fundamental freedoms of the Data subject;
b) to obtain, on request, at reasonable intervals and without excessive delay, confirmation of the Processing of Personal data relating to them, the communication in an intelligible form of the data processed, and all available information on their origin, on the retention period as well as any other information that the Data importer is required to provide in order to ensure the transparency of Processing in accordance with Clause 10.1;
c) to obtain, on request, information on the reasoning underlying the Processing where the results of such Processing are applied to them;
d) to object at any time, on grounds relating to their situation, to the Processing of Personal data concerning them, unless the Data importer demonstrates legitimate grounds for the Processing which override their interests, rights and fundamental freedoms;
e) to obtain, on request without excessive delay, rectification of their Personal data that is incorrect or out of date, or erasure if their Personal data are being, or have been, processed contrary to these Clauses;
f) to obtain a copy of these Clauses, provided that the Data importer may redact any information contained in the Annexes of these Clauses that it or, following consultation, the Data exporter has reasonably identified as a trade secret or other confidential information. Parties should, in such cases of redaction, provide a meaningful summary of the Clause so that the Data subject should be able to understand their content and exercise their rights;
g) to be provided with information on a contact person under the control of the Data importer, whose responsibility is to ensure compliance with letters (a) to (f) of this Clause. Data subjects shall be free to turn to the contact person at any time and at no cost in relation to the Data processing, including Onward transfers, and where applicable, to obtain assistance in exercising their rights.

18.5 The exercise of these rights shall be free of charge.

18.6 The Data importer may restrict or refuse the exercise of those rights if such restriction or refusal is provided for by its domestic law, such restriction or refusal respects the essence of fundamental rights and freedoms and constitutes a necessary and proportionate measure in a democratic society for:

a) the protection of national security, defence, public safety, public order or public policy; important economic and financial interests of the State, the impartiality and independence of the judiciary or the prevention, investigation, and prosecution of criminal offenses and the execution of criminal penalties, and other essential objectives of general public interest;
b) the protection of the Data subject or the rights and fundamental freedoms of others, notably freedom of expression;
c) archiving purposes in the public interest, scientific or historical research purposes or statistical purposes when there is no recognizable risk of infringement of the interests, rights, and fundamental freedoms of Data subjects.

Clause 19. Redress for the Data Subject

19.1 Where the Data subject invokes a Third-party beneficiary right pursuant to Clause 7, the Data importer shall accept the decision of the Data subject to lodge a complaint with the competent Supervisory authority/ies pursuant to Clause 21, and/or to refer the dispute to the competent courts pursuant to Clause 26.

Clause 20. Liability of the Parties

20.1 Each Party shall be liable to the other Party/ies for any damages it causes the other Party/ies by any breach of these Clauses.

20.2 Each Party shall be liable to the Data subject, and the Data subject shall be entitled to receive compensation, for any material or non-material damages that the Party causes the Data subject by breaching these Clauses. This is without prejudice to the liability of the Data exporter or the Data importer under the Applicable law or the law applicable to the Data importer.

20.3 Where more than one Party is responsible for any damage caused to the Data subject as a result of a breach of these Clauses, all responsible Parties shall be jointly and severally liable and the Data subject is entitled to bring an action in court against any of these Parties.

20.4 The Parties agree that, if one Party is held liable under the previous paragraph, it shall be entitled to claim back from the other Party/ies that part of the compensation corresponding to the other Party's/Parties' responsibility for the damage.

20.5 The Controller remains responsible for the Processing where it engages a Processor to act on its behalf. The Parties may not invoke the conduct of a Processor or sub-Processor to avoid their own liability.

Clause 21. Supervisory Authority

21.1 The Supervisory authority/ies with responsibility for ensuring compliance by the Data exporter with the Applicable law as regards the Transfer shall act as competent Supervisory authority/ies.

21.2 The Data importer agrees to submit itself to the jurisdiction of and cooperate with the competent Supervisory authority in any procedures aimed at ensuring compliance with these Clauses, and to abide by its decision. In particular, the Data importer agrees to respond to enquiries, submit to review or audits, and comply with the measures adopted by the Supervisory authority, including remedial and compensatory measures. It shall provide the Supervisory authority with written confirmation that the necessary actions have been taken.

SECTION III—LOCAL LAWS AND OBLIGATIONS IN CASE OF ACCESS BY PUBLIC AUTHORITIES

Clause 22. Local Laws and Practices Affecting Compliance with the Clauses

22.1 The Parties warrant that they have no reason to believe that the laws and practices in the country of destination applicable to the Processing by the Data importer, including any requirements to disclose Personal data or measures authorizing access by public authorities, prevent the Data importer from fulfilling its obligations under these Clauses. This is based on the understanding that laws and practices that respect the essence of human rights and fundamental freedoms and do not exceed what is necessary and proportionate in a democratic society to safeguard one of the objectives listed in International Human Rights law, are not in contradiction with these Clauses.

22.2 The Parties declare that in providing the warranty pursuant to previous paragraph, they have taken due account in particular of the following elements:

a) the specific circumstances of the Transfer;
b) the laws (including case law) and practices in the country of destination relevant in the specific circumstances of the Transfer;
c) any relevant contractual, technical or organizational safeguards put in place to supplement the safeguards under these Clauses.

22.3 The Data importer warrants that, in carrying out the assessment pursuant to paragraph 22.2, it has made its best efforts to provide the Data exporter with relevant information and agrees that it will continue to cooperate with the Data exporter in ensuring compliance with these Clauses.

22.4 The Parties shall document the assessment pursuant to paragraph 22.2 and make it available to the competent Supervisory authority on request.

Clause 23. Obligations of the Data Importer in Case of Access by Public Authorities

23.1 Notification

a) In so far as domestic law of Data importer allows, the Data importer shall notify the Data exporter and, where possible the Data subject promptly or use its best efforts to do so if it is compelled to preserve, grant access, make available or disclose Personal data transferred from the Data exporter to a Third party including to a public authority.
b) If the Data importer is prohibited from notifying the Data exporter and/or the Data subject, then in so far domestic law allows it agrees to use its best efforts to obtain a waiver of the prohibition with a view to communicating as much information as possible. The Data importer agrees to document its efforts in order to be able to demonstrate them to the Data exporter, on request.

c) Where permissible under the laws of the country of destination, the Data importer agrees to provide the Data exporter, on request, with as much relevant information as possible on any requests for disclosure it has received (in particular, number of requests, type of data requested, requesting authority/ies, whether requests have been challenged, and the outcome of such challenges, etc.).

d) The Data importer agrees to preserve the information pursuant to paragraphs (a) to (c) for the duration of the contract and make it available to the competent Supervisory authority on request.

e) Paragraph (a), (b), and (d) are without prejudice to the obligation of the Data importer pursuant to Clause 22.5 and Clause 24 to inform the Data exporter promptly where it is unable to comply with these Clauses.

23.2. Review of legality and data minimization

a) The Data importer shall review the legality of any request for disclosure, in particular whether it is within the powers granted to the requesting public authority, and to challenge the request if, after careful assessment, it concludes that there are reasonable grounds to consider that the request is unlawful under the laws of the country of destination, applicable obligations under international law and principles of international comity. The Data importer shall, under the same conditions and in line with its domestic legislation pursue possibilities of appeal. Pending the determination of any challenge (including on appeal, as relevant) the Data importer shall, to the extent available under domestic legislation, seek interim measures to suspend the effects of the request. These requirements are without prejudice to the obligations of the Data importer under Clause 22.5 and Clause 24.1.

b) The Data importer shall document its legal assessment and any challenge to the request for disclosure and, to the extent permissible under the laws of the country of destination, shall make the relevant documentation available to the Data exporter. It shall also make it available to the competent Supervisory authority on request.

c) When responding to a request for disclosure, the Data importer shall, having complied with the duty in 23.2, and confirm the lawfulness of the request provide, only the information which is necessary to respond to the request, in accordance with the domestic legislation.

SECTION IV—FINAL PROVISIONS

Clause 24. Non-compliance with the Clauses and Termination

24.1 Each Party shall promptly inform the other Party/ies if it is unable to comply with these Clauses, for whatever reason.

24.2 In the event that the Data exporter has clear information that the Data importer is in breach of these Clauses or unable to comply with these Clauses, the Data exporter shall suspend the transfer of Personal data to the Data importer under these Clauses until compliance is again ensured or the contract is terminated. This is without prejudice to Clause 22.6.

24.3 The Data exporter shall be entitled to terminate the contract, insofar as it concerns the Processing of Personal data under these Clauses, where:

a) the Data exporter has suspended the Transfer of Personal data to the Data importer pursuant to paragraph 24.2 and compliance with the Clauses is not restored within a reasonable time and in any event within one month of suspension;

b) the Data importer is in substantial or persistent breach of these Clauses; or

c) the Data importer fails to comply with a binding decision of a competent court or a competent Supervisory authority regarding its obligations under these Clauses.

In these cases, it shall inform the competent Supervisory authority of such non-compliance. Where the contract involves more than two Parties, the Data exporter may exercise this right to termination only with respect to the non-compliant Party, unless the Parties have agreed otherwise.

24.4 Personal data that has been transferred prior to the termination of the contract pursuant to paragraph 24.3 shall at the choice of the Data exporter immediately be returned to the Data exporter or deleted in its entirety. The same shall apply to any copies of the data. The Data importer shall certify the deletion of the data to the Data exporter. Until the data is deleted or returned, the Data importer shall continue to ensure compliance with these Clauses. In case of local laws applicable to the Data importer that prohibit the return or deletion of the transferred Personal data, the Data importer warrants that it will continue to ensure compliance with these Clauses and will only process the data to the extent and for as long as required under that local law. The Data exporter should be notified of the relevant local law and the required retention period. Only the minimum amount of Personal data should be retained to comply with domestic law.

Clause 25. Governing Law

These Clauses shall be governed by the law of the country of the Data exporter.

Clause 26. Choice of Forum and Jurisdiction

26.1 Any dispute arising from these Clauses shall be resolved by the courts of [____].

26.2 Data subjects may also bring legal proceedings against the Data exporter and/or Data importer before the courts of the country in which they have their habitual residence.

26.3 The Parties agree to submit themselves to the jurisdiction of such courts.

Clause 27. Arbitration Clause

Option 1: WIPO Rules
Any dispute, controversy or claim arising under, out of or relating to this contract and any subsequent amendments of this contract, including, without limitation, its formation, validity, binding effect, interpretation, performance, breach or termination, as well as non-contractual claims, shall be submitted to mediation in accordance with the WIPO Mediation Rules. The place of mediation shall be [specify place]. The language to be used in the mediation shall be [specify language].

If, and to the extent that, any such dispute, controversy or claim has not been settled pursuant to the mediation within [60][90] days of the commencement of the mediation, it shall, upon the filing of a Request for Arbitration by either party, be referred to and finally determined by arbitration in accordance with the WIPO [Expedited] Arbitration Rules. Alternatively, if, before the expiration of the said period of [60][90] days, either party fails to participate or to continue to participate in the mediation, the dispute, controversy or claim shall, upon the filing of a Request for Arbitration by the other party, be referred to and finally determined by arbitration in accordance with the WIPO [Expedited] Arbitration Rules. [The arbitral tribunal shall consist of [a sole arbitrator][three arbitrators].]* The place of arbitration shall be [specify place]. The language to be used in the arbitral proceedings shall be [specify language]. The dispute, controversy or claim referred to arbitration shall be decided in accordance with the law of [specify jurisdiction]. (* The WIPO Expedited Arbitration Rules provide that the arbitral tribunal shall consist of a sole arbitrator.)

Option 2: ICC Rules
If the Parties are unable to resolve any difference they may have, the dispute shall be finally settled under the Rules of Arbitration (hereinafter, the 'Rules') of the International Chamber of Commerce ('ICC') by three arbitrators designated by the Parties. Each Party shall designate one arbitrator. The third arbitrator shall be designated by the two arbitrators designated by the Parties. If either Party fails to designate an arbitrator within thirty days after the filing of the dispute with the ICC, such arbitrator shall be appointed in the manner prescribed by the Rules. An arbitration proceeding hereunder shall be conducted in [City, Country], and shall be conducted in [specify language]. The decision or award of the arbitrators shall be in writing and is final and binding on both Parties.

By the signatures of their authorized representatives below, the Data exporter and the Data importer agree to be bound by these MCC.
Data exporter name:
Main address:
Key contact:

Data importer information:
Main address:
Key contact:

Signed for and on behalf of the Data exporter Signed:
Date of signature [MM/DD/YEAR] Full name:
Job title:

Signed for and on behalf of the Data importer Signed:
Date of signature [MM/DD/YEAR] Full name:
Job title:

Annex 1.1

Information about the transfers
[NOTE: It must be possible to clearly distinguish the information applicable to each transfer or category of transfers and, in this regard, to determine the respective role(s) of the Parties as data exporter(s) and/or data importer(s). This does not necessarily require completing and signing separate annexes for each transfer/category of transfers and/or contractual relationship, where this transparency can achieved through one set of annexes. However, where necessary to ensure sufficient clarity, separate sets of annexes should be used].

Description of the transfer:

- The categories of Data subjects whose data are transferred;
- The categories of Personal data transferred;
- The Special categories of data transferred (where applicable) and the restrictions or safeguards applied, which take full account of the nature of the data and the risks involved, such as, for example, strict purpose limitation, lawful basis for the processing (ex: explicit consent of the Data subject) access restrictions (including access only for staff who have received specific training), restrictions regarding further disclosure, retention of records of data sharing, restrictions on Onward transfers, specific organizational or technical security measures (ex: data encryption, pseudonymization) or additional security measures;
- The frequency of data transfers (e.g. whether data are transferred once or continuously);
- The nature of the Processing;
- The purpose(s) of the data Transfer and further processing;
- The period for which the Personal data will be stored or, where this is not possible, the criteria for determining this period;

Annex 1.2

Signature form

[Term: Start date [MM/DD/YEAR]—End date [MM/DD/YEAR]]

Data exporter information Full legal name:
Trading name (if different):

Main address (if a company registered address):
Official registration number (if any):
Key contact (full name, job title, contact details including email):

Data importer information Full legal name:
Trading name (if different):
Main address (if a company registered address)::
Official registration number (if any):
Key contact (full name, job title, contact details including email):

By the signatures of their authorized representatives below, the parties agree to be bound by these Model Contractual Clauses (hereinafter 'the Clauses').

Signed for and on behalf of the Data exporter Signed:
Date of signature [MM/DD/YEAR] Full name:
Job title:

Signed for and on behalf of the Data importer Signed:
Date of signature [MM/DD/YEAR] Full name:
Job title:

Annex 1.3

Security measures
This annex has to be completed and updated by the Data importer. The technical and organizational measures must be described in specific (and not generic) terms. It must be clearly indicated which measures apply to each transfer/set of transfers.

Examples of possible measures:
Measures of pseudonymization and encryption of Personal data

Measures for ensuring ongoing confidentiality, integrity, availability and resilience of Processing systems and services

Measures for ensuring the ability to restore the availability and access to Personal data in a timely manner in the event of a physical or technical incident

Processes for regularly testing, assessing and evaluating the effectiveness of technical and organizational measures in order to ensure the security of the Processing

Measures for user identification and authorization

Measures for the protection of Personal data during transmission

Measures for the protection of Personal data during storage

Measures for ensuring physical security of locations at which Personal data are processed

Measures for ensuring events logging

Measures for ensuring system configuration, including default configuration

Measures for internal IT and IT security governance and management

Measures for certification/assurance of processes and products

Measures for ensuring data minimization

Measures for ensuring data quality

Measures for ensuring limited data retention

Measures for ensuring accountability

Measures for allowing data portability and ensuring erasure

Index

For the benefit of digital users, indexed terms that span two pages (e.g., 52–53) may, on occasion, appear on only one of those pages.